尾田栄一郎

There's this Japanese legend called the "Standing Death of Benkei." I think it's the coolest way for a man to die. The death of the great Whitebeard in the previous volume epitomizes this saying. And while we're talking about the great warrior Benkei, I just want to say he and I are just alike. Yeah. I heard this thing about him and it's quite a coincidence--we both feel like crying when we bump our shins. We're so much alike! That's what it means to be a man among men. All right! Let's start volume 60!

—Eiichiro Oda, 2010

Eiichiro Oda began his manga career at the age of 17, when his one-shot cowboy manga **Wanted!** won second place in the coveted Tezuka manga awards. Oda went on to work as an assistant to some of the biggest manga artists in the industry, including Nobuhiro Watsuki, before winning the Hop Step Award for new artists. His pirate adventure **One Piece**, which debuted in **Weekly Shonen Jump** in 1997, quickly became one of the most popular manga in Japan.

ONE PIECE VOL. 60
PARAMOUNT WAR PART 4

SHONEN JUMP Manga Edition

This graphic novel contains material that was originally published in English in SHONEN JUMP #101–104. Artwork in the magazine may have been slightly altered from that presented here.

STORY AND ART BY EIICHIRO ODA

English Adaptation/Lance Caselman
Translation/Laabaman, HC Language Solutions, Inc.
Touch-up Art & Lettering/Vanessa Satone
Design/Fawn Lau
Editor/Alexis Kirsch

Printed in the U.S.A.

Published by VIZ Media, LLC
P.O. Box 77010
San Francisco, CA 94107

10 9 8 7 6 5 4 3 2 1
First printing, January 2012

www.viz.com

THE WORLD'S MOST POPULAR MANGA
www.shonenjump.com

SHONEN JUMP MANGA

ONE PIECE

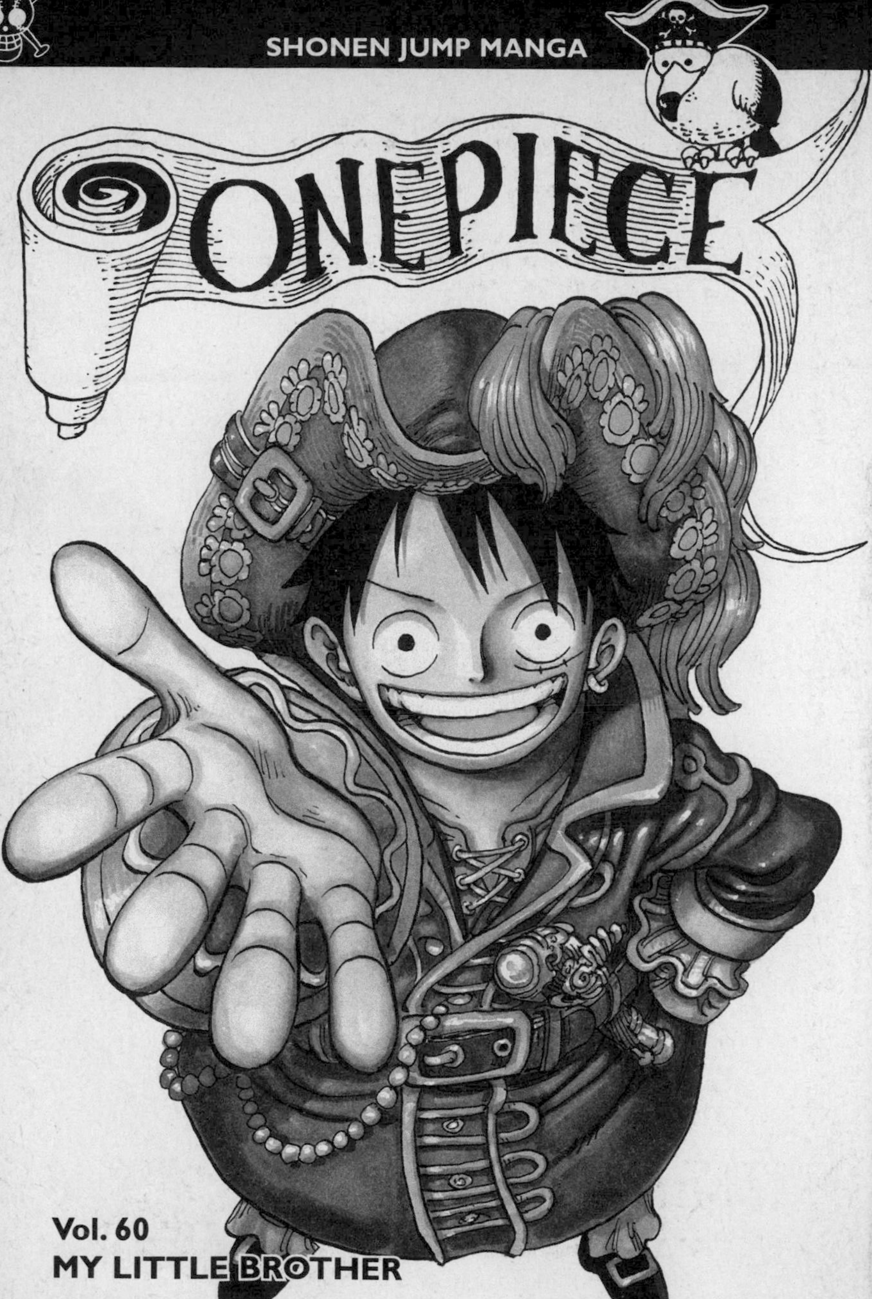

Vol. 60

MY LITTLE BROTHER

STORY AND ART BY

EIICHIRO ODA

Characters

Monkey D. Luffy
(from ten years ago)

A boy who dreams of becoming the Pirate King. With no one else to depend on, he sincerely wants to become friends with Ace.

Young boy from Windmill Village

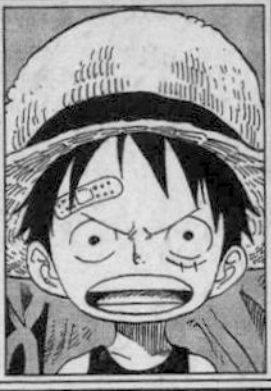

Portgaz D. Ace
(from ten years ago)

Gold Roger's son. He began his life with Dadan three years before Luffy came along.

Young boy who lives on Mt. Corvo

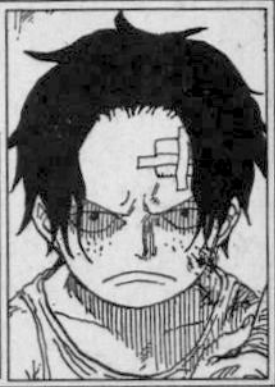

Sabo
(from ten years ago)

Ace's best friend. He and Ace are saving money to become pirates.

Young boy from Grey Terminal

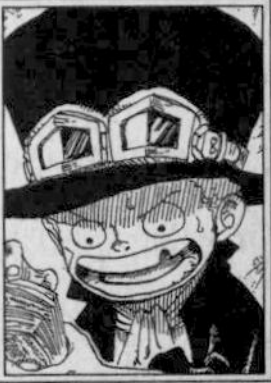

Monkey D. Garp
(from ten years ago)

Luffy's grandfather. Roger entrusted Ace to him, but he turned Ace over to Dadan's care.

Navy officer

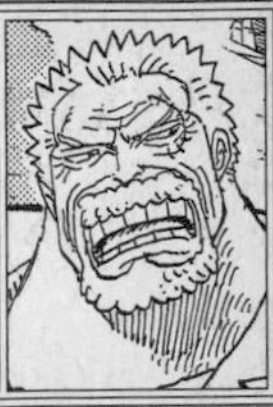

Curly Dadan
(from ten years ago)

A bandit who Garp entrusted with Luffy and Ace.

Leader of the Dadan gang

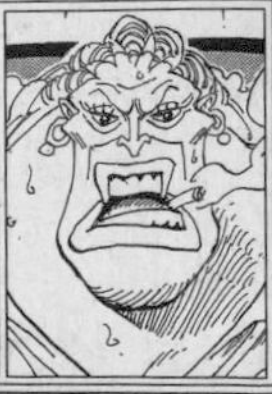

Straw Hat Crew

Roronoa Zolo

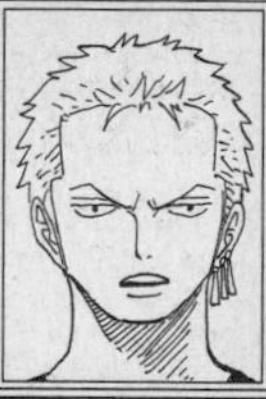

He was sent off to the ruins of the Muggy Kingdom on Gloom Island. He is currently with Perona.

Fighter, Bounty: 120 million berries

Tony Tony Chopper

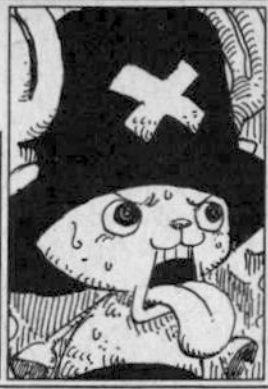

Currently in the Birdie Kingdom, where birds rule over the people. Some say this island is a Treasure Island.

Ship's Doctor, Bounty: 50 berries

Nami

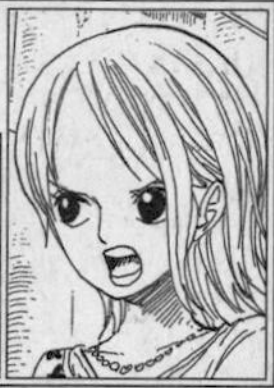

She is currently in Weatheria, a country on a small sky island, where people study the science of weather.

Navigator, Bounty: 16 million berries

Nico Robin

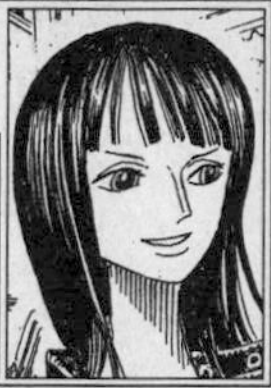

Currently in the country on a bridge called Tequila Wolf. She was enslaved but later freed by the Revolutionary Army.

Archeologist, Bounty: 80 million berries

Usopp

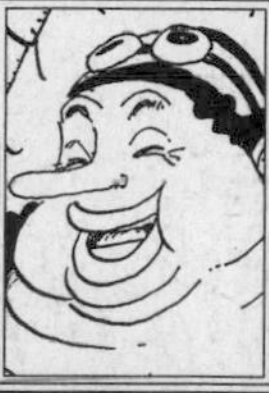

He is currently with Heracles in the bandit forest of Glinston in the Bowin Islands.

Sniper, Bounty: 30 million berries

Franky

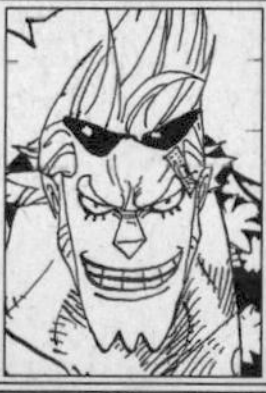

Currently on the Mechanical Island, birthplace of the genius Dr. Vegapunk in the Future Land Baldimore.

Shipwright, Bounty: 44 million berries

Sanji

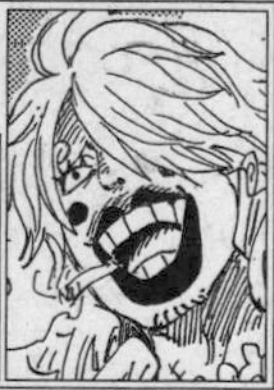

He is on dreamy Peachy Island, known as the second "Island of Women." Is he now a maiden in the infamous Kamabakka Kingdom?!

Cook, Bounty: 77 million berries

Brook

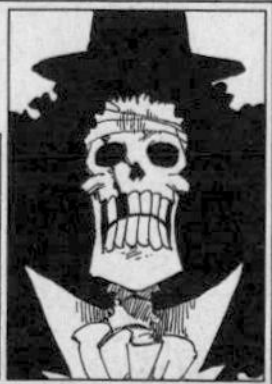

In Hungeria, the impoverished country of Lazy Bones Island. He is currently worshipped by locals as the devil lord.

Musician, Bounty: 33 million berries

Story

In an attempt to prevent the execution of his brother, Ace, Luffy fights his way to Navy Headquarters where he is joined by Whitebeard and his pirates. But waiting for them there are the most powerful warriors the Navy can muster. A battle erupts such as the world has never seen! With the help of his allies, Luffy struggles to pass the Navy's fearsome defenses and rescue Ace. But at the last moment, Ace suffers a mortal wound from Akainu and dies before Luffy's eyes. The great pirate Whitebeard is killed as well in this legendary battle.

Luffy is spirited away to the Island of Women where he recovers, but the loss of his brother torments him. What is the nature of the bond between Luffy and Ace? Now, for the first time, the secrets of their past are revealed! It all begins ten years ago...

PARAMOUNT WAR

ONE PIECE

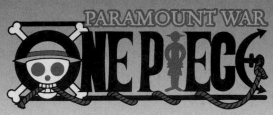

Vol. 60
My Little Brother

CONTENTS

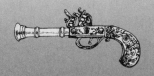

Chapter 585:
BROTHERLY PACT

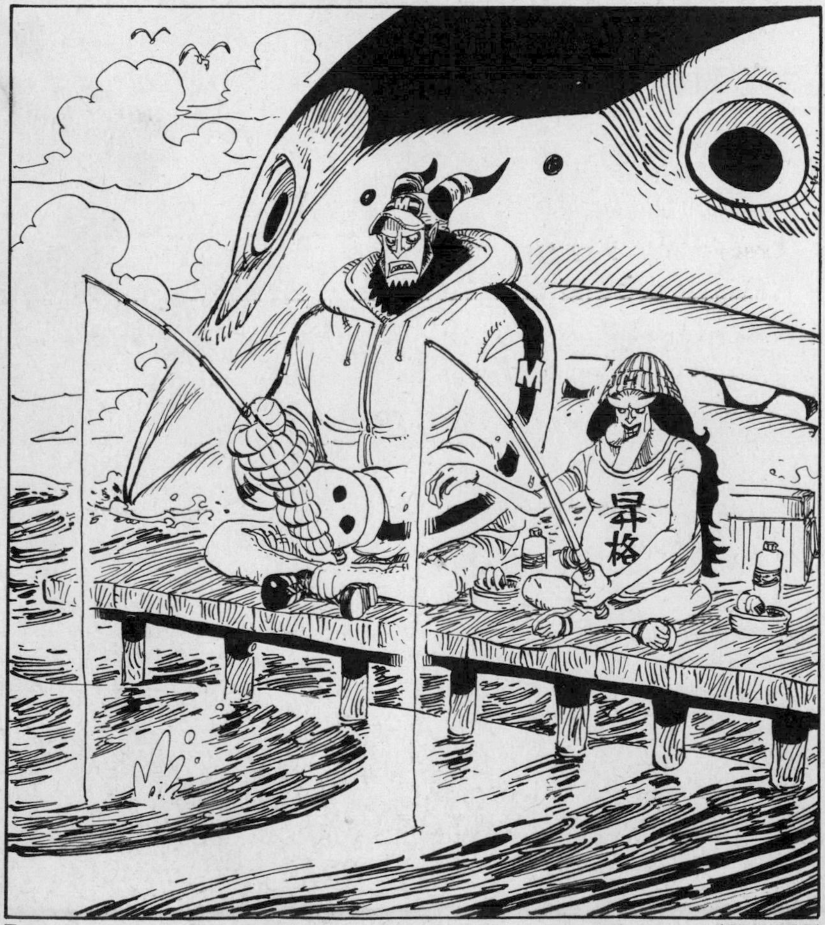
昇格

*PROMOTION

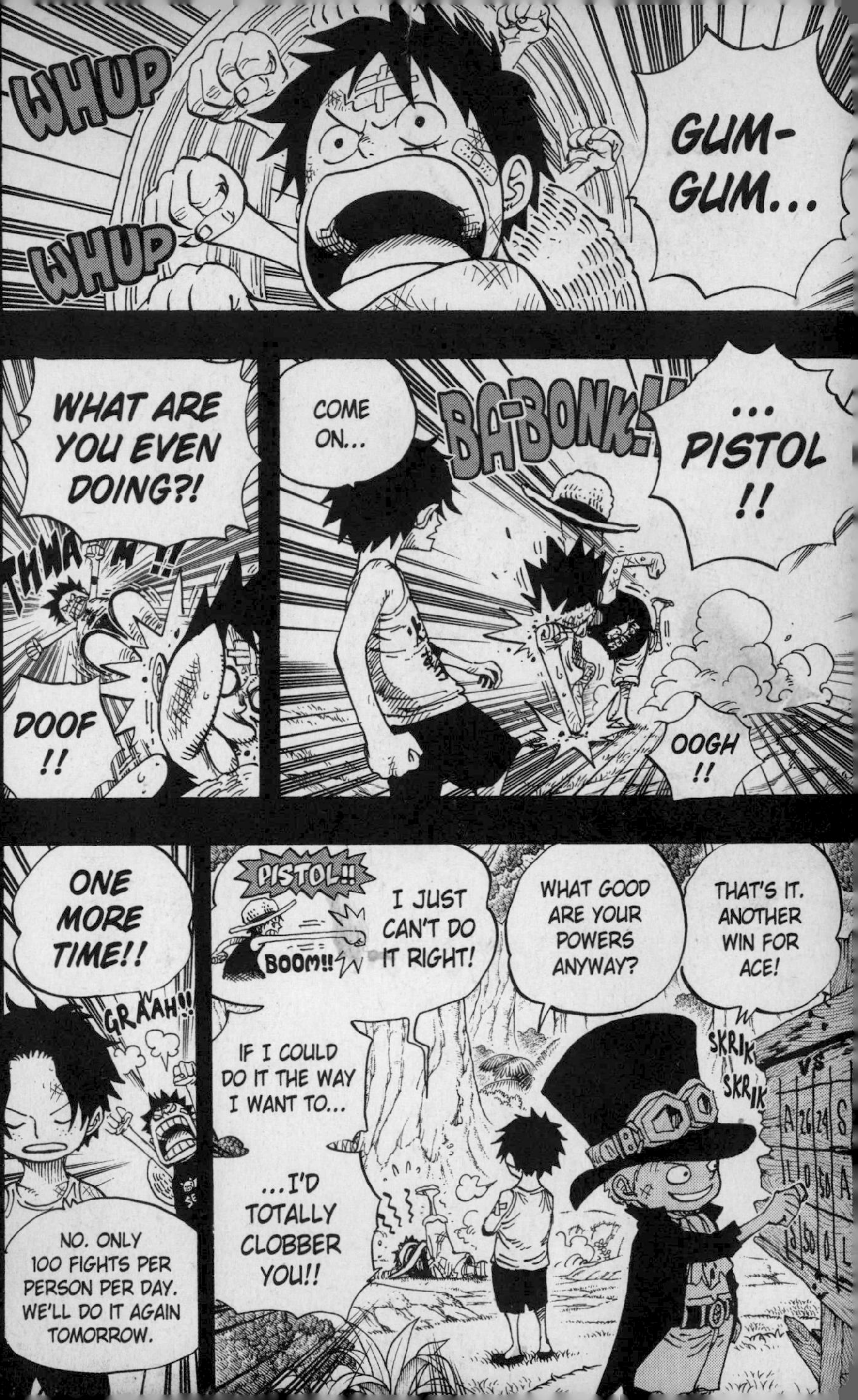
GUM-GUM...
WHUP
WHUP
...PISTOL!!
BA-BONK!!
COME ON...
OOGH!!
WHAT ARE YOU EVEN DOING?!
THWA M!!
DOOF!!
THAT'S IT. ANOTHER WIN FOR ACE!
WHAT GOOD ARE YOUR POWERS ANYWAY?
I JUST CAN'T DO IT RIGHT!
PISTOL!!
BOOM!!
SKRIK
SKRIK
IF I COULD DO IT THE WAY I WANT TO...
...I'D TOTALLY CLOBBER YOU!!
ONE MORE TIME!!
GRAAH!!
NO. ONLY 100 FIGHTS PER PERSON PER DAY. WE'LL DO IT AGAIN TOMORROW.

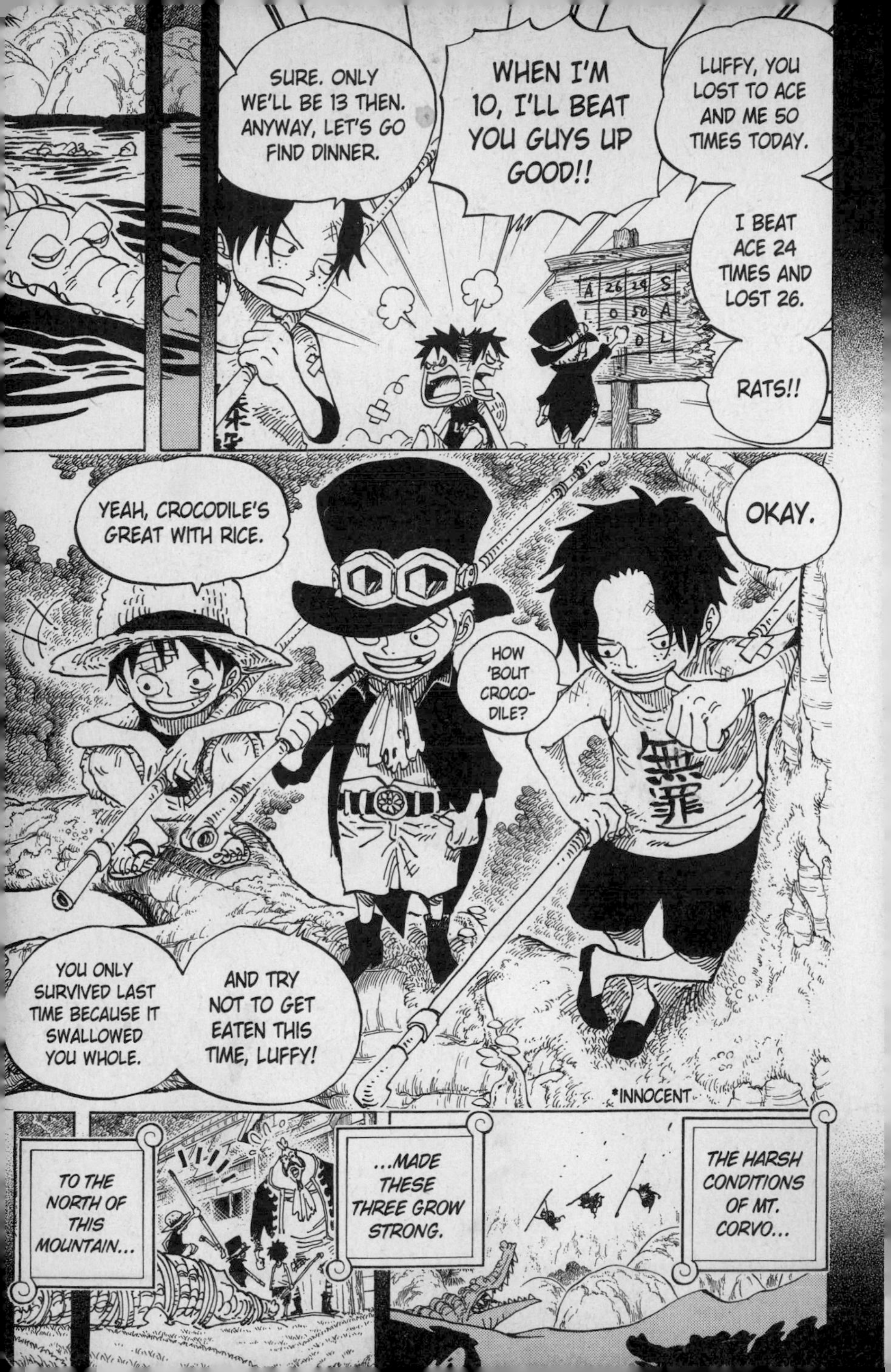
LUFFY, YOU LOST TO ACE AND ME 50 TIMES TODAY.
I BEAT ACE 24 TIMES AND LOST 26.
RATS!!
WHEN I'M 10, I'LL BEAT YOU GUYS UP GOOD!!
SURE. ONLY WE'LL BE 13 THEN. ANYWAY, LET'S GO FIND DINNER.
OKAY.
HOW 'BOUT CROCODILE?
YEAH, CROCODILE'S GREAT WITH RICE.
AND TRY NOT TO GET EATEN THIS TIME, LUFFY!
YOU ONLY SURVIVED LAST TIME BECAUSE IT SWALLOWED YOU WHOLE.
*INNOCENT
THE HARSH CONDITIONS OF MT. CORVO...
...MADE THESE THREE GROW STRONG.
TO THE NORTH OF THIS MOUNTAIN...

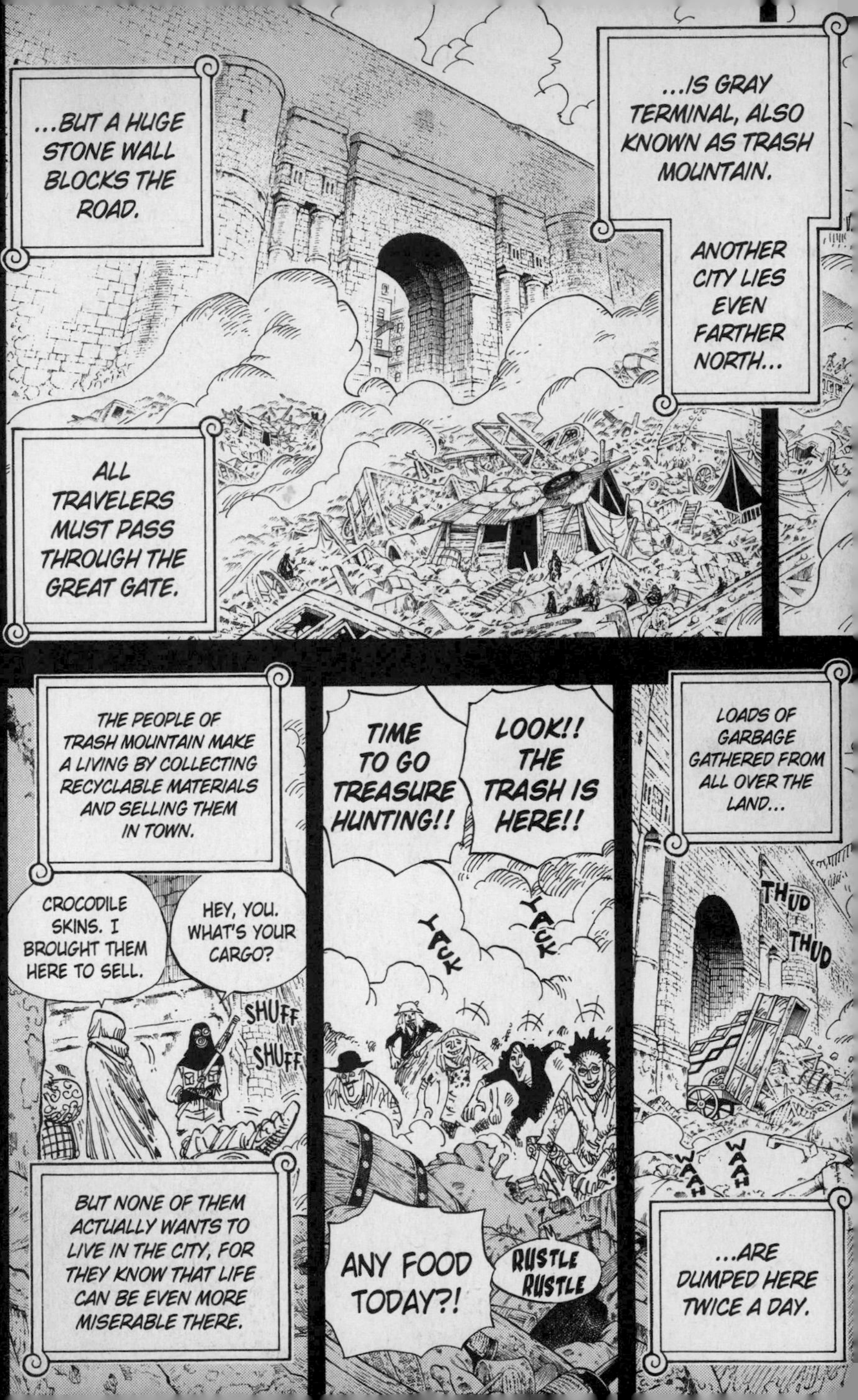

...IS GRAY TERMINAL, ALSO KNOWN AS TRASH MOUNTAIN.
ANOTHER CITY LIES EVEN FARTHER NORTH...
...BUT A HUGE STONE WALL BLOCKS THE ROAD.
ALL TRAVELERS MUST PASS THROUGH THE GREAT GATE.
LOADS OF GARBAGE GATHERED FROM ALL OVER THE LAND...
THUD
THUD
WAAH
WAAH
...ARE DUMPED HERE TWICE A DAY.
LOOK!! THE TRASH IS HERE!!
TIME TO GO TREASURE HUNTING!!
YACK
YACK
RUSTLE RUSTLE
ANY FOOD TODAY?!
THE PEOPLE OF TRASH MOUNTAIN MAKE A LIVING BY COLLECTING RECYCLABLE MATERIALS AND SELLING THEM IN TOWN.
HEY, YOU. WHAT'S YOUR CARGO?
CROCODILE SKINS. I BROUGHT THEM HERE TO SELL.
SHUFF
SHUFF
BUT NONE OF THEM ACTUALLY WANTS TO LIVE IN THE CITY, FOR THEY KNOW THAT LIFE CAN BE EVEN MORE MISERABLE THERE.

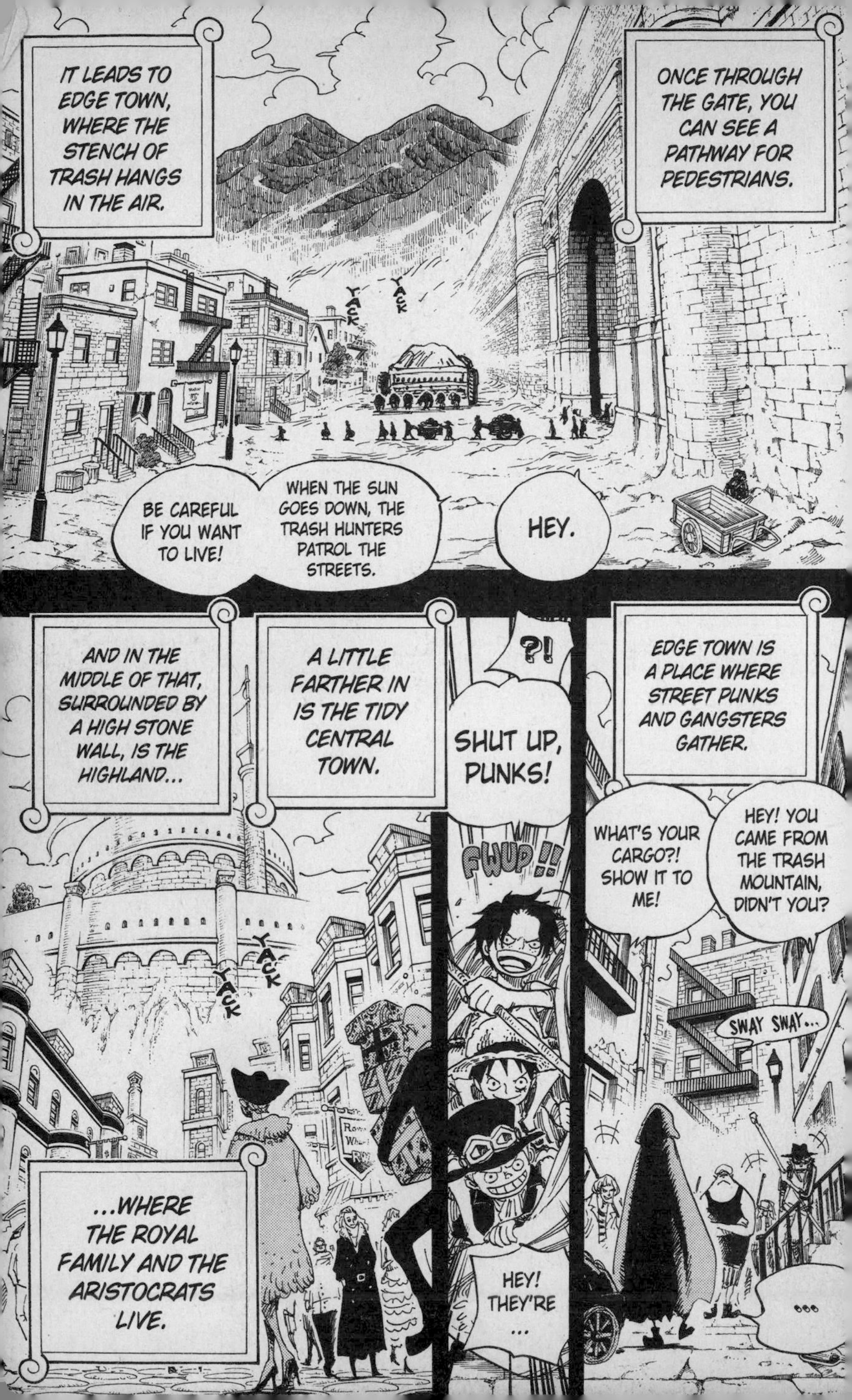
ONCE THROUGH THE GATE, YOU CAN SEE A PATHWAY FOR PEDESTRIANS.
IT LEADS TO EDGE TOWN, WHERE THE STENCH OF TRASH HANGS IN THE AIR.
YACK
YACK
HEY.
WHEN THE SUN GOES DOWN, THE TRASH HUNTERS PATROL THE STREETS.
BE CAREFUL IF YOU WANT TO LIVE!
EDGE TOWN IS A PLACE WHERE STREET PUNKS AND GANGSTERS GATHER.
HEY! YOU CAME FROM THE TRASH MOUNTAIN, DIDN'T YOU?
WHAT'S YOUR CARGO?! SHOW IT TO ME!
SWAY SWAY...
...
?!
SHUT UP, PUNKS!
FWUP!!
HEY! THEY'RE ...
A LITTLE FARTHER IN IS THE TIDY CENTRAL TOWN.
AND IN THE MIDDLE OF THAT, SURROUNDED BY A HIGH STONE WALL, IS THE HIGHLAND...
YACK
YACK
...WHERE THE ROYAL FAMILY AND THE ARISTOCRATS LIVE.

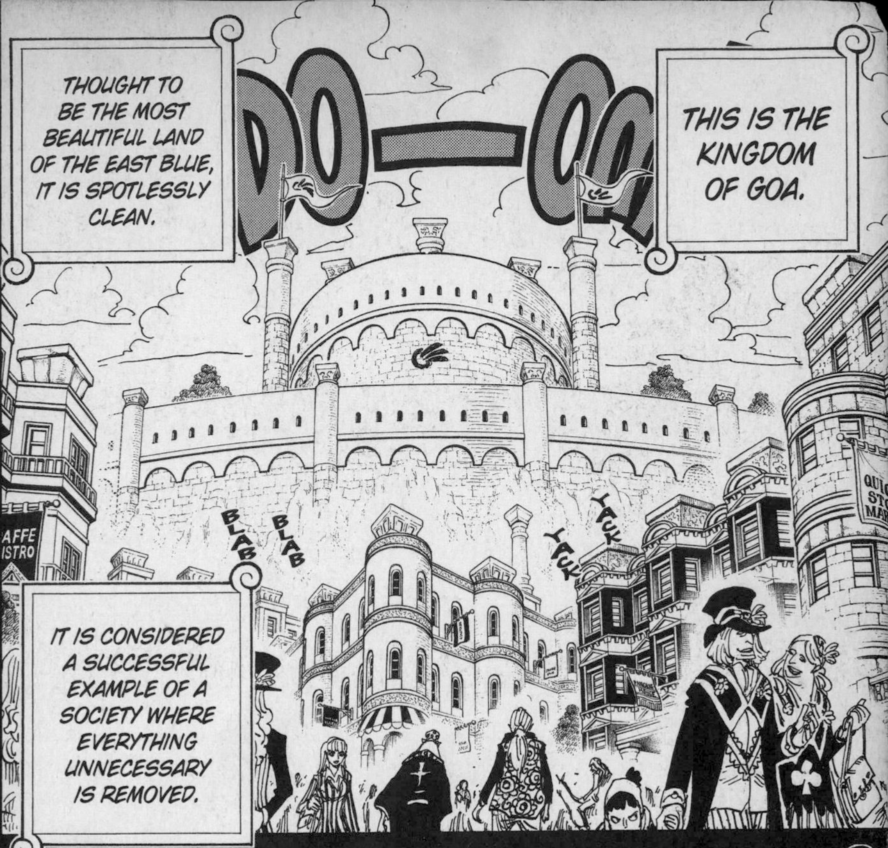
THIS IS THE KINGDOM OF GOA.
THOUGHT TO BE THE MOST BEAUTIFUL LAND OF THE EAST BLUE, IT IS SPOTLESSLY CLEAN.
DO—OO
YACK YACK
BLAB BLAB
IT IS CONSIDERED A SUCCESSFUL EXAMPLE OF A SOCIETY WHERE EVERYTHING UNNECESSARY IS REMOVED.

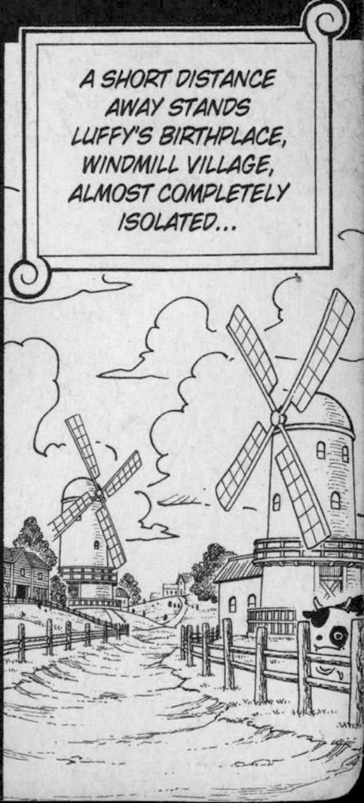
A SHORT DISTANCE AWAY STANDS LUFFY'S BIRTHPLACE, WINDMILL VILLAGE, ALMOST COMPLETELY ISOLATED...

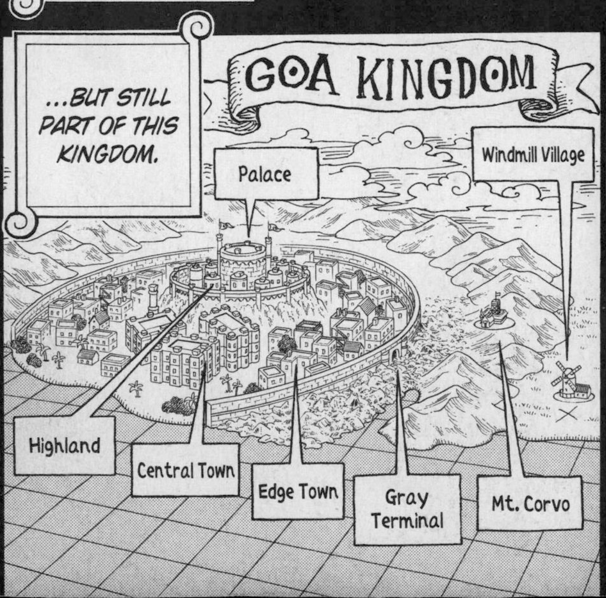
...BUT STILL PART OF THIS KINGDOM.
GOA KINGDOM
Windmill Village
Palace
Highland
Central Town
Edge Town
Gray Terminal
Mt. Corvo

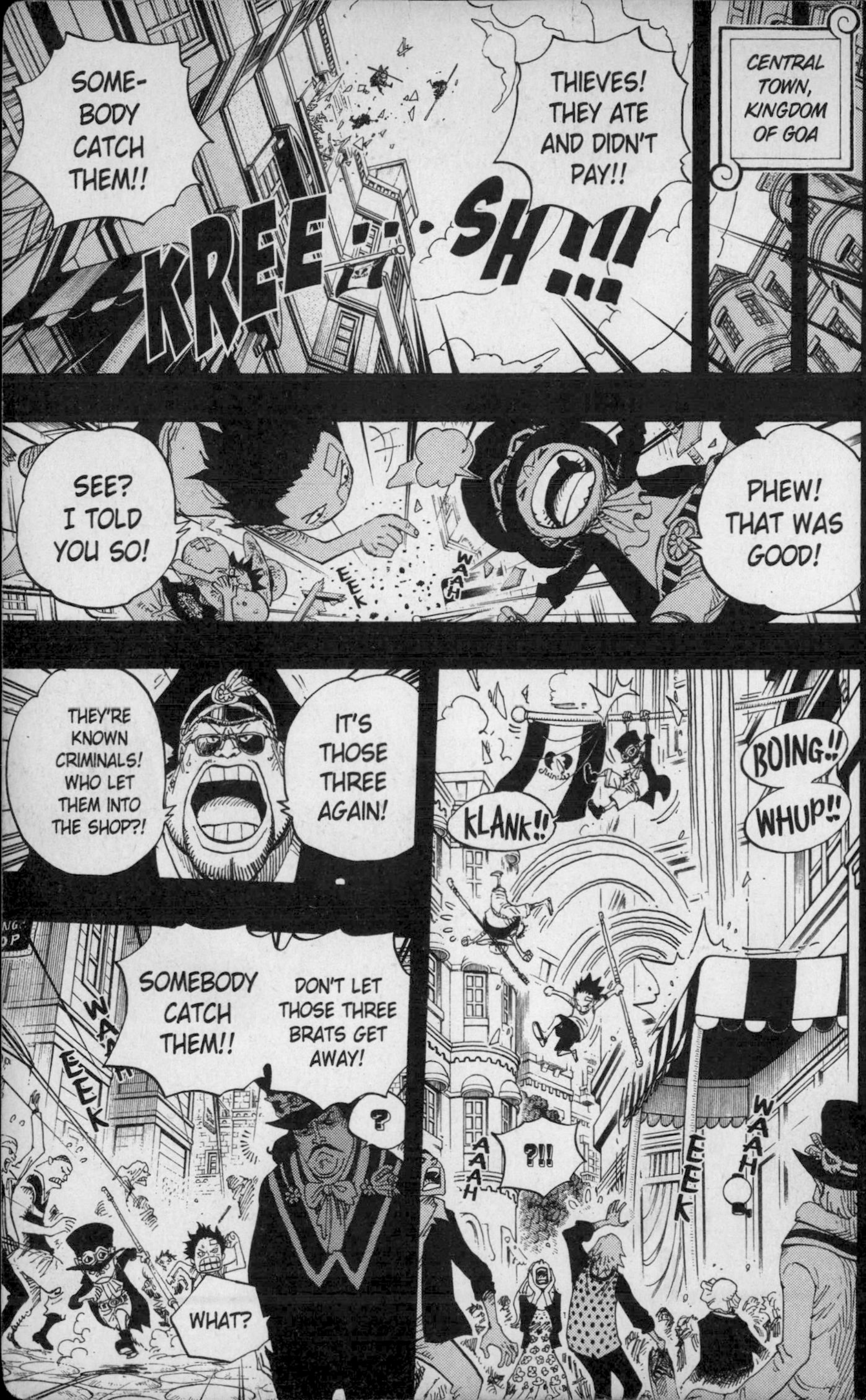
CENTRAL TOWN, KINGDOM OF GOA
THIEVES! THEY ATE AND DIDN'T PAY!!
SOME-BODY CATCH THEM!!
KREE---SH!!!
PHEW! THAT WAS GOOD!
WAAH
EEK
SEE? I TOLD YOU SO!
BOING!!
WHUP!!
KLANK!!
?!!
WAAH
EEK
AAAH
IT'S THOSE THREE AGAIN!
THEY'RE KNOWN CRIMINALS! WHO LET THEM INTO THE SHOP?!
DON'T LET THOSE THREE BRATS GET AWAY!
SOMEBODY CATCH THEM!!
?
WAAH
EEK
WHAT?

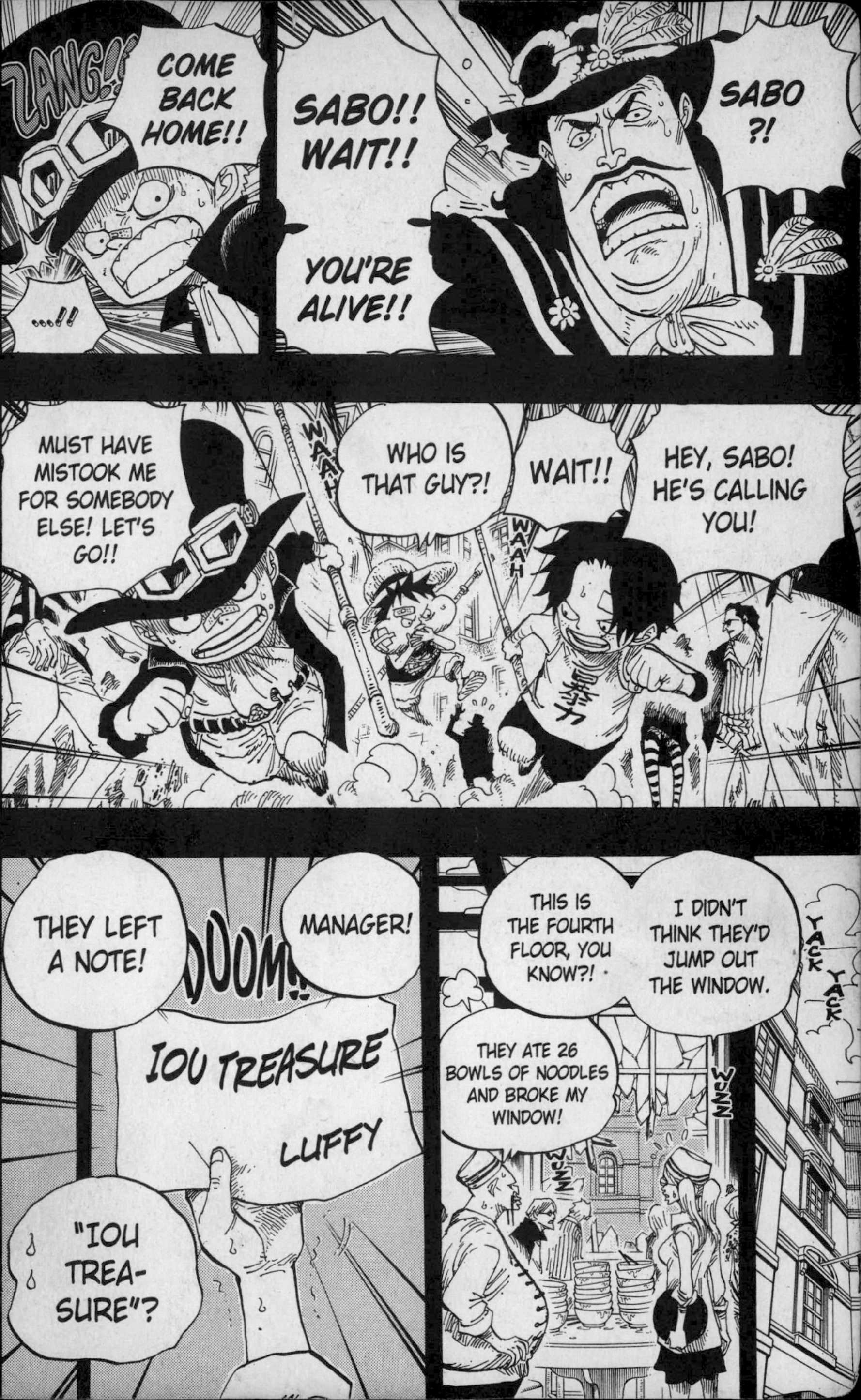
SABO ?!
SABO!! WAIT!!
YOU'RE ALIVE!!
ZANG!!
COME BACK HOME!!
...!!
HEY, SABO! HE'S CALLING YOU!
WAIT!!
WAAAH
WHO IS THAT GUY?!
WAAAH
MUST HAVE MISTOOK ME FOR SOMEBODY ELSE! LET'S GO!!
I DIDN'T THINK THEY'D JUMP OUT THE WINDOW.
THIS IS THE FOURTH FLOOR, YOU KNOW?!
YACK YACK
THEY ATE 26 BOWLS OF NOODLES AND BROKE MY WINDOW!
WUZZ
WUZZ
MANAGER!
THEY LEFT A NOTE!
DOOM!!
IOU TREASURE
LUFFY
"IOU TREA-SURE"?

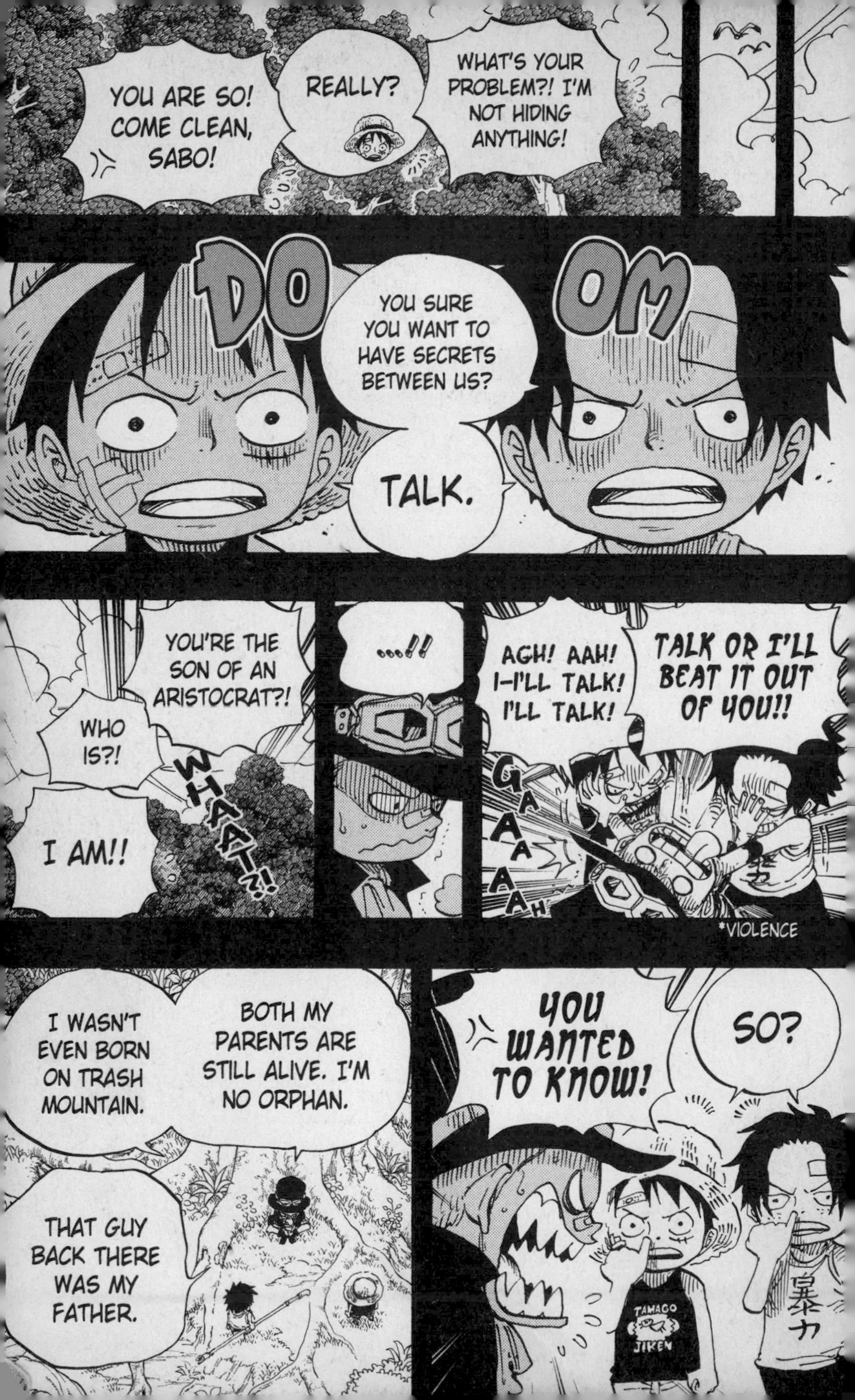
WHAT'S YOUR PROBLEM?! I'M NOT HIDING ANYTHING!
REALLY?
YOU ARE SO! COME CLEAN, SABO!
DOOM
YOU SURE YOU WANT TO HAVE SECRETS BETWEEN US?
TALK.
TALK OR I'LL BEAT IT OUT OF YOU!!
AGH! AAH! I-I'LL TALK! I'LL TALK!
GAAAAAAH
...!!
YOU'RE THE SON OF AN ARISTOCRAT?!
WHO IS?!
WHAAT?!
I AM!!
SO?
YOU WANTED TO KNOW!
TAMAGO JIKEN
暴力
*VIOLENCE
BOTH MY PARENTS ARE STILL ALIVE. I'M NO ORPHAN.
I WASN'T EVEN BORN ON TRASH MOUNTAIN.
THAT GUY BACK THERE WAS MY FATHER.

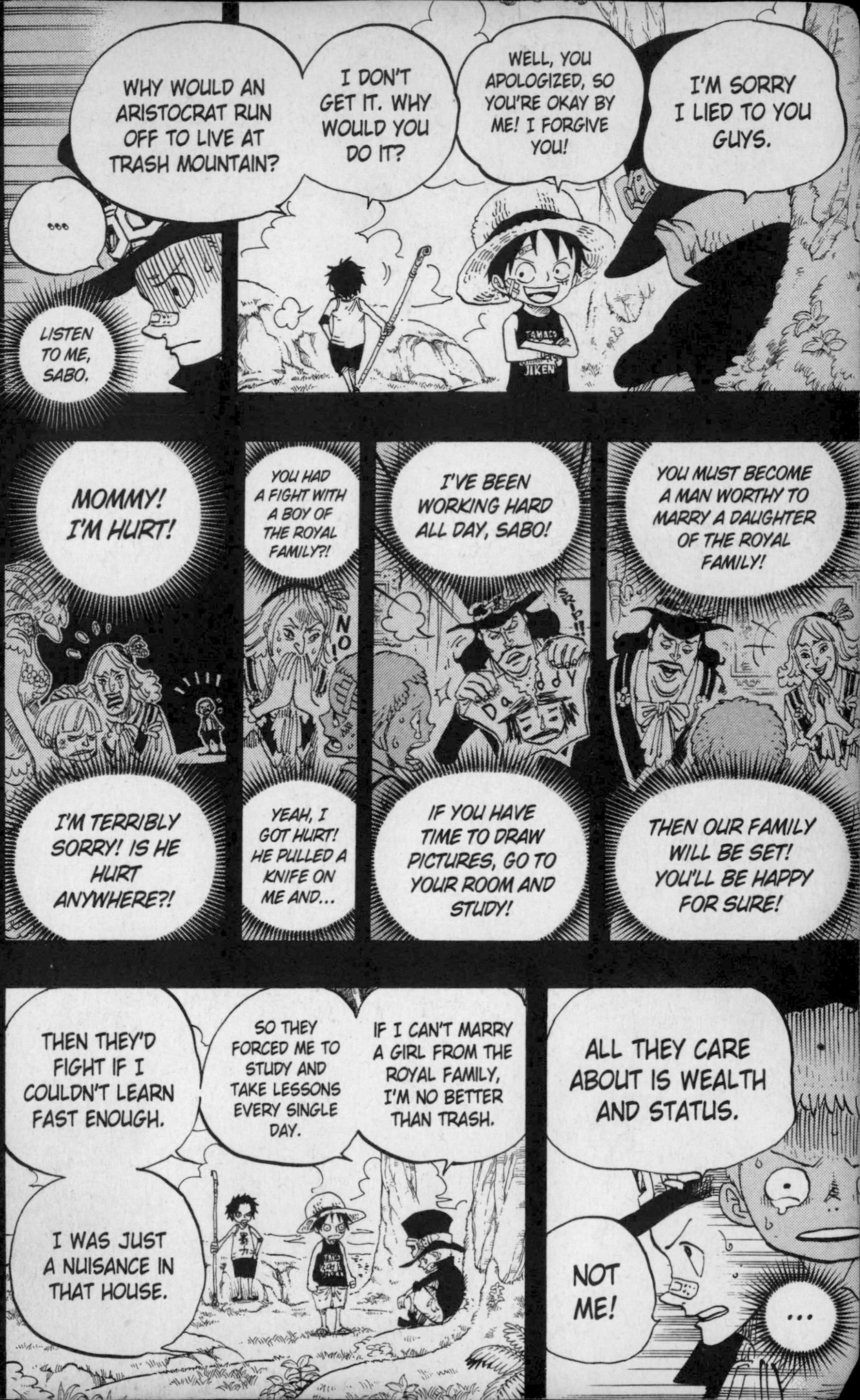
I'M SORRY I LIED TO YOU GUYS.
WELL, YOU APOLOGIZED, SO YOU'RE OKAY BY ME! I FORGIVE YOU!
I DON'T GET IT. WHY WOULD YOU DO IT?
WHY WOULD AN ARISTOCRAT RUN OFF TO LIVE AT TRASH MOUNTAIN?
...
LISTEN TO ME, SABO.
YOU MUST BECOME A MAN WORTHY TO MARRY A DAUGHTER OF THE ROYAL FAMILY!
THEN OUR FAMILY WILL BE SET! YOU'LL BE HAPPY FOR SURE!
I'VE BEEN WORKING HARD ALL DAY, SABO!
SRIP!!
IF YOU HAVE TIME TO DRAW PICTURES, GO TO YOUR ROOM AND STUDY!
YOU HAD A FIGHT WITH A BOY OF THE ROYAL FAMILY?!
NO!
YEAH, I GOT HURT! HE PULLED A KNIFE ON ME AND...
MOMMY! I'M HURT!
I'M TERRIBLY SORRY! IS HE HURT ANYWHERE?!
ALL THEY CARE ABOUT IS WEALTH AND STATUS.
...
NOT ME!
IF I CAN'T MARRY A GIRL FROM THE ROYAL FAMILY, I'M NO BETTER THAN TRASH.
SO THEY FORCED ME TO STUDY AND TAKE LESSONS EVERY SINGLE DAY.
THEN THEY'D FIGHT IF I COULDN'T LEARN FAST ENOUGH.
I WAS JUST A NUISANCE IN THAT HOUSE.

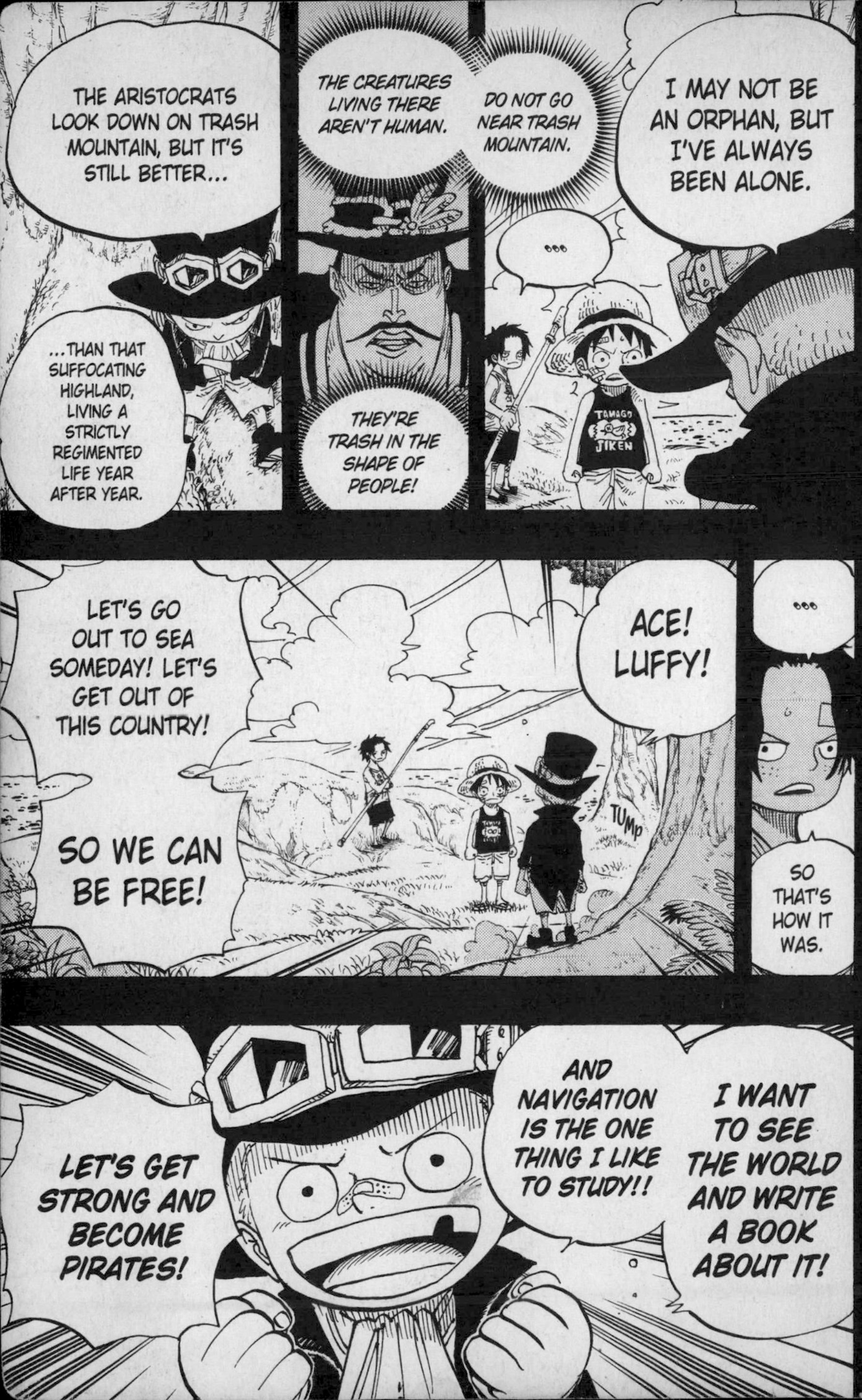
I MAY NOT BE AN ORPHAN, BUT I'VE ALWAYS BEEN ALONE.
...
DO NOT GO NEAR TRASH MOUNTAIN.
THE CREATURES LIVING THERE AREN'T HUMAN.
THEY'RE TRASH IN THE SHAPE OF PEOPLE!
THE ARISTOCRATS LOOK DOWN ON TRASH MOUNTAIN, BUT IT'S STILL BETTER...
...THAN THAT SUFFOCATING HIGHLAND, LIVING A STRICTLY REGIMENTED LIFE YEAR AFTER YEAR.
...
SO THAT'S HOW IT WAS.
ACE! LUFFY!
TUMP
LET'S GO OUT TO SEA SOMEDAY! LET'S GET OUT OF THIS COUNTRY!
SO WE CAN BE FREE!
I WANT TO SEE THE WORLD AND WRITE A BOOK ABOUT IT!
AND NAVIGATION IS THE ONE THING I LIKE TO STUDY!!
LET'S GET STRONG AND BECOME PIRATES!

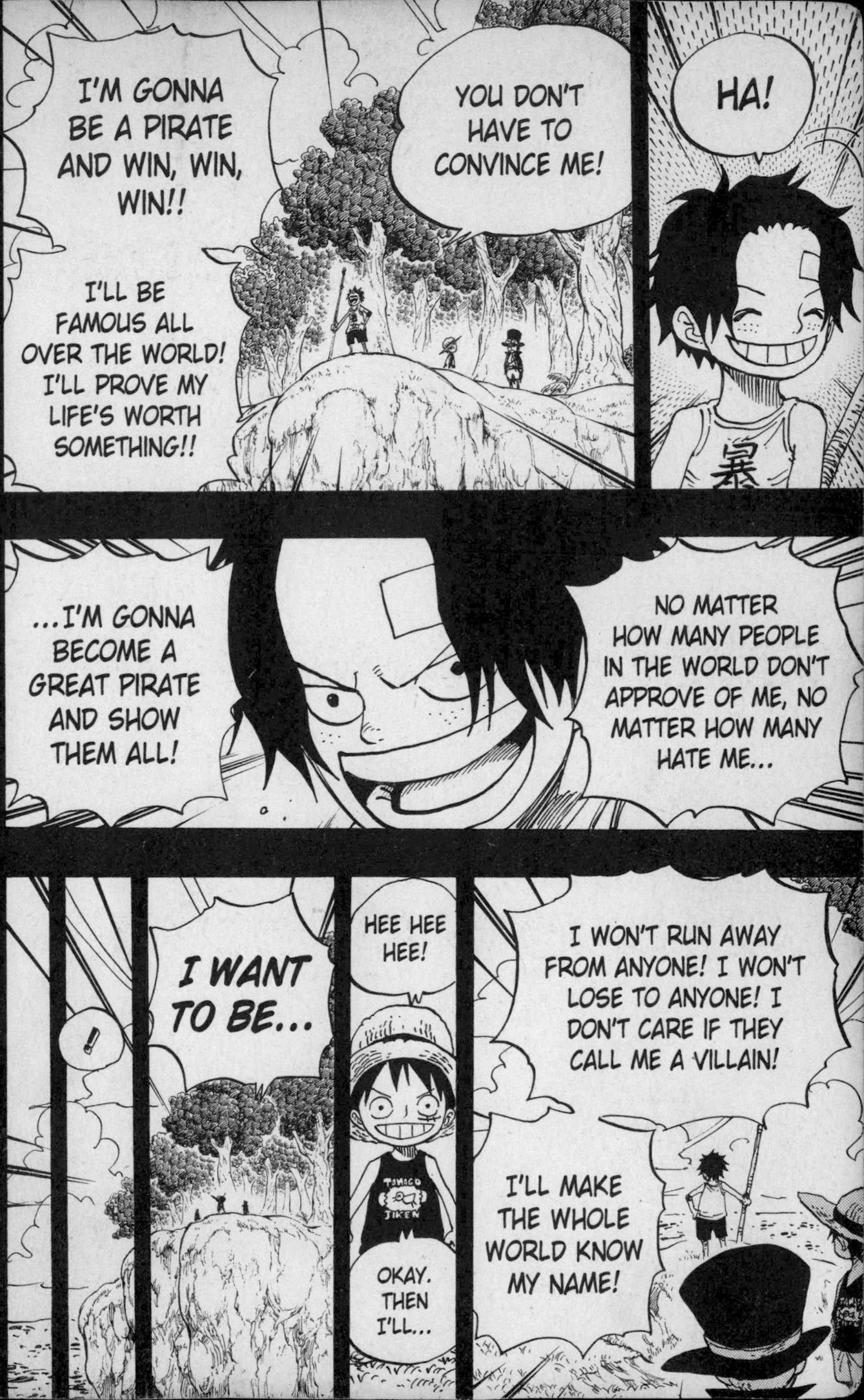
HA!
YOU DON'T HAVE TO CONVINCE ME!
I'M GONNA BE A PIRATE AND WIN, WIN, WIN!!
I'LL BE FAMOUS ALL OVER THE WORLD! I'LL PROVE MY LIFE'S WORTH SOMETHING!!
NO MATTER HOW MANY PEOPLE IN THE WORLD DON'T APPROVE OF ME, NO MATTER HOW MANY HATE ME...
...I'M GONNA BECOME A GREAT PIRATE AND SHOW THEM ALL!
I WON'T RUN AWAY FROM ANYONE! I WON'T LOSE TO ANYONE! I DON'T CARE IF THEY CALL ME A VILLAIN!
I'LL MAKE THE WHOLE WORLD KNOW MY NAME!
HEE HEE HEE!
OKAY. THEN I'LL...
I WANT TO BE...
!

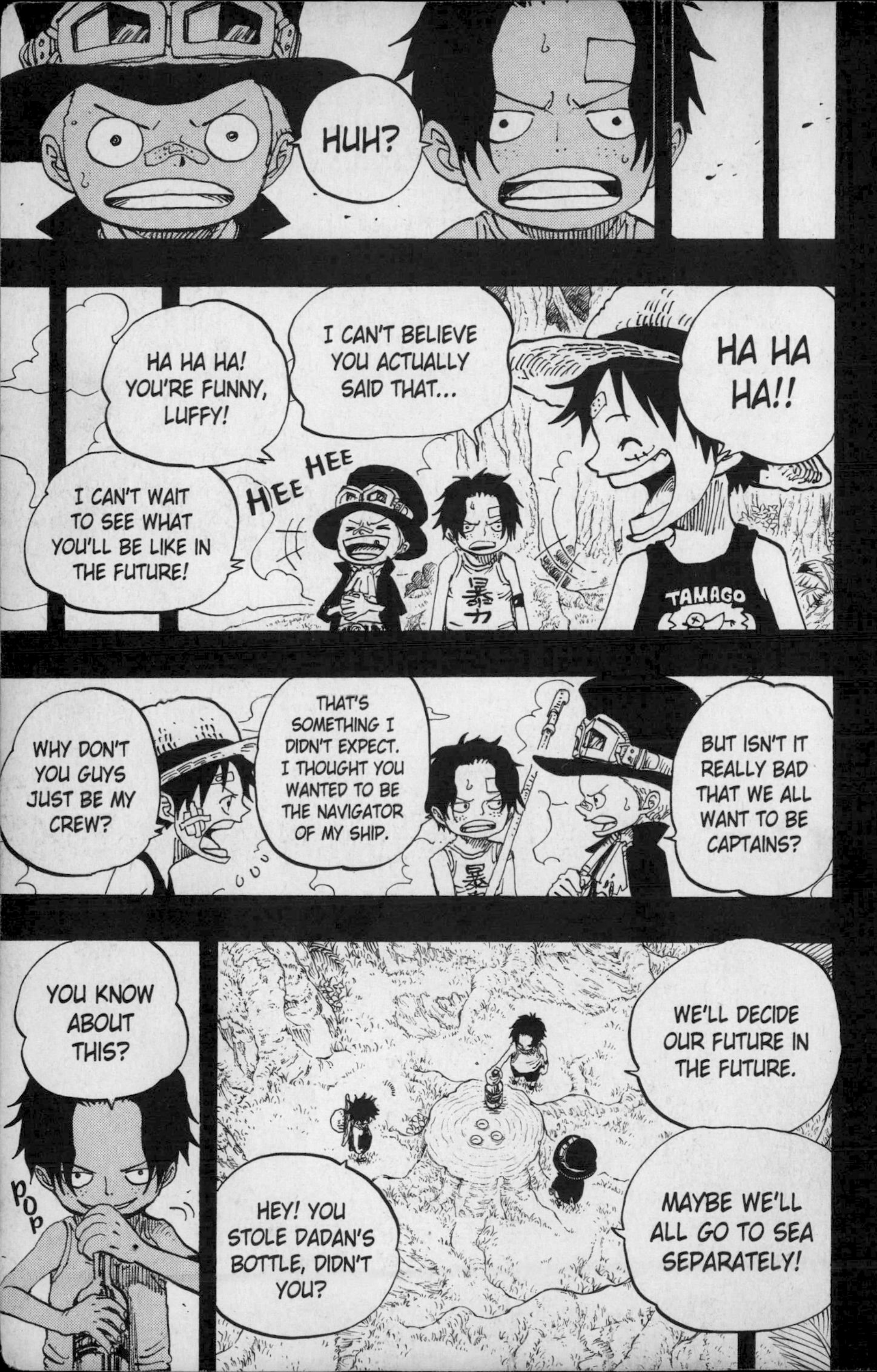
HUH?
HA HA HA!!
I CAN'T BELIEVE YOU ACTUALLY SAID THAT...
HA HA HA! YOU'RE FUNNY, LUFFY!
HEE HEE
I CAN'T WAIT TO SEE WHAT YOU'LL BE LIKE IN THE FUTURE!
TAMAGO
BUT ISN'T IT REALLY BAD THAT WE ALL WANT TO BE CAPTAINS?
THAT'S SOMETHING I DIDN'T EXPECT. I THOUGHT YOU WANTED TO BE THE NAVIGATOR OF MY SHIP.
WHY DON'T YOU GUYS JUST BE MY CREW?
WE'LL DECIDE OUR FUTURE IN THE FUTURE.
MAYBE WE'LL ALL GO TO SEA SEPARATELY!
HEY! YOU STOLE DADAN'S BOTTLE, DIDN'T YOU?
YOU KNOW ABOUT THIS?
POP

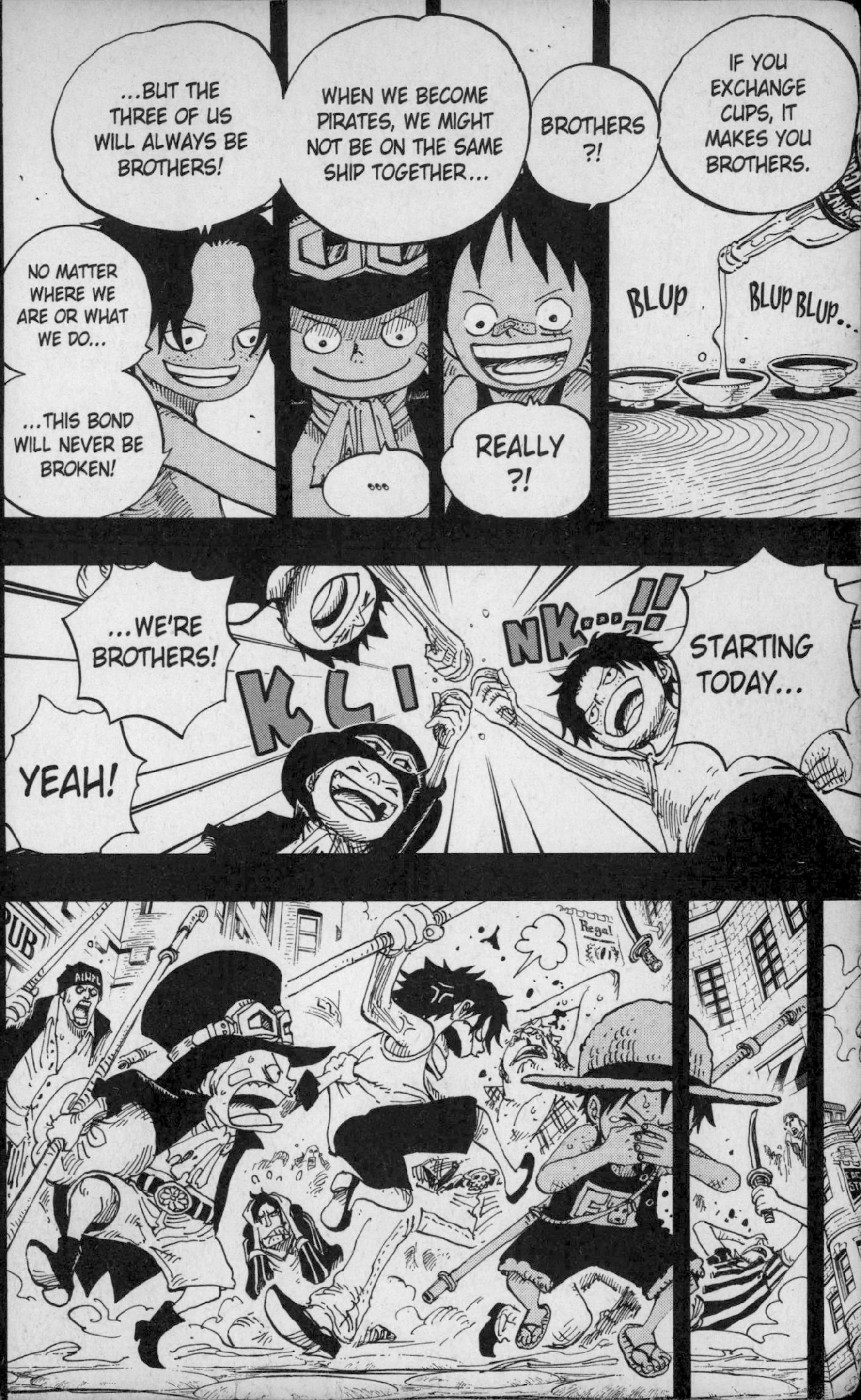
IF YOU EXCHANGE CUPS, IT MAKES YOU BROTHERS.
BLUP
BLUP BLUP...
BROTHERS ?!
REALLY ?!
WHEN WE BECOME PIRATES, WE MIGHT NOT BE ON THE SAME SHIP TOGETHER...
...
...BUT THE THREE OF US WILL ALWAYS BE BROTHERS!
NO MATTER WHERE WE ARE OR WHAT WE DO...
...THIS BOND WILL NEVER BE BROKEN!
STARTING TODAY...
KLI
NK...!!
...WE'RE BROTHERS!
YEAH!
Regal
PUB

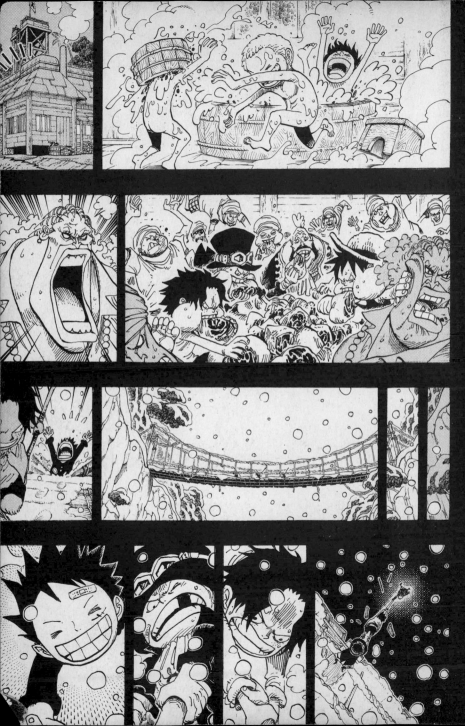

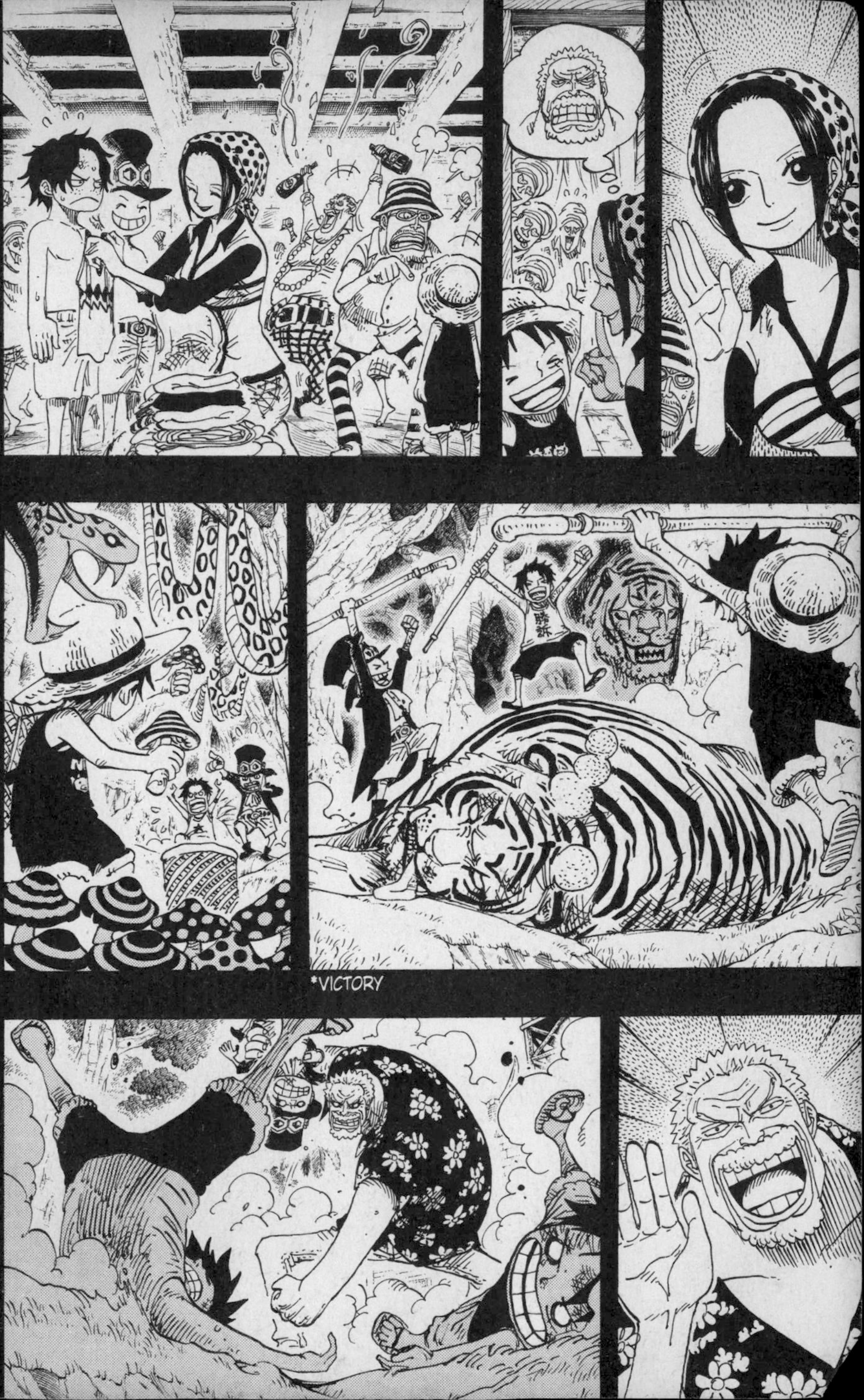
勝訴
*VICTORY

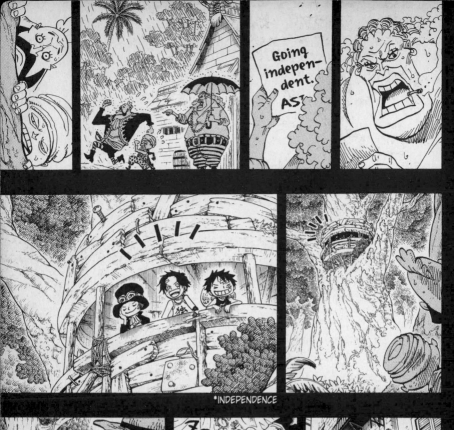

Going independ—dent. AS[*]

*INDEPENDENCE

*PILLAGE

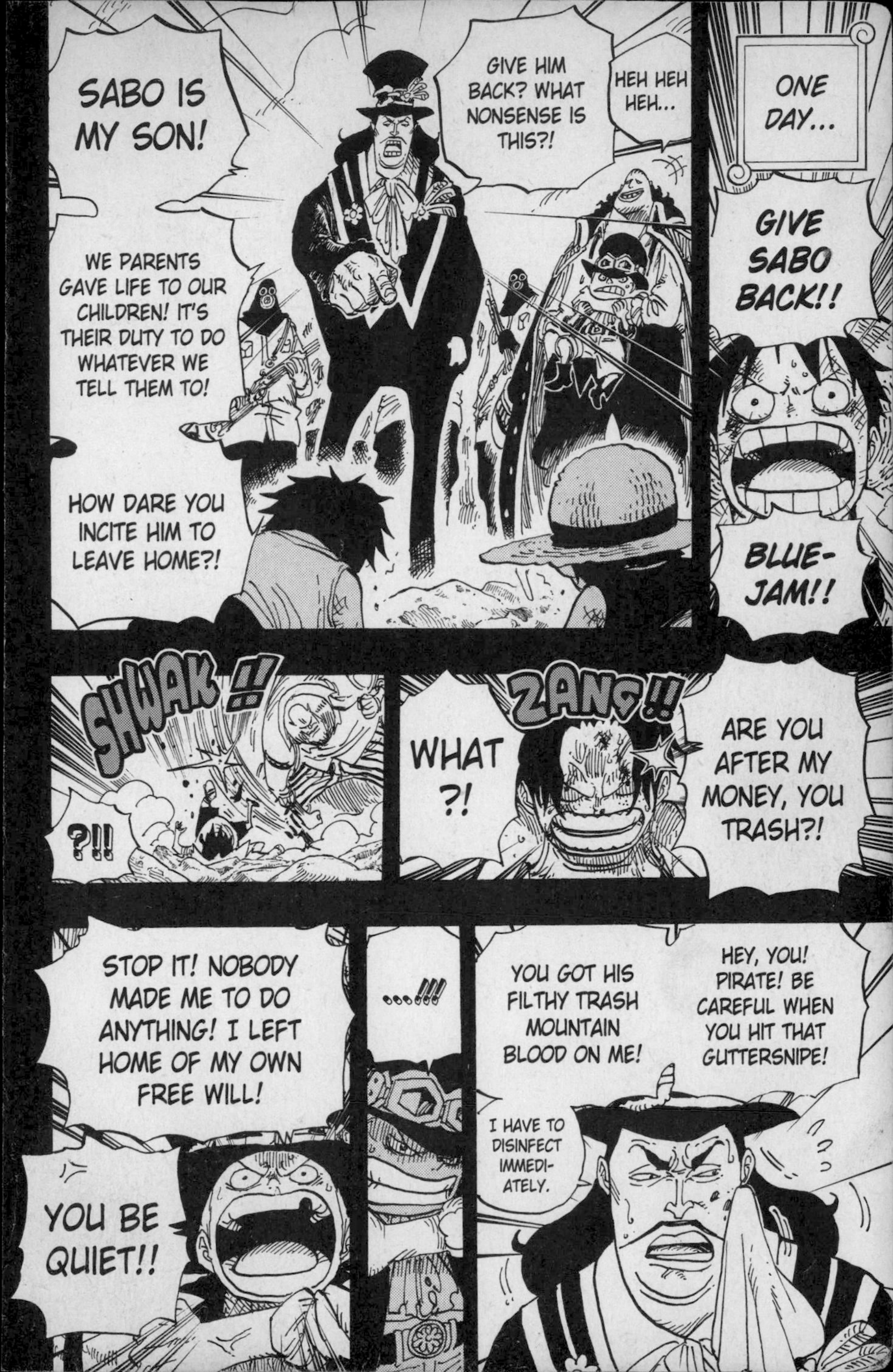

ONE DAY...
GIVE SABO BACK!!
BLUE-JAM!!
HEH HEH HEH...
GIVE HIM BACK? WHAT NONSENSE IS THIS?!
SABO IS MY SON!
WE PARENTS GAVE LIFE TO OUR CHILDREN! IT'S THEIR DUTY TO DO WHATEVER WE TELL THEM TO!
HOW DARE YOU INCITE HIM TO LEAVE HOME?!
ZANG!!
ARE YOU AFTER MY MONEY, YOU TRASH?!
WHAT ?!
SHWAK!!
?!!
HEY, YOU! PIRATE! BE CAREFUL WHEN YOU HIT THAT GUTTERSNIPE!
YOU GOT HIS FILTHY TRASH MOUNTAIN BLOOD ON ME!
I HAVE TO DISINFECT IMMEDI-ATELY.
...!!!
STOP IT! NOBODY MADE ME TO DO ANYTHING! I LEFT HOME OF MY OWN FREE WILL!
YOU BE QUIET!!

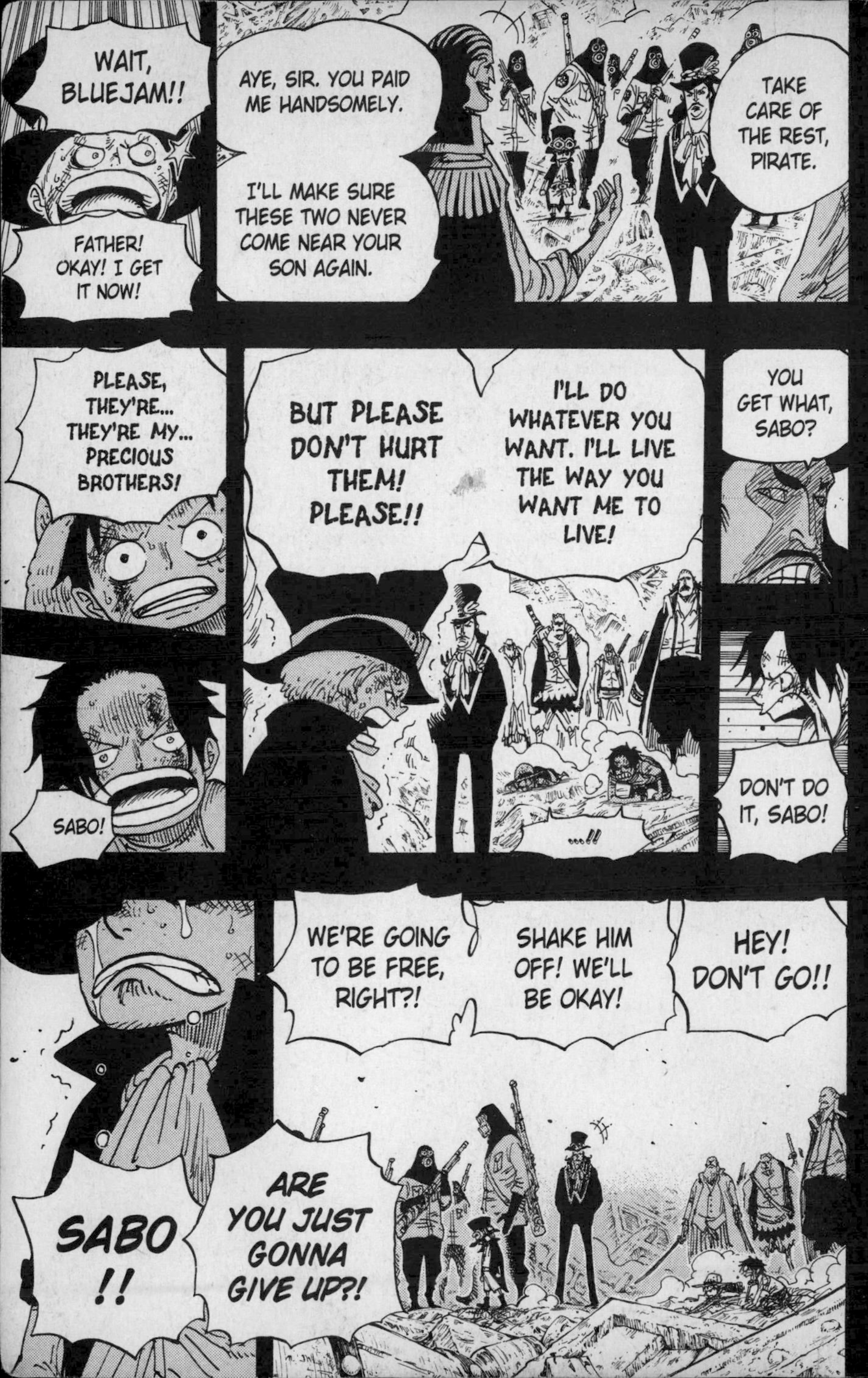
TAKE CARE OF THE REST, PIRATE.
AYE, SIR. YOU PAID ME HANDSOMELY.
I'LL MAKE SURE THESE TWO NEVER COME NEAR YOUR SON AGAIN.
WAIT, BLUEJAM!!
FATHER! OKAY! I GET IT NOW!
YOU GET WHAT, SABO?
DON'T DO IT, SABO!
I'LL DO WHATEVER YOU WANT. I'LL LIVE THE WAY YOU WANT ME TO LIVE!
BUT PLEASE DON'T HURT THEM! PLEASE!!
...!!
PLEASE, THEY'RE... THEY'RE MY... PRECIOUS BROTHERS!
SABO!
HEY! DON'T GO!!
SHAKE HIM OFF! WE'LL BE OKAY!
WE'RE GOING TO BE FREE, RIGHT?!
ARE YOU JUST GONNA GIVE UP?!
SABO!!

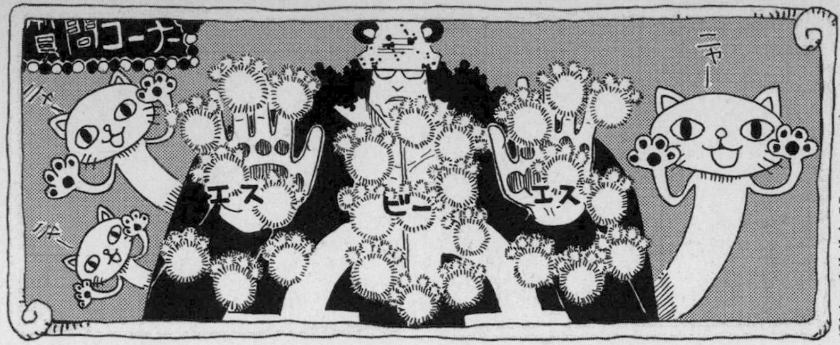
エス
ビー
エス
ニャー

(Shinokibibi, Kanagawa)

Reader (Q): Odacchi! Let's take a picture together! We'll take it when we say, *"ONE PIECE!"* ✌ klik♡ Oh, by the way, let's start the Question Corner! Yay! I said it!

--One Piece LOVE

Oda (A): Okay! ONE PIECE! ✌ Hey!! It already started!

Q: Hello! I have a question for Franky! My friend keeps shooting Coup de Vent at me during class! But I can't shoot my own Coup de Vent. (sweat drop) What's the proper counterattack?

--Ms. Birthday♡

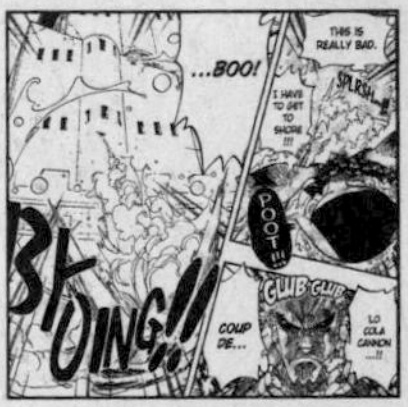
THIS IS REALLY BAD.
SPLRSH!!
I HAVE TO GET TO SHORE !!!
...BOO!
POOT!!!
BYOING!!
LO COLA CANNON ...!!
GLUB GLUB
COUP DE...

A: Shoot back with a "Coup de Boo." Right, Franky?

Franky: Yeah!

Q: Why does Admiral of the Fleet Sengoku get salmon roe on his head when he uses his powers?

--TomoP

A: What nice weather we're having today. Whoa, we caught a big one out at sea today! And I got some fresh salmon roe! Let's put some on top of the rice! Time to eat!♡ What's this I'm eating, a Sengoku Bowl?! It's not salmon roe, by the way. This is bad. Sengoku is starting to look like food to me.

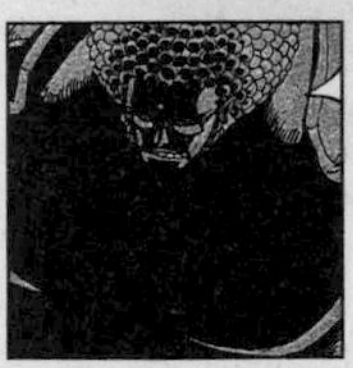

Q: Mr. Oda, what is Admiral of the Fleet Sengoku's power? I really want to know.

--SOD

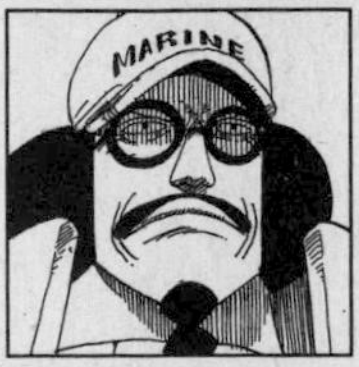
MARINE

A: See? If you ask like a normal human being, I'll answer like one. I gave him that look on a whim, but if you really want to know, he's actually a mythical beast zoan-type like Marco. His Devil Fruit is a Human-Human Fruit, model Buddha. I'm not sure if I can call Buddha a mythical beast or human, but it's just a biological category. Please leave it at that.

Chapter 586: CITY OF STENCH

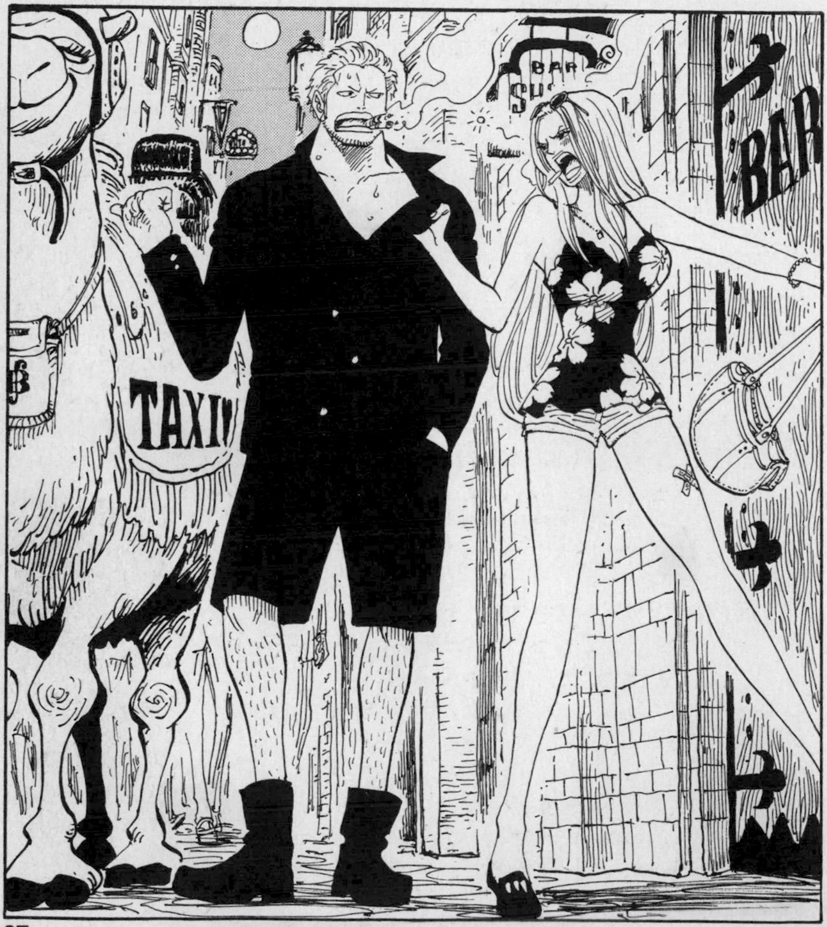
BAR
BAR
TAXI

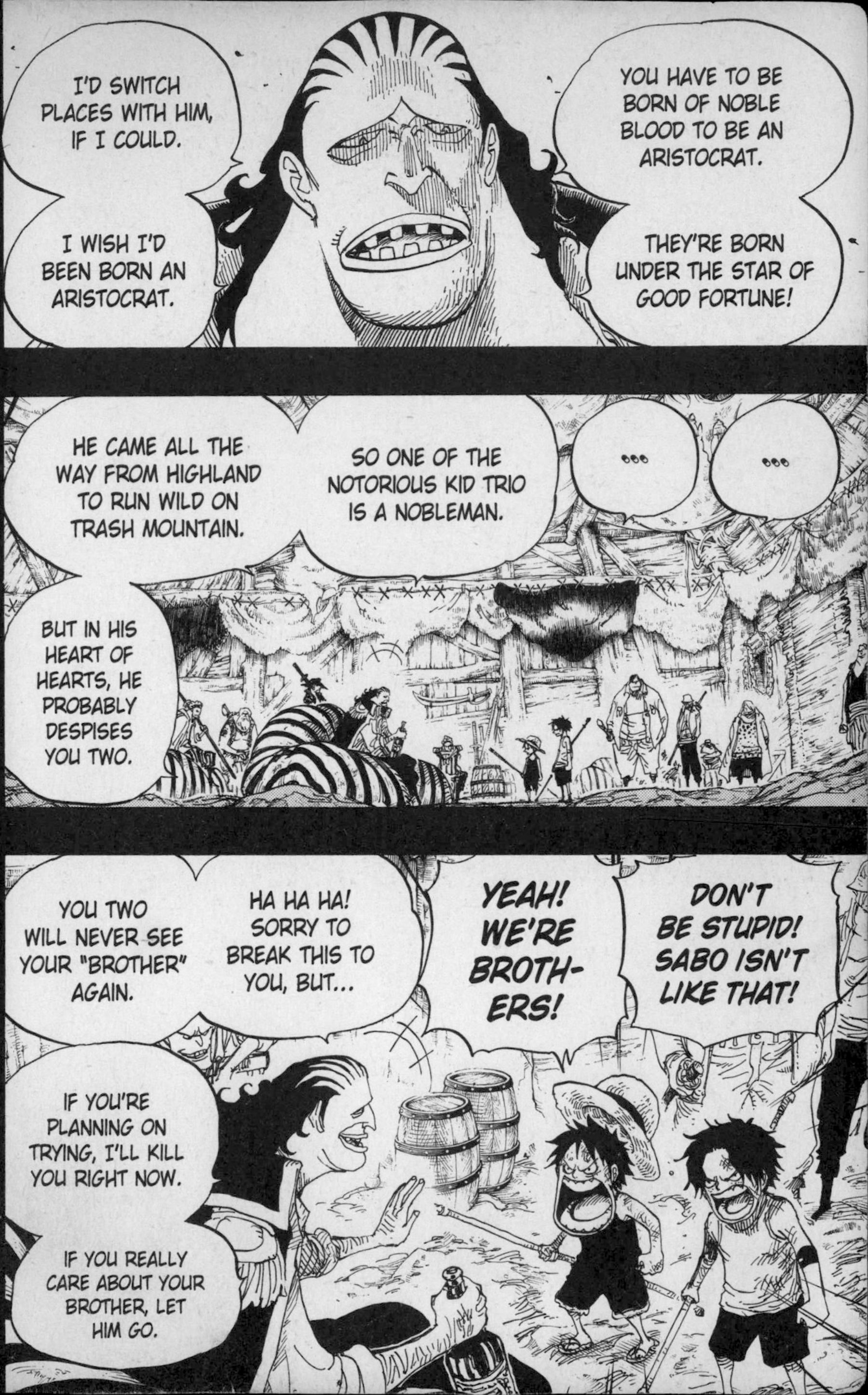
YOU HAVE TO BE BORN OF NOBLE BLOOD TO BE AN ARISTOCRAT.
THEY'RE BORN UNDER THE STAR OF GOOD FORTUNE!
I'D SWITCH PLACES WITH HIM, IF I COULD.
I WISH I'D BEEN BORN AN ARISTOCRAT.
...
...
SO ONE OF THE NOTORIOUS KID TRIO IS A NOBLEMAN.
HE CAME ALL THE WAY FROM HIGHLAND TO RUN WILD ON TRASH MOUNTAIN.
BUT IN HIS HEART OF HEARTS, HE PROBABLY DESPISES YOU TWO.
DON'T BE STUPID! SABO ISN'T LIKE THAT!
YEAH! WE'RE BROTH-ERS!
HA HA HA! SORRY TO BREAK THIS TO YOU, BUT...
YOU TWO WILL NEVER SEE YOUR "BROTHER" AGAIN.
IF YOU'RE PLANNING ON TRYING, I'LL KILL YOU RIGHT NOW.
IF YOU REALLY CARE ABOUT YOUR BROTHER, LET HIM GO.

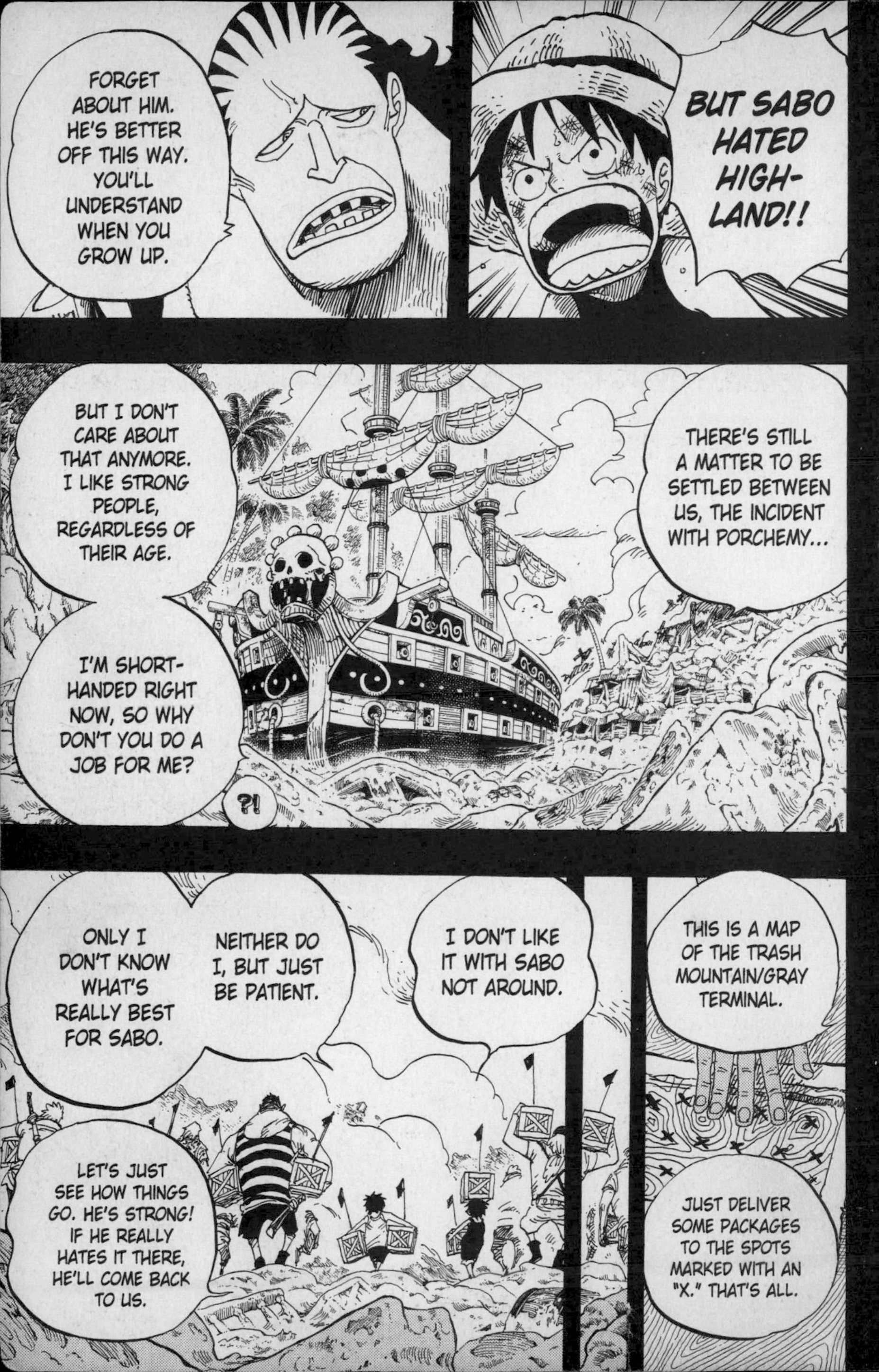
BUT SABO HATED HIGH-LAND!!
FORGET ABOUT HIM. HE'S BETTER OFF THIS WAY. YOU'LL UNDERSTAND WHEN YOU GROW UP.
THERE'S STILL A MATTER TO BE SETTLED BETWEEN US, THE INCIDENT WITH PORCHEMY...
BUT I DON'T CARE ABOUT THAT ANYMORE. I LIKE STRONG PEOPLE, REGARDLESS OF THEIR AGE.
I'M SHORT-HANDED RIGHT NOW, SO WHY DON'T YOU DO A JOB FOR ME?
?!
THIS IS A MAP OF THE TRASH MOUNTAIN/GRAY TERMINAL.
JUST DELIVER SOME PACKAGES TO THE SPOTS MARKED WITH AN "X." THAT'S ALL.
I DON'T LIKE IT WITH SABO NOT AROUND.
NEITHER DO I, BUT JUST BE PATIENT.
ONLY I DON'T KNOW WHAT'S REALLY BEST FOR SABO.
LET'S JUST SEE HOW THINGS GO. HE'S STRONG! IF HE REALLY HATES IT THERE, HE'LL COME BACK TO US.

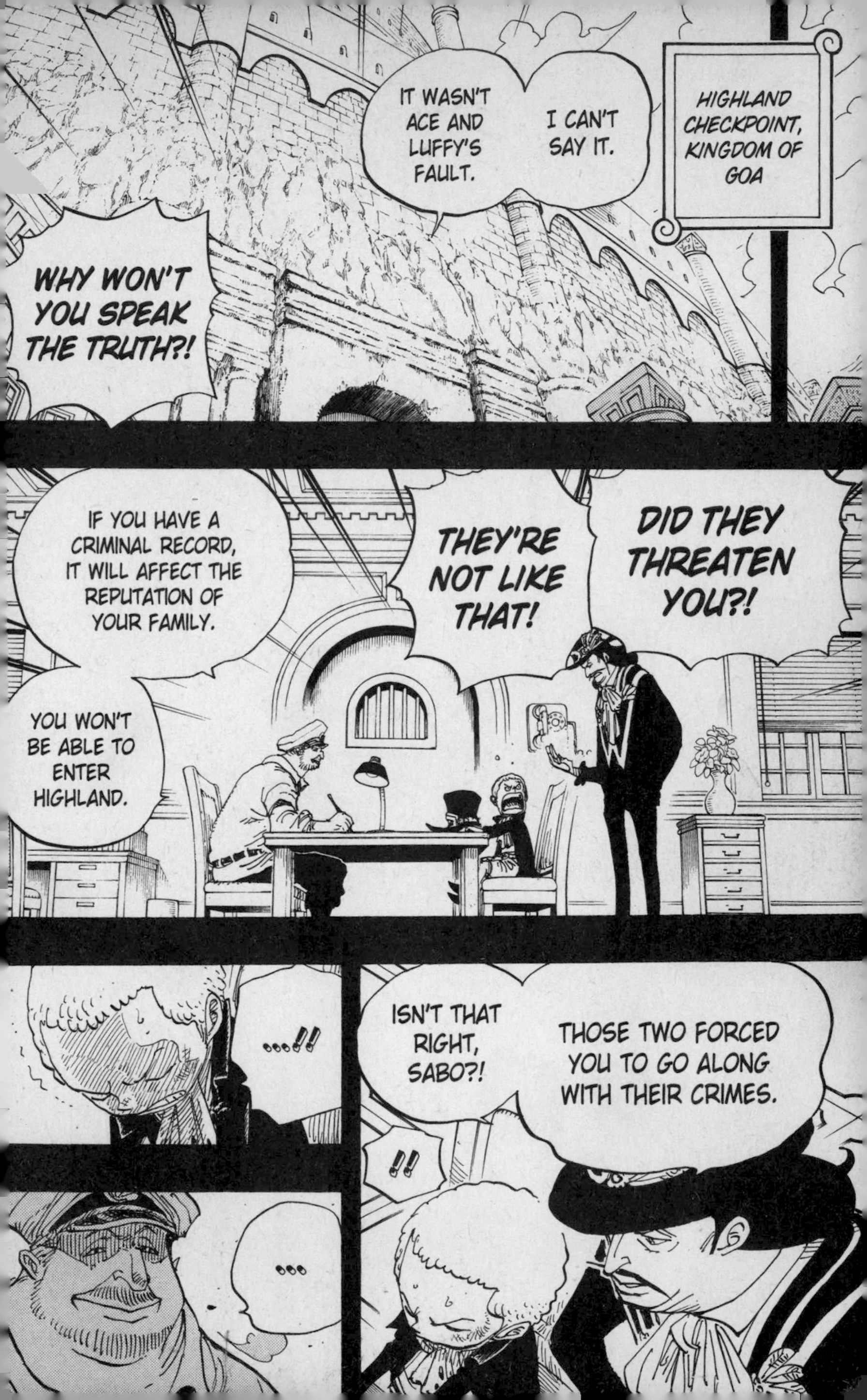
HIGHLAND CHECKPOINT, KINGDOM OF GOA
I CAN'T SAY IT.
IT WASN'T ACE AND LUFFY'S FAULT.
WHY WON'T YOU SPEAK THE TRUTH?!
DID THEY THREATEN YOU?!
THEY'RE NOT LIKE THAT!
IF YOU HAVE A CRIMINAL RECORD, IT WILL AFFECT THE REPUTATION OF YOUR FAMILY.
YOU WON'T BE ABLE TO ENTER HIGHLAND.
THOSE TWO FORCED YOU TO GO ALONG WITH THEIR CRIMES.
ISN'T THAT RIGHT, SABO?!
!!
...!!
...

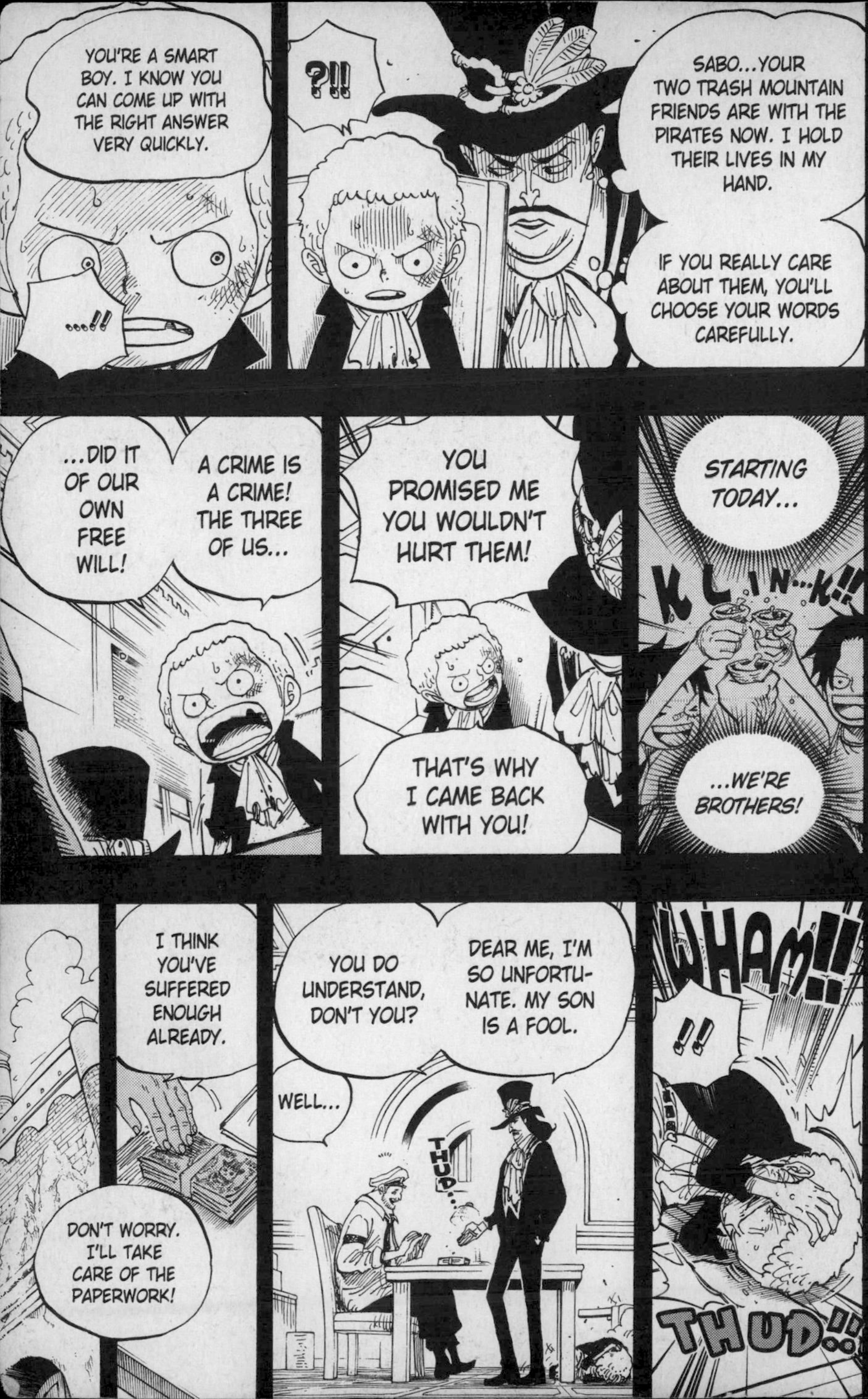
SABO...YOUR TWO TRASH MOUNTAIN FRIENDS ARE WITH THE PIRATES NOW. I HOLD THEIR LIVES IN MY HAND.
?!!
IF YOU REALLY CARE ABOUT THEM, YOU'LL CHOOSE YOUR WORDS CAREFULLY.
YOU'RE A SMART BOY. I KNOW YOU CAN COME UP WITH THE RIGHT ANSWER VERY QUICKLY.
...!!
STARTING TODAY...
KLIN...K!!
...WE'RE BROTHERS!
YOU PROMISED ME YOU WOULDN'T HURT THEM!
THAT'S WHY I CAME BACK WITH YOU!
A CRIME IS A CRIME! THE THREE OF US...
...DID IT OF OUR OWN FREE WILL!
WHAM!!
!!
THUD!!
DEAR ME, I'M SO UNFORTU-NATE. MY SON IS A FOOL.
YOU DO UNDERSTAND, DON'T YOU?
WELL...
THUD...
I THINK YOU'VE SUFFERED ENOUGH ALREADY.
DON'T WORRY. I'LL TAKE CARE OF THE PAPERWORK!

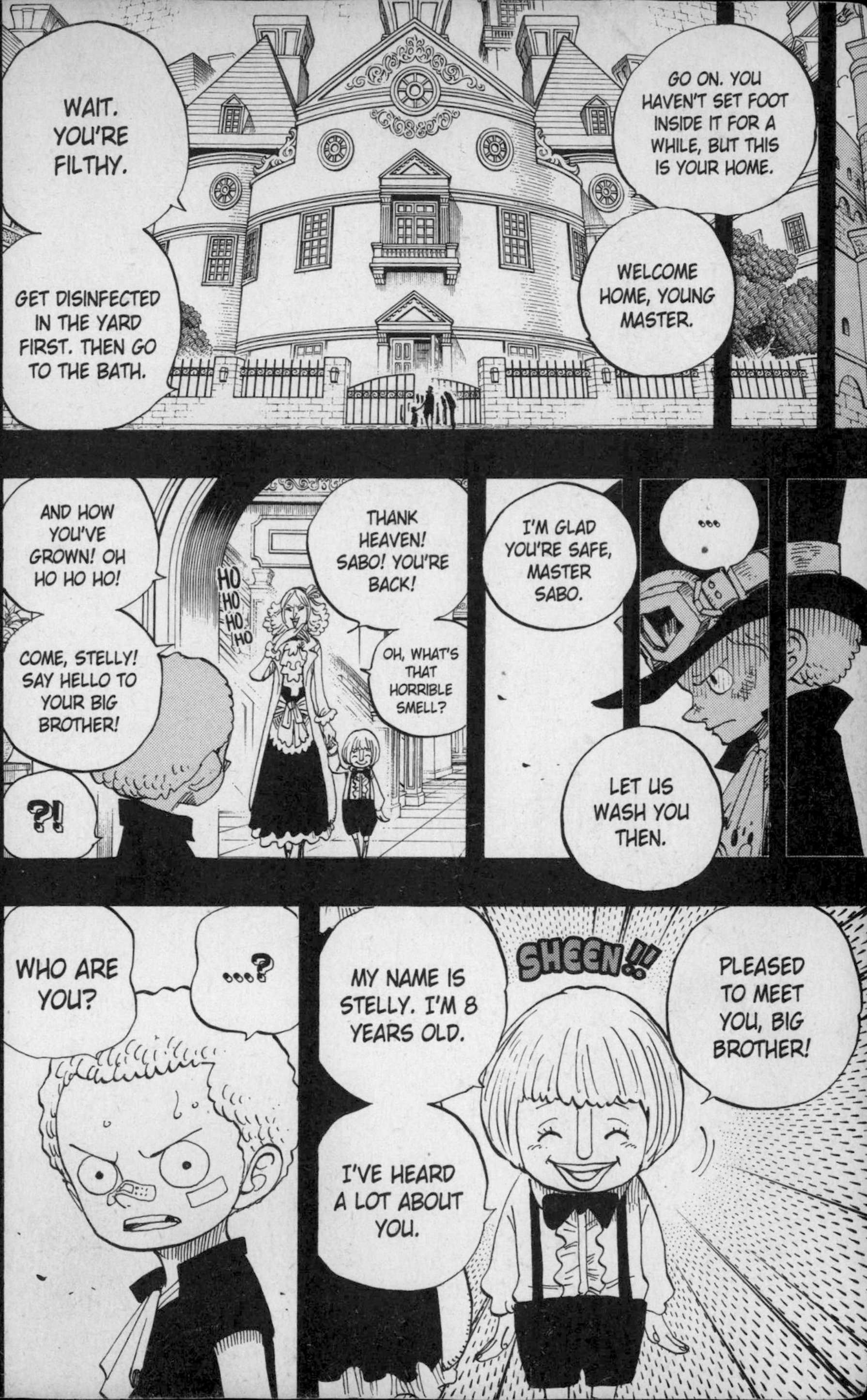

GO ON. YOU HAVEN'T SET FOOT INSIDE IT FOR A WHILE, BUT THIS IS YOUR HOME.
WELCOME HOME, YOUNG MASTER.
WAIT. YOU'RE FILTHY.
GET DISINFECTED IN THE YARD FIRST. THEN GO TO THE BATH.
...
I'M GLAD YOU'RE SAFE, MASTER SABO.
LET US WASH YOU THEN.
THANK HEAVEN! SABO! YOU'RE BACK!
OH, WHAT'S THAT HORRIBLE SMELL?
AND HOW YOU'VE GROWN! OH HO HO HO!
HO HO HO HO
COME, STELLY! SAY HELLO TO YOUR BIG BROTHER!
?!
SHEEN!!
PLEASED TO MEET YOU, BIG BROTHER!
MY NAME IS STELLY. I'M 8 YEARS OLD.
I'VE HEARD A LOT ABOUT YOU.
...?
WHO ARE YOU?

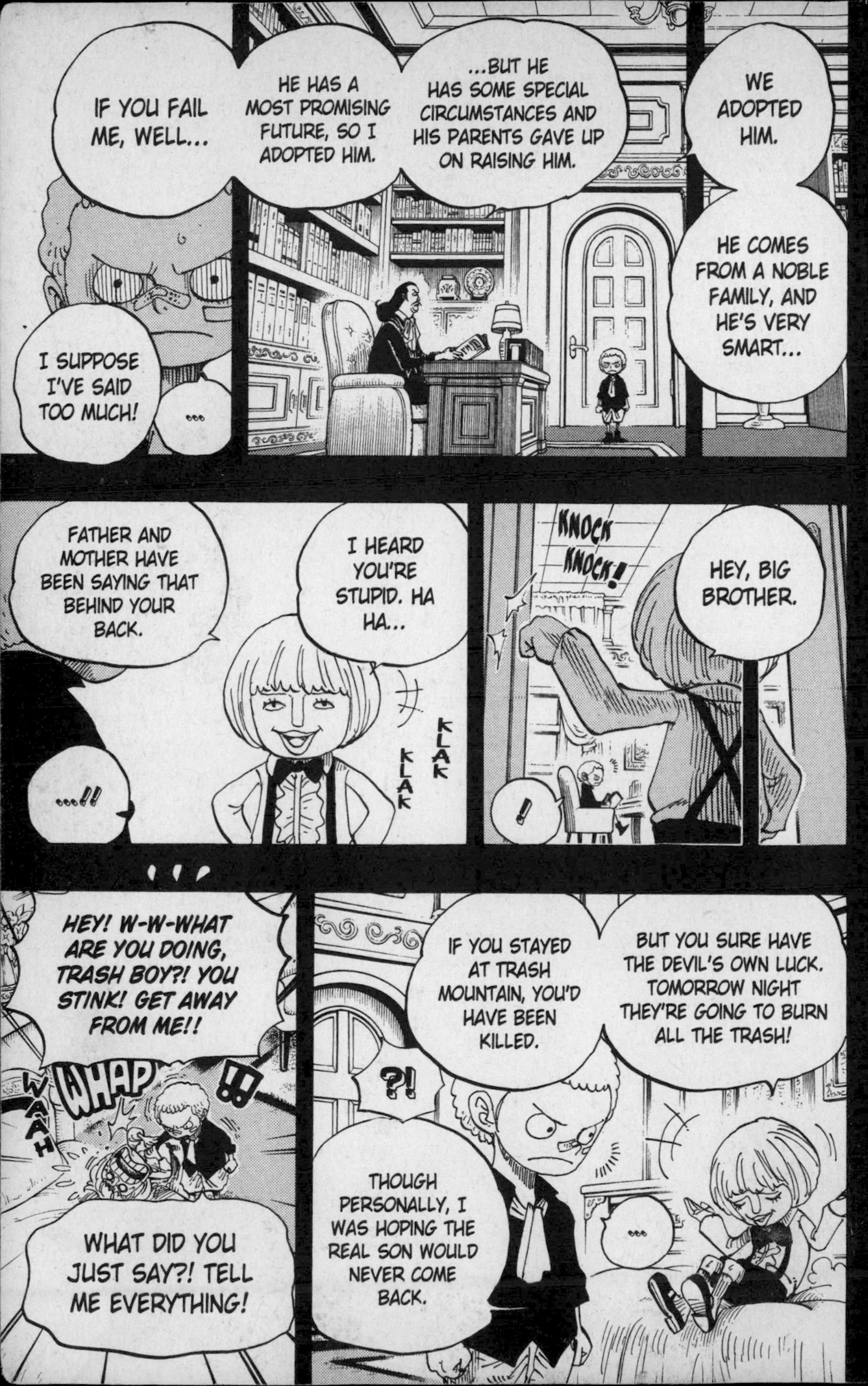
WE ADOPTED HIM.
HE COMES FROM A NOBLE FAMILY, AND HE'S VERY SMART...
...BUT HE HAS SOME SPECIAL CIRCUMSTANCES AND HIS PARENTS GAVE UP ON RAISING HIM.
HE HAS A MOST PROMISING FUTURE, SO I ADOPTED HIM.
IF YOU FAIL ME, WELL...
I SUPPOSE I'VE SAID TOO MUCH!
...
KNOCK KNOCK!
HEY, BIG BROTHER.
!
I HEARD YOU'RE STUPID. HA HA...
KLAK KLAK
FATHER AND MOTHER HAVE BEEN SAYING THAT BEHIND YOUR BACK.
...!!
BUT YOU SURE HAVE THE DEVIL'S OWN LUCK. TOMORROW NIGHT THEY'RE GOING TO BURN ALL THE TRASH!
IF YOU STAYED AT TRASH MOUNTAIN, YOU'D HAVE BEEN KILLED.
?!
THOUGH PERSONALLY, I WAS HOPING THE REAL SON WOULD NEVER COME BACK.
...
HEY! W-W-WHAT ARE YOU DOING, TRASH BOY?! YOU STINK! GET AWAY FROM ME!!
WHAP
WAAH
!!
WHAT DID YOU JUST SAY?! TELL ME EVERYTHING!

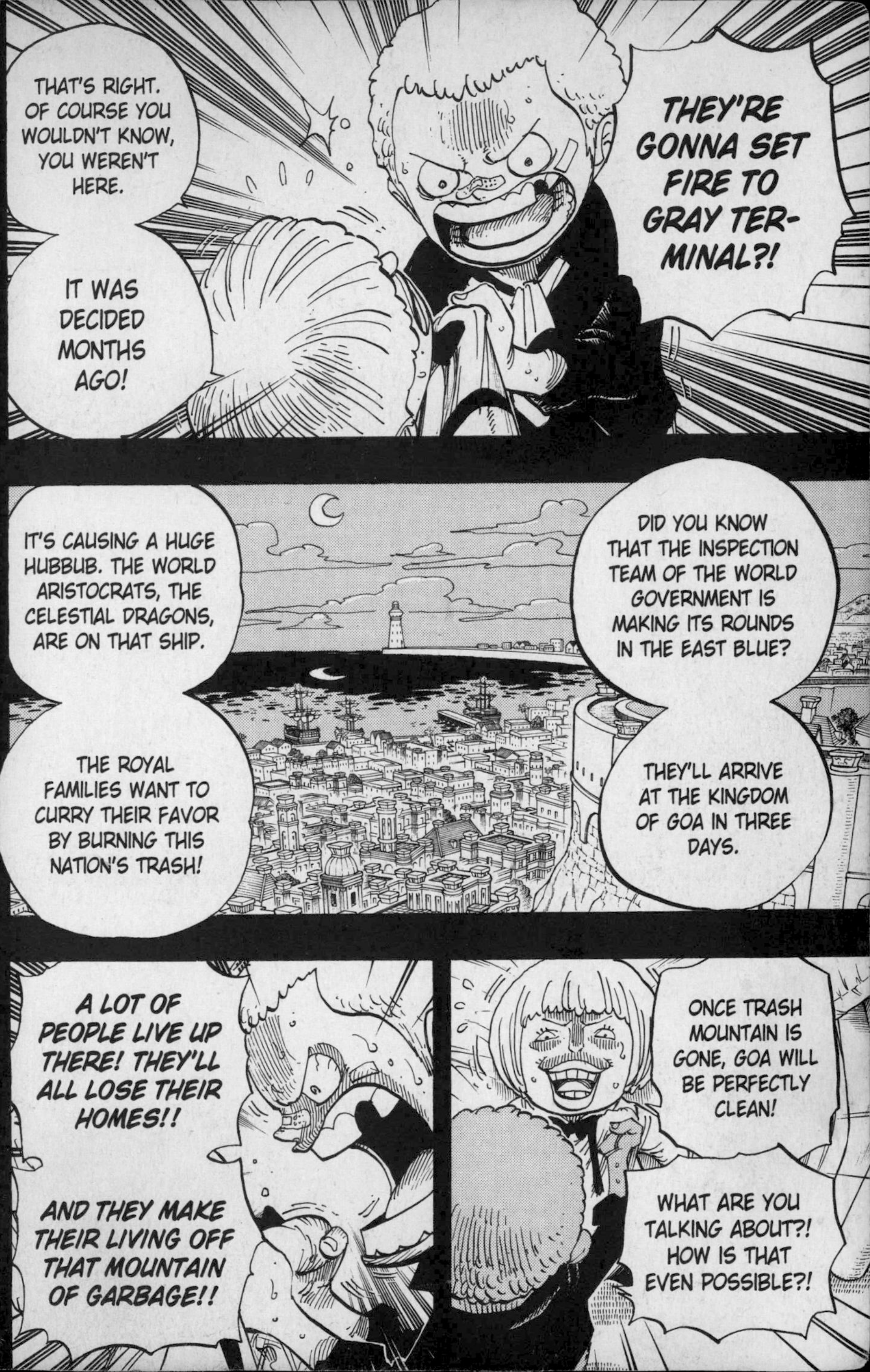
THEY'RE GONNA SET FIRE TO GRAY TER-MINAL?!
THAT'S RIGHT. OF COURSE YOU WOULDN'T KNOW, YOU WEREN'T HERE.
IT WAS DECIDED MONTHS AGO!
DID YOU KNOW THAT THE INSPECTION TEAM OF THE WORLD GOVERNMENT IS MAKING ITS ROUNDS IN THE EAST BLUE?
THEY'LL ARRIVE AT THE KINGDOM OF GOA IN THREE DAYS.
IT'S CAUSING A HUGE HUBBUB. THE WORLD ARISTOCRATS, THE CELESTIAL DRAGONS, ARE ON THAT SHIP.
THE ROYAL FAMILIES WANT TO CURRY THEIR FAVOR BY BURNING THIS NATION'S TRASH!
ONCE TRASH MOUNTAIN IS GONE, GOA WILL BE PERFECTLY CLEAN!
WHAT ARE YOU TALKING ABOUT?! HOW IS THAT EVEN POSSIBLE?!
A LOT OF PEOPLE LIVE UP THERE! THEY'LL ALL LOSE THEIR HOMES!!
AND THEY MAKE THEIR LIVING OFF THAT MOUNTAIN OF GARBAGE!!

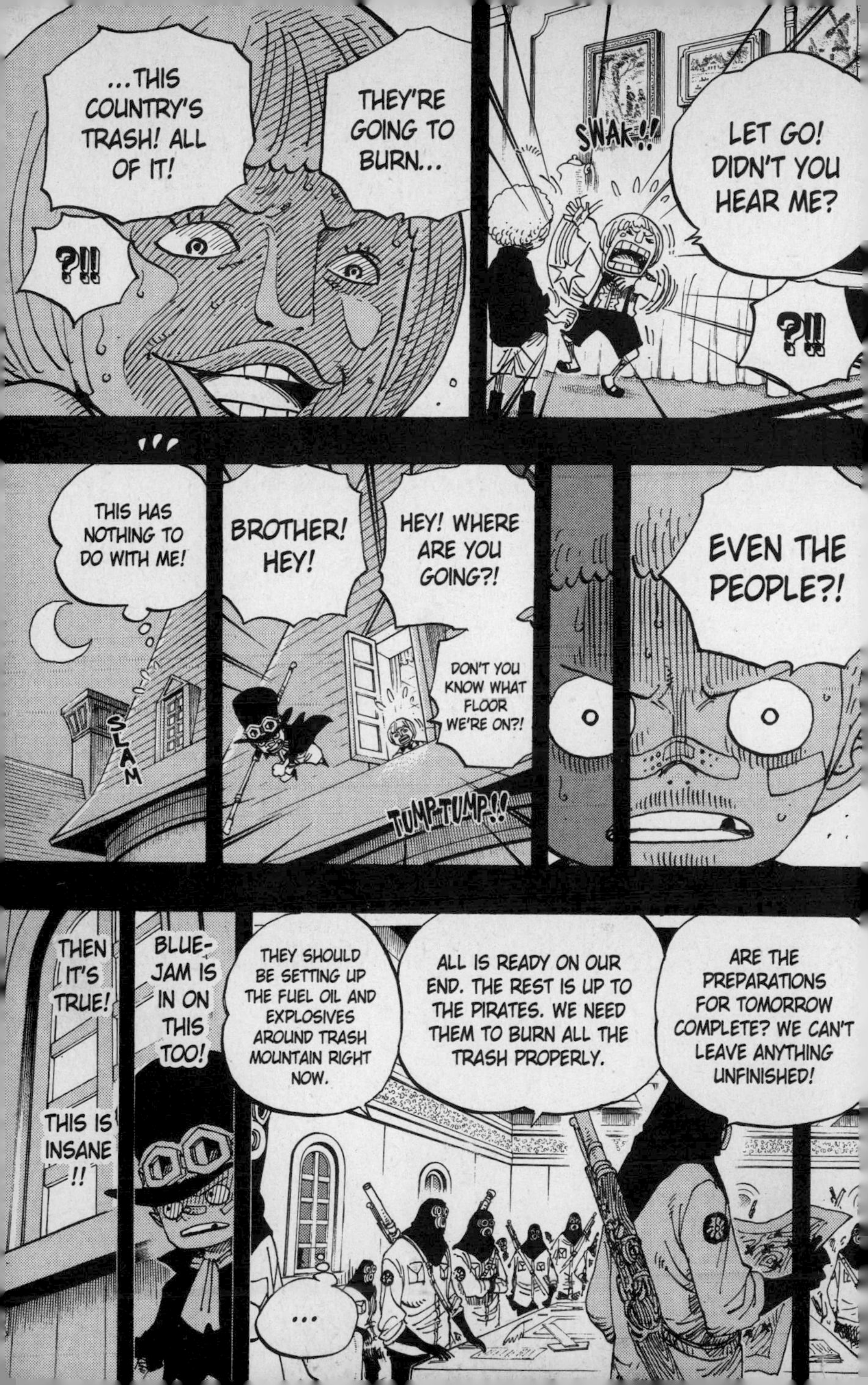
SWAK!!
LET GO! DIDN'T YOU HEAR ME?
?!!
THEY'RE GOING TO BURN...
...THIS COUNTRY'S TRASH! ALL OF IT!
?!!
EVEN THE PEOPLE?!
HEY! WHERE ARE YOU GOING?!
BROTHER! HEY!
DON'T YOU KNOW WHAT FLOOR WE'RE ON?!
TUMP TUMP!!
THIS HAS NOTHING TO DO WITH ME!
SLAM
ARE THE PREPARATIONS FOR TOMORROW COMPLETE? WE CAN'T LEAVE ANYTHING UNFINISHED!
ALL IS READY ON OUR END. THE REST IS UP TO THE PIRATES. WE NEED THEM TO BURN ALL THE TRASH PROPERLY.
THEY SHOULD BE SETTING UP THE FUEL OIL AND EXPLOSIVES AROUND TRASH MOUNTAIN RIGHT NOW.
...
BLUE-JAM IS IN ON THIS TOO!
THEN IT'S TRUE!
THIS IS INSANE!!

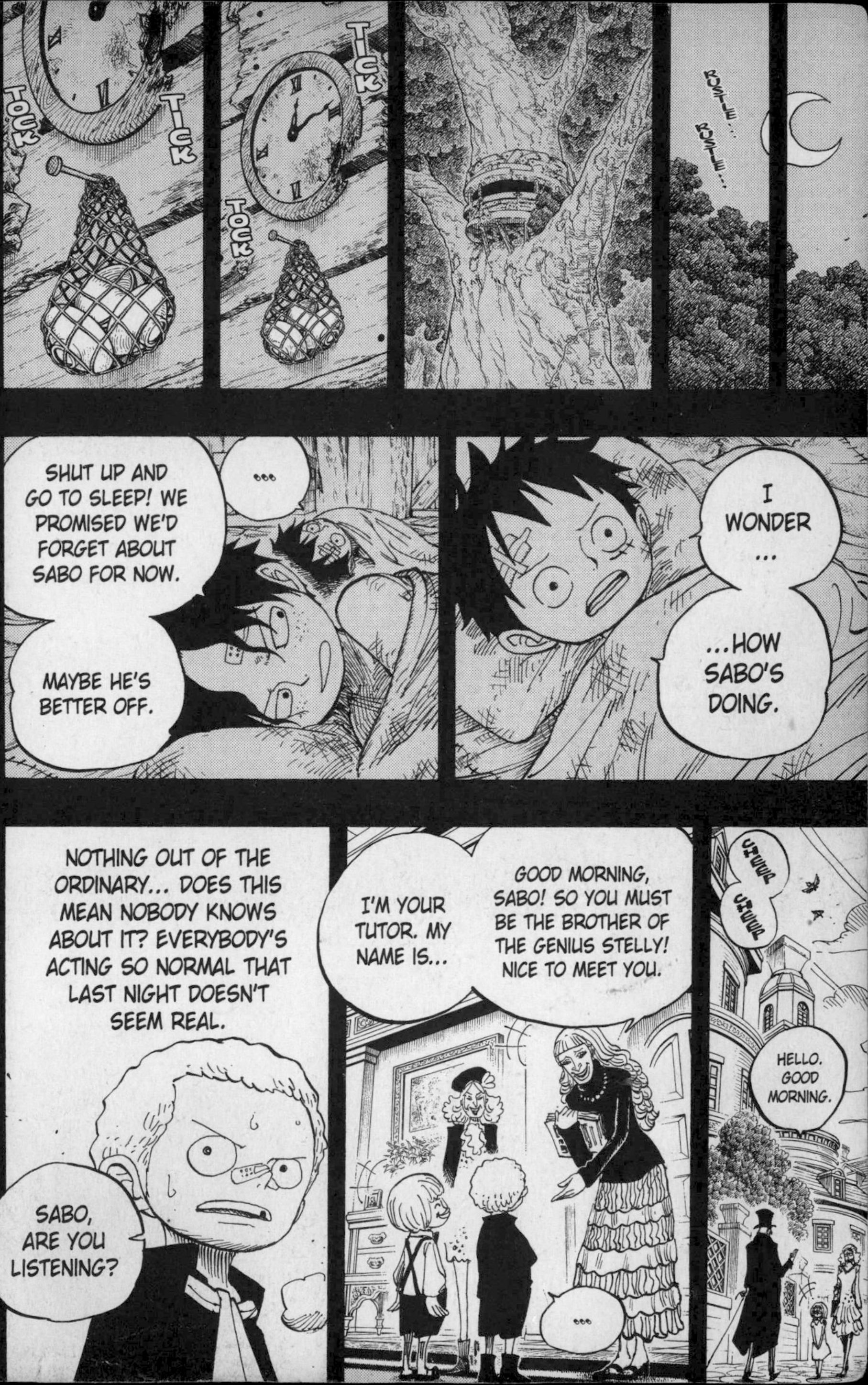
RUSTLE...
RUSTLE...
TICK
TOCK
TICK
TOCK
I WONDER...
...HOW SABO'S DOING.
...
SHUT UP AND GO TO SLEEP! WE PROMISED WE'D FORGET ABOUT SABO FOR NOW.
MAYBE HE'S BETTER OFF.
CHEEP
CHEEP
HELLO. GOOD MORNING.
GOOD MORNING, SABO! SO YOU MUST BE THE BROTHER OF THE GENIUS STELLY! NICE TO MEET YOU.
I'M YOUR TUTOR. MY NAME IS...
...
NOTHING OUT OF THE ORDINARY... DOES THIS MEAN NOBODY KNOWS ABOUT IT? EVERYBODY'S ACTING SO NORMAL THAT LAST NIGHT DOESN'T SEEM REAL.
SABO, ARE YOU LISTENING?

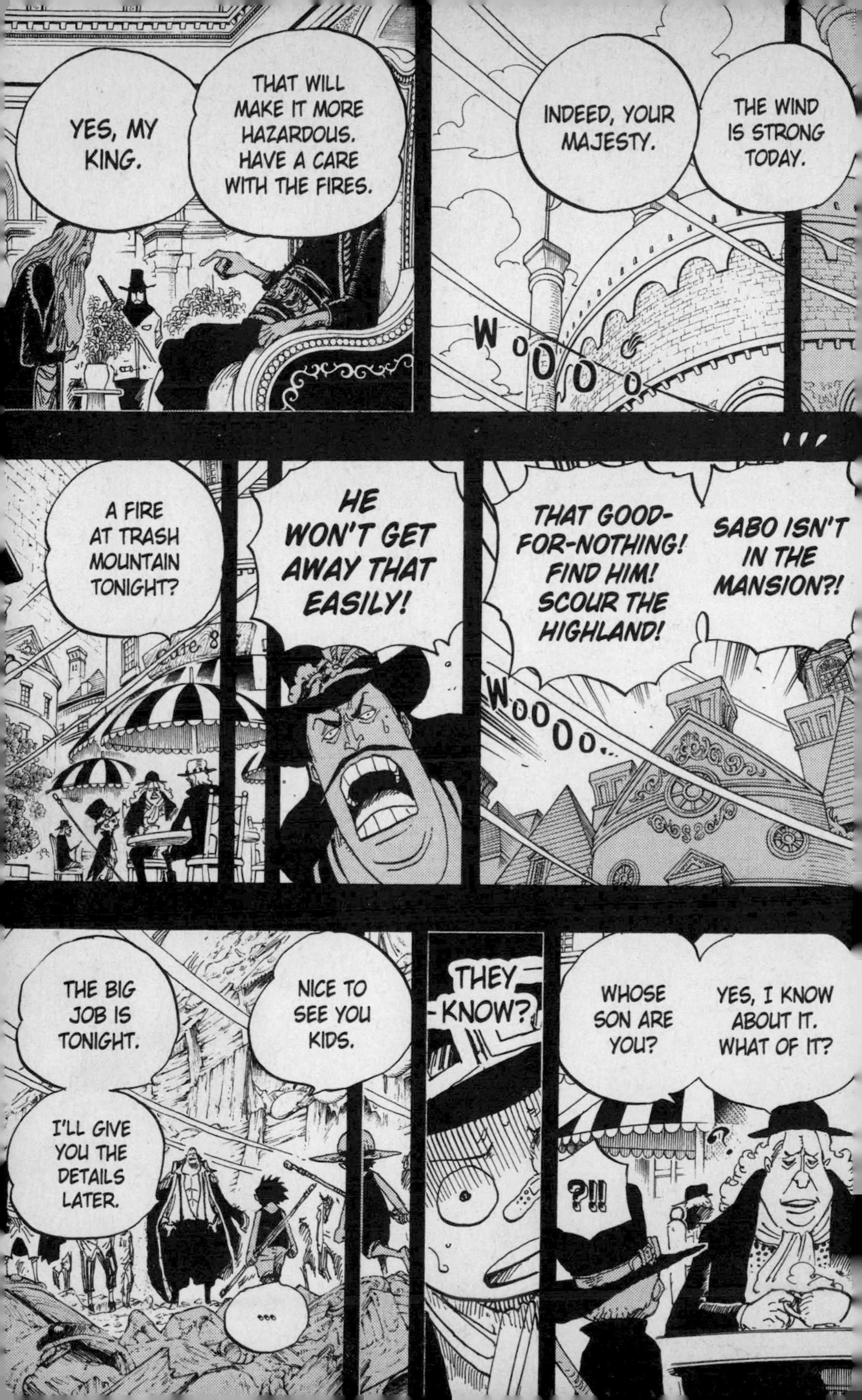
THE WIND IS STRONG TODAY.
INDEED, YOUR MAJESTY.
WOOOOO
THAT WILL MAKE IT MORE HAZARDOUS. HAVE A CARE WITH THE FIRES.
YES, MY KING.
SABO ISN'T IN THE MANSION?!
THAT GOOD-FOR-NOTHING! FIND HIM! SCOUR THE HIGHLAND!
WOOOOO...
HE WON'T GET AWAY THAT EASILY!
A FIRE AT TRASH MOUNTAIN TONIGHT?
YES, I KNOW ABOUT IT. WHAT OF IT?
WHOSE SON ARE YOU?
?!!
THEY KNOW?
NICE TO SEE YOU KIDS.
THE BIG JOB IS TONIGHT.
I'LL GIVE YOU THE DETAILS LATER.
...

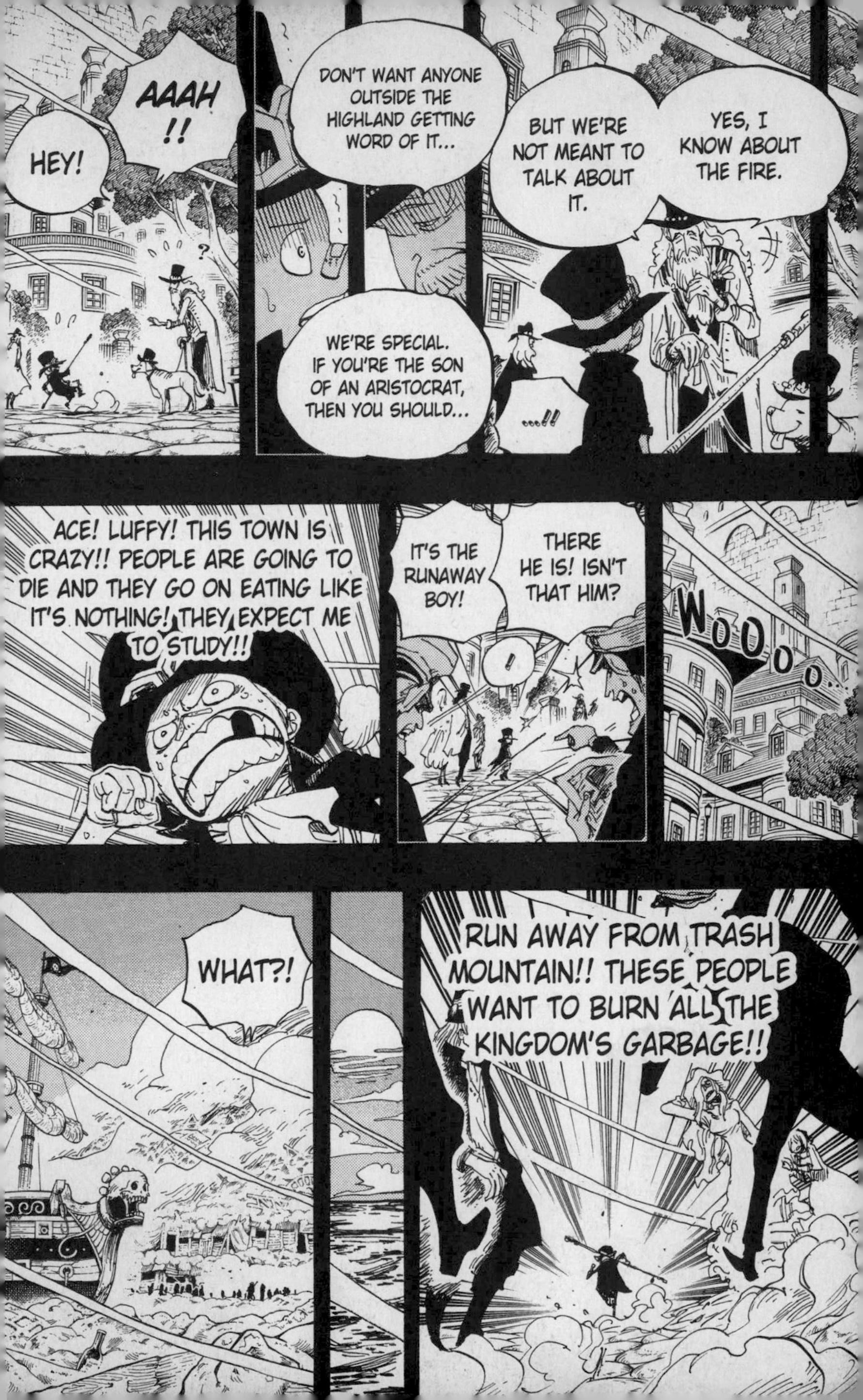
YES, I KNOW ABOUT THE FIRE.
BUT WE'RE NOT MEANT TO TALK ABOUT IT.
...!!
DON'T WANT ANYONE OUTSIDE THE HIGHLAND GETTING WORD OF IT...
WE'RE SPECIAL. IF YOU'RE THE SON OF AN ARISTOCRAT, THEN YOU SHOULD...
AAAH!!
HEY!
?
WOOOO...
THERE HE IS! ISN'T THAT HIM?
IT'S THE RUNAWAY BOY!
!
ACE! LUFFY! THIS TOWN IS CRAZY!! PEOPLE ARE GOING TO DIE AND THEY GO ON EATING LIKE IT'S NOTHING! THEY EXPECT ME TO STUDY!!
RUN AWAY FROM TRASH MOUNTAIN!! THESE PEOPLE WANT TO BURN ALL THE KINGDOM'S GARBAGE!!
WHAT?!

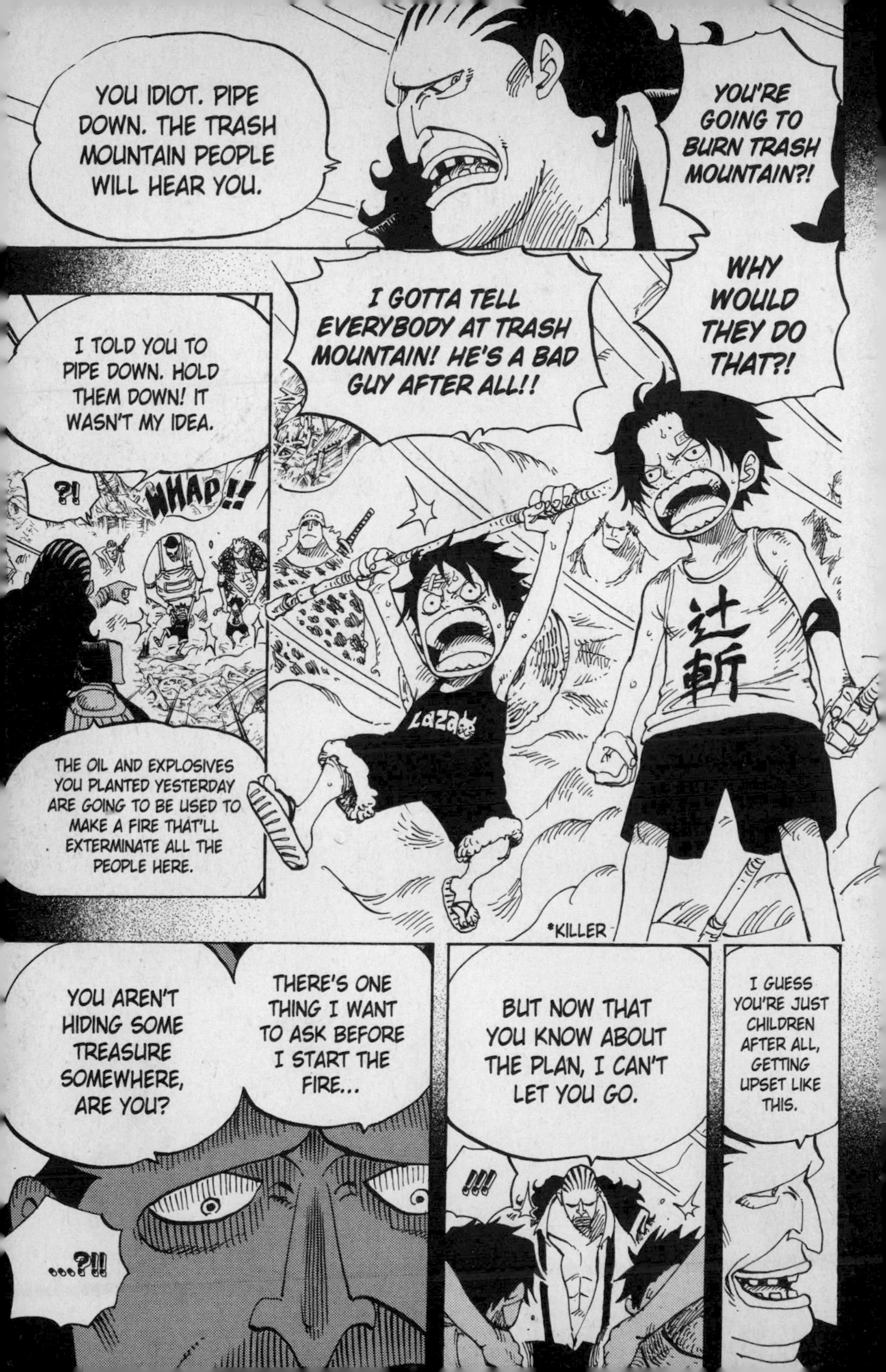
YOU'RE GOING TO BURN TRASH MOUNTAIN?!
YOU IDIOT. PIPE DOWN. THE TRASH MOUNTAIN PEOPLE WILL HEAR YOU.
WHY WOULD THEY DO THAT?!
I GOTTA TELL EVERYBODY AT TRASH MOUNTAIN! HE'S A BAD GUY AFTER ALL!!
辻斬
*KILLER
I TOLD YOU TO PIPE DOWN. HOLD THEM DOWN! IT WASN'T MY IDEA.
?!
WHAP!!
THE OIL AND EXPLOSIVES YOU PLANTED YESTERDAY ARE GOING TO BE USED TO MAKE A FIRE THAT'LL EXTERMINATE ALL THE PEOPLE HERE.
I GUESS YOU'RE JUST CHILDREN AFTER ALL, GETTING UPSET LIKE THIS.
BUT NOW THAT YOU KNOW ABOUT THE PLAN, I CAN'T LET YOU GO.
!!!
THERE'S ONE THING I WANT TO ASK BEFORE I START THE FIRE...
YOU AREN'T HIDING SOME TREASURE SOMEWHERE, ARE YOU?
...?!!

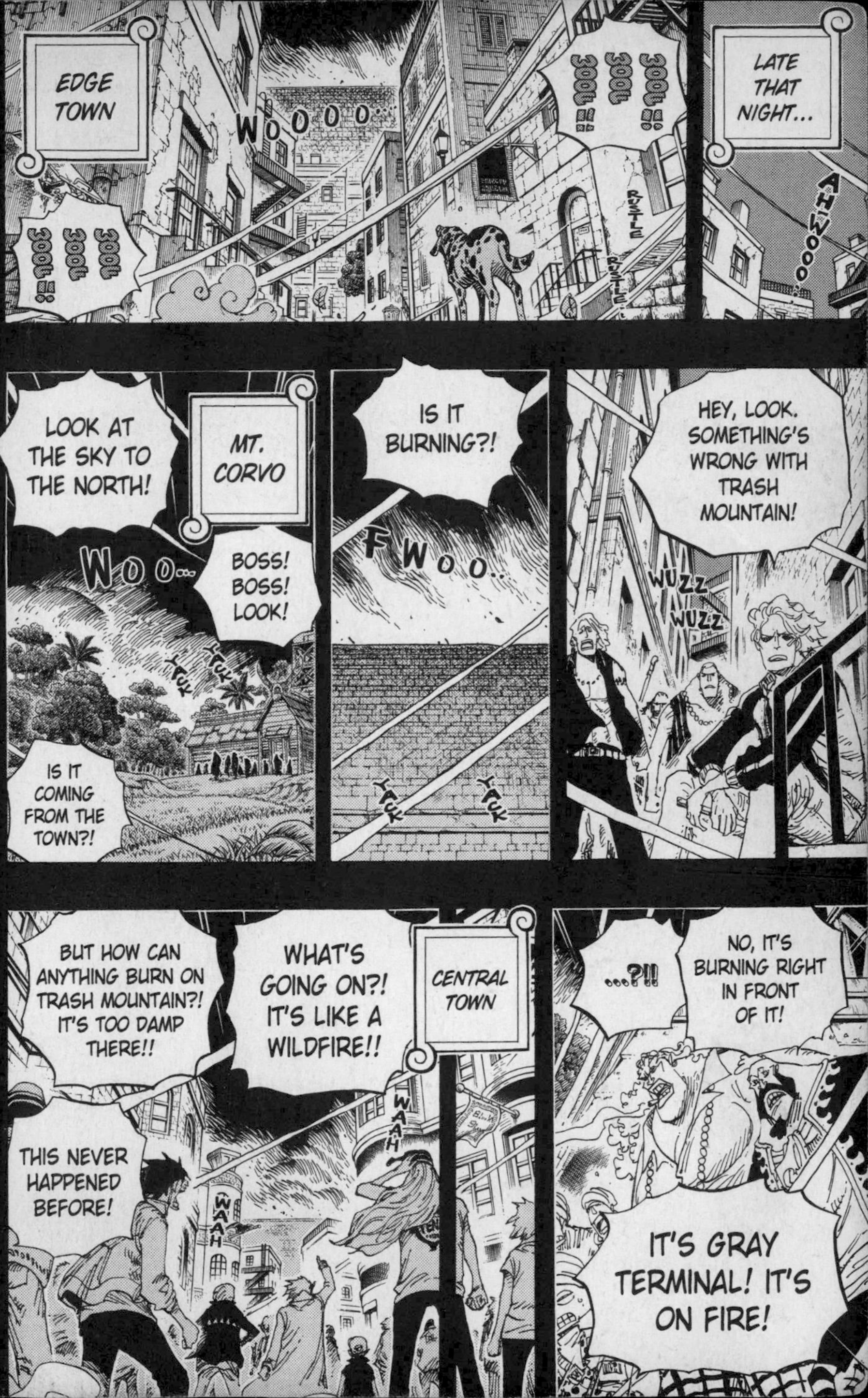
LATE THAT NIGHT...
AHWOOO...
WOOF!! WOOF!! WOOF!!
RUSTLE
RUSTLE...
WOOOO...
EDGE TOWN
WOOF!! WOOF!! WOOF!!
HEY, LOOK. SOMETHING'S WRONG WITH TRASH MOUNTAIN!
WUZZ WUZZ
IS IT BURNING?!
FWOO...
YACK
YACK
MT. CORVO
LOOK AT THE SKY TO THE NORTH!
BOSS! BOSS! LOOK!
WOO...
YACK YACK
IS IT COMING FROM THE TOWN?!
NO, IT'S BURNING RIGHT IN FRONT OF IT!
...?!!
IT'S GRAY TERMINAL! IT'S ON FIRE!
CENTRAL TOWN
WHAT'S GOING ON?! IT'S LIKE A WILDFIRE!!
BUT HOW CAN ANYTHING BURN ON TRASH MOUNTAIN?! IT'S TOO DAMP THERE!!
WAAH
THIS NEVER HAPPENED BEFORE!
WAAH

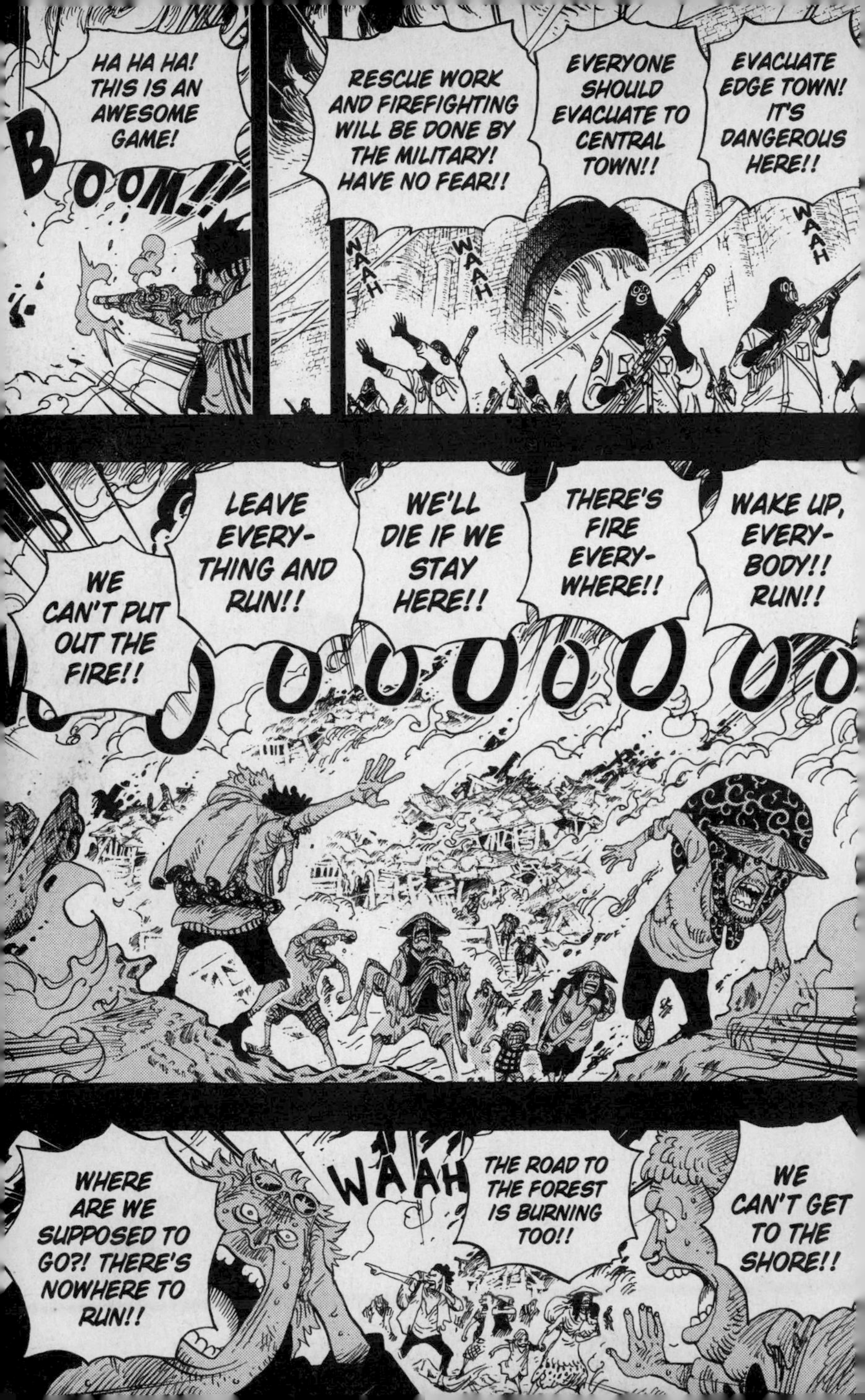
EVACUATE EDGE TOWN! IT'S DANGEROUS HERE!!
WAAH
EVERYONE SHOULD EVACUATE TO CENTRAL TOWN!!
RESCUE WORK AND FIREFIGHTING WILL BE DONE BY THE MILITARY! HAVE NO FEAR!!
WAAH
WAAH
HA HA HA! THIS IS AN AWESOME GAME!
BOOM!!
WAKE UP, EVERY-BODY!! RUN!!
THERE'S FIRE EVERY-WHERE!!
WE'LL DIE IF WE STAY HERE!!
LEAVE EVERY-THING AND RUN!!
WE CAN'T PUT OUT THE FIRE!!
WE CAN'T GET TO THE SHORE!!
THE ROAD TO THE FOREST IS BURNING TOO!!
WAAH
WHERE ARE WE SUPPOSED TO GO?! THERE'S NOWHERE TO RUN!!

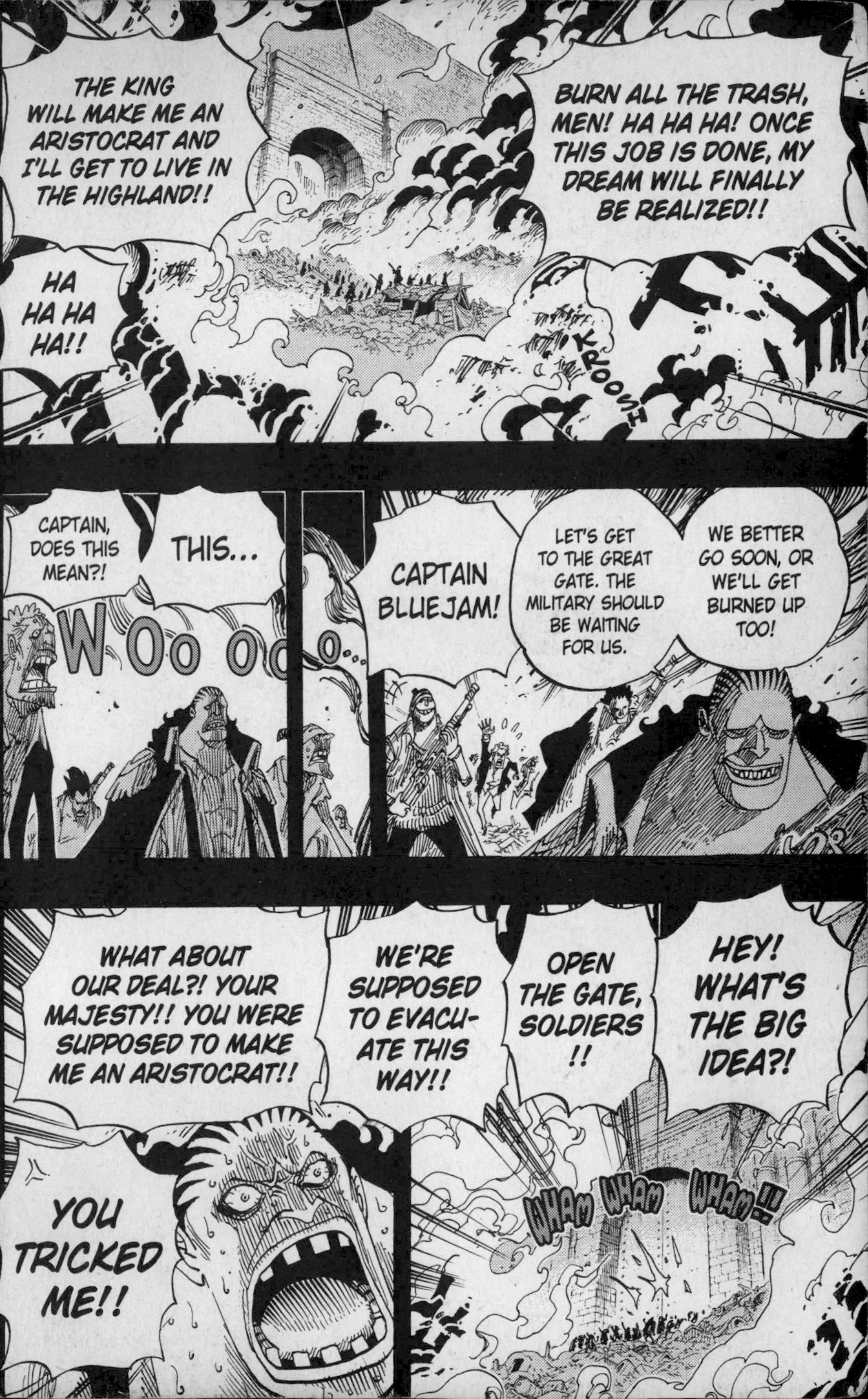
BURN ALL THE TRASH, MEN! HA HA HA! ONCE THIS JOB IS DONE, MY DREAM WILL FINALLY BE REALIZED!!
THE KING WILL MAKE ME AN ARISTOCRAT AND I'LL GET TO LIVE IN THE HIGHLAND!!
KROOSH
HA HA HA HA!!
WE BETTER GO SOON, OR WE'LL GET BURNED UP TOO!
LET'S GET TO THE GREAT GATE. THE MILITARY SHOULD BE WAITING FOR US.
CAPTAIN BLUEJAM!
THIS...
CAPTAIN, DOES THIS MEAN?!
WOoo ooo...
HEY! WHAT'S THE BIG IDEA?!
OPEN THE GATE, SOLDIERS!!
WE'RE SUPPOSED TO EVACUATE THIS WAY!!
WHAT ABOUT OUR DEAL?! YOUR MAJESTY!! YOU WERE SUPPOSED TO MAKE ME AN ARISTOCRAT!!
WHAM WHAM WHAM!!
YOU TRICKED ME!!

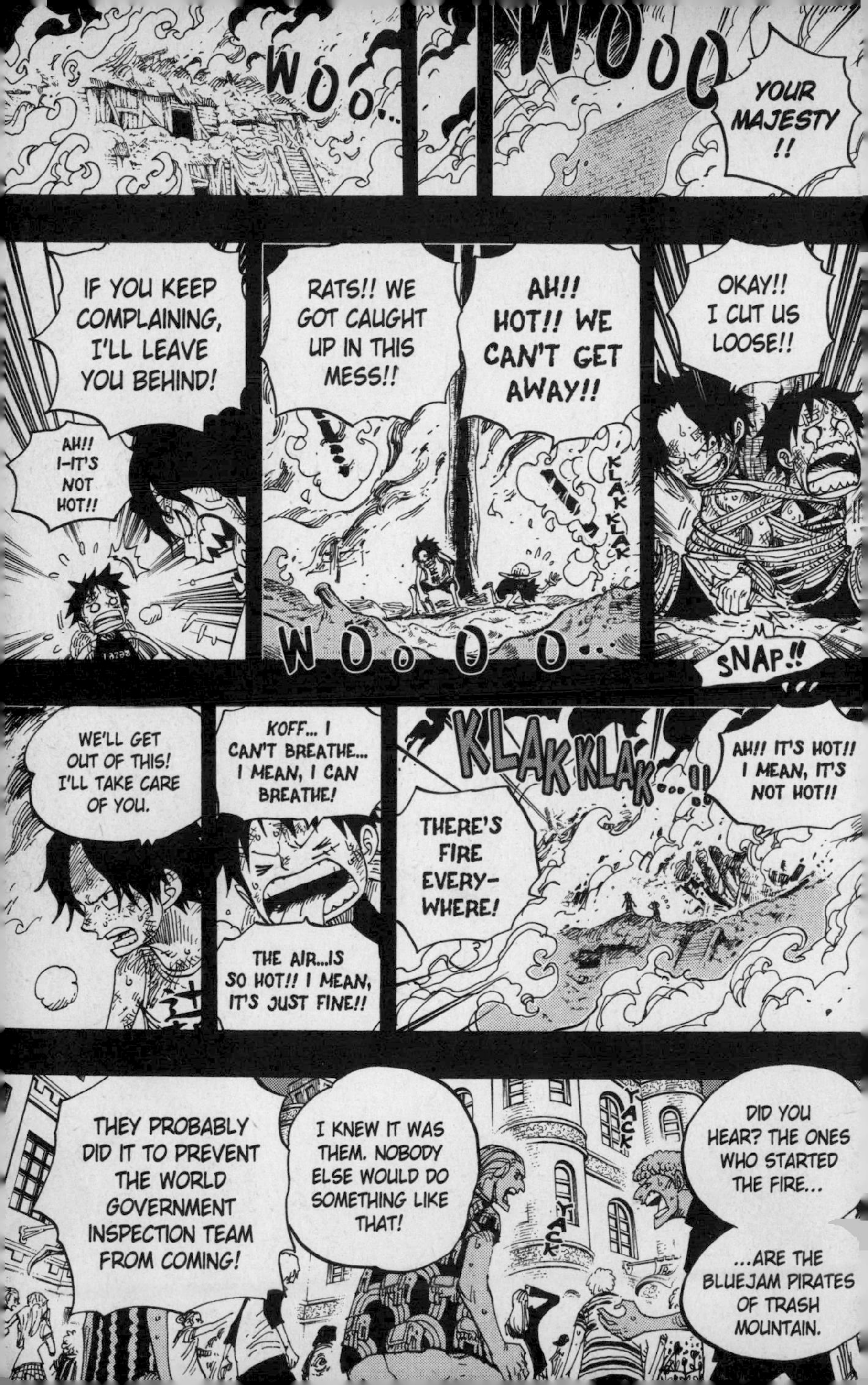
WOOO
YOUR MAJESTY !!
WOO...
OKAY!! I CUT US LOOSE!!
SNAP!!
AH!! HOT!! WE CAN'T GET AWAY!!
RATS!! WE GOT CAUGHT UP IN THIS MESS!!
KLAK KLAK
WO.OO..
IF YOU KEEP COMPLAINING, I'LL LEAVE YOU BEHIND!
AH!! I-IT'S NOT HOT!!
KLAK KLAK...!!
AH!! IT'S HOT!! I MEAN, IT'S NOT HOT!!
THERE'S FIRE EVERY-WHERE!
KOFF... I CAN'T BREATHE... I MEAN, I CAN BREATHE!
THE AIR...IS SO HOT!! I MEAN, IT'S JUST FINE!!
WE'LL GET OUT OF THIS! I'LL TAKE CARE OF YOU.
DID YOU HEAR? THE ONES WHO STARTED THE FIRE...
...ARE THE BLUEJAM PIRATES OF TRASH MOUNTAIN.
YACK
YACK
I KNEW IT WAS THEM. NOBODY ELSE WOULD DO SOMETHING LIKE THAT!
THEY PROBABLY DID IT TO PREVENT THE WORLD GOVERNMENT INSPECTION TEAM FROM COMING!

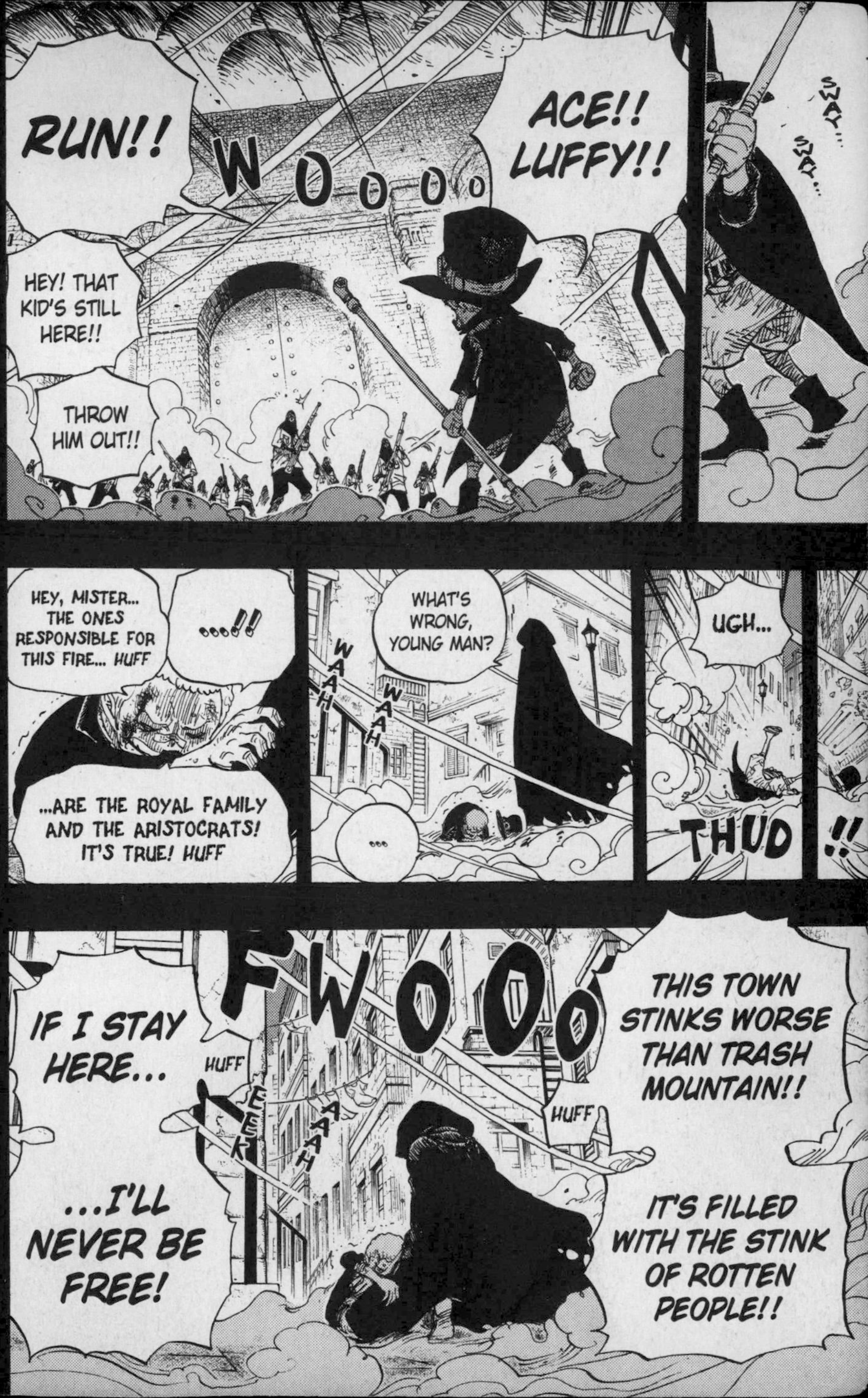
SWAY... SWAY...
ACE!! LUFFY!!
WOOOO
RUN!!
HEY! THAT KID'S STILL HERE!!
THROW HIM OUT!!
!!
UGH...
THUD
WHAT'S WRONG, YOUNG MAN?
WAAAH
WAAAH
...
...!!
HEY, MISTER... THE ONES RESPONSIBLE FOR THIS FIRE... HUFF
...ARE THE ROYAL FAMILY AND THE ARISTOCRATS! IT'S TRUE! HUFF
THIS TOWN STINKS WORSE THAN TRASH MOUNTAIN!!
FWOOOO
HUFF
IF I STAY HERE...
HUFF
EEEK
AAAAH
IT'S FILLED WITH THE STINK OF ROTTEN PEOPLE!!
...I'LL NEVER BE FREE!

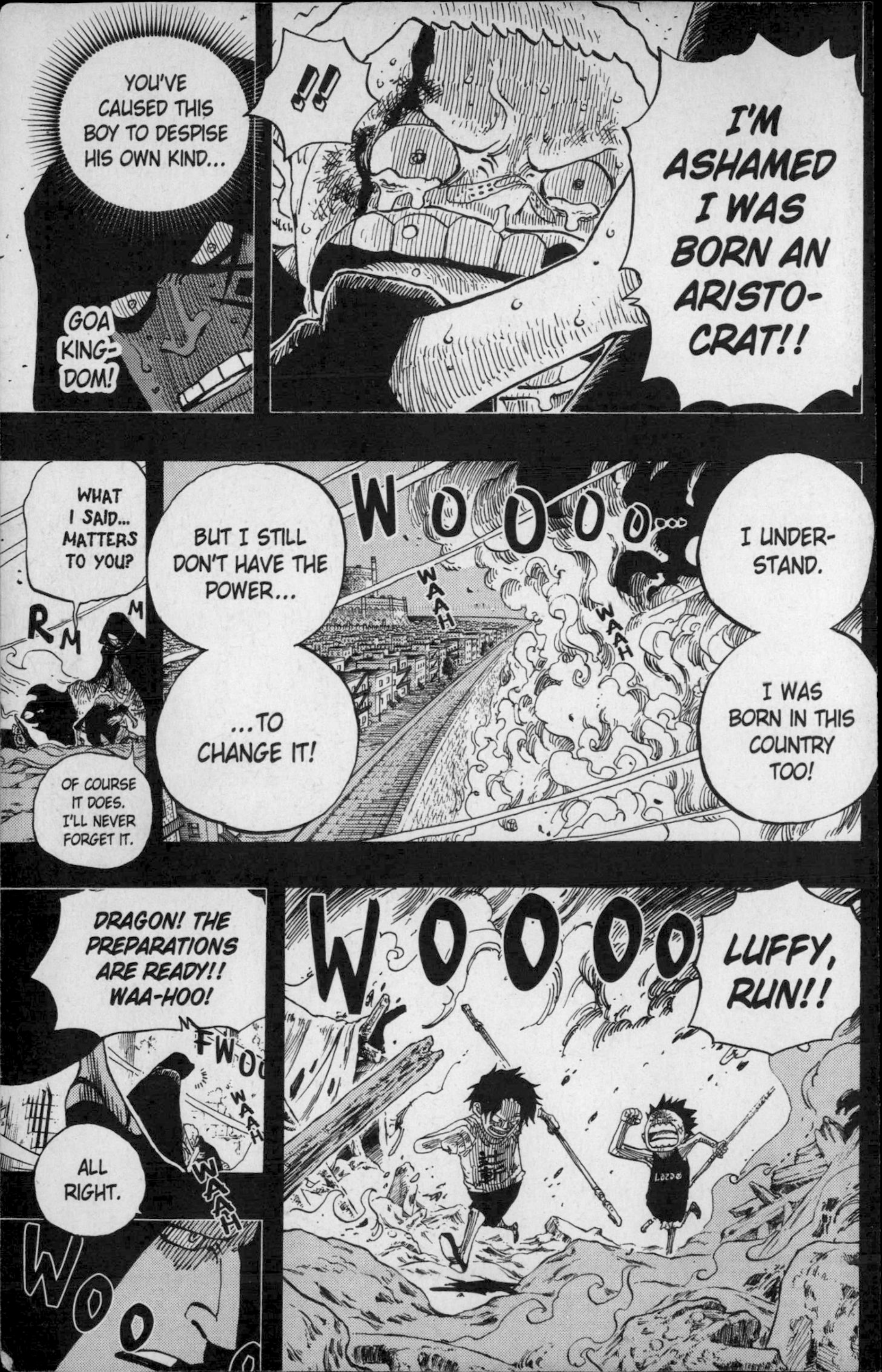
!!
I'M ASHAMED I WAS BORN AN ARISTO-CRAT!!
YOU'VE CAUSED THIS BOY TO DESPISE HIS OWN KIND...
GOA KING-DOM!
I UNDER-STAND.
I WAS BORN IN THIS COUNTRY TOO!
WOOOO...
WAAH
WAAH
BUT I STILL DON'T HAVE THE POWER...
...TO CHANGE IT!
WHAT I SAID... MATTERS TO YOU?
RMM
OF COURSE IT DOES. I'LL NEVER FORGET IT.
LUFFY, RUN!!
WOOOO
DRAGON! THE PREPARATIONS ARE READY!! WAA-HOO!
FWOO
WAAH
ALL RIGHT.
WAAH
WOO

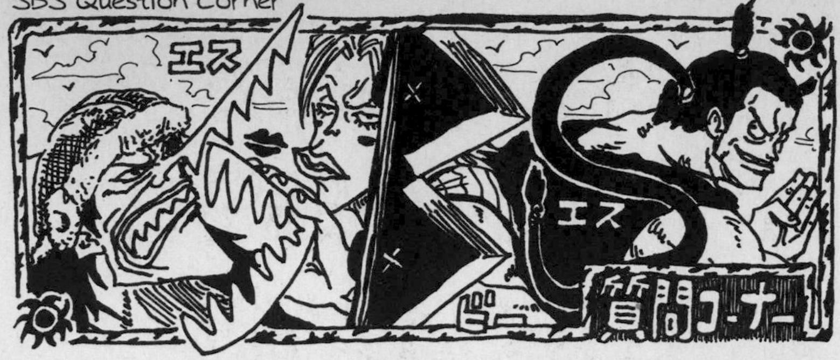
エス
ビー
エス
質問コーナー

(92, Akita)

Q: In volume 56, on page 195, what's that thing Buggy is chanting? Is that like "Open Sesame" or something?

--Ace LOVE

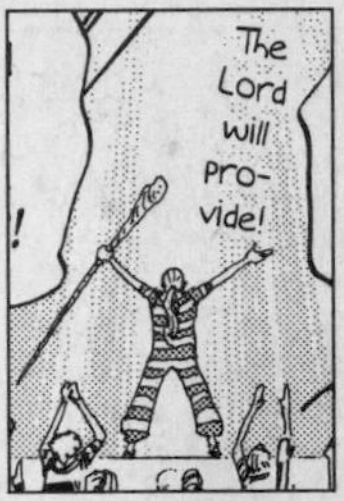
The Lord will provide!
!

A: Oh, that? I don't really know too much about it, but haven't you ever heard of it? Christmas choirs sing it all the time. You might not really know what it means, but I put it in there to give a sort of divine air to Buggy. It's really no big deal. But if you have to know, it's the Japanese lyrics to "Joy to the World." If you have time on your hands, look it up.

Q: While reading the Navy vs. the Whitebeard Pirates battle in volume 58, I got swallowed up by the war! I forgot to breath and I di-die--

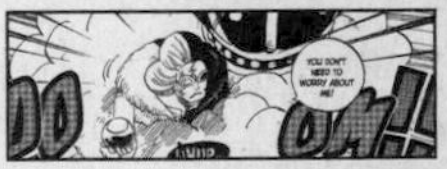
YOU DON'T NEED TO WORRY ABOUT ME!
DO
OM!

DIDN'T DIE!

I have a question. In volume 58, Inazuma the Revolutionary popped out of Iva's head! Does this mean you can live inside Iva's head?! Please tell me. It's a once in a lifetime wish of mine to know.

--Corona

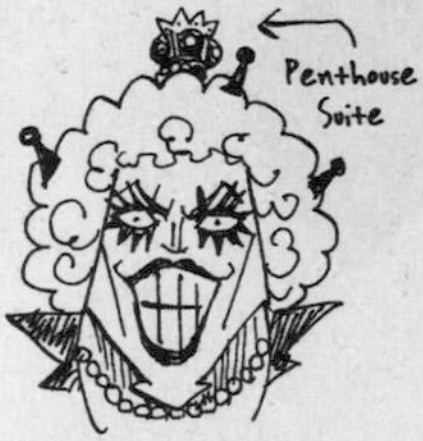
Penthouse Suite

A: You can stay in there for 5,000 berries per person per night. The limit is three people, mind you. If you see the ocean while he's moving around, we will charge you an additional Ocean View fee. The penthouse suite in his crown is a very spacious area. For groups of 30 or more, we provide an Emporio Face-Growth Hormone as an added bonus. Please call for more details.

Q: Is it possible for a woman to become an editor of *One Piece?* Or are all the editors of boys' comics supposed to be men?

--Uekiman

A: A beautiful babe with big knockers is fine by me! If I had an editor like that, I'd work even harder! Only I think I might not draw as fast! But to be honest, the editorial department of Jump is filled with perverts. I think it's in your best interests to stay away from there.

Chapter 587:
I WILL NEVER RUN AWAY

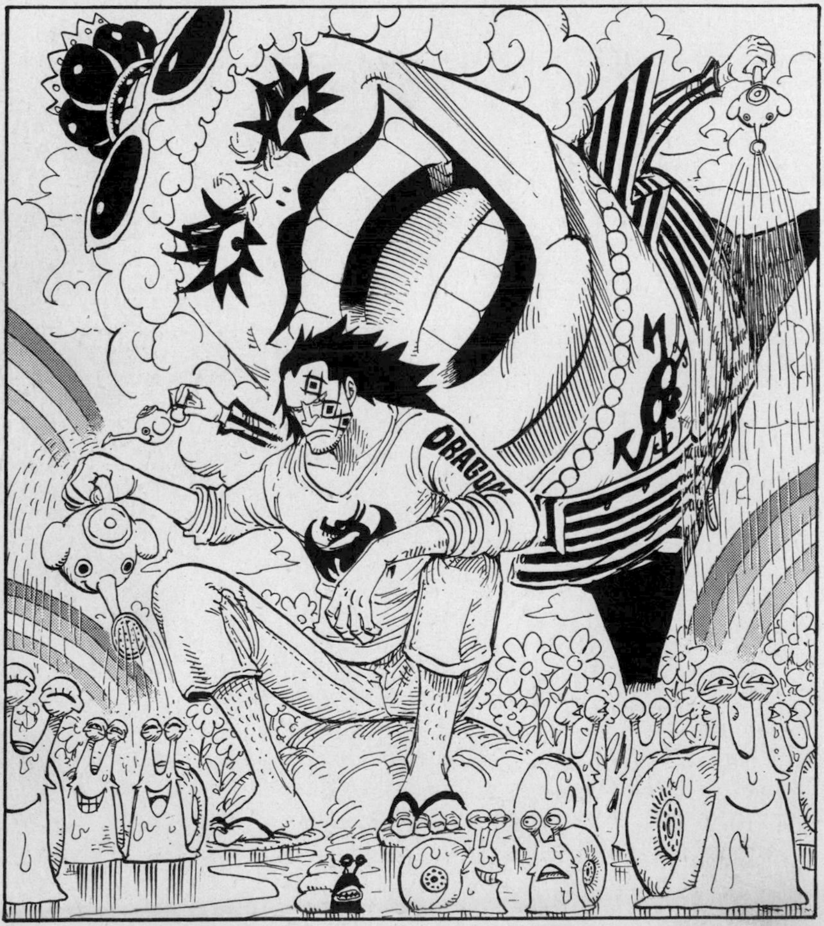
DRAGON

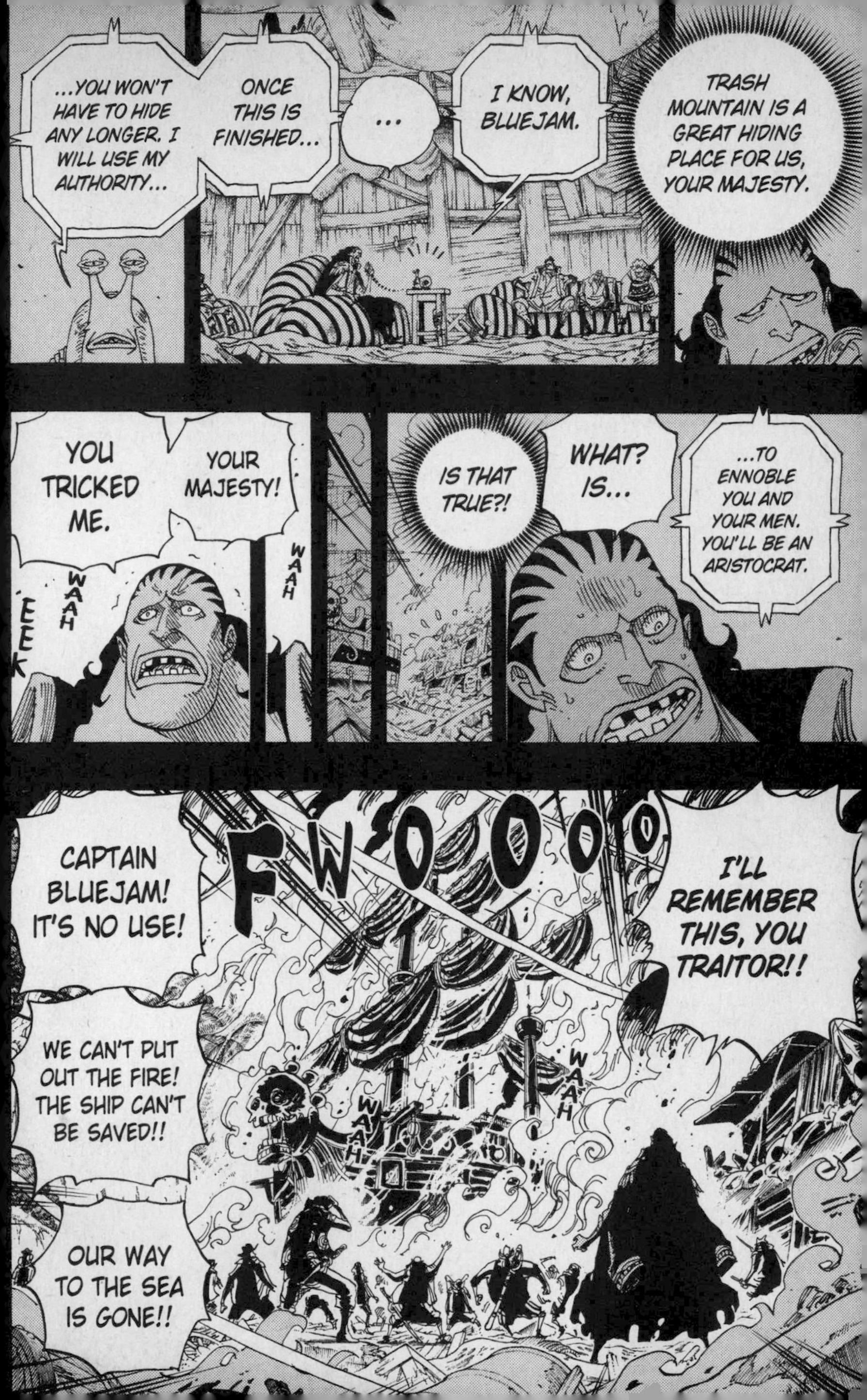
TRASH MOUNTAIN IS A GREAT HIDING PLACE FOR US, YOUR MAJESTY.
I KNOW, BLUEJAM.
...
ONCE THIS IS FINISHED...
...YOU WON'T HAVE TO HIDE ANY LONGER. I WILL USE MY AUTHORITY...
...TO ENNOBLE YOU AND YOUR MEN. YOU'LL BE AN ARISTOCRAT.
WHAT? IS...
IS THAT TRUE?!
WAAH
YOUR MAJESTY!
YOU TRICKED ME.
WAAH
EEEK
FWOOOO
I'LL REMEMBER THIS, YOU TRAITOR!!
CAPTAIN BLUEJAM! IT'S NO USE!
WAAH
WAAH
WE CAN'T PUT OUT THE FIRE! THE SHIP CAN'T BE SAVED!!
OUR WAY TO THE SEA IS GONE!!

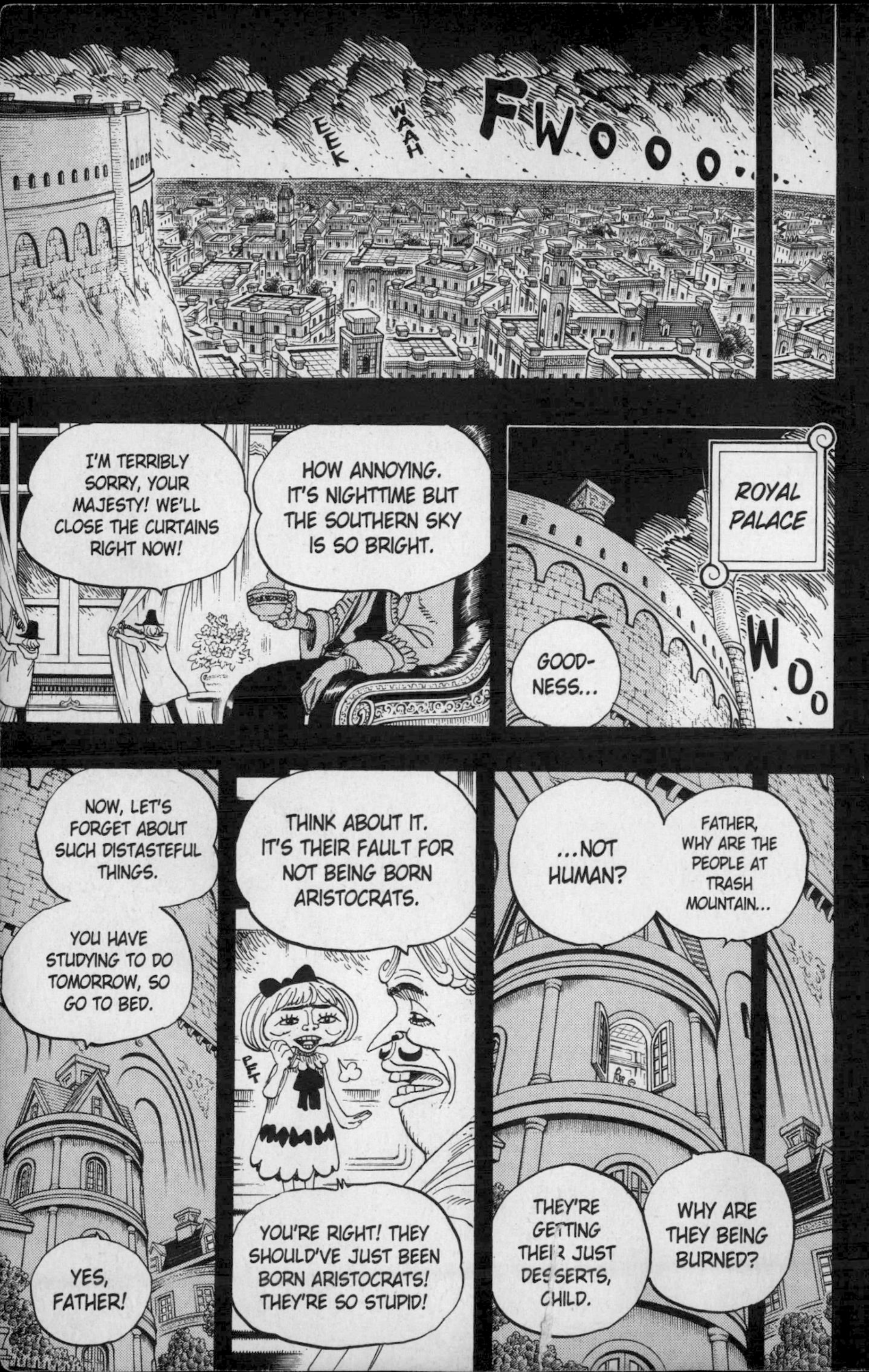
FWOOO...
WAAH
EEK
ROYAL PALACE
WOO
GOOD-NESS...
HOW ANNOYING. IT'S NIGHTTIME BUT THE SOUTHERN SKY IS SO BRIGHT.
I'M TERRIBLY SORRY, YOUR MAJESTY! WE'LL CLOSE THE CURTAINS RIGHT NOW!
FATHER, WHY ARE THE PEOPLE AT TRASH MOUNTAIN...
...NOT HUMAN?
WHY ARE THEY BEING BURNED?
THEY'RE GETTING THEIR JUST DESSERTS, CHILD.
THINK ABOUT IT. IT'S THEIR FAULT FOR NOT BEING BORN ARISTOCRATS.
YOU'RE RIGHT! THEY SHOULD'VE JUST BEEN BORN ARISTOCRATS! THEY'RE SO STUPID!
NOW, LET'S FORGET ABOUT SUCH DISTASTEFUL THINGS.
YOU HAVE STUDYING TO DO TOMORROW, SO GO TO BED.
YES, FATHER!

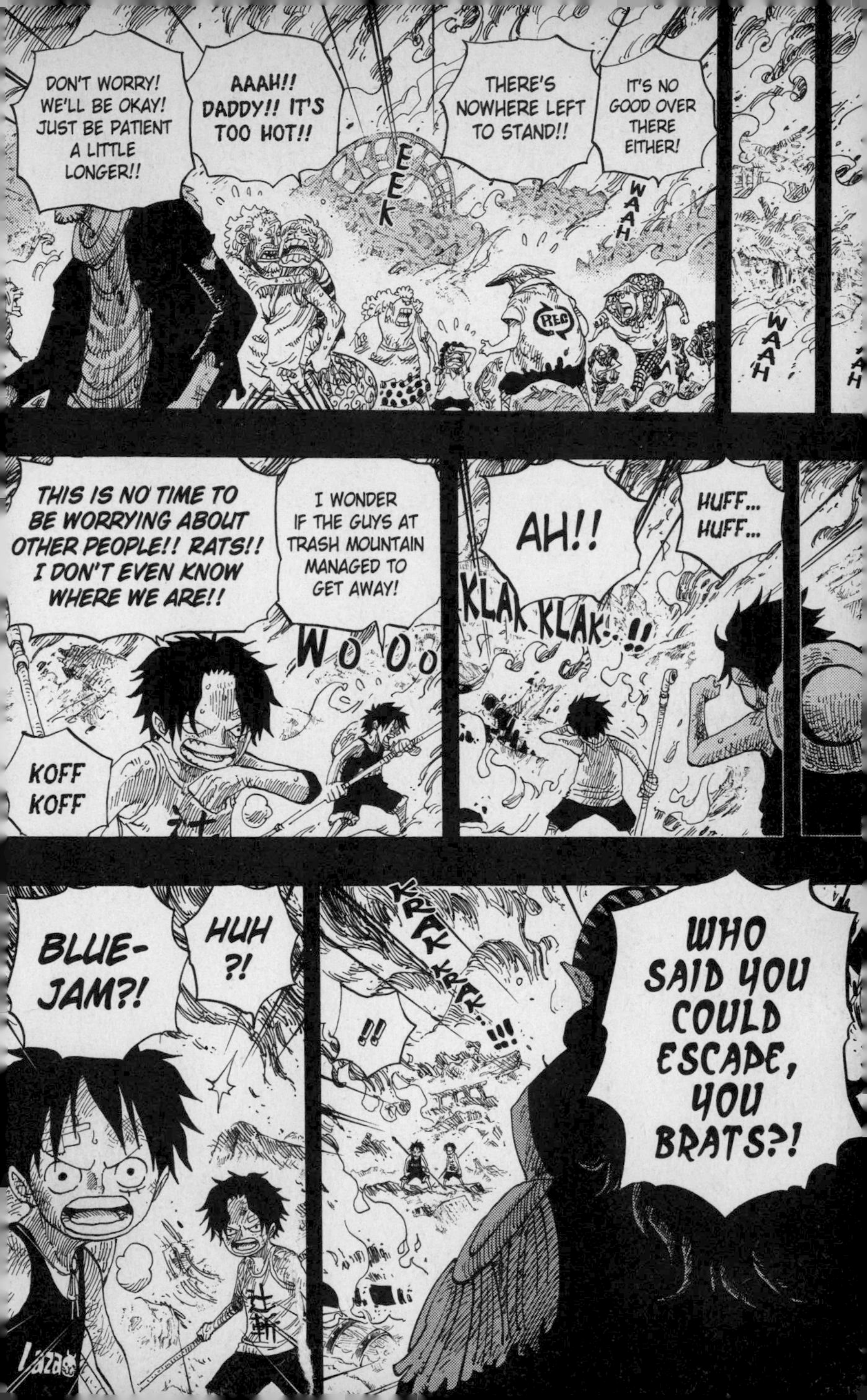
WAAH
IT'S NO GOOD OVER THERE EITHER!
WAAH
THERE'S NOWHERE LEFT TO STAND!!
EEK
AAAH!! DADDY!! IT'S TOO HOT!!
DON'T WORRY! WE'LL BE OKAY! JUST BE PATIENT A LITTLE LONGER!!
HUFF... HUFF...
AH!!
KLAK KLAK..!!
I WONDER IF THE GUYS AT TRASH MOUNTAIN MANAGED TO GET AWAY!
THIS IS NO TIME TO BE WORRYING ABOUT OTHER PEOPLE!! RATS!! I DON'T EVEN KNOW WHERE WE ARE!!
WOOO
KOFF KOFF
WHO SAID YOU COULD ESCAPE, YOU BRATS?!
KRAK KRAK..!!!
!!
HUH ?!
BLUE-JAM?!

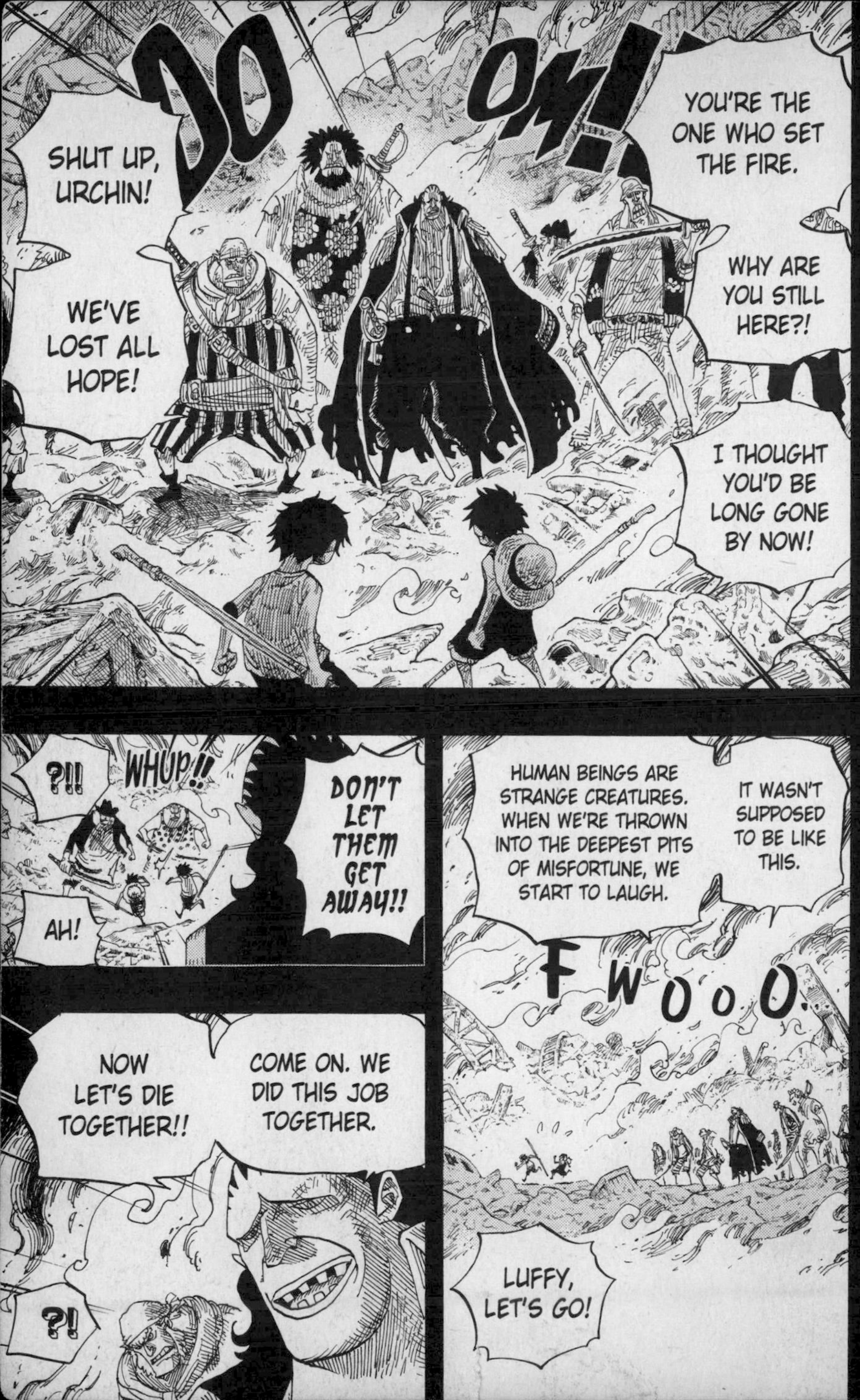
DOOON!
YOU'RE THE ONE WHO SET THE FIRE.
WHY ARE YOU STILL HERE?!
I THOUGHT YOU'D BE LONG GONE BY NOW!
SHUT UP, URCHIN!
WE'VE LOST ALL HOPE!
IT WASN'T SUPPOSED TO BE LIKE THIS.
HUMAN BEINGS ARE STRANGE CREATURES. WHEN WE'RE THROWN INTO THE DEEPEST PITS OF MISFORTUNE, WE START TO LAUGH.
FWOOO
LUFFY, LET'S GO!
DON'T LET THEM GET AWAY!!
WHUP!!
?!!
AH!
COME ON. WE DID THIS JOB TOGETHER.
NOW LET'S DIE TOGETHER!!
?!

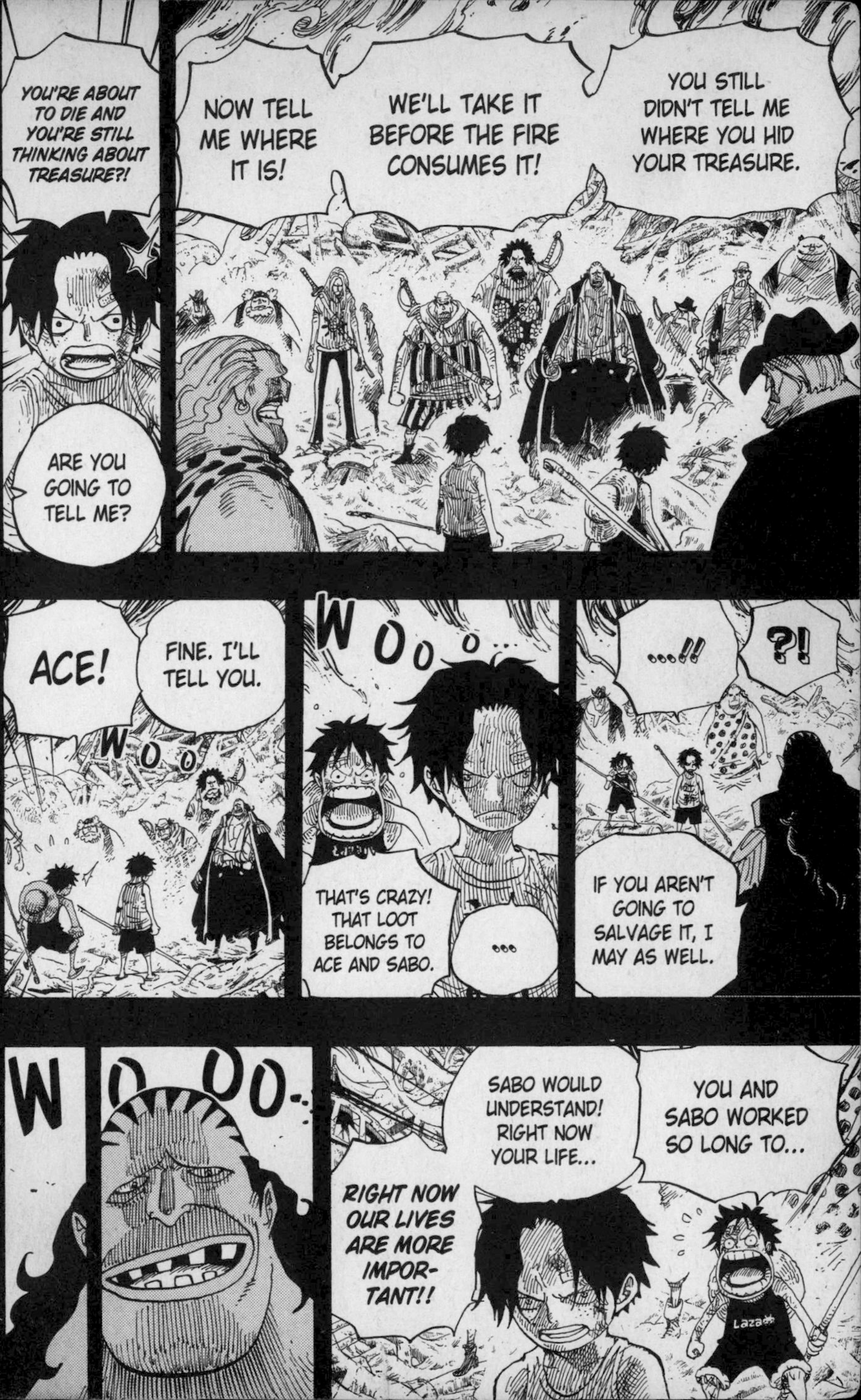
YOU STILL DIDN'T TELL ME WHERE YOU HID YOUR TREASURE.
WE'LL TAKE IT BEFORE THE FIRE CONSUMES IT!
NOW TELL ME WHERE IT IS!
YOU'RE ABOUT TO DIE AND YOU'RE STILL THINKING ABOUT TREASURE?!
ARE YOU GOING TO TELL ME?
?!
...!!
IF YOU AREN'T GOING TO SALVAGE IT, I MAY AS WELL.
WOOO...
THAT'S CRAZY! THAT LOOT BELONGS TO ACE AND SABO.
...
FINE. I'LL TELL YOU.
ACE!
WOO
YOU AND SABO WORKED SO LONG TO...
SABO WOULD UNDERSTAND! RIGHT NOW YOUR LIFE...
RIGHT NOW OUR LIVES ARE MORE IMPORTANT!!
WOOOO..

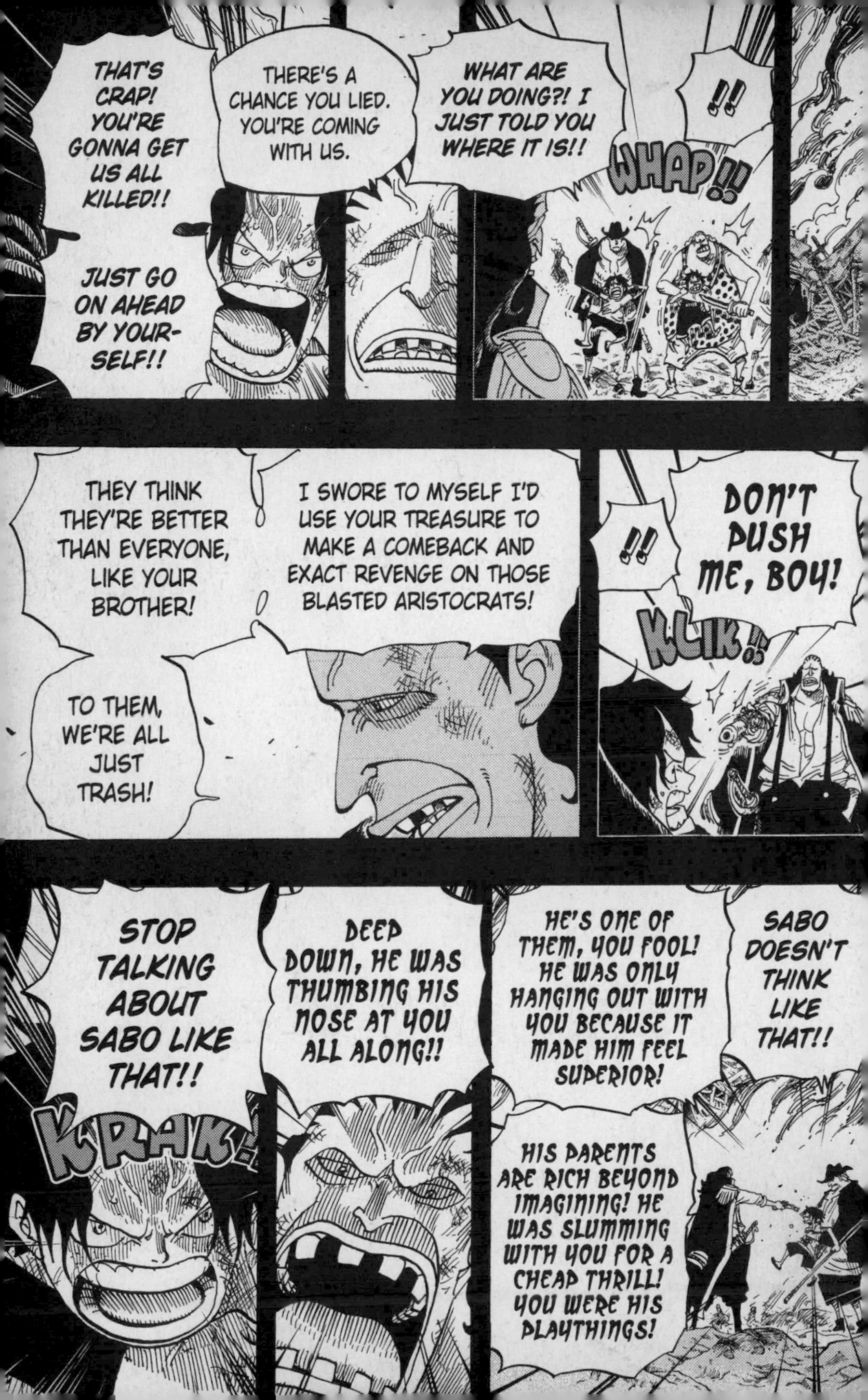
!!
WHAP!!
WHAT ARE YOU DOING?! I JUST TOLD YOU WHERE IT IS!!
THERE'S A CHANCE YOU LIED. YOU'RE COMING WITH US.
THAT'S CRAP! YOU'RE GONNA GET US ALL KILLED!!
JUST GO ON AHEAD BY YOUR-SELF!!
DON'T PUSH ME, BOY!
!!
KLIK!!
I SWORE TO MYSELF I'D USE YOUR TREASURE TO MAKE A COMEBACK AND EXACT REVENGE ON THOSE BLASTED ARISTOCRATS!
THEY THINK THEY'RE BETTER THAN EVERYONE, LIKE YOUR BROTHER!
TO THEM, WE'RE ALL JUST TRASH!
SABO DOESN'T THINK LIKE THAT!!
HE'S ONE OF THEM, YOU FOOL! HE WAS ONLY HANGING OUT WITH YOU BECAUSE IT MADE HIM FEEL SUPERIOR!
HIS PARENTS ARE RICH BEYOND IMAGINING! HE WAS SLUMMING WITH YOU FOR A CHEAP THRILL! YOU WERE HIS PLAYTHINGS!
DEEP DOWN, HE WAS THUMBING HIS NOSE AT YOU ALL ALONG!!
STOP TALKING ABOUT SABO LIKE THAT!!
KRAK!

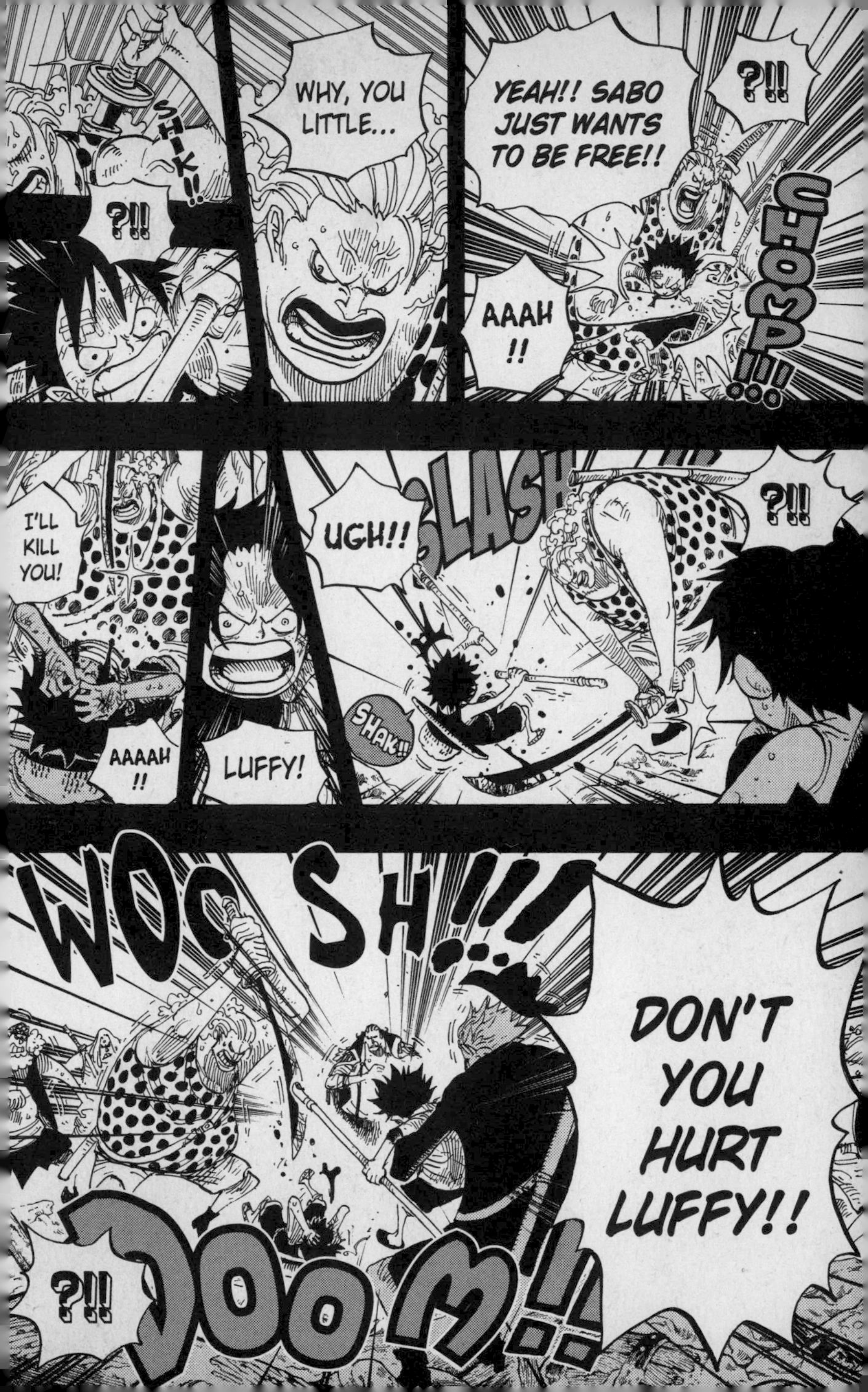
?!!
YEAH!! SABO JUST WANTS TO BE FREE!!
CHOMP!!!
AAAH !!
WHY, YOU LITTLE...
SHIK!!
?!!
?!!
SLASH
UGH!!
SHAK!!
LUFFY!
I'LL KILL YOU!
AAAAH !!
WOOSH!!!
DON'T YOU HURT LUFFY!!
?!!
DOOM!!

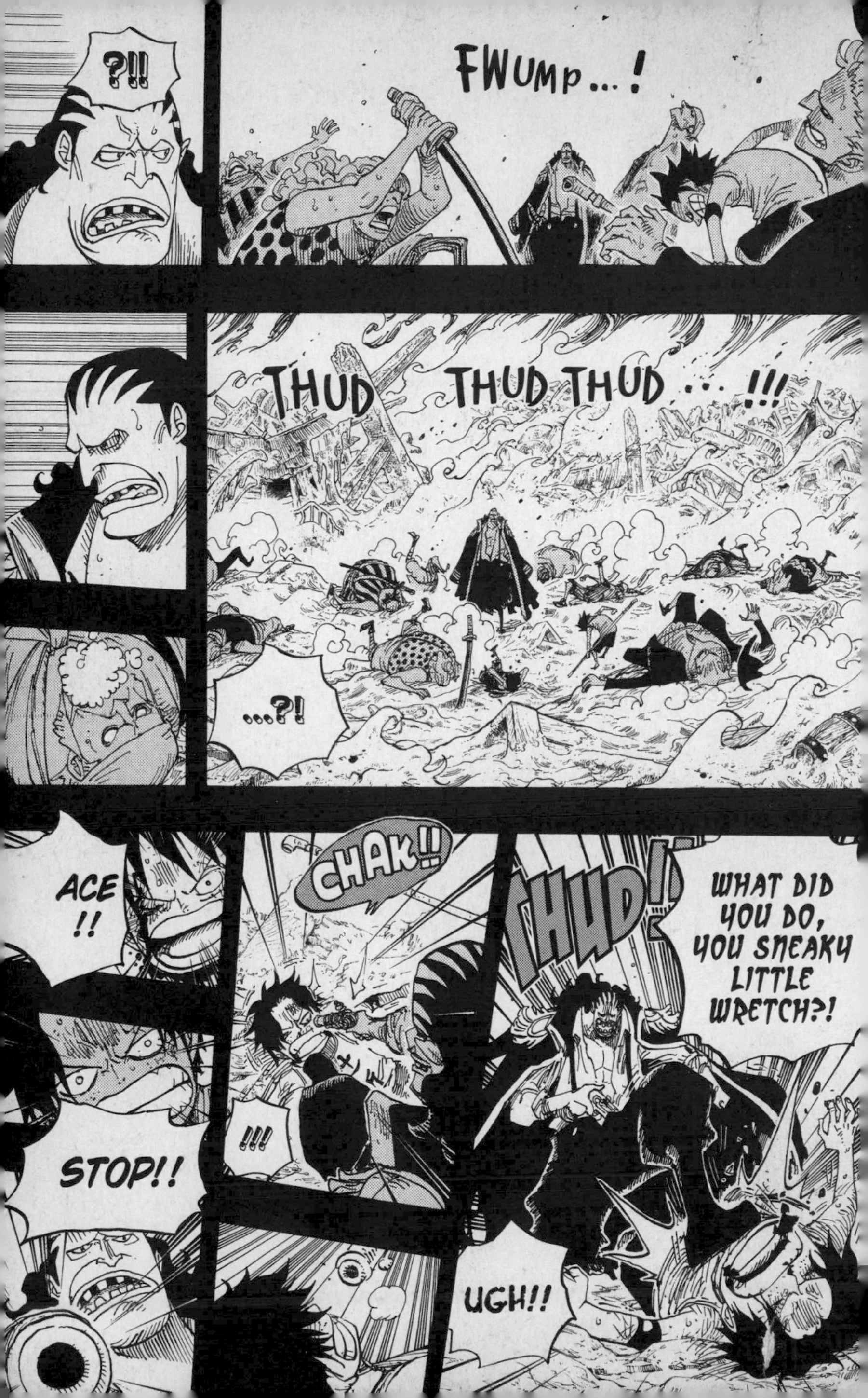
FWUMP...!
?!!
THUD THUD THUD...!!!
...?!
THUD!!
WHAT DID YOU DO, YOU SNEAKY LITTLE WRETCH?!
UGH!!
CHAK!!
!!!
ACE!!
STOP!!

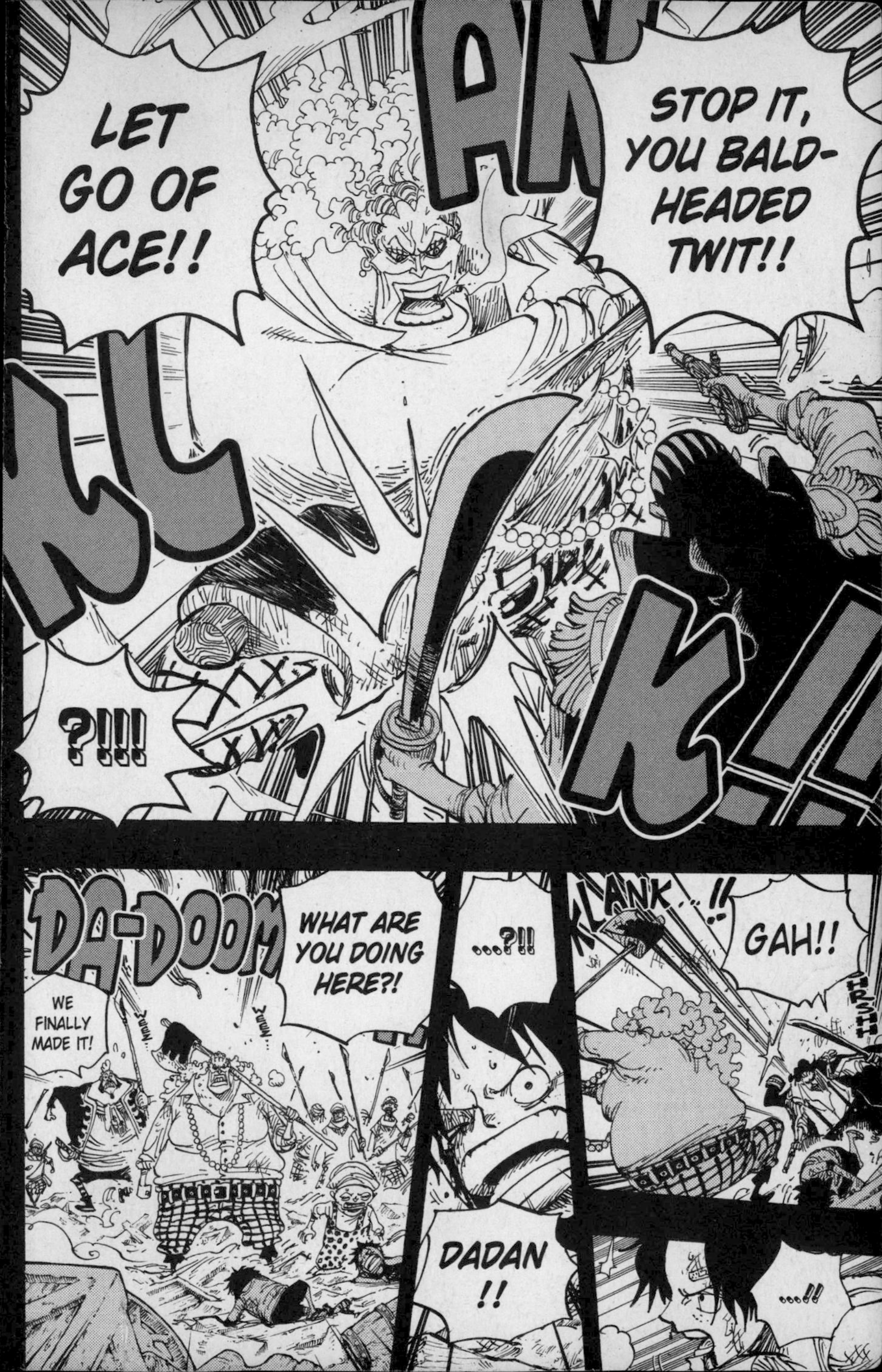
STOP IT, YOU BALD-HEADED TWIT!!
LET GO OF ACE!!
?!!!
KLANK...!!
GAH!!
HRSHH
...!!
...?!!
WHAT ARE YOU DOING HERE?!
DADAN!!
DA-DOOM
WE FINALLY MADE IT!

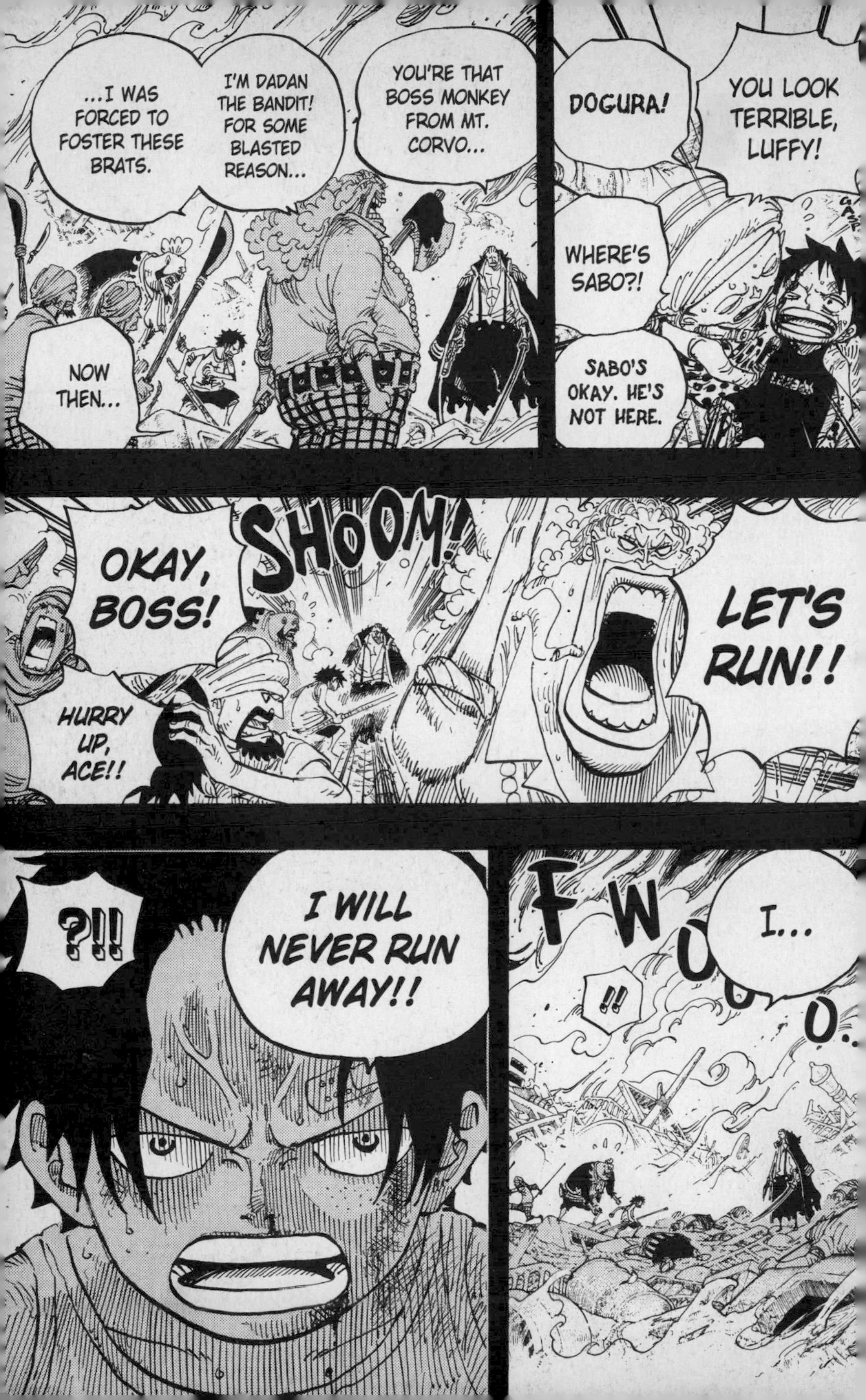
YOU LOOK TERRIBLE, LUFFY!
DOGURA!
WHERE'S SABO?!
SABO'S OKAY. HE'S NOT HERE.
YOU'RE THAT BOSS MONKEY FROM MT. CORVO...
I'M DADAN THE BANDIT! FOR SOME BLASTED REASON...
...I WAS FORCED TO FOSTER THESE BRATS.
NOW THEN...
LET'S RUN!!
SHOOM!
OKAY, BOSS!
HURRY UP, ACE!!
I...
FWOOOO...
!!
I WILL NEVER RUN AWAY!!
?!!

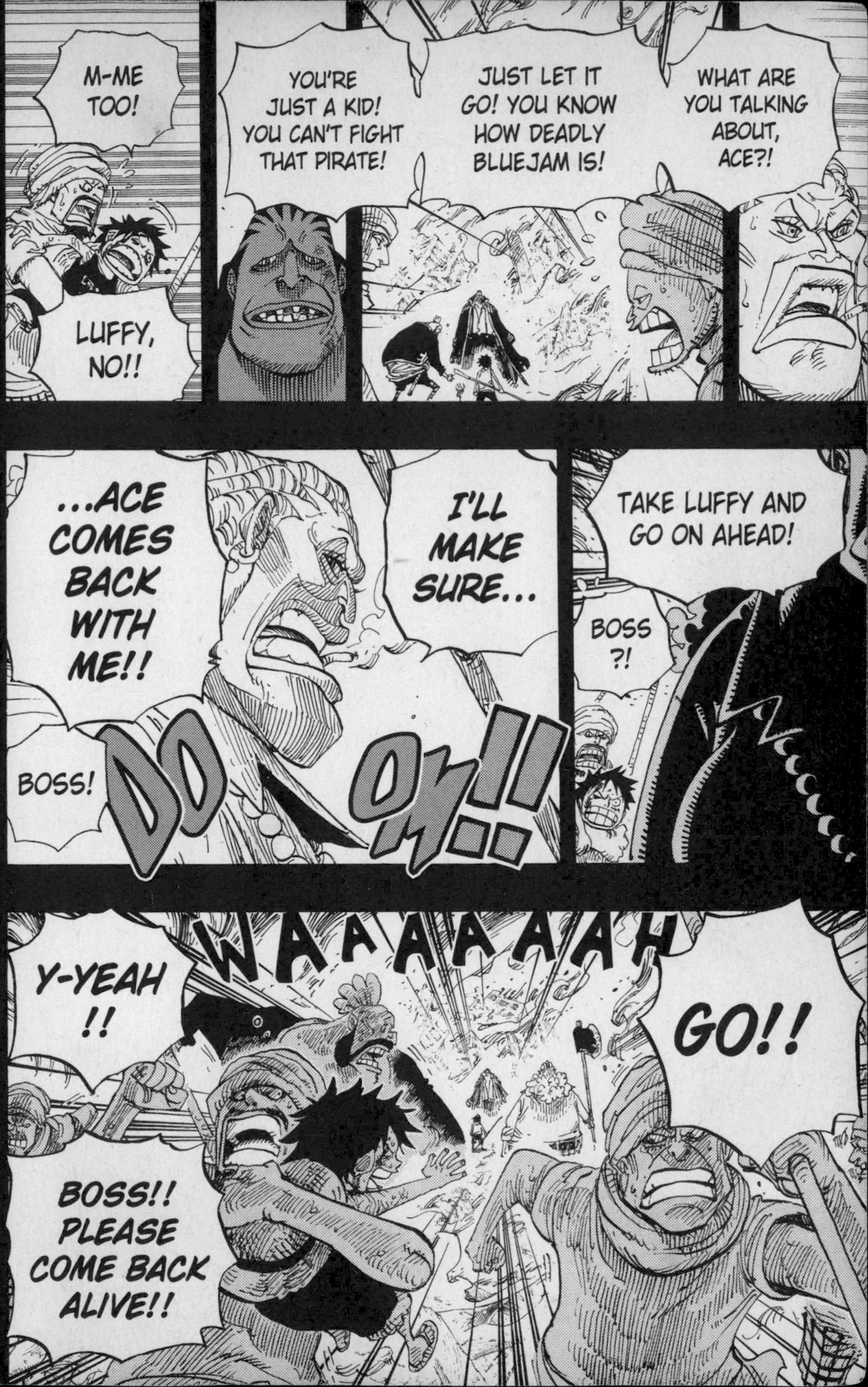
WHAT ARE YOU TALKING ABOUT, ACE?!
JUST LET IT GO! YOU KNOW HOW DEADLY BLUEJAM IS!
YOU'RE JUST A KID! YOU CAN'T FIGHT THAT PIRATE!
M-ME TOO!
LUFFY, NO!!
TAKE LUFFY AND GO ON AHEAD!
BOSS ?!
I'LL MAKE SURE...
...ACE COMES BACK WITH ME!!
DOOM!!
BOSS!
WAAAAAAAH
GO!!
Y-YEAH !!
BOSS!! PLEASE COME BACK ALIVE!!

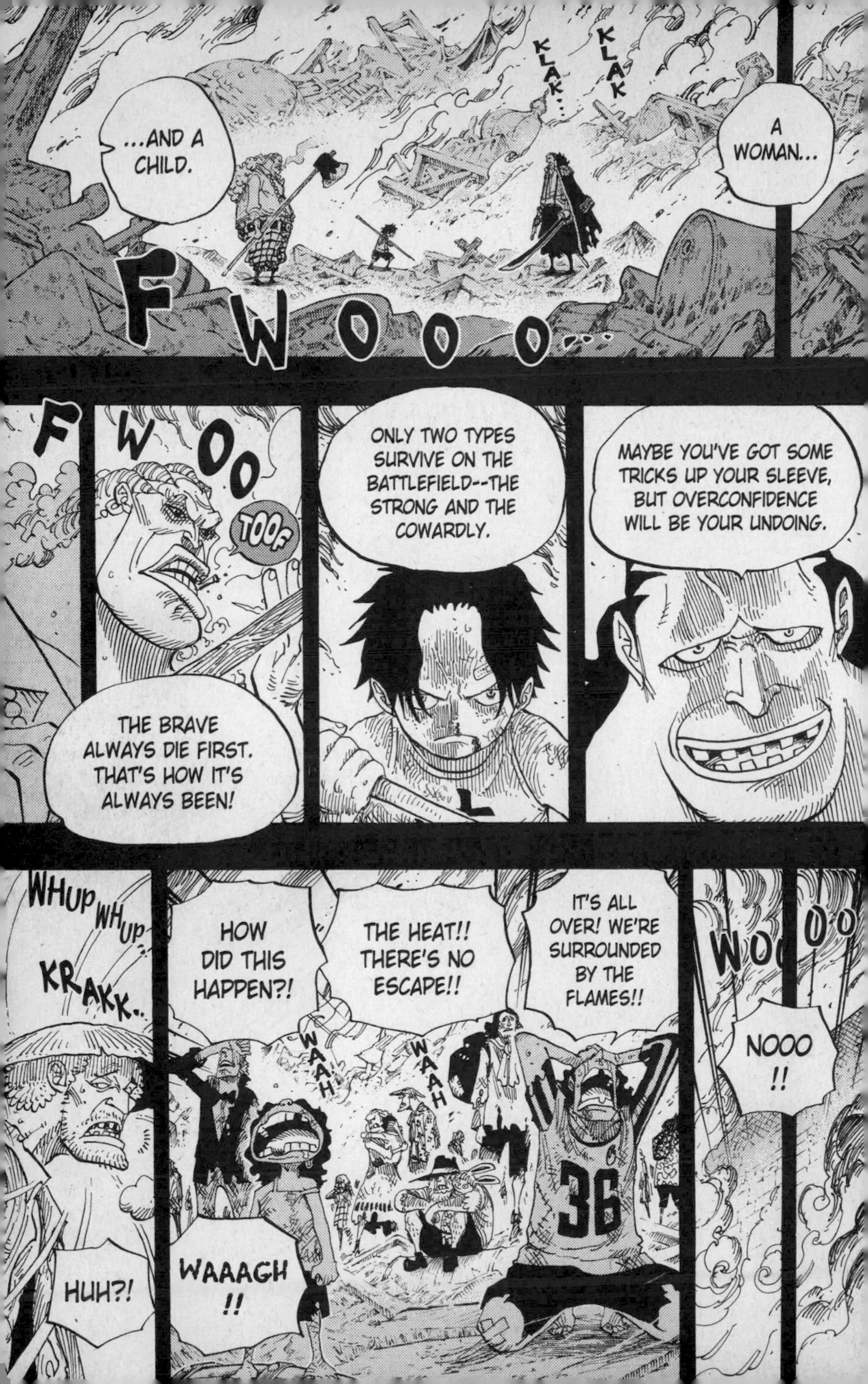
A WOMAN...
KLAK KLAK...
...AND A CHILD.
FWOOO...
MAYBE YOU'VE GOT SOME TRICKS UP YOUR SLEEVE, BUT OVERCONFIDENCE WILL BE YOUR UNDOING.
ONLY TWO TYPES SURVIVE ON THE BATTLEFIELD--THE STRONG AND THE COWARDLY.
FWOO
TOOF
THE BRAVE ALWAYS DIE FIRST. THAT'S HOW IT'S ALWAYS BEEN!
WOOOO
NOOO !!
IT'S ALL OVER! WE'RE SURROUNDED BY THE FLAMES!!
THE HEAT!! THERE'S NO ESCAPE!!
WAAH
WAAH
HOW DID THIS HAPPEN?!
WAAAGH !!
WHUP WHUP
KRAKK..
HUH?!

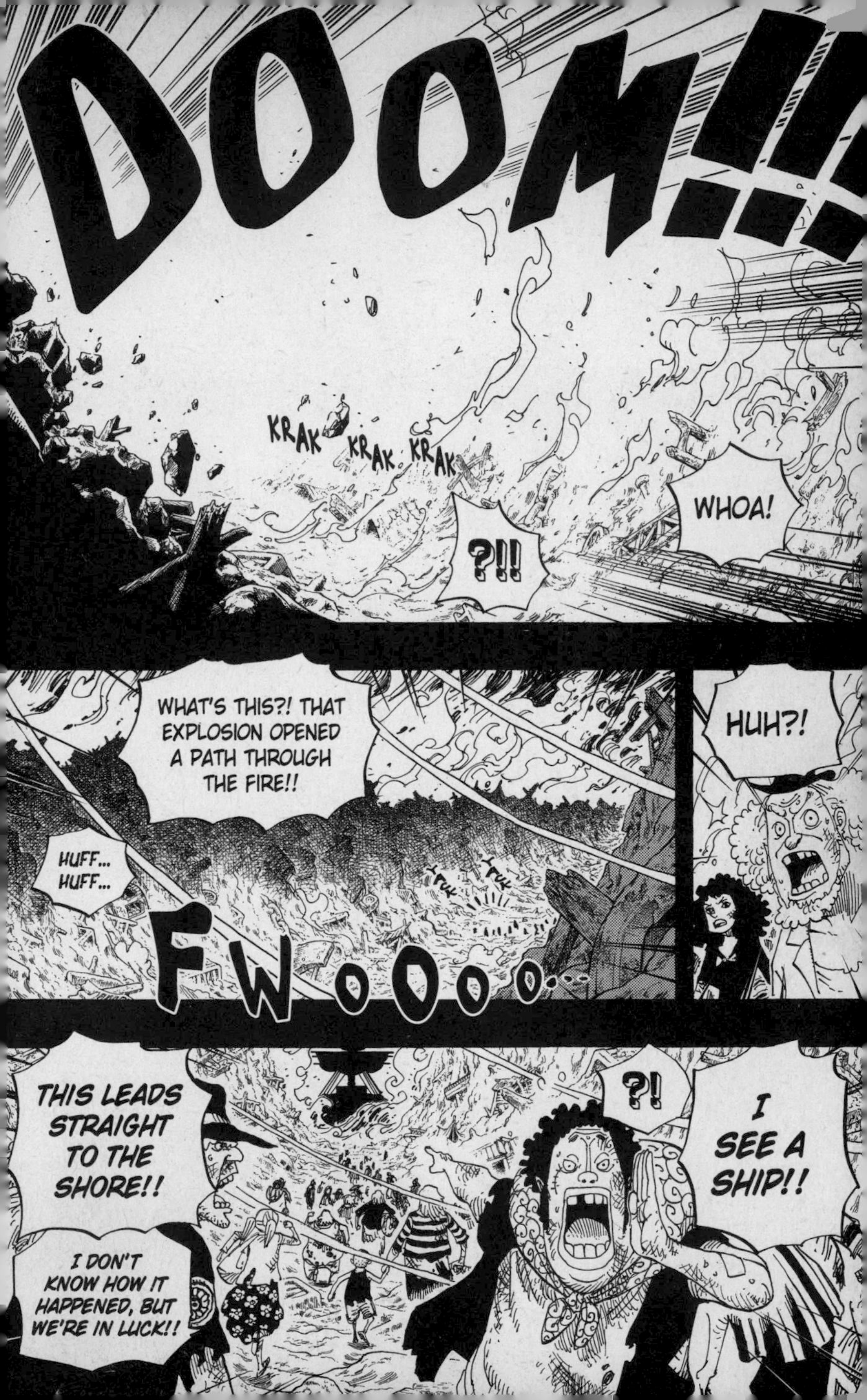
DOOM!!!
WHOA!
?!!
KRAK KRAK KRAK
HUH?!
WHAT'S THIS?! THAT EXPLOSION OPENED A PATH THROUGH THE FIRE!!
HUFF... HUFF...
FWOOOO
I SEE A SHIP!!
?!
THIS LEADS STRAIGHT TO THE SHORE!!
I DON'T KNOW HOW IT HAPPENED, BUT WE'RE IN LUCK!!

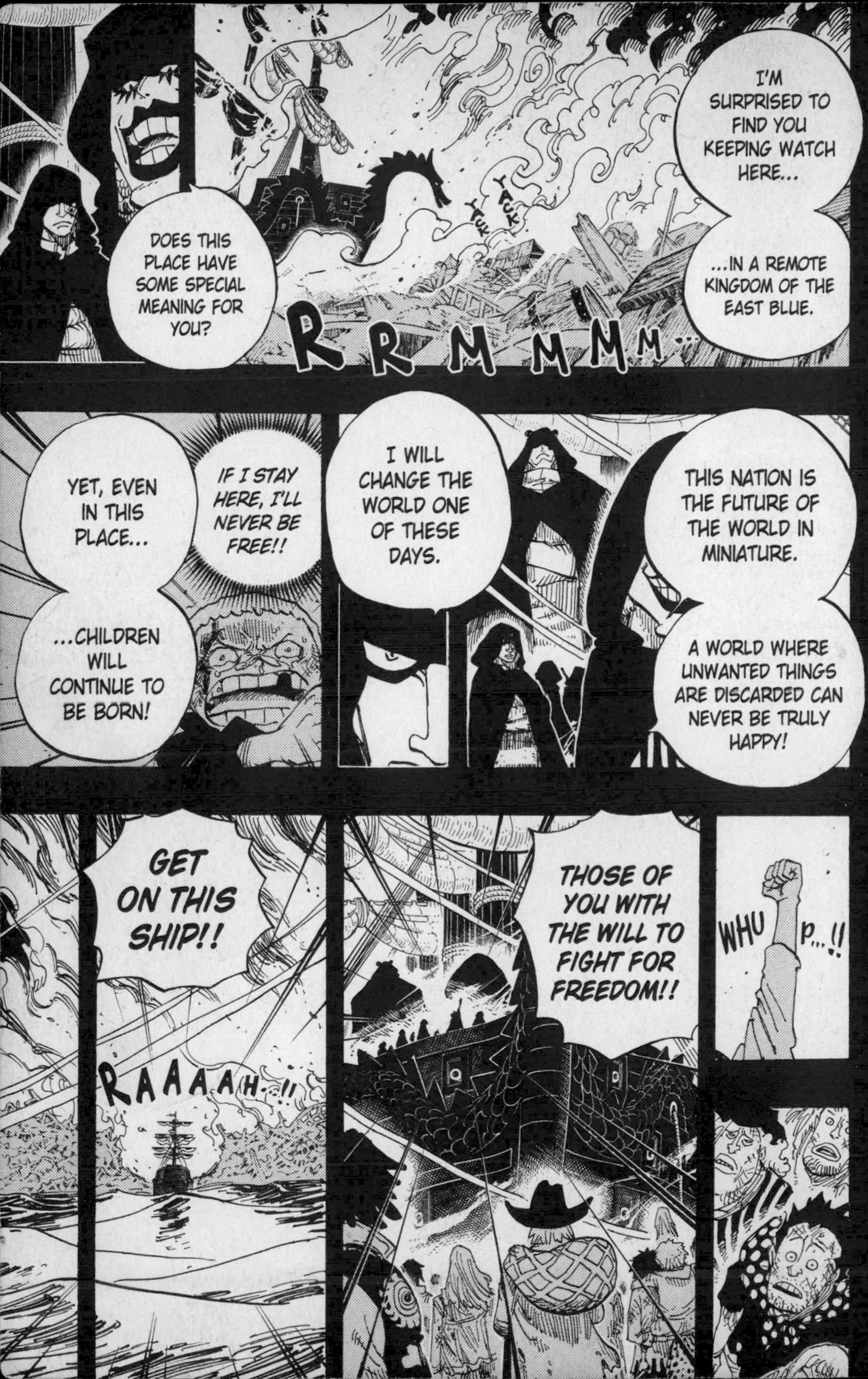
I'M SURPRISED TO FIND YOU KEEPING WATCH HERE...
...IN A REMOTE KINGDOM OF THE EAST BLUE.
YACK YACK
RRMMMM...
DOES THIS PLACE HAVE SOME SPECIAL MEANING FOR YOU?
THIS NATION IS THE FUTURE OF THE WORLD IN MINIATURE.
A WORLD WHERE UNWANTED THINGS ARE DISCARDED CAN NEVER BE TRULY HAPPY!
I WILL CHANGE THE WORLD ONE OF THESE DAYS.
IF I STAY HERE, I'LL NEVER BE FREE!!
YET, EVEN IN THIS PLACE...
...CHILDREN WILL CONTINUE TO BE BORN!
WHUp...!!
THOSE OF YOU WITH THE WILL TO FIGHT FOR FREEDOM!!
GET ON THIS SHIP!!
RAAAAH...!!

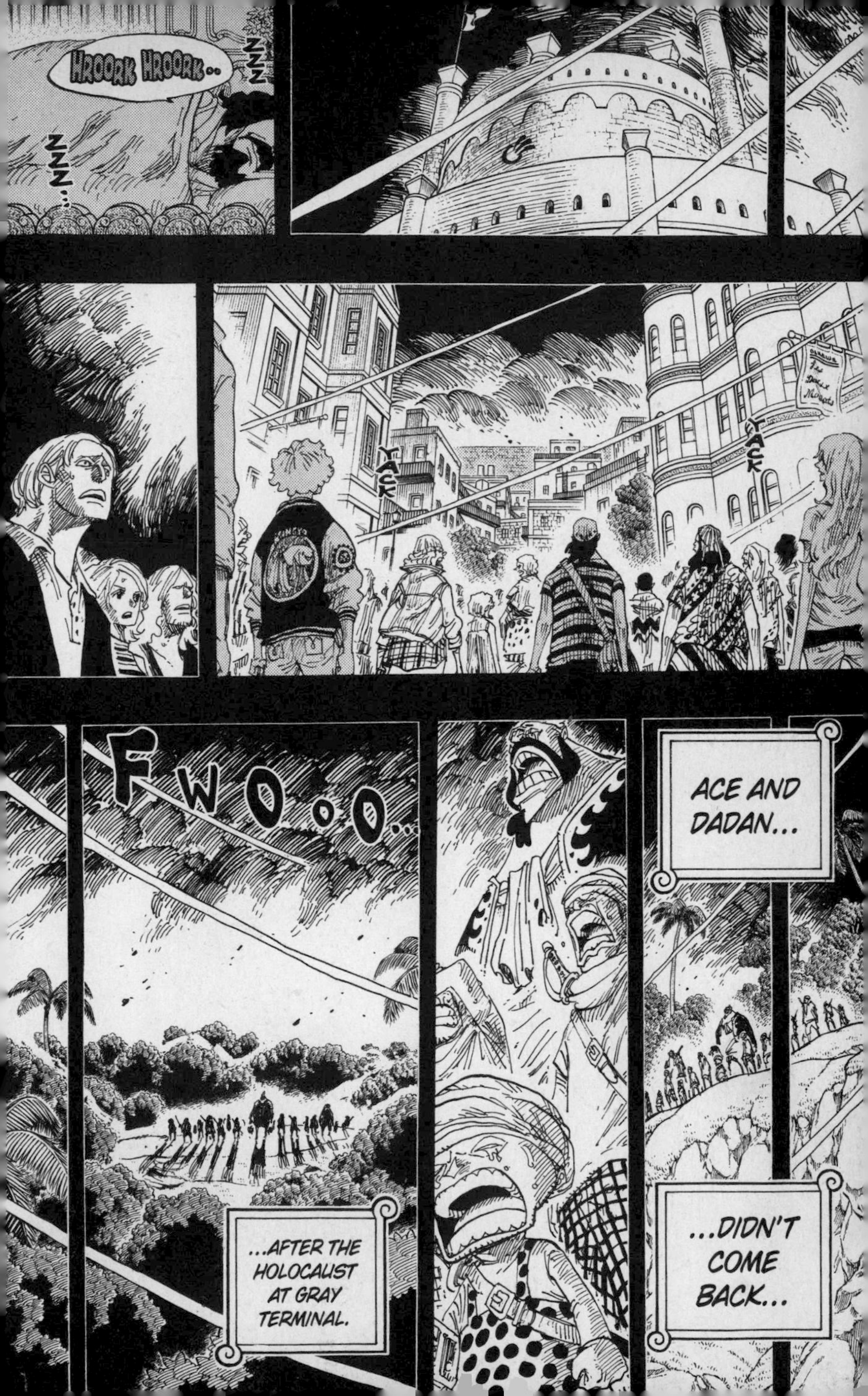
HROOAK HROOAK..
ZZZ
ZZZ...
YACK
YACK
ACE AND DADAN...
...DIDN'T COME BACK...
FWOO...
...AFTER THE HOLOCAUST AT GRAY TERMINAL.

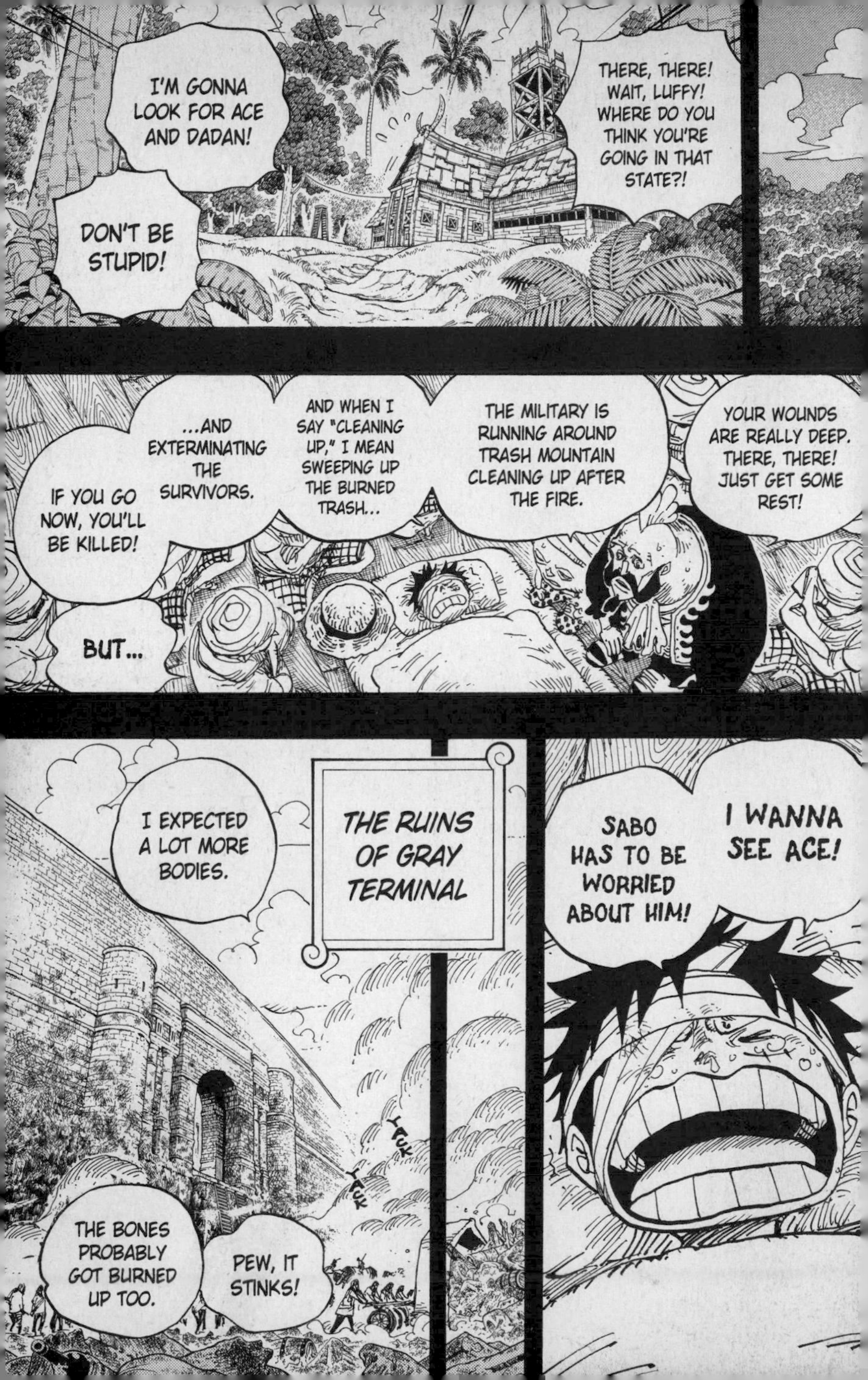
THERE, THERE! WAIT, LUFFY! WHERE DO YOU THINK YOU'RE GOING IN THAT STATE?!
I'M GONNA LOOK FOR ACE AND DADAN!
DON'T BE STUPID!
YOUR WOUNDS ARE REALLY DEEP. THERE, THERE! JUST GET SOME REST!
THE MILITARY IS RUNNING AROUND TRASH MOUNTAIN CLEANING UP AFTER THE FIRE.
AND WHEN I SAY "CLEANING UP," I MEAN SWEEPING UP THE BURNED TRASH...
...AND EXTERMINATING THE SURVIVORS.
IF YOU GO NOW, YOU'LL BE KILLED!
BUT...
I WANNA SEE ACE!
SABO HAS TO BE WORRIED ABOUT HIM!
THE RUINS OF GRAY TERMINAL
I EXPECTED A LOT MORE BODIES.
YUCK
YUCK
PEW, IT STINKS!
THE BONES PROBABLY GOT BURNED UP TOO.

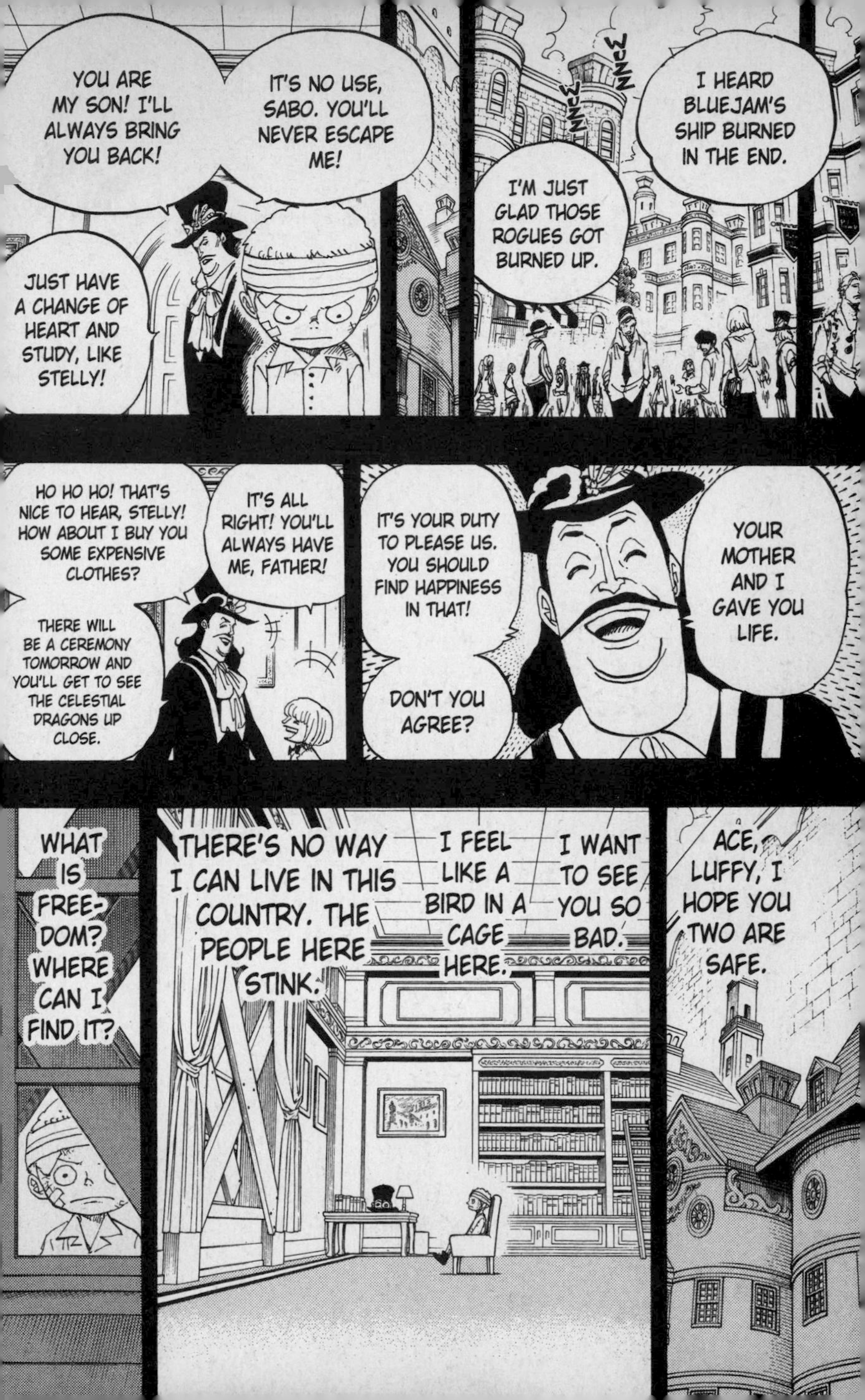
I HEARD BLUEJAM'S SHIP BURNED IN THE END.
I'M JUST GLAD THOSE ROGUES GOT BURNED UP.
IT'S NO USE, SABO. YOU'LL NEVER ESCAPE ME!
YOU ARE MY SON! I'LL ALWAYS BRING YOU BACK!
JUST HAVE A CHANGE OF HEART AND STUDY, LIKE STELLY!
YOUR MOTHER AND I GAVE YOU LIFE.
IT'S YOUR DUTY TO PLEASE US. YOU SHOULD FIND HAPPINESS IN THAT!
DON'T YOU AGREE?
IT'S ALL RIGHT! YOU'LL ALWAYS HAVE ME, FATHER!
HO HO HO! THAT'S NICE TO HEAR, STELLY! HOW ABOUT I BUY YOU SOME EXPENSIVE CLOTHES?
THERE WILL BE A CEREMONY TOMORROW AND YOU'LL GET TO SEE THE CELESTIAL DRAGONS UP CLOSE.
ACE, LUFFY, I HOPE YOU TWO ARE SAFE.
I WANT TO SEE YOU SO BAD.
I FEEL LIKE A BIRD IN A CAGE HERE.
THERE'S NO WAY I CAN LIVE IN THIS COUNTRY. THE PEOPLE HERE STINK.
WHAT IS FREEDOM? WHERE CAN I FIND IT?

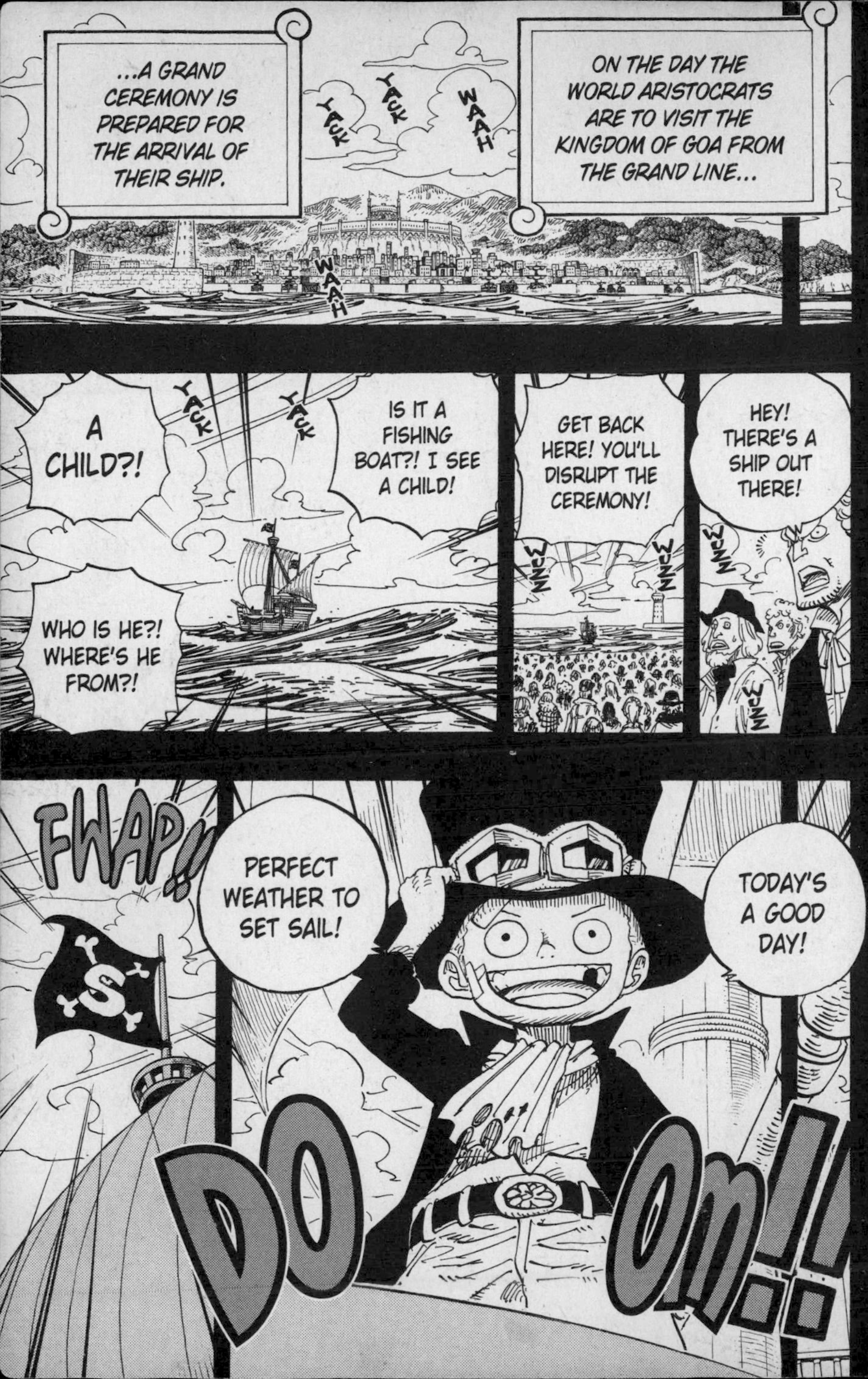
ON THE DAY THE WORLD ARISTOCRATS ARE TO VISIT THE KINGDOM OF GOA FROM THE GRAND LINE...
WAAH
YACK
YACK
...A GRAND CEREMONY IS PREPARED FOR THE ARRIVAL OF THEIR SHIP.
WAAAH
HEY! THERE'S A SHIP OUT THERE!
WUZZ
WUZZ
GET BACK HERE! YOU'LL DISRUPT THE CEREMONY!
WUZZ
WUZZ
IS IT A FISHING BOAT?! I SEE A CHILD!
YACK
YACK
A CHILD?!
WHO IS HE?! WHERE'S HE FROM?!
TODAY'S A GOOD DAY!
PERFECT WEATHER TO SET SAIL!
FWAP!!
DOOM!!

SABO'S OCEAN

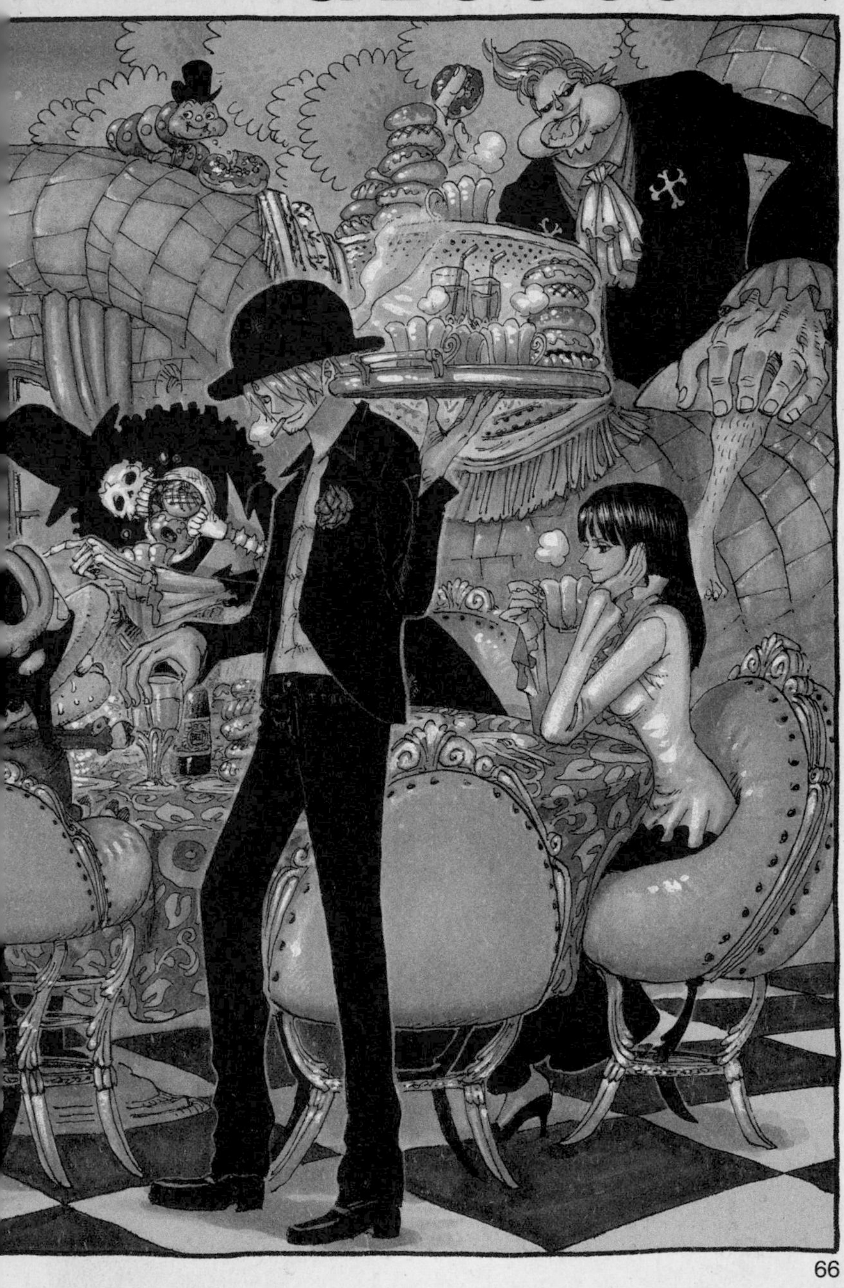

Chapter 588:

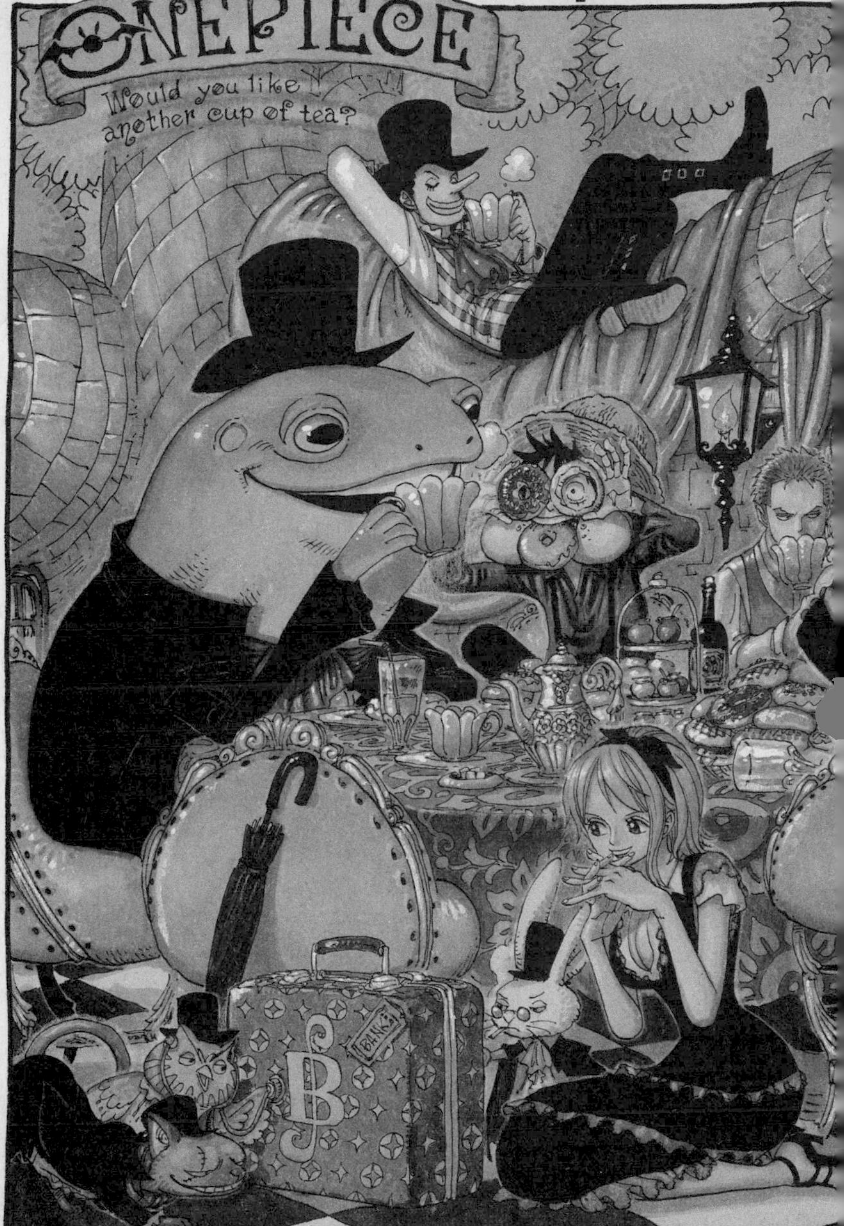
ONE PIECE
Would you like another cup of tea?
BANK
B

vol.60
ONE PIECE

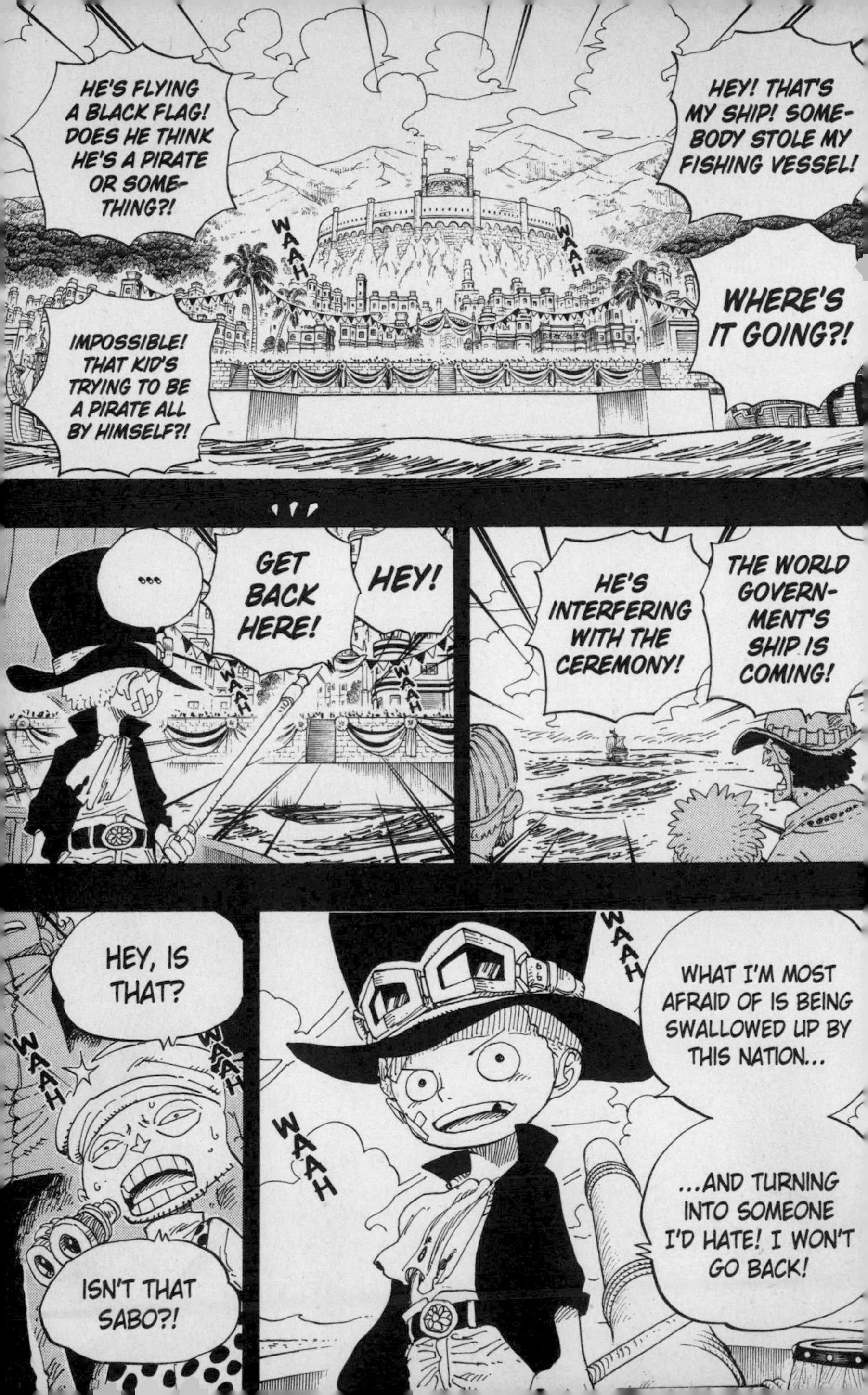
HEY! THAT'S MY SHIP! SOMEBODY STOLE MY FISHING VESSEL!
WHERE'S IT GOING?!
WAAH
WAAH
HE'S FLYING A BLACK FLAG! DOES HE THINK HE'S A PIRATE OR SOMETHING?!
IMPOSSIBLE! THAT KID'S TRYING TO BE A PIRATE ALL BY HIMSELF?!
THE WORLD GOVERNMENT'S SHIP IS COMING!
HE'S INTERFERING WITH THE CEREMONY!
HEY!
GET BACK HERE!
WAAH
WAAH
...
WAAH
WHAT I'M MOST AFRAID OF IS BEING SWALLOWED UP BY THIS NATION...
...AND TURNING INTO SOMEONE I'D HATE! I WON'T GO BACK!
WAAH
HEY, IS THAT?
WAAH
WAAH
ISN'T THAT SABO?!

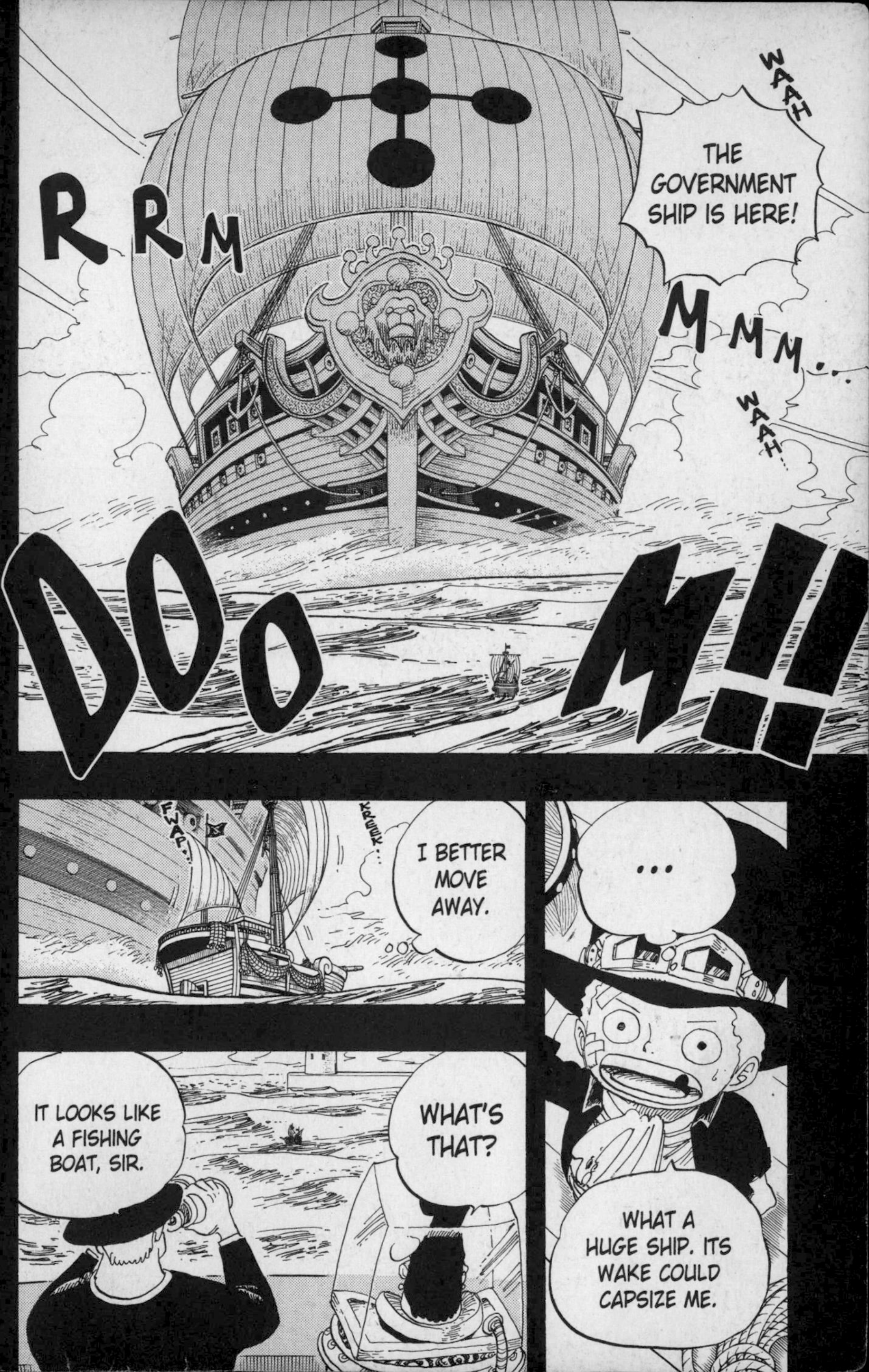
WAAAH
THE GOVERNMENT SHIP IS HERE!
RRM
MMMM...
WAAAH...
DOOM!!
...
WHAT A HUGE SHIP. ITS WAKE COULD CAPSIZE ME.
KREEK...
FWAP...
I BETTER MOVE AWAY.
WHAT'S THAT?
IT LOOKS LIKE A FISHING BOAT, SIR.

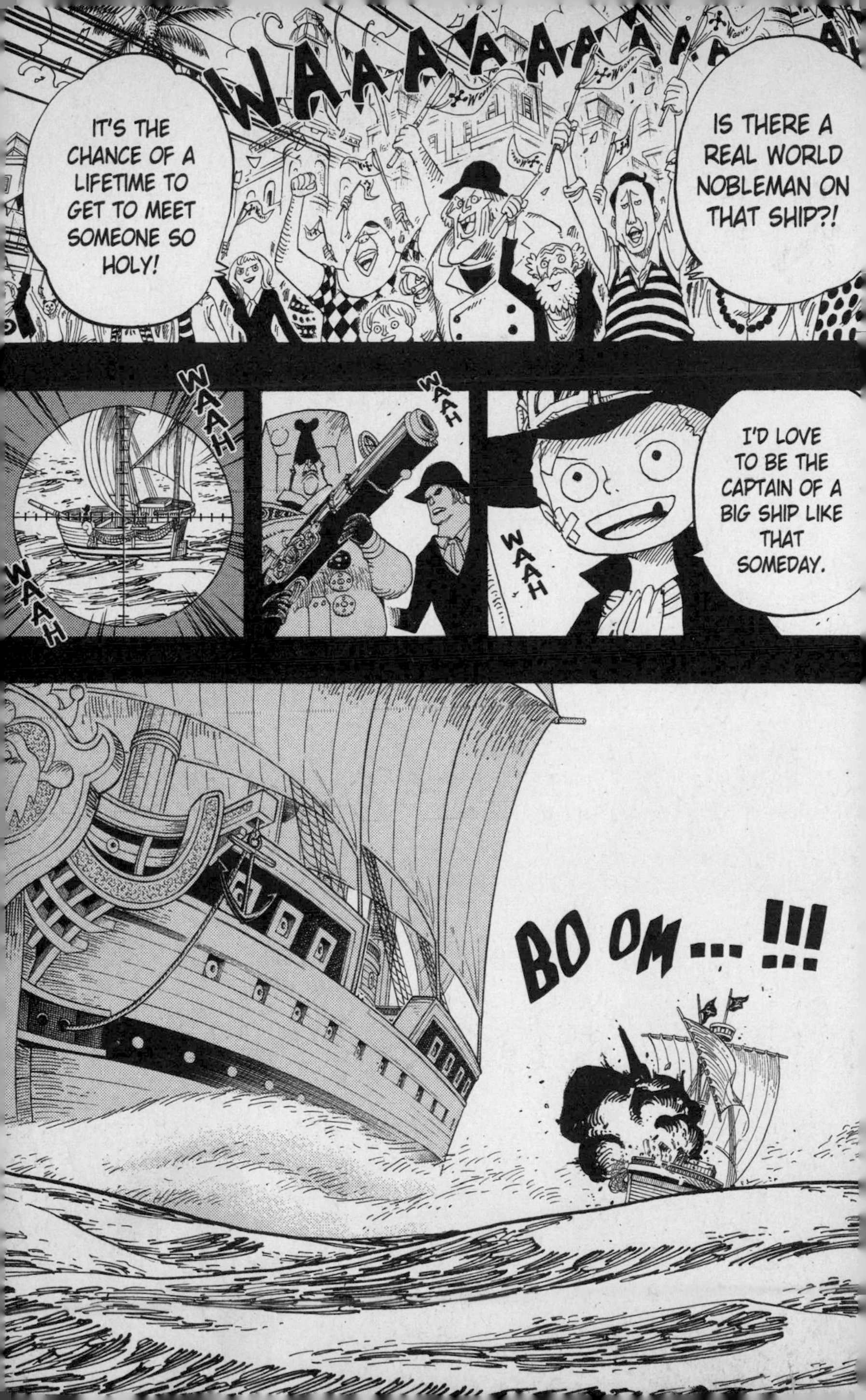
WAAAAAAA
IS THERE A REAL WORLD NOBLEMAN ON THAT SHIP?!
IT'S THE CHANCE OF A LIFETIME TO GET TO MEET SOMEONE SO HOLY!
I'D LOVE TO BE THE CAPTAIN OF A BIG SHIP LIKE THAT SOMEDAY.
WAAH
WAAH
WAAH
WAAH
BOOM...!!!

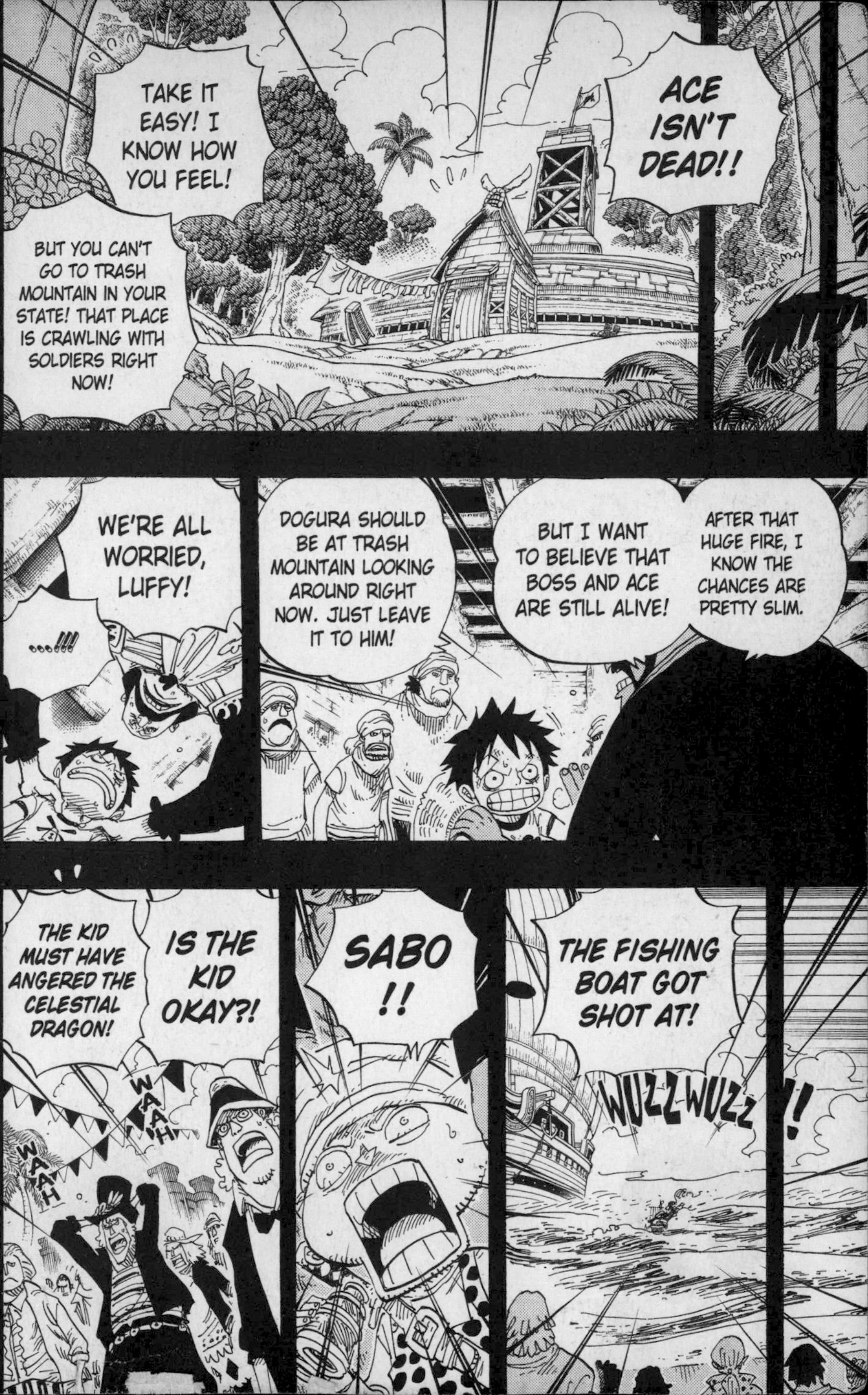
ACE ISN'T DEAD!!
TAKE IT EASY! I KNOW HOW YOU FEEL!
BUT YOU CAN'T GO TO TRASH MOUNTAIN IN YOUR STATE! THAT PLACE IS CRAWLING WITH SOLDIERS RIGHT NOW!
AFTER THAT HUGE FIRE, I KNOW THE CHANCES ARE PRETTY SLIM.
BUT I WANT TO BELIEVE THAT BOSS AND ACE ARE STILL ALIVE!
DOGURA SHOULD BE AT TRASH MOUNTAIN LOOKING AROUND RIGHT NOW. JUST LEAVE IT TO HIM!
WE'RE ALL WORRIED, LUFFY!
...!!!
THE FISHING BOAT GOT SHOT AT!
WUZZ WUZZz!
SABO!!
IS THE KID OKAY?!
THE KID MUST HAVE ANGERED THE CELESTIAL DRAGON!
WAAH
WAAH

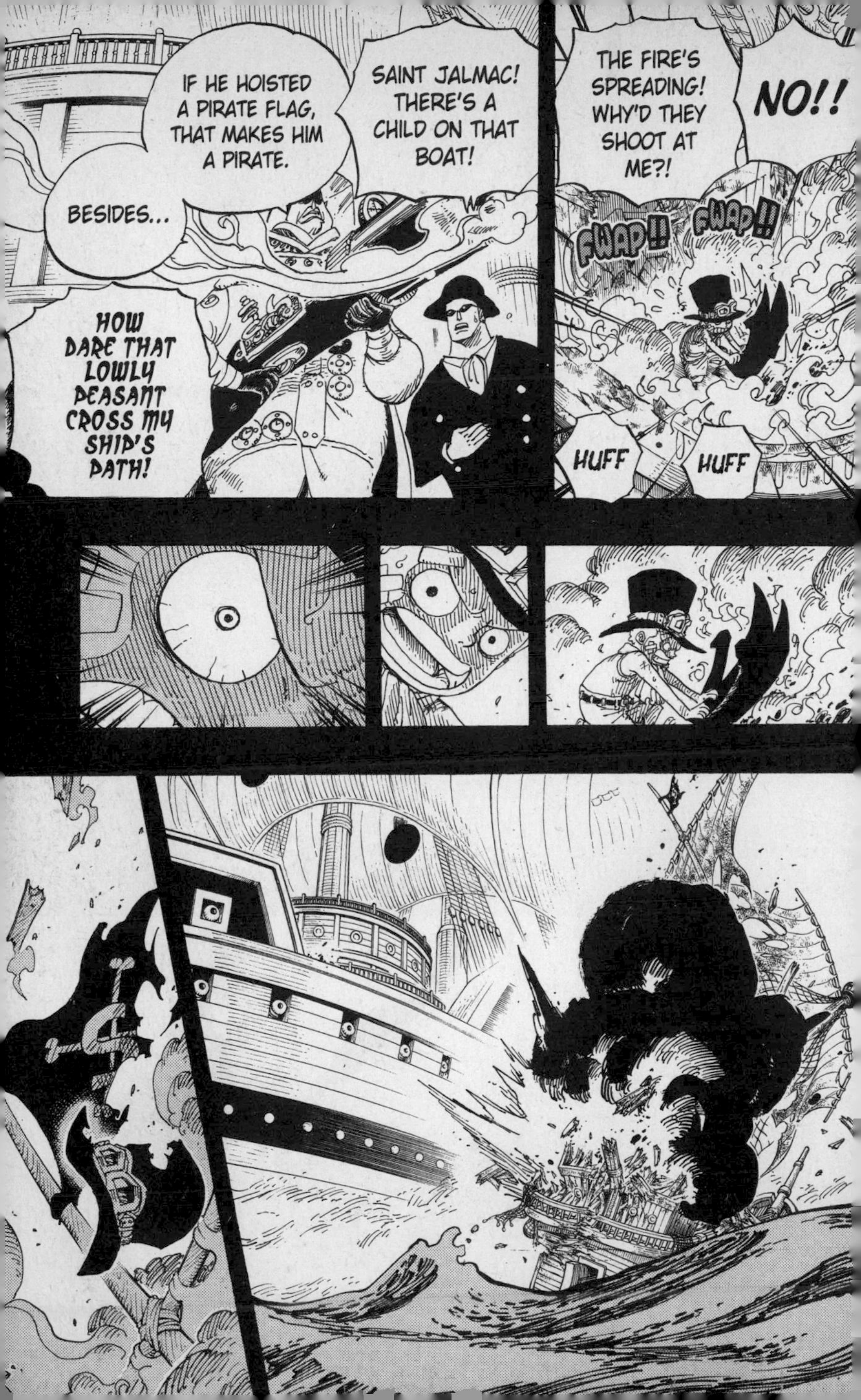
NO!!
THE FIRE'S SPREADING! WHY'D THEY SHOOT AT ME?!
FWAP!! FWAP!!
HUFF HUFF
SAINT JALMAC! THERE'S A CHILD ON THAT BOAT!
IF HE HOISTED A PIRATE FLAG, THAT MAKES HIM A PIRATE.
BESIDES...
HOW DARE THAT LOWLY PEASANT CROSS MY SHIP'S PATH!

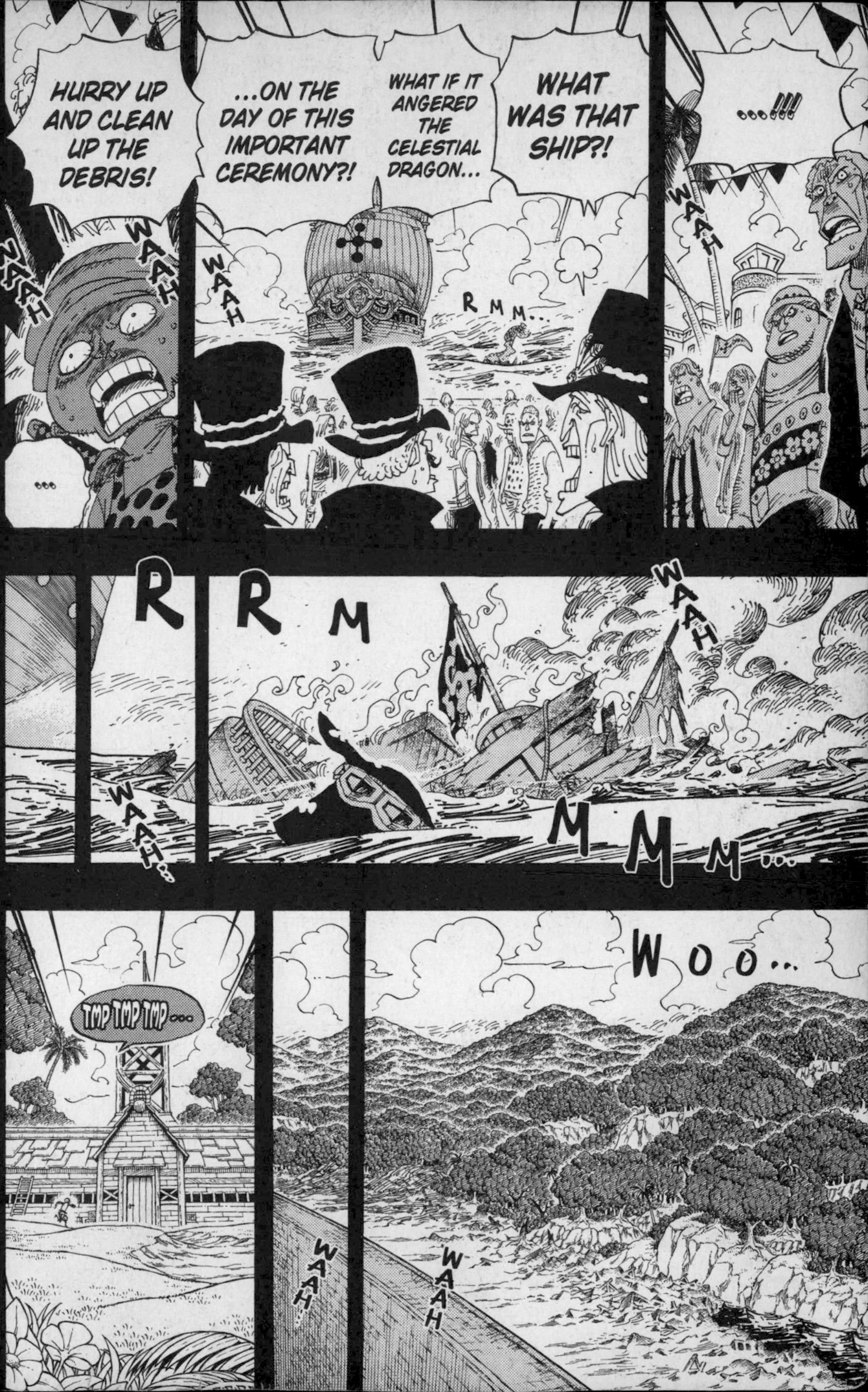
...!!!
WAAH
WHAT WAS THAT SHIP?!
WHAT IF IT ANGERED THE CELESTIAL DRAGON...
...ON THE DAY OF THIS IMPORTANT CEREMONY?!
RMM...
WAAH
HURRY UP AND CLEAN UP THE DEBRIS!
WAAH
WAAH
...
WAAH
RRM
MMM...
WAAH...
WOO...
WAAH
WAAH...
TMP TMP TMP...

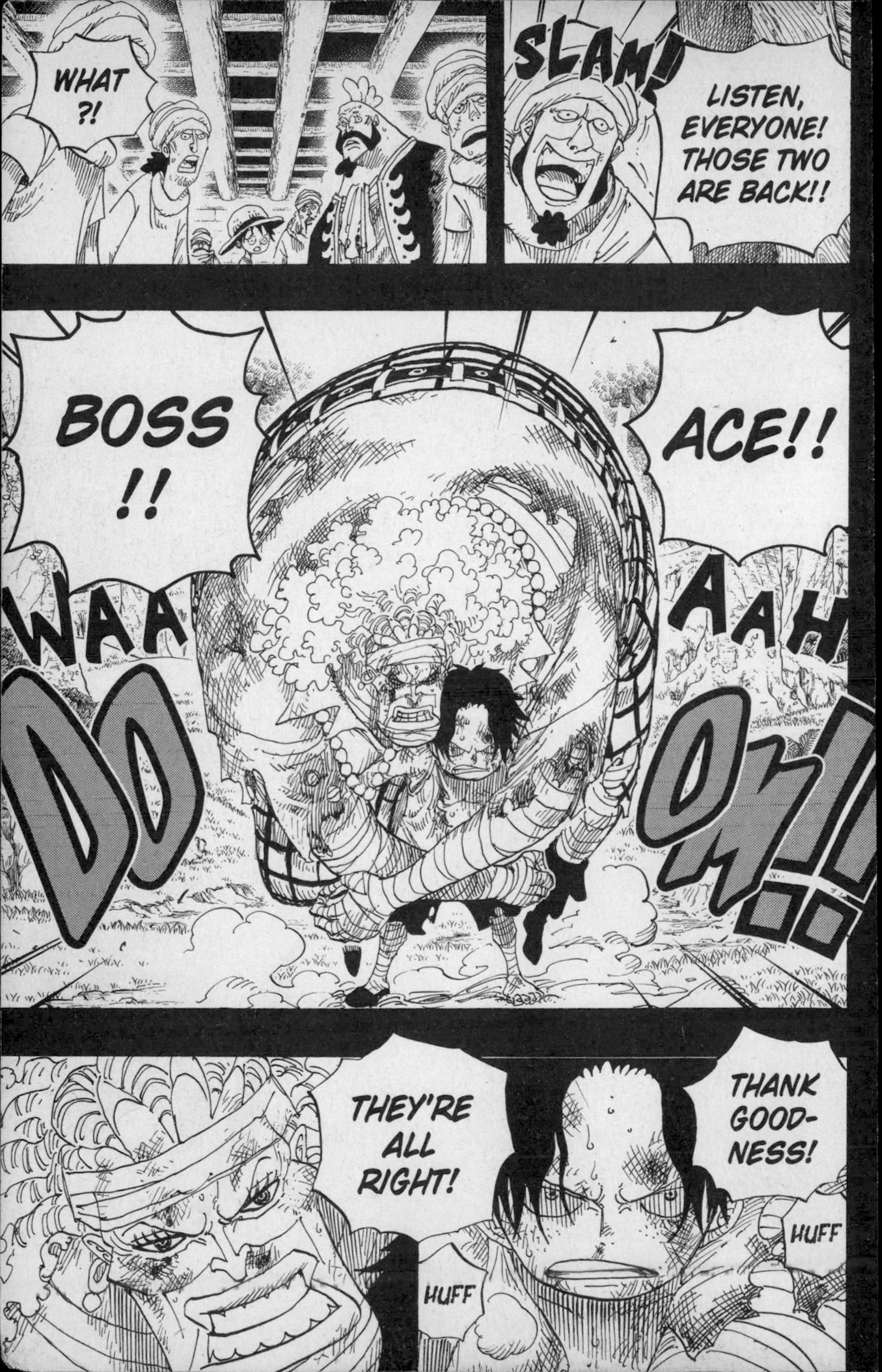
SLAM!
LISTEN, EVERYONE! THOSE TWO ARE BACK!!
WHAT ?!
ACE!!
BOSS !!
AAH
WAA
OH!!
DO
THANK GOOD-NESS!
HUFF
THEY'RE ALL RIGHT!
HUFF

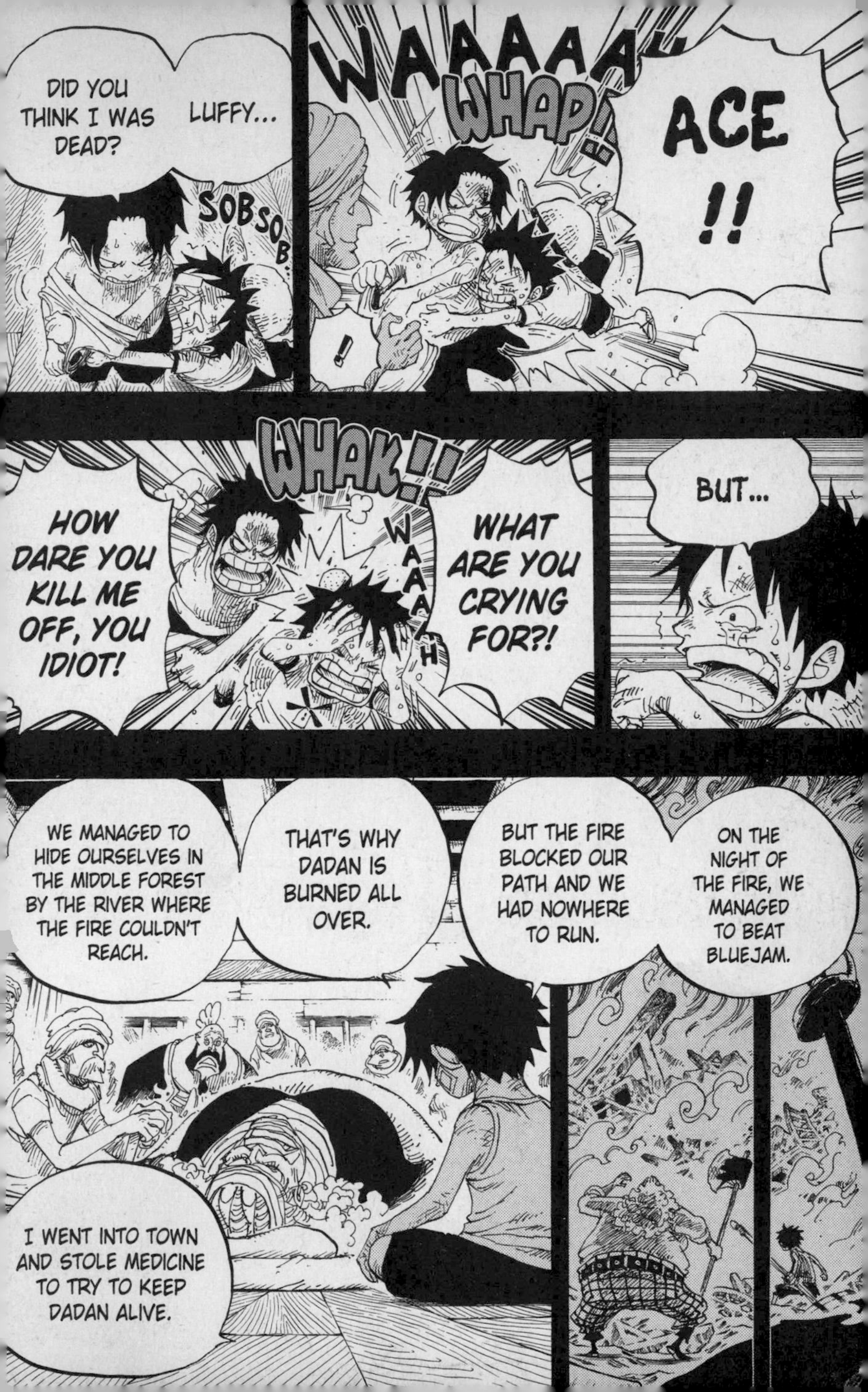
ACE !!
WAAAAAH
WHAP!!
!
LUFFY...
DID YOU THINK I WAS DEAD?
SOB SOB
BUT...
WHAT ARE YOU CRYING FOR?!
WHAK!!
WAAAAH
HOW DARE YOU KILL ME OFF, YOU IDIOT!
ON THE NIGHT OF THE FIRE, WE MANAGED TO BEAT BLUEJAM.
BUT THE FIRE BLOCKED OUR PATH AND WE HAD NOWHERE TO RUN.
THAT'S WHY DADAN IS BURNED ALL OVER.
WE MANAGED TO HIDE OURSELVES IN THE MIDDLE FOREST BY THE RIVER WHERE THE FIRE COULDN'T REACH.
I WENT INTO TOWN AND STOLE MEDICINE TO TRY TO KEEP DADAN ALIVE.

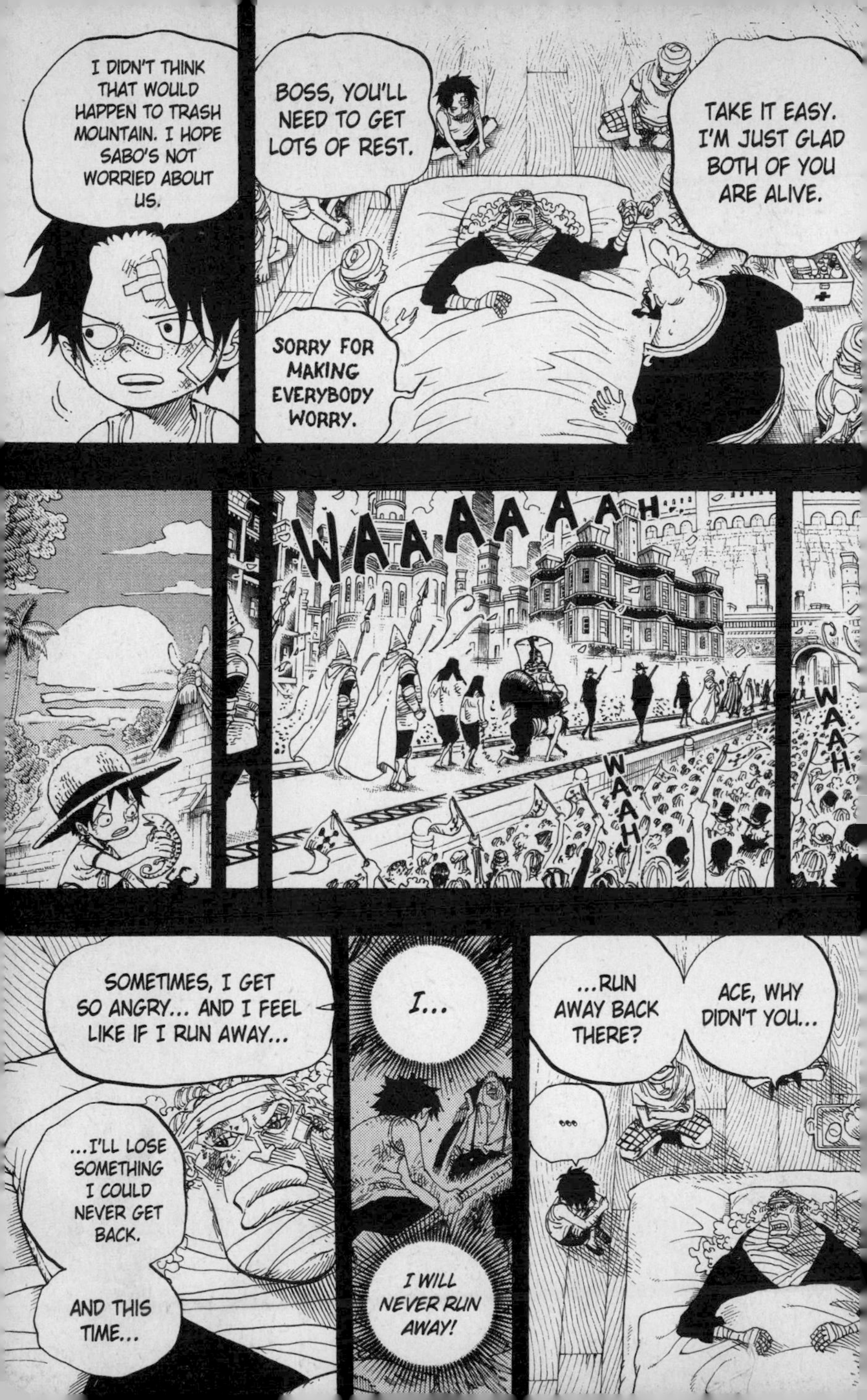
TAKE IT EASY. I'M JUST GLAD BOTH OF YOU ARE ALIVE.
BOSS, YOU'LL NEED TO GET LOTS OF REST.
SORRY FOR MAKING EVERYBODY WORRY.
I DIDN'T THINK THAT WOULD HAPPEN TO TRASH MOUNTAIN. I HOPE SABO'S NOT WORRIED ABOUT US.
WAAH
WAAAAAAH
WAAH
ACE, WHY DIDN'T YOU...
...RUN AWAY BACK THERE?
...
I...
I WILL NEVER RUN AWAY!
SOMETIMES, I GET SO ANGRY... AND I FEEL LIKE IF I RUN AWAY...
...I'LL LOSE SOMETHING I COULD NEVER GET BACK.
AND THIS TIME...

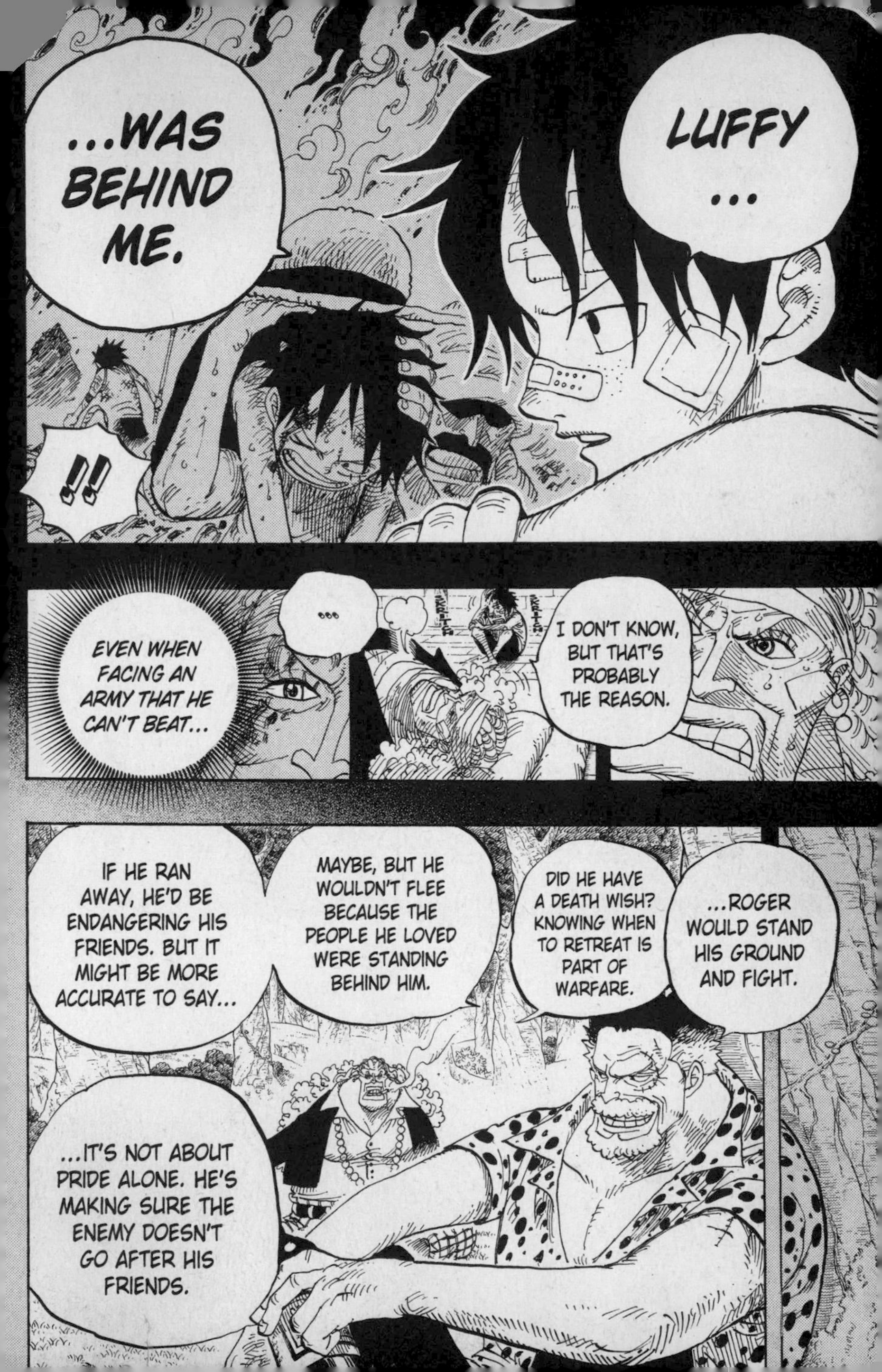
LUFFY ...
...WAS BEHIND ME.
!!
SKRITCH
SKRITCH
I DON'T KNOW, BUT THAT'S PROBABLY THE REASON.
...
EVEN WHEN FACING AN ARMY THAT HE CAN'T BEAT...
...ROGER WOULD STAND HIS GROUND AND FIGHT.
DID HE HAVE A DEATH WISH? KNOWING WHEN TO RETREAT IS PART OF WARFARE.
MAYBE, BUT HE WOULDN'T FLEE BECAUSE THE PEOPLE HE LOVED WERE STANDING BEHIND HIM.
IF HE RAN AWAY, HE'D BE ENDANGERING HIS FRIENDS. BUT IT MIGHT BE MORE ACCURATE TO SAY...
...IT'S NOT ABOUT PRIDE ALONE. HE'S MAKING SURE THE ENEMY DOESN'T GO AFTER HIS FRIENDS.

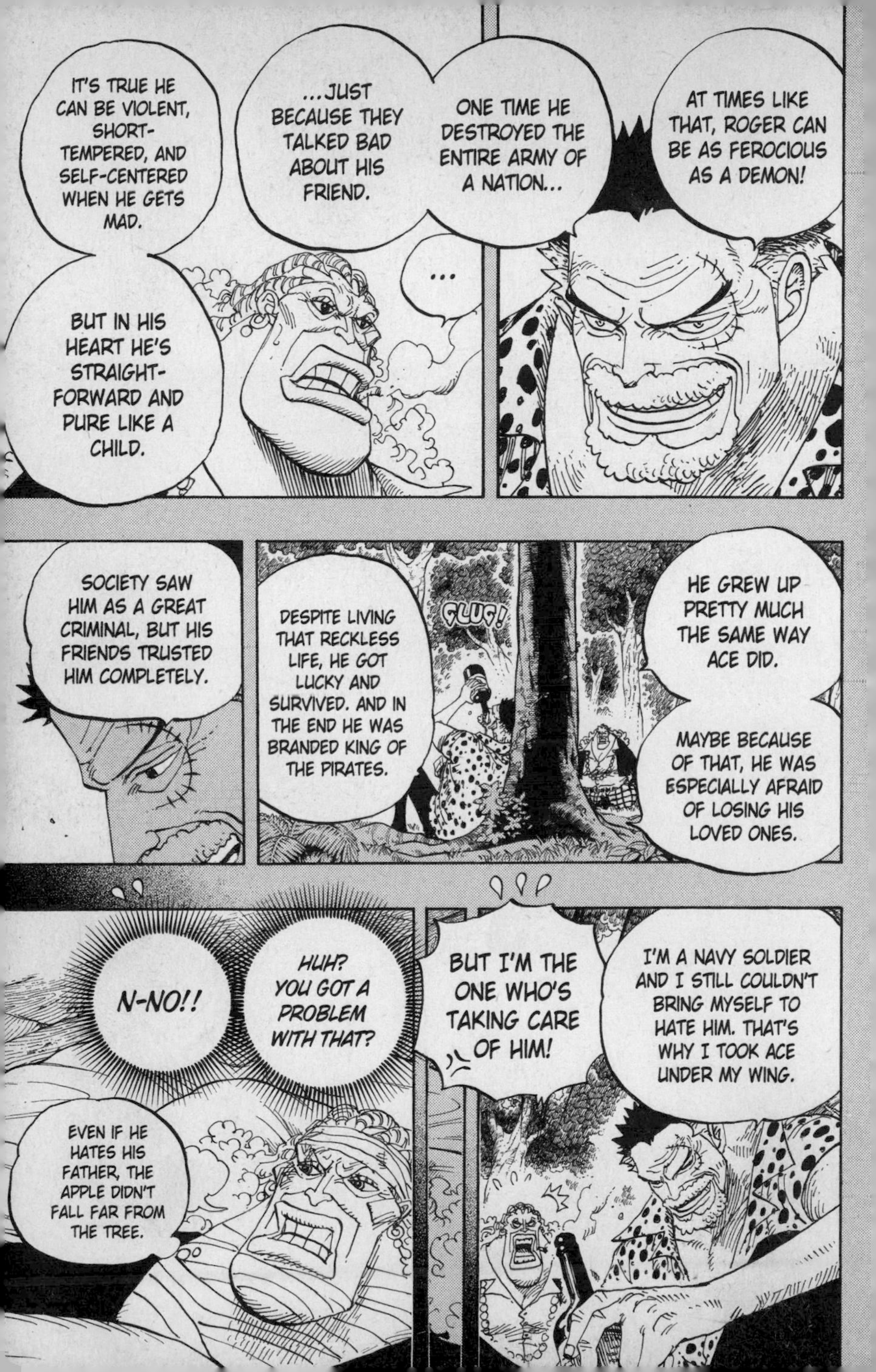
AT TIMES LIKE THAT, ROGER CAN BE AS FEROCIOUS AS A DEMON!
ONE TIME HE DESTROYED THE ENTIRE ARMY OF A NATION...
...JUST BECAUSE THEY TALKED BAD ABOUT HIS FRIEND.
...
IT'S TRUE HE CAN BE VIOLENT, SHORT-TEMPERED, AND SELF-CENTERED WHEN HE GETS MAD.
BUT IN HIS HEART HE'S STRAIGHT-FORWARD AND PURE LIKE A CHILD.
HE GREW UP PRETTY MUCH THE SAME WAY ACE DID.
MAYBE BECAUSE OF THAT, HE WAS ESPECIALLY AFRAID OF LOSING HIS LOVED ONES.
GLUG!
DESPITE LIVING THAT RECKLESS LIFE, HE GOT LUCKY AND SURVIVED. AND IN THE END HE WAS BRANDED KING OF THE PIRATES.
SOCIETY SAW HIM AS A GREAT CRIMINAL, BUT HIS FRIENDS TRUSTED HIM COMPLETELY.
I'M A NAVY SOLDIER AND I STILL COULDN'T BRING MYSELF TO HATE HIM. THAT'S WHY I TOOK ACE UNDER MY WING.
BUT I'M THE ONE WHO'S TAKING CARE OF HIM!
HUH? YOU GOT A PROBLEM WITH THAT?
N-NO!!
EVEN IF HE HATES HIS FATHER, THE APPLE DIDN'T FALL FAR FROM THE TREE.

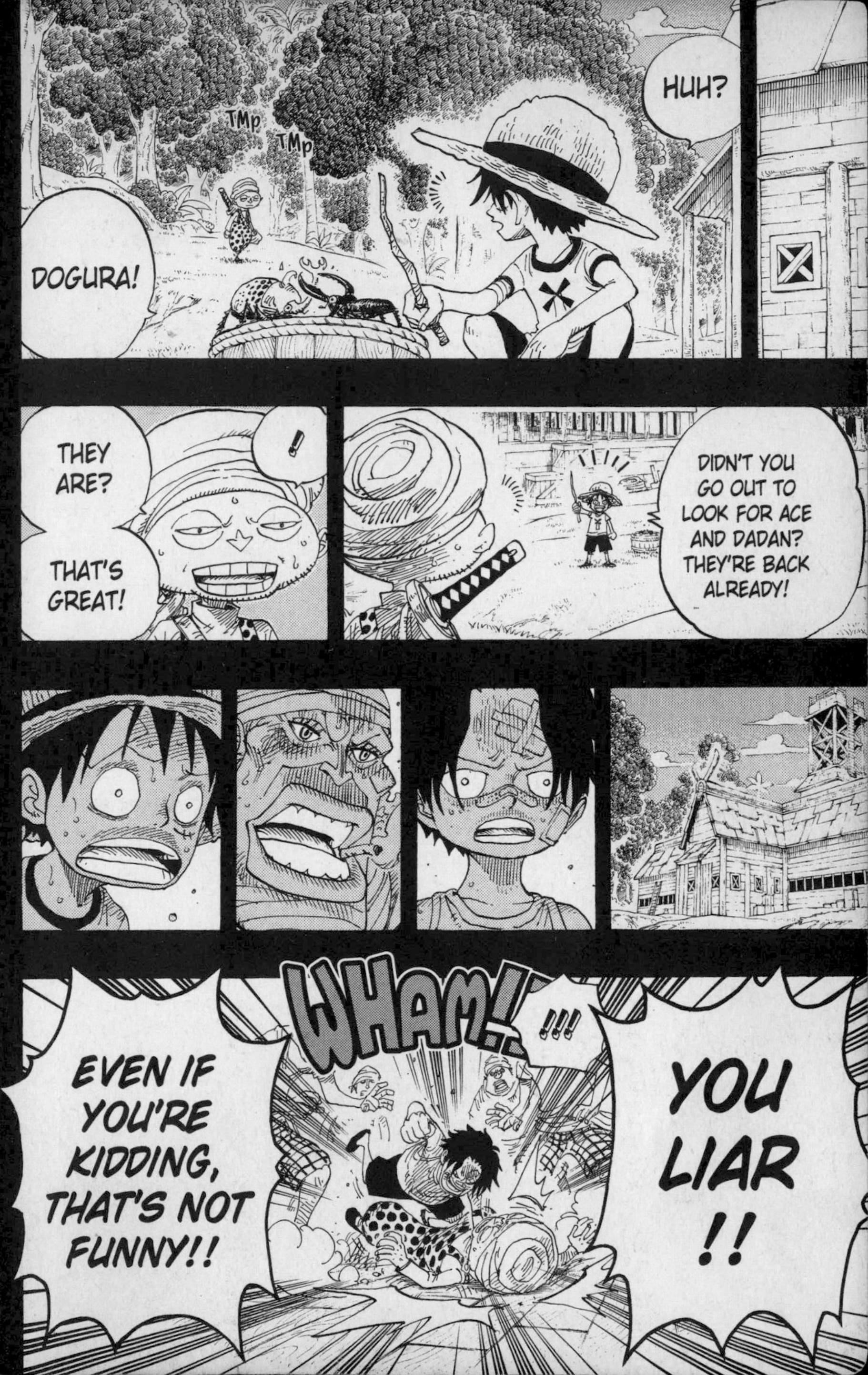
HUH?
TMp
TMp
DOGURA!
DIDN'T YOU GO OUT TO LOOK FOR ACE AND DADAN? THEY'RE BACK ALREADY!
!
THEY ARE?
THAT'S GREAT!
YOU LIAR!!
WHAM!!
!!!
EVEN IF YOU'RE KIDDING, THAT'S NOT FUNNY!!

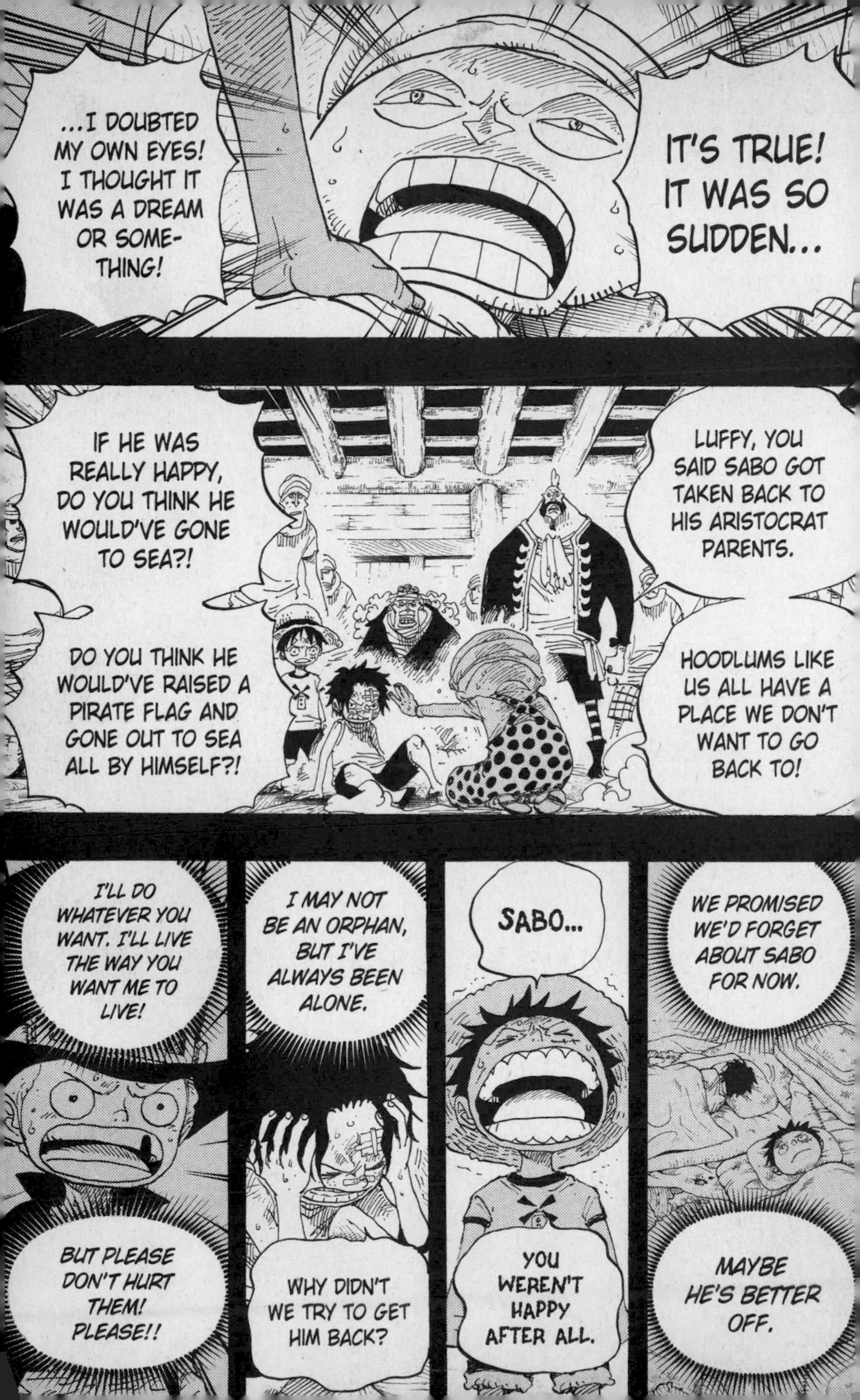
IT'S TRUE! IT WAS SO SUDDEN...
...I DOUBTED MY OWN EYES! I THOUGHT IT WAS A DREAM OR SOME-THING!
LUFFY, YOU SAID SABO GOT TAKEN BACK TO HIS ARISTOCRAT PARENTS.
HOODLUMS LIKE US ALL HAVE A PLACE WE DON'T WANT TO GO BACK TO!
IF HE WAS REALLY HAPPY, DO YOU THINK HE WOULD'VE GONE TO SEA?!
DO YOU THINK HE WOULD'VE RAISED A PIRATE FLAG AND GONE OUT TO SEA ALL BY HIMSELF?!
WE PROMISED WE'D FORGET ABOUT SABO FOR NOW.
MAYBE HE'S BETTER OFF.
SABO...
YOU WEREN'T HAPPY AFTER ALL.
I MAY NOT BE AN ORPHAN, BUT I'VE ALWAYS BEEN ALONE.
WHY DIDN'T WE TRY TO GET HIM BACK?
I'LL DO WHATEVER YOU WANT. I'LL LIVE THE WAY YOU WANT ME TO LIVE!
BUT PLEASE DON'T HURT THEM! PLEASE!!

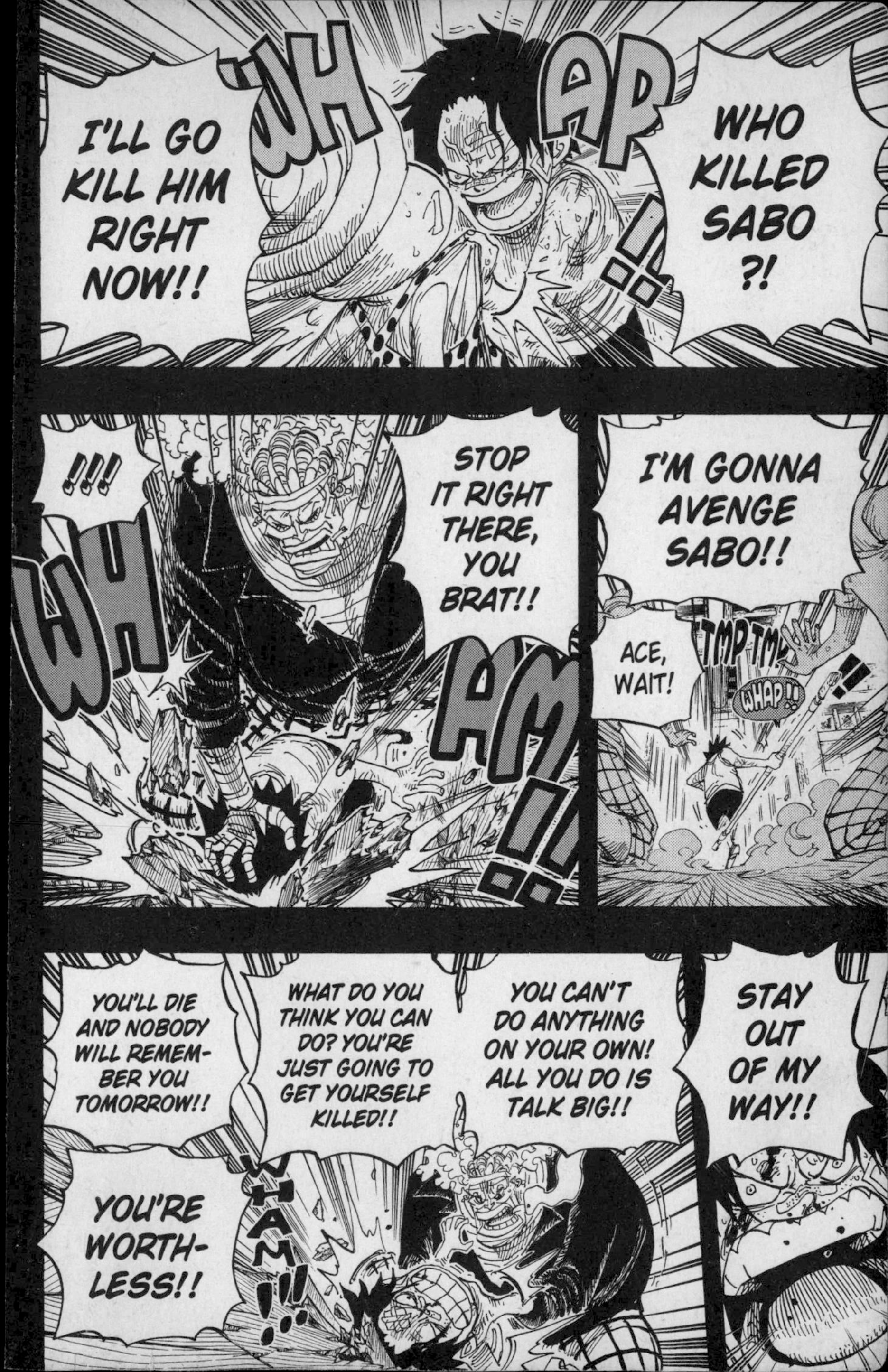
WHO KILLED SABO ?!
WHAP!!
I'LL GO KILL HIM RIGHT NOW!!
I'M GONNA AVENGE SABO!!
TMP TMP
WHAP!!
ACE, WAIT!
STOP IT RIGHT THERE, YOU BRAT!!
!!!
WHAM!!
STAY OUT OF MY WAY!!
YOU CAN'T DO ANYTHING ON YOUR OWN! ALL YOU DO IS TALK BIG!!
WHAT DO YOU THINK YOU CAN DO? YOU'RE JUST GOING TO GET YOURSELF KILLED!!
YOU'LL DIE AND NOBODY WILL REMEMBER YOU TOMORROW!!
WHAM!!
YOU'RE WORTHLESS!!

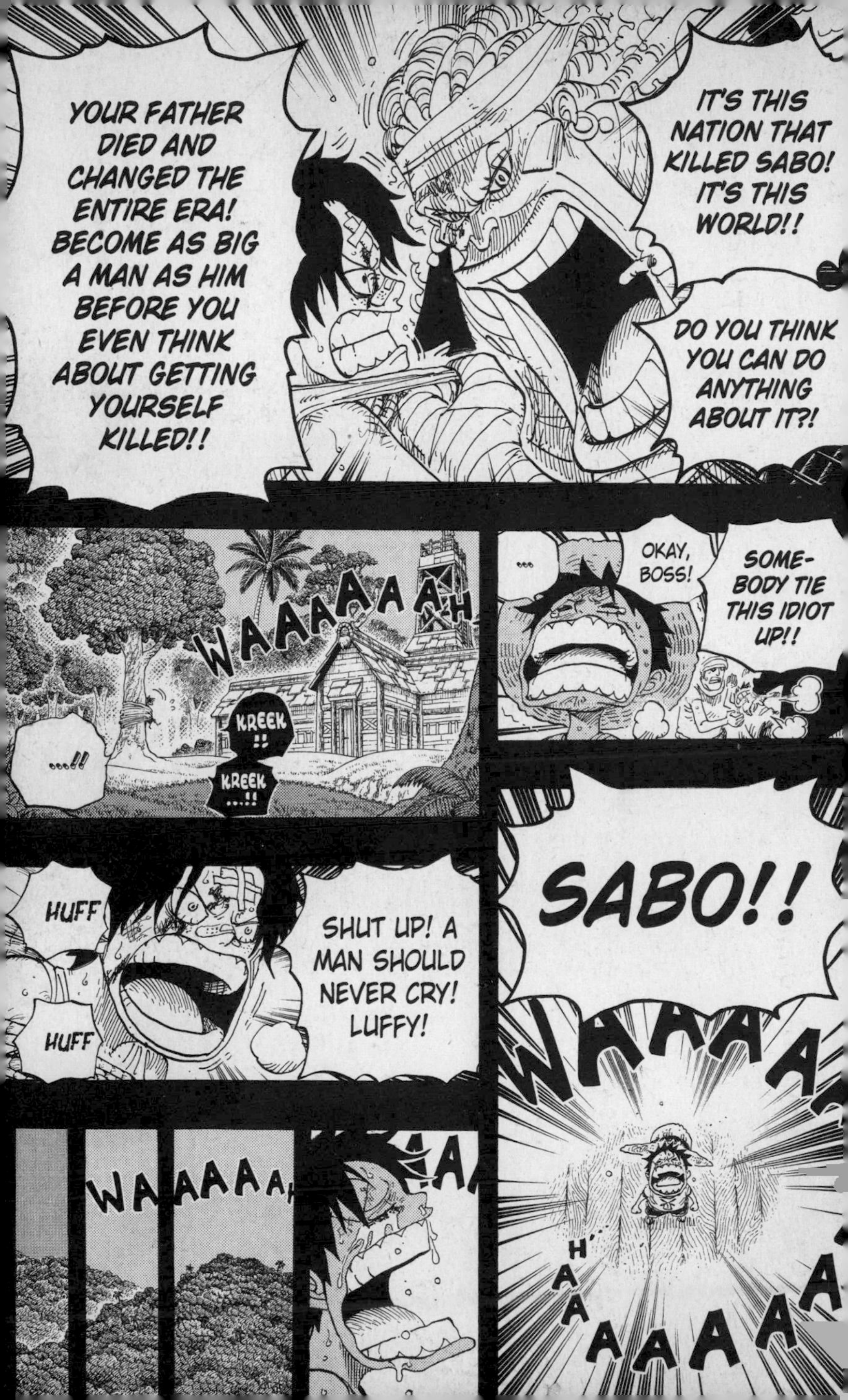
IT'S THIS NATION THAT KILLED SABO! IT'S THIS WORLD!!
DO YOU THINK YOU CAN DO ANYTHING ABOUT IT?!
YOUR FATHER DIED AND CHANGED THE ENTIRE ERA! BECOME AS BIG A MAN AS HIM BEFORE YOU EVEN THINK ABOUT GETTING YOURSELF KILLED!!
SOME-BODY TIE THIS IDIOT UP!!
OKAY, BOSS!
...
SABO!!
WAAAAAH
HAAAAAAA
WAAAAAAH
KREEK !!
KREEK ...!!
...!!
SHUT UP! A MAN SHOULD NEVER CRY! LUFFY!
HUFF
HUFF
WAAAAAH

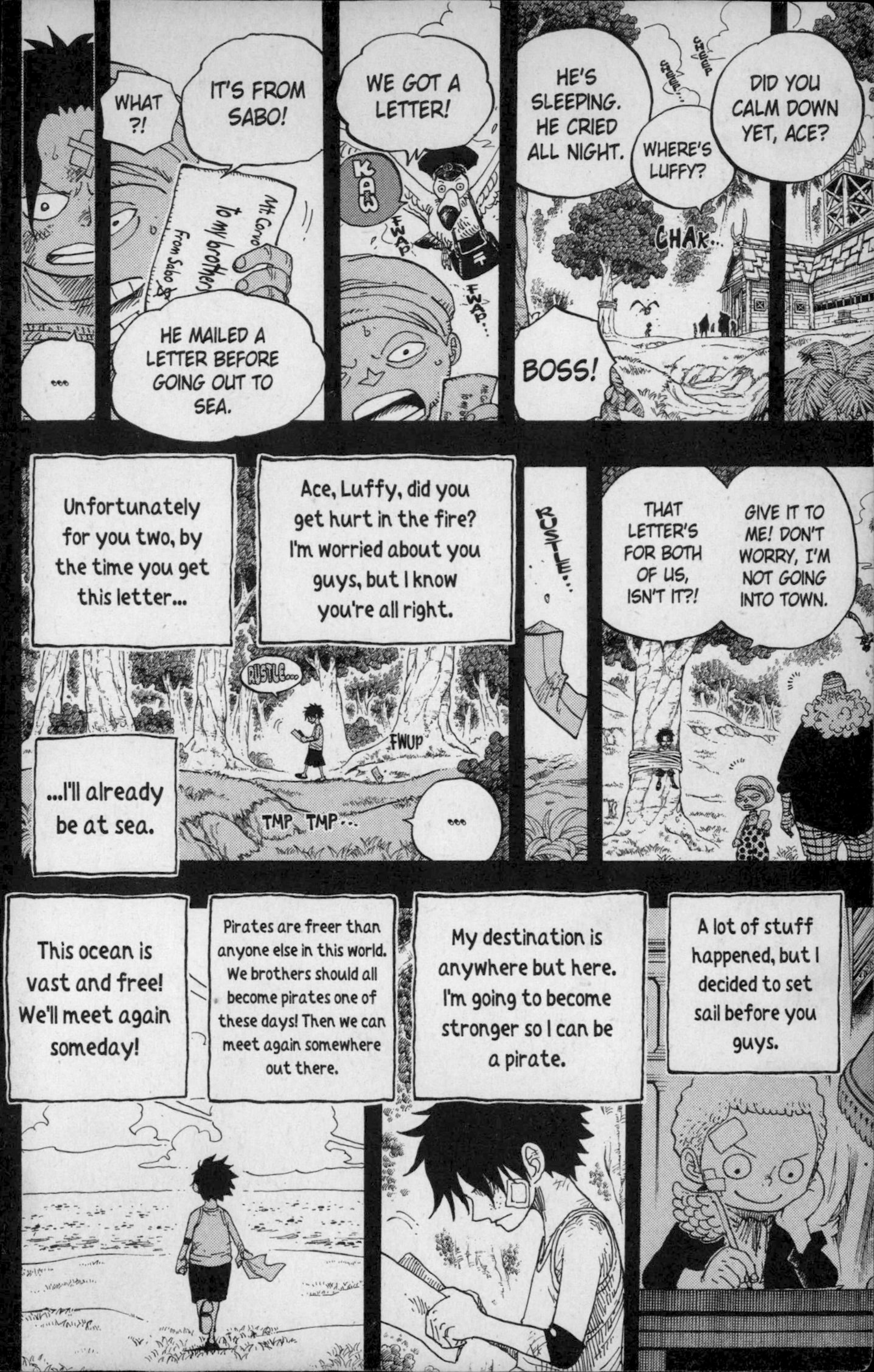

DID YOU CALM DOWN YET, ACE?
WHERE'S LUFFY?
HE'S SLEEPING. HE CRIED ALL NIGHT.
CHAK...
BOSS!
WE GOT A LETTER!
KAW
FWAP
FWAP...
IT'S FROM SABO!
WHAT ?!
Mt. Corvo
to my brothers
from Sabo
HE MAILED A LETTER BEFORE GOING OUT TO SEA.
...
GIVE IT TO ME! DON'T WORRY, I'M NOT GOING INTO TOWN.
THAT LETTER'S FOR BOTH OF US, ISN'T IT?!
RUSTLE...
Ace, Luffy, did you get hurt in the fire? I'm worried about you guys, but I know you're all right.
Unfortunately for you two, by the time you get this letter...
RUSTLE...
FWUP
...I'll already be at sea.
TMP TMP...
...
A lot of stuff happened, but I decided to set sail before you guys.
My destination is anywhere but here. I'm going to become stronger so I can be a pirate.
Pirates are freer than anyone else in this world. We brothers should all become pirates one of these days! Then we can meet again somewhere out there.
This ocean is vast and free! We'll meet again someday!

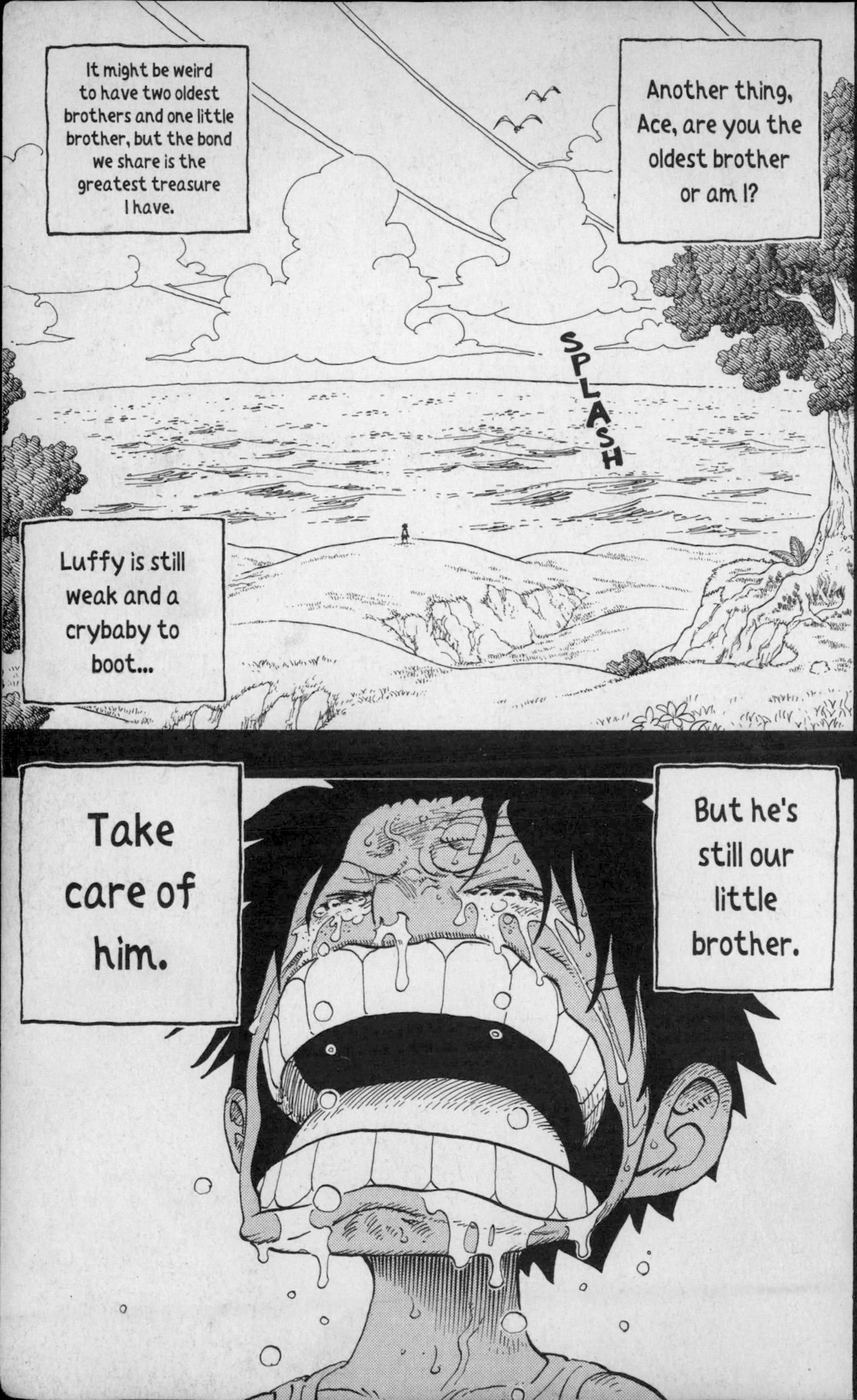

Another thing, Ace, are you the oldest brother or am I?
It might be weird to have two oldest brothers and one little brother, but the bond we share is the greatest treasure I have.
SPLASH
Luffy is still weak and a crybaby to boot...
But he's still our little brother.
Take care of him.

Chapter 589: WILL OF THE WINDS

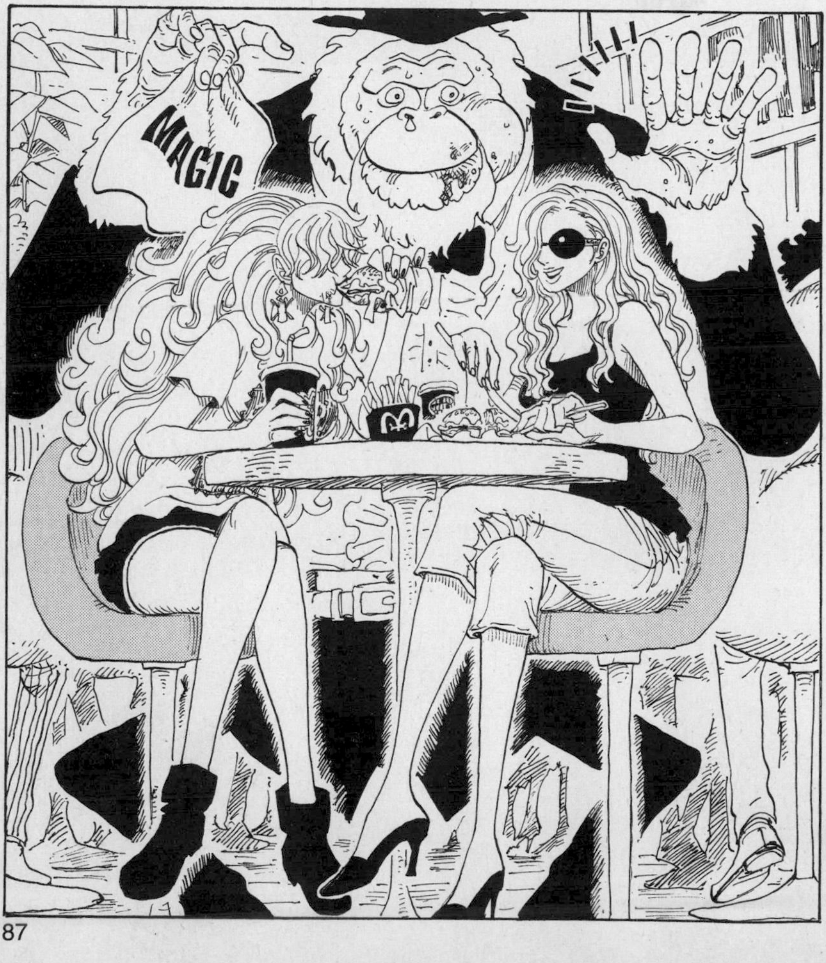
MAGIC

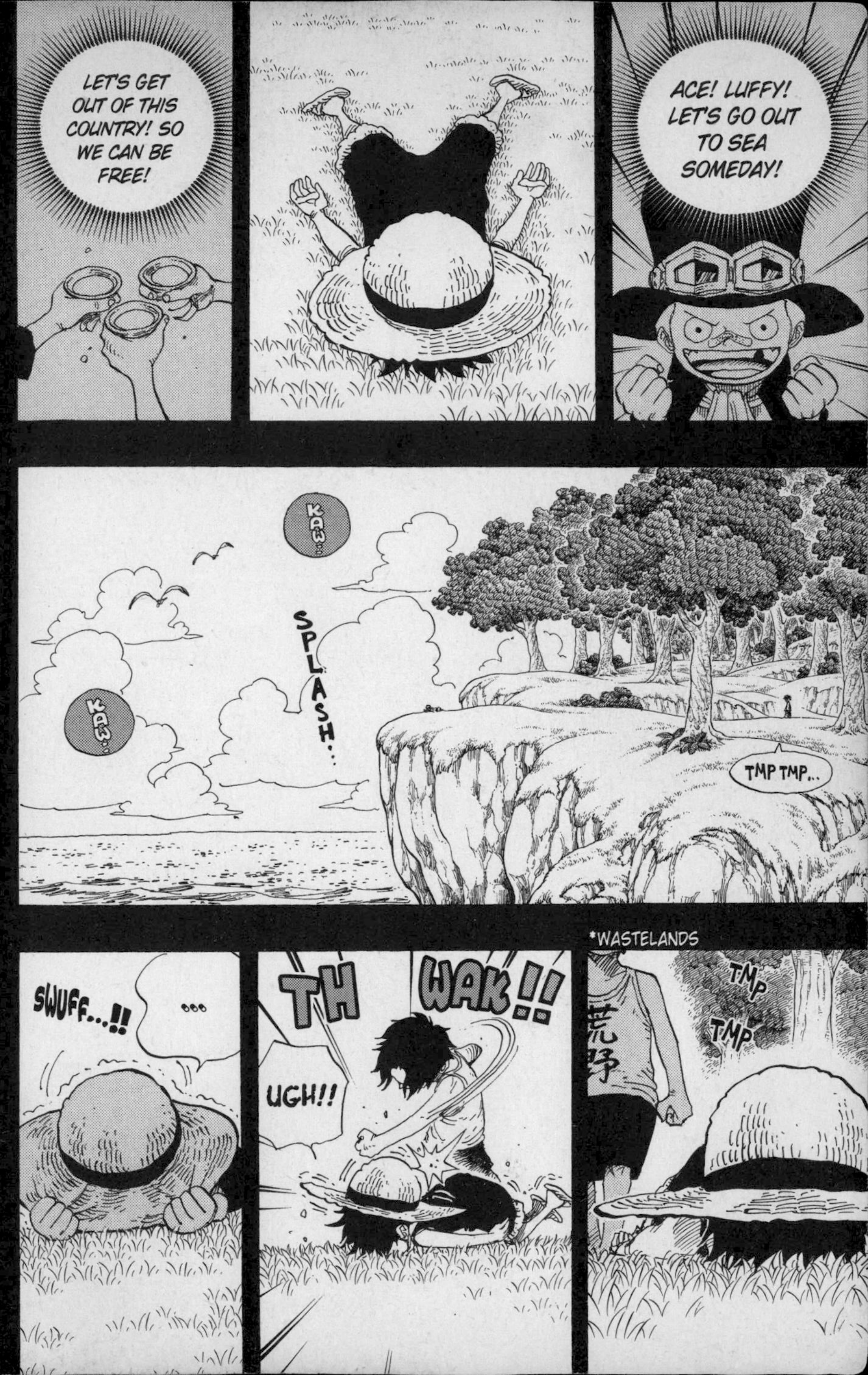
ACE! LUFFY! LET'S GO OUT TO SEA SOMEDAY!
LET'S GET OUT OF THIS COUNTRY! SO WE CAN BE FREE!
TMP TMP...
KAW...
SPLASH...
KAW...
*WASTELANDS
TMP TMP
荒野
THWAK!!
UGH!!
...
SWUFF...!!

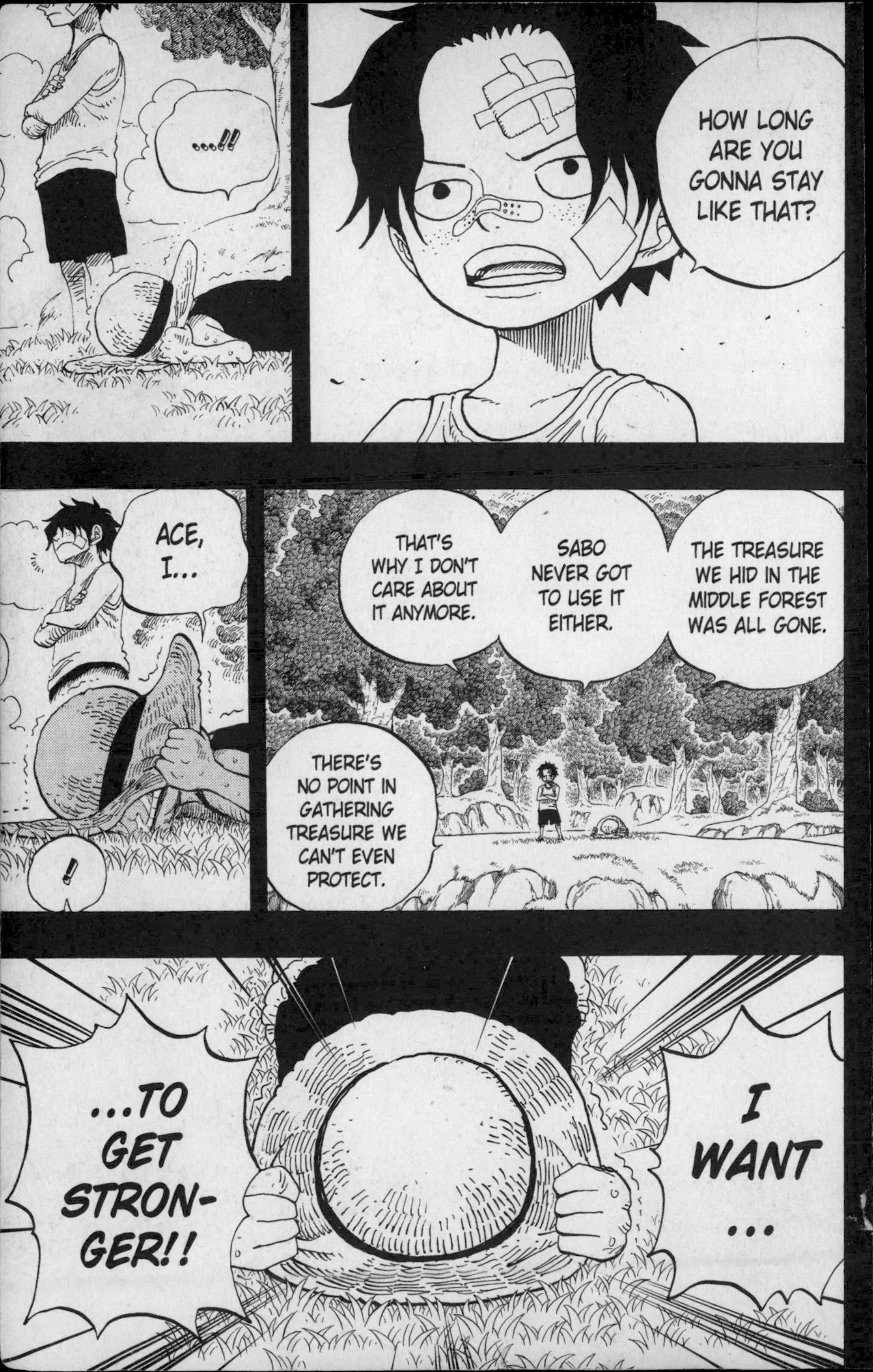
HOW LONG ARE YOU GONNA STAY LIKE THAT?
...!!
THE TREASURE WE HID IN THE MIDDLE FOREST WAS ALL GONE.
SABO NEVER GOT TO USE IT EITHER.
THAT'S WHY I DON'T CARE ABOUT IT ANYMORE.
THERE'S NO POINT IN GATHERING TREASURE WE CAN'T EVEN PROTECT.
ACE, I...
!
I WANT...
...TO GET STRON-GER!!

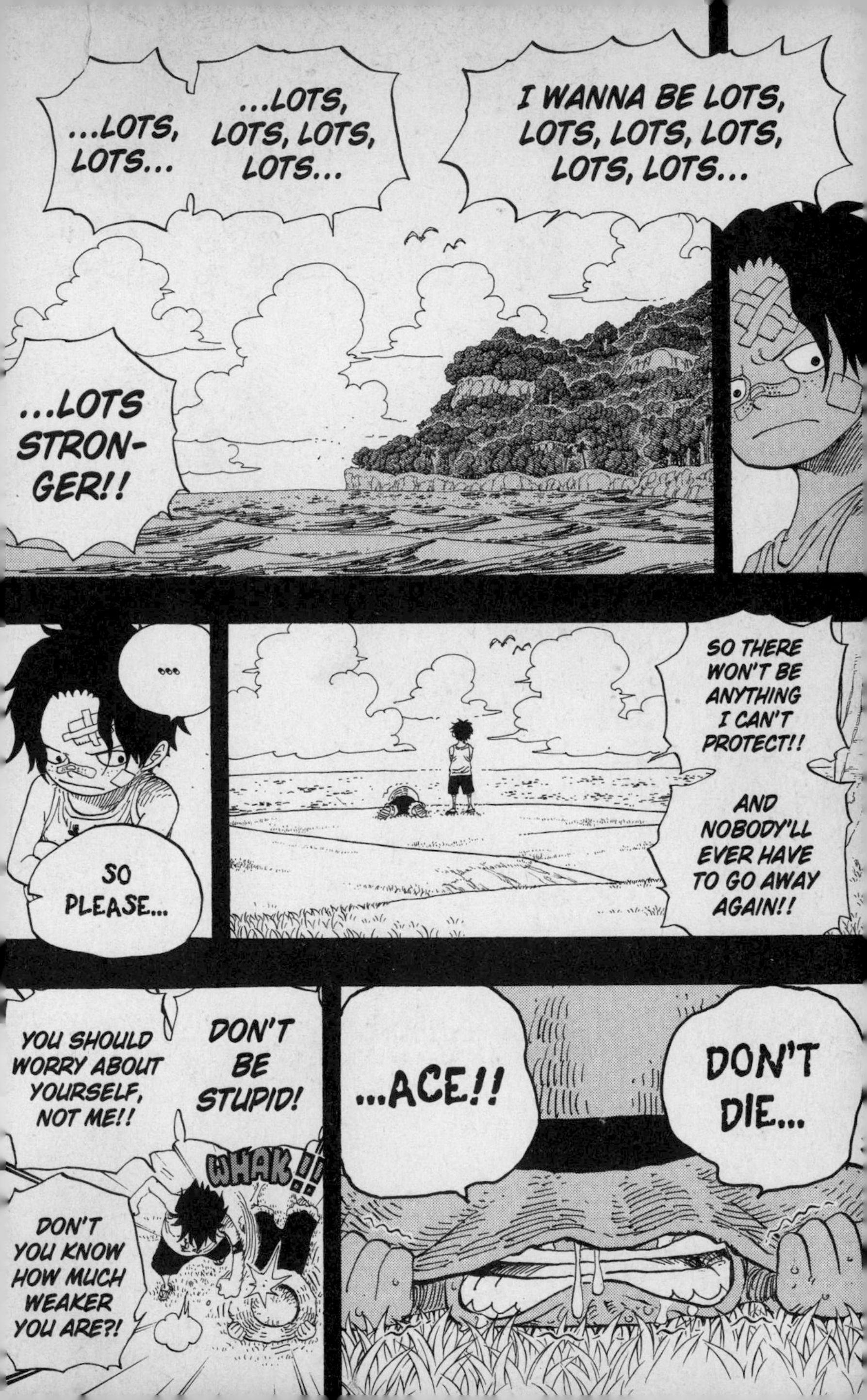
I WANNA BE LOTS, LOTS, LOTS, LOTS, LOTS, LOTS...
...LOTS, LOTS, LOTS, LOTS...
...LOTS, LOTS...
...LOTS STRON-GER!!
SO THERE WON'T BE ANYTHING I CAN'T PROTECT!!
AND NOBODY'LL EVER HAVE TO GO AWAY AGAIN!!
...
SO PLEASE...
DON'T DIE...
...ACE!!
DON'T BE STUPID!
YOU SHOULD WORRY ABOUT YOURSELF, NOT ME!!
WHAK!!
DON'T YOU KNOW HOW MUCH WEAKER YOU ARE?!

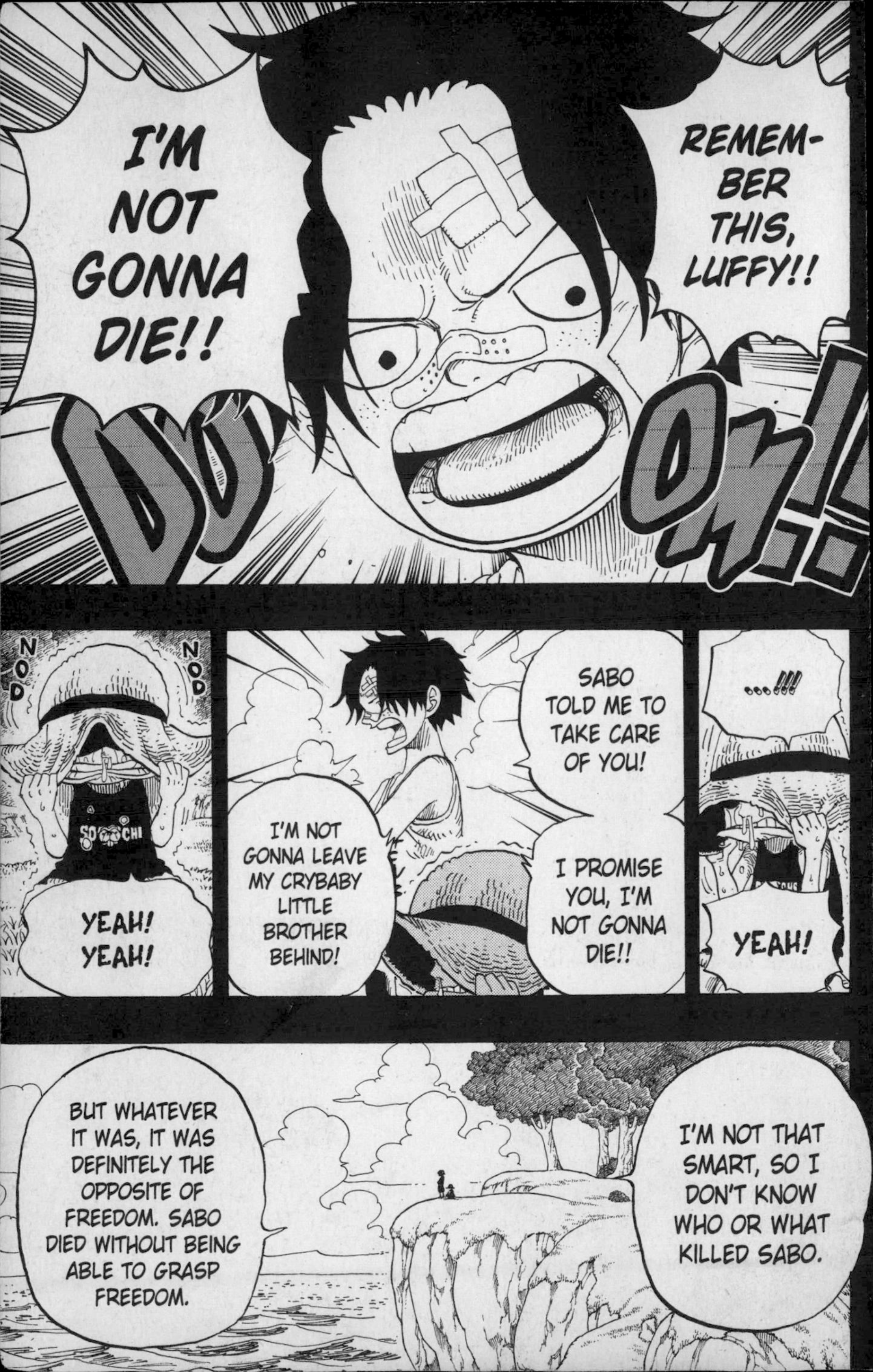

REMEMBER THIS, LUFFY!!
I'M NOT GONNA DIE!!
DOON!!
...!!!
YEAH!
SABO TOLD ME TO TAKE CARE OF YOU!
I PROMISE YOU, I'M NOT GONNA DIE!!
I'M NOT GONNA LEAVE MY CRYBABY LITTLE BROTHER BEHIND!
NOD
NOD
YEAH! YEAH!
I'M NOT THAT SMART, SO I DON'T KNOW WHO OR WHAT KILLED SABO.
BUT WHATEVER IT WAS, IT WAS DEFINITELY THE OPPOSITE OF FREEDOM. SABO DIED WITHOUT BEING ABLE TO GRASP FREEDOM.

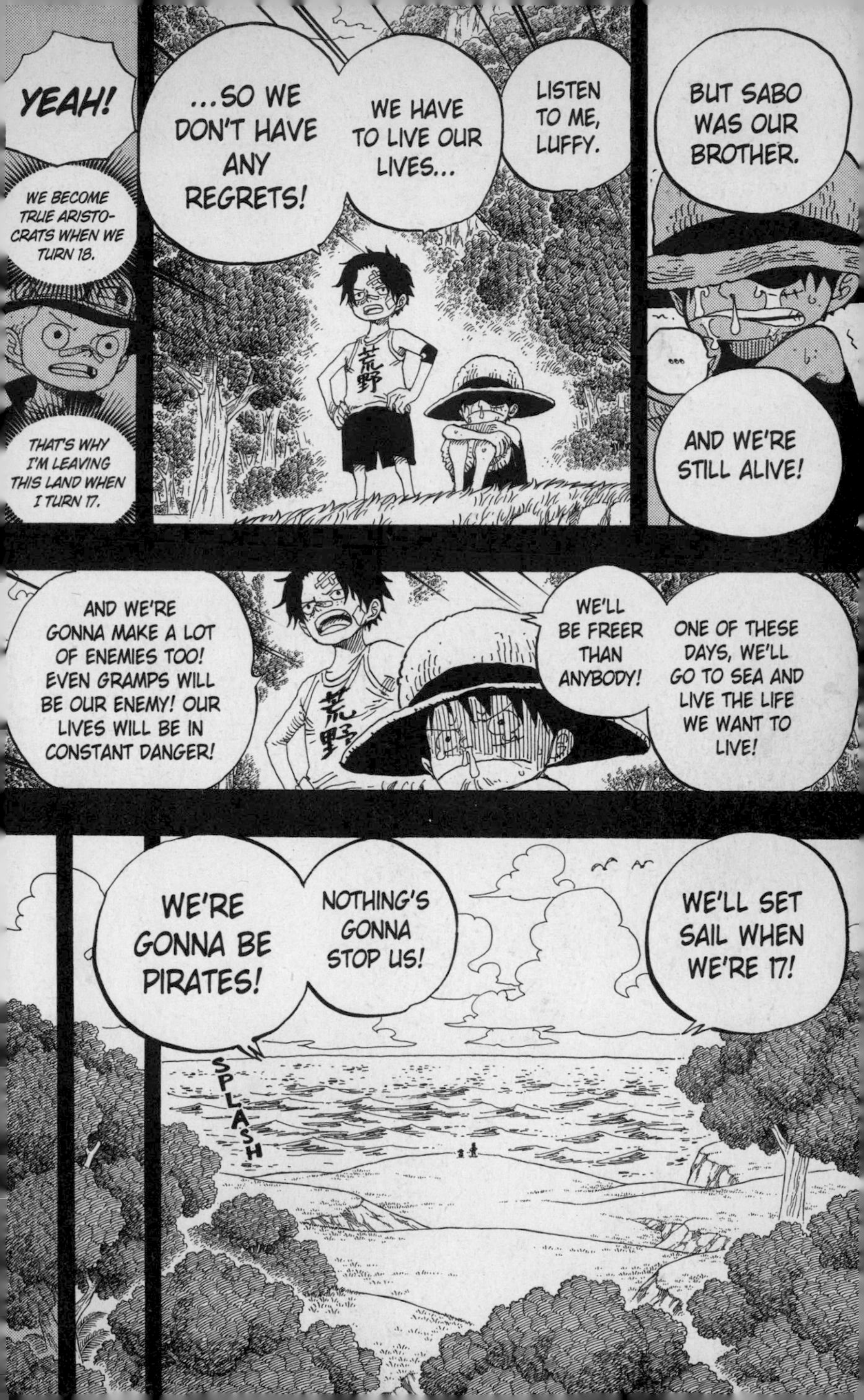
BUT SABO WAS OUR BROTHER.
...
AND WE'RE STILL ALIVE!
LISTEN TO ME, LUFFY.
WE HAVE TO LIVE OUR LIVES...
...SO WE DON'T HAVE ANY REGRETS!
YEAH!
WE BECOME TRUE ARISTO-CRATS WHEN WE TURN 18.
THAT'S WHY I'M LEAVING THIS LAND WHEN I TURN 17.
ONE OF THESE DAYS, WE'LL GO TO SEA AND LIVE THE LIFE WE WANT TO LIVE!
WE'LL BE FREER THAN ANYBODY!
AND WE'RE GONNA MAKE A LOT OF ENEMIES TOO! EVEN GRAMPS WILL BE OUR ENEMY! OUR LIVES WILL BE IN CONSTANT DANGER!
WE'LL SET SAIL WHEN WE'RE 17!
NOTHING'S GONNA STOP US!
WE'RE GONNA BE PIRATES!
SPLASH

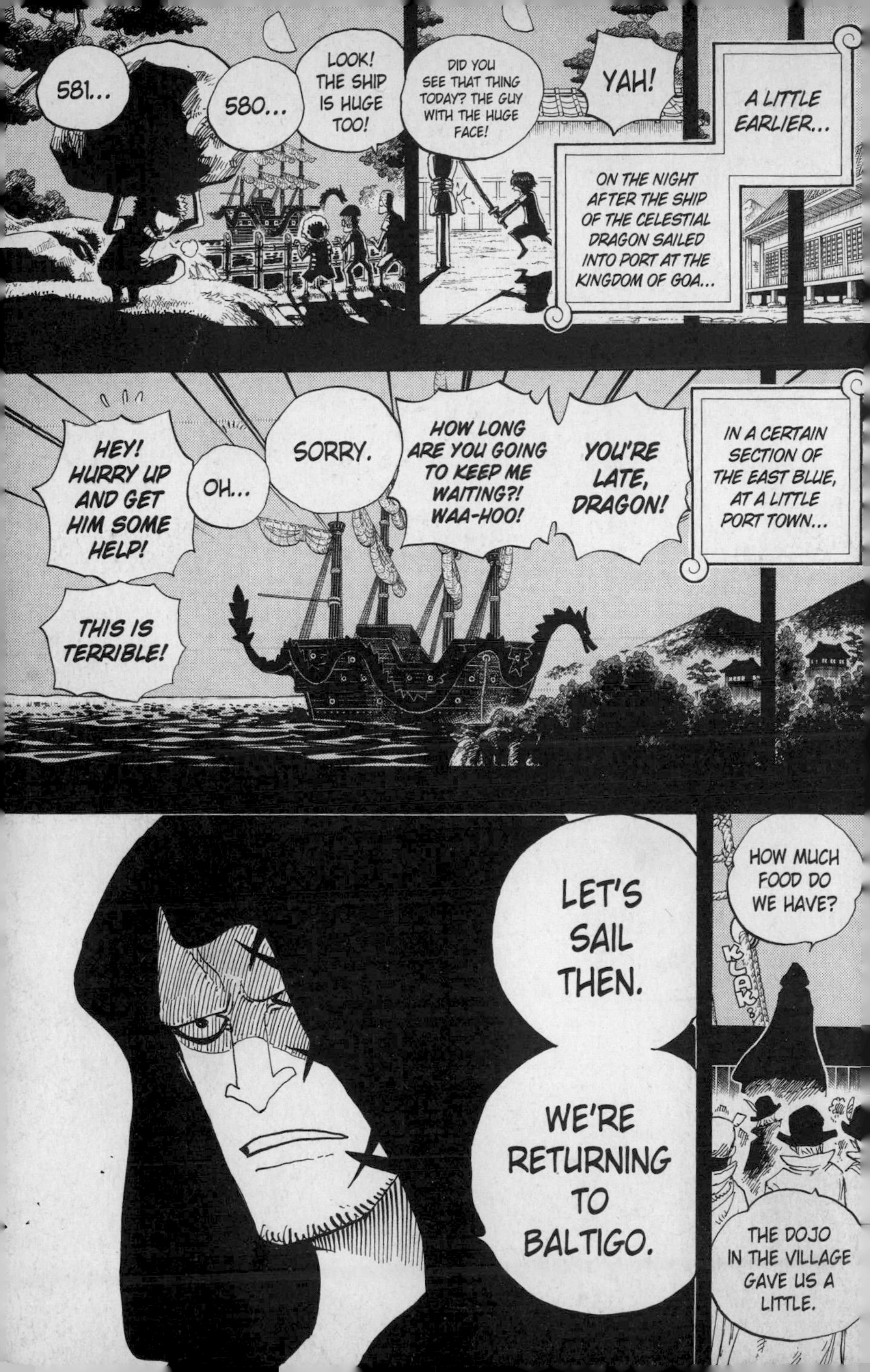
A LITTLE EARLIER...
ON THE NIGHT AFTER THE SHIP OF THE CELESTIAL DRAGON SAILED INTO PORT AT THE KINGDOM OF GOA...
YAH!
DID YOU SEE THAT THING TODAY? THE GUY WITH THE HUGE FACE!
LOOK! THE SHIP IS HUGE TOO!
580...
581...
IN A CERTAIN SECTION OF THE EAST BLUE, AT A LITTLE PORT TOWN...
YOU'RE LATE, DRAGON!
HOW LONG ARE YOU GOING TO KEEP ME WAITING?! WAA-HOO!
SORRY.
OH...
HEY! HURRY UP AND GET HIM SOME HELP!
THIS IS TERRIBLE!
HOW MUCH FOOD DO WE HAVE?
THE DOJO IN THE VILLAGE GAVE US A LITTLE.
LET'S SAIL THEN.
WE'RE RETURNING TO BALTIGO.

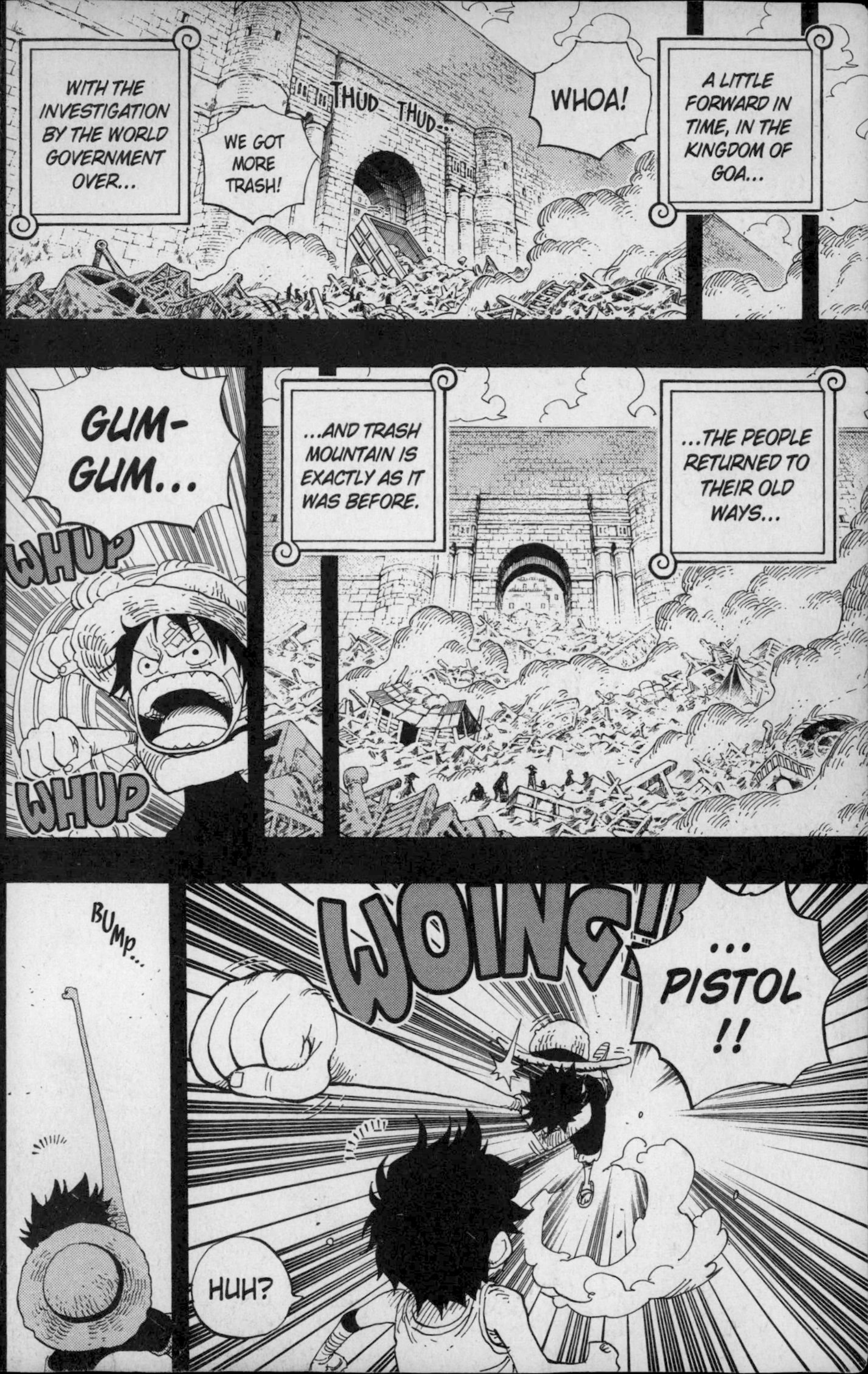
A LITTLE FORWARD IN TIME, IN THE KINGDOM OF GOA...
WHOA!
THUD THUD...
WE GOT MORE TRASH!
WITH THE INVESTIGATION BY THE WORLD GOVERNMENT OVER...
...THE PEOPLE RETURNED TO THEIR OLD WAYS...
...AND TRASH MOUNTAIN IS EXACTLY AS IT WAS BEFORE.
GUM-GUM...
WHUP
WHUP
WOING!!
...PISTOL!!
HUH?
BUMP...

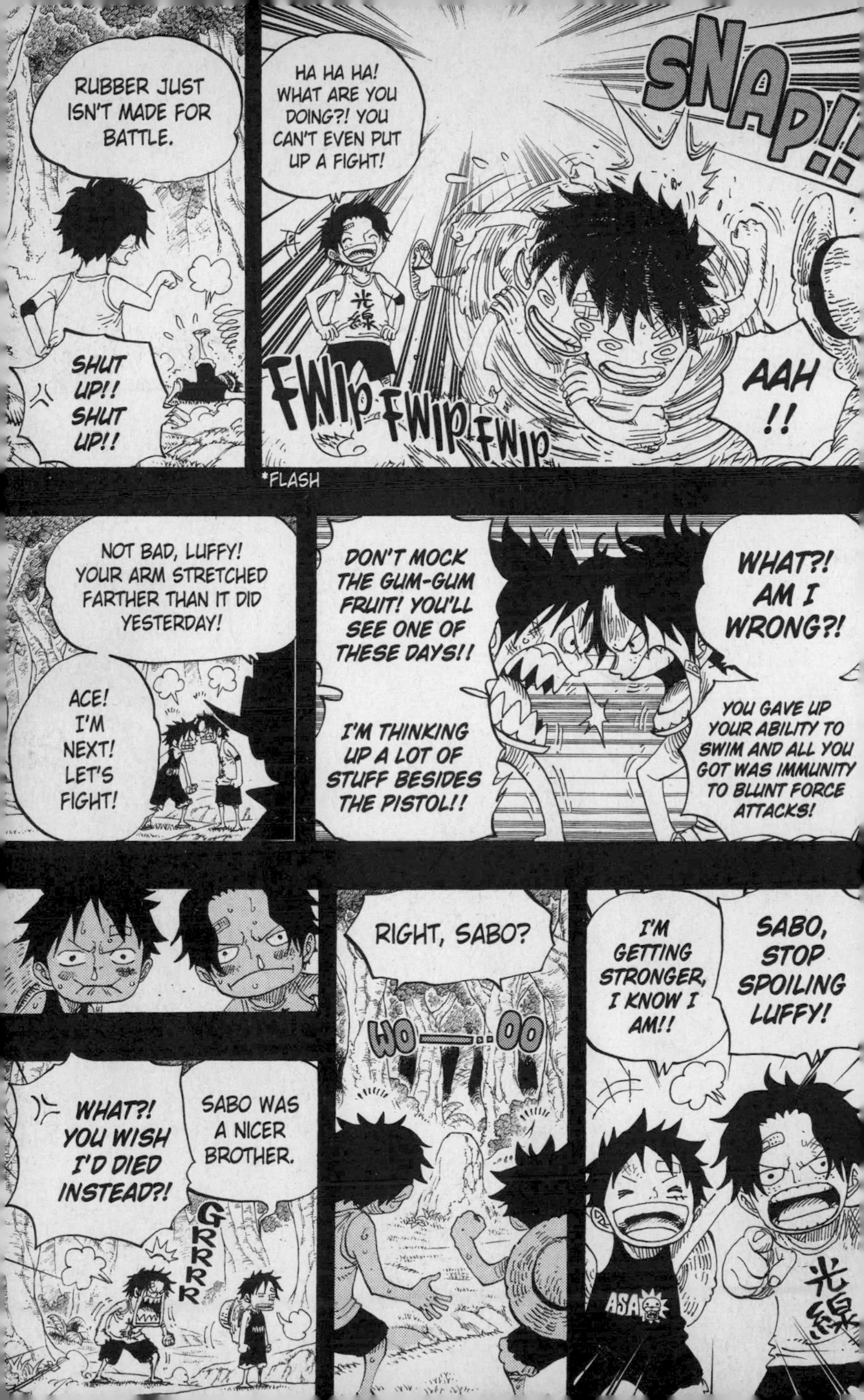
SNAP!!
HA HA HA! WHAT ARE YOU DOING?! YOU CAN'T EVEN PUT UP A FIGHT!
光線
AAH!!
FWIP FWIP FWIP
*FLASH
RUBBER JUST ISN'T MADE FOR BATTLE.
SHUT UP!! SHUT UP!!
WHAT?! AM I WRONG?!
DON'T MOCK THE GUM-GUM FRUIT! YOU'LL SEE ONE OF THESE DAYS!!
YOU GAVE UP YOUR ABILITY TO SWIM AND ALL YOU GOT WAS IMMUNITY TO BLUNT FORCE ATTACKS!
I'M THINKING UP A LOT OF STUFF BESIDES THE PISTOL!!
NOT BAD, LUFFY! YOUR ARM STRETCHED FARTHER THAN IT DID YESTERDAY!
ACE! I'M NEXT! LET'S FIGHT!
SABO, STOP SPOILING LUFFY!
I'M GETTING STRONGER, I KNOW I AM!!
光線
ASA
RIGHT, SABO?
WO——OO
SABO WAS A NICER BROTHER.
WHAT?! YOU WISH I'D DIED INSTEAD?!
GRRRR

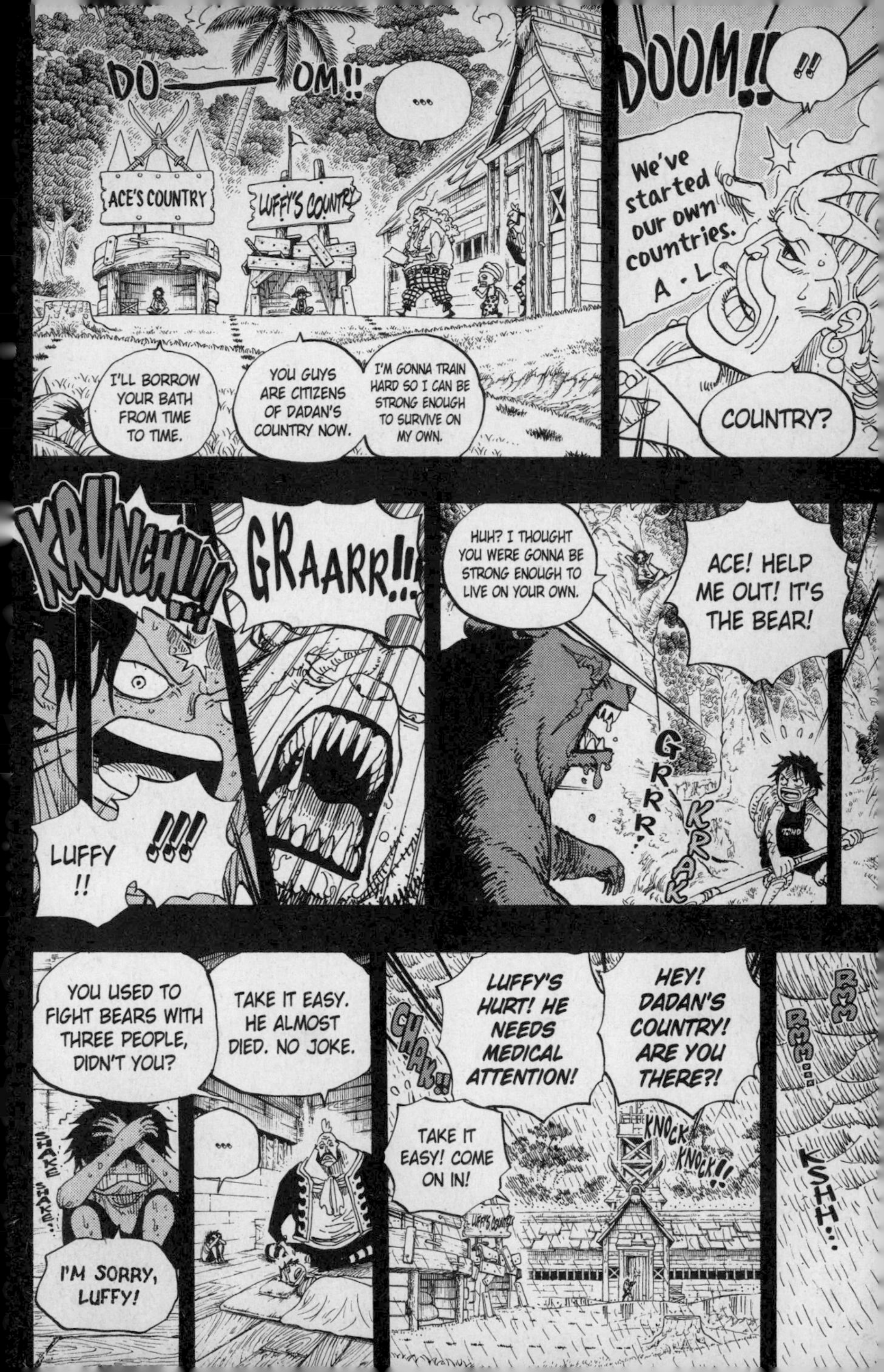
!!
DOOM!!
We've started our own countries.
A・L
COUNTRY?
...
DO——OM!!
ACE'S COUNTRY
LUFFY'S COUNTRY
I'M GONNA TRAIN HARD SO I CAN BE STRONG ENOUGH TO SURVIVE ON MY OWN.
YOU GUYS ARE CITIZENS OF DADAN'S COUNTRY NOW.
I'LL BORROW YOUR BATH FROM TIME TO TIME.
ACE! HELP ME OUT! IT'S THE BEAR!
HUH? I THOUGHT YOU WERE GONNA BE STRONG ENOUGH TO LIVE ON YOUR OWN.
KRAK
GRRRR
GRAARR!!!
KRUNCH!!!
!!!
LUFFY !!
RMM
RMM...
KSHH...
HEY! DADAN'S COUNTRY! ARE YOU THERE?!
LUFFY'S HURT! HE NEEDS MEDICAL ATTENTION!
KNOCK KNOCK!!
CHAK!!
TAKE IT EASY! COME ON IN!
LUFFY'S COUNTRY
TAKE IT EASY. HE ALMOST DIED. NO JOKE.
...
YOU USED TO FIGHT BEARS WITH THREE PEOPLE, DIDN'T YOU?
SHAKE
SHAKE...
I'M SORRY, LUFFY!

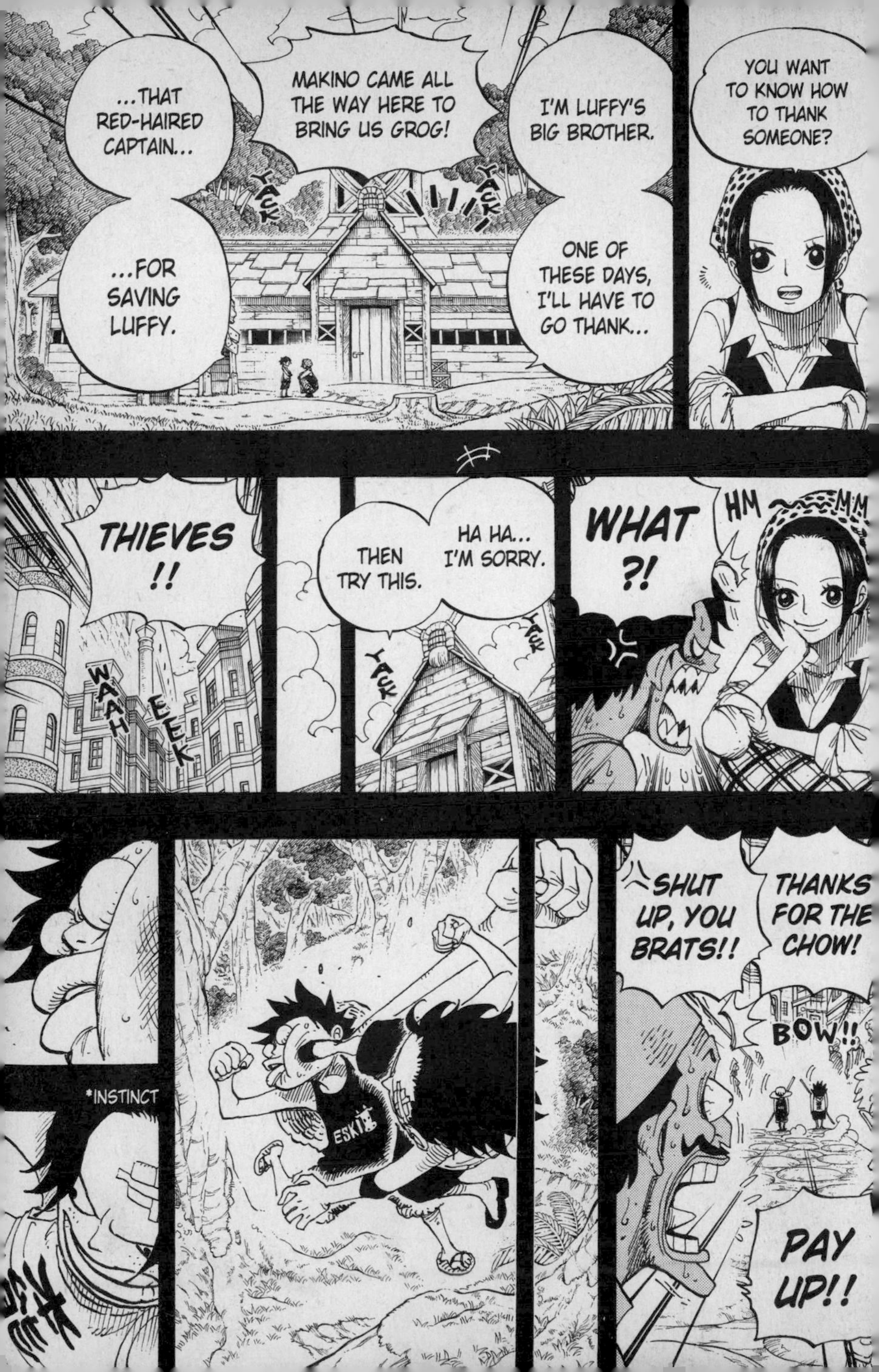
YOU WANT TO KNOW HOW TO THANK SOMEONE?
I'M LUFFY'S BIG BROTHER.
MAKINO CAME ALL THE WAY HERE TO BRING US GROG!
YACK
YACK
ONE OF THESE DAYS, I'LL HAVE TO GO THANK...
...THAT RED-HAIRED CAPTAIN...
...FOR SAVING LUFFY.
HM~MM
WHAT ?!
HA HA... I'M SORRY.
THEN TRY THIS.
YACK
YACK
THIEVES !!
WAAH
EEEK
THANKS FOR THE CHOW!
SHUT UP, YOU BRATS!!
BOW!!
PAY UP!!
ESKI
*INSTINCT

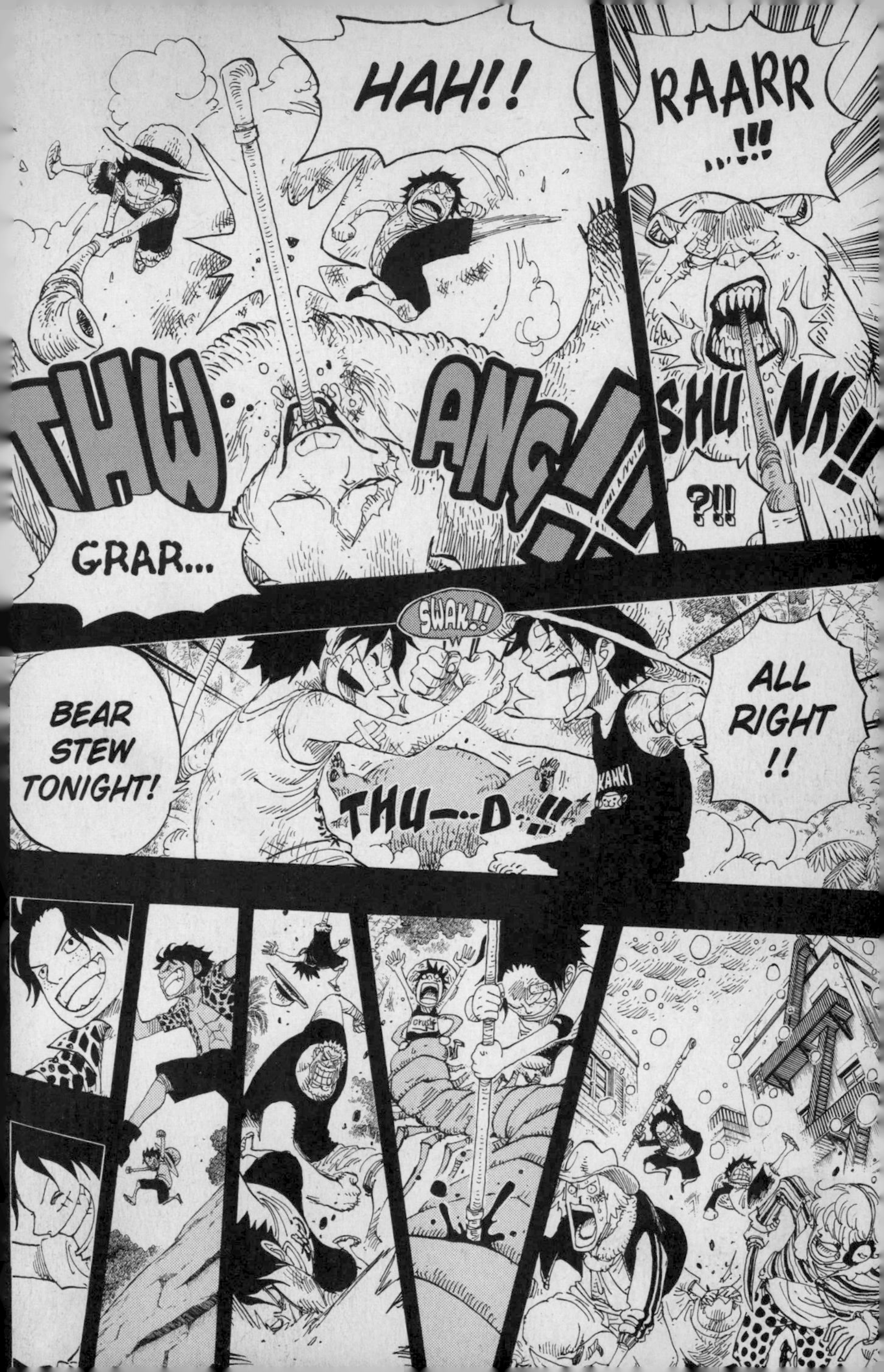
RAARR !!!
SHU NK!!
?!!
HAH!!
THW ANG!!
GRAR...
SWAK!!
ALL RIGHT !!
BEAR STEW TONIGHT!
THU—..D..!!

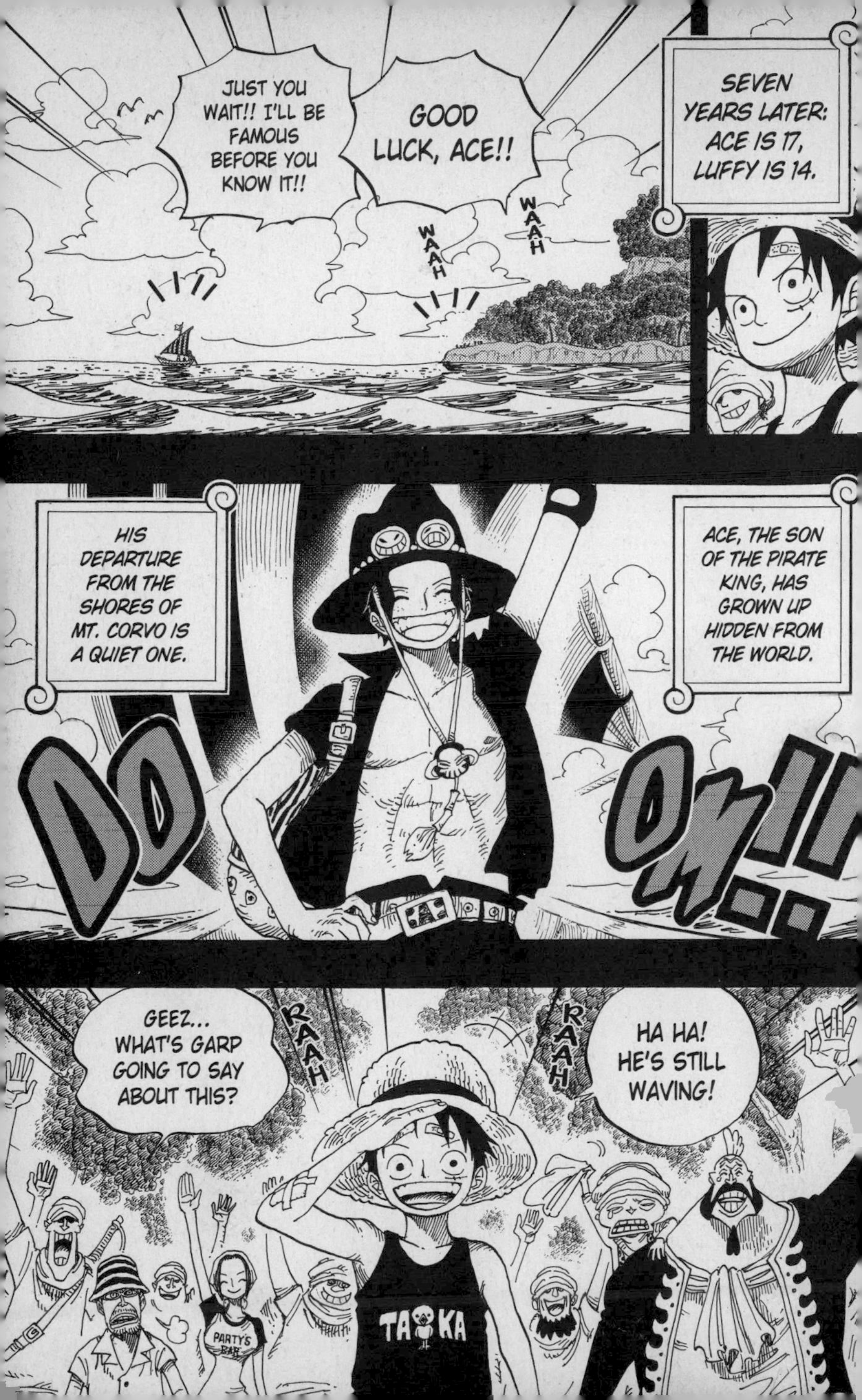
SEVEN YEARS LATER: ACE IS 17, LUFFY IS 14.
GOOD LUCK, ACE!!
WAAH
WAAH
JUST YOU WAIT!! I'LL BE FAMOUS BEFORE YOU KNOW IT!!
ACE, THE SON OF THE PIRATE KING, HAS GROWN UP HIDDEN FROM THE WORLD.
HIS DEPARTURE FROM THE SHORES OF MT. CORVO IS A QUIET ONE.
DOON!!..
HA HA! HE'S STILL WAVING!
RAAH
RAAH
GEEZ... WHAT'S GARP GOING TO SAY ABOUT THIS?
TAKA
PARTY'S BAR

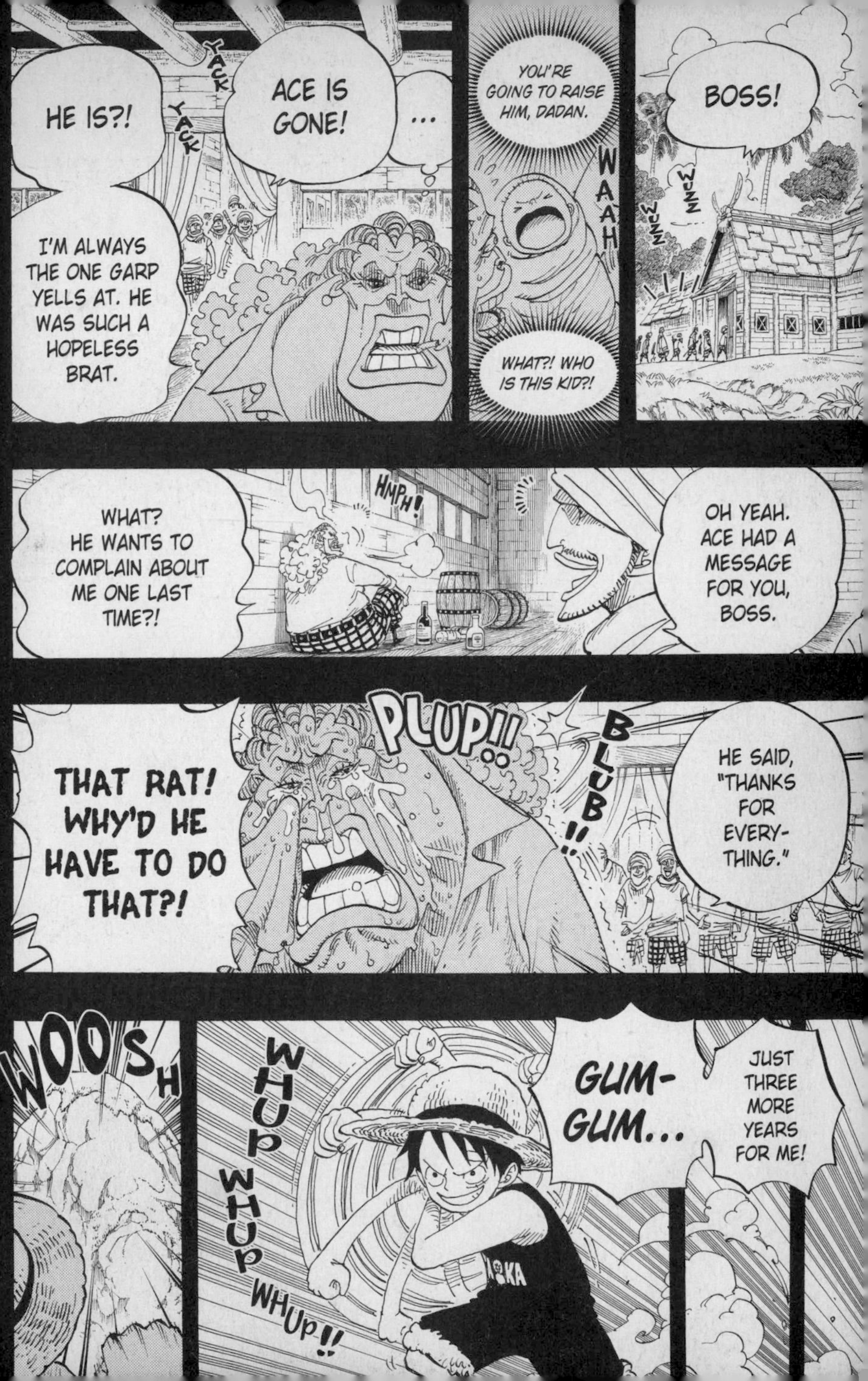
BOSS!
WUZZ
WUZZ
YOU'RE GOING TO RAISE HIM, DADAN.
WAAH
WHAT?! WHO IS THIS KID?!
...
ACE IS GONE!
YACK
YACK
HE IS?!
I'M ALWAYS THE ONE GARP YELLS AT. HE WAS SUCH A HOPELESS BRAT.
OH YEAH. ACE HAD A MESSAGE FOR YOU, BOSS.
HMPH!
WHAT? HE WANTS TO COMPLAIN ABOUT ME ONE LAST TIME?!
HE SAID, "THANKS FOR EVERYTHING."
BLUB!!
PLUP!!
THAT RAT! WHY'D HE HAVE TO DO THAT?!
JUST THREE MORE YEARS FOR ME!
GUM-GUM...
WHUP
WHUP
WHUP!!
WOOSH

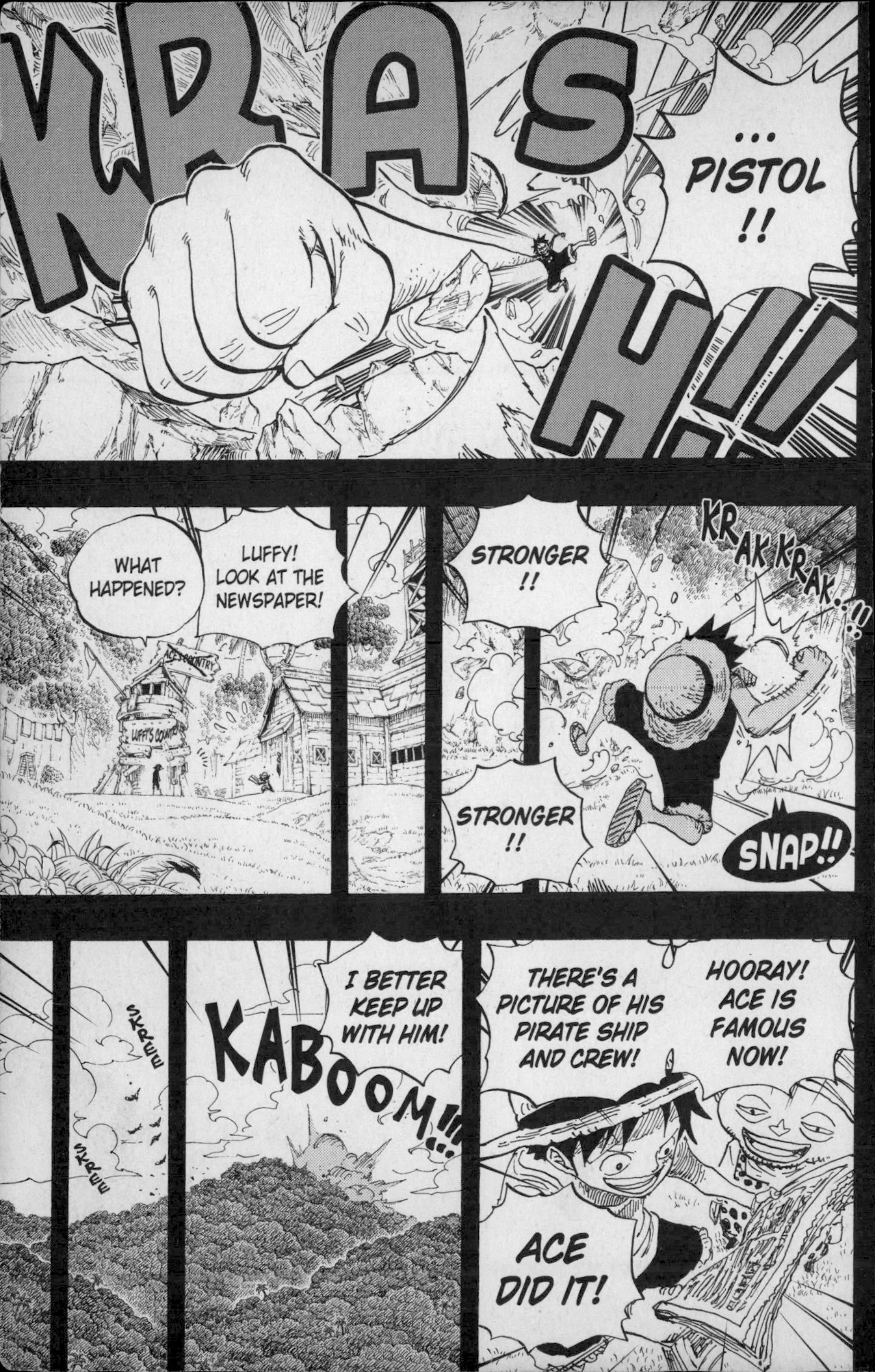
... PISTOL !!
KRASH!!
KRAK KRAK..!!
STRONGER !!
SNAP!!
STRONGER !!
LUFFY! LOOK AT THE NEWSPAPER!
WHAT HAPPENED?
ACE'S COUNTRY
LUFFY'S COUNTRY
HOORAY! ACE IS FAMOUS NOW!
THERE'S A PICTURE OF HIS PIRATE SHIP AND CREW!
ACE DID IT!
I BETTER KEEP UP WITH HIM!
KABOOM!!!
SKREE
SKREE

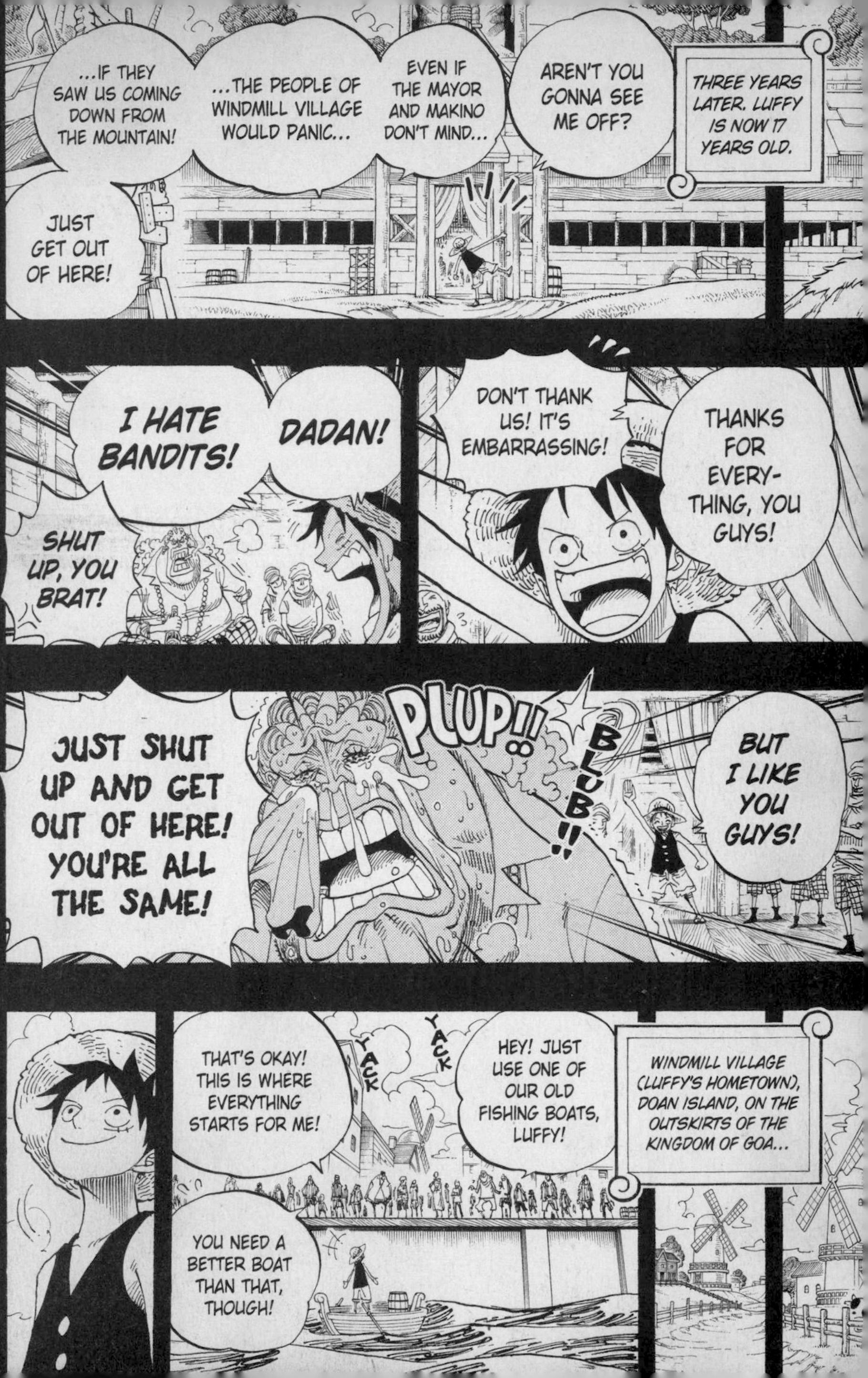
THREE YEARS LATER. LUFFY IS NOW 17 YEARS OLD.
AREN'T YOU GONNA SEE ME OFF?
EVEN IF THE MAYOR AND MAKINO DON'T MIND...
...THE PEOPLE OF WINDMILL VILLAGE WOULD PANIC...
...IF THEY SAW US COMING DOWN FROM THE MOUNTAIN!
JUST GET OUT OF HERE!
THANKS FOR EVERY-THING, YOU GUYS!
DON'T THANK US! IT'S EMBARRASSING!
DADAN!
I HATE BANDITS!
SHUT UP, YOU BRAT!
BUT I LIKE YOU GUYS!
BLUB!!
PLUP!!
JUST SHUT UP AND GET OUT OF HERE! YOU'RE ALL THE SAME!
WINDMILL VILLAGE (LUFFY'S HOMETOWN), DOAN ISLAND, ON THE OUTSKIRTS OF THE KINGDOM OF GOA...
HEY! JUST USE ONE OF OUR OLD FISHING BOATS, LUFFY!
YACK
YACK
THAT'S OKAY! THIS IS WHERE EVERYTHING STARTS FOR ME!
YOU NEED A BETTER BOAT THAN THAT, THOUGH!

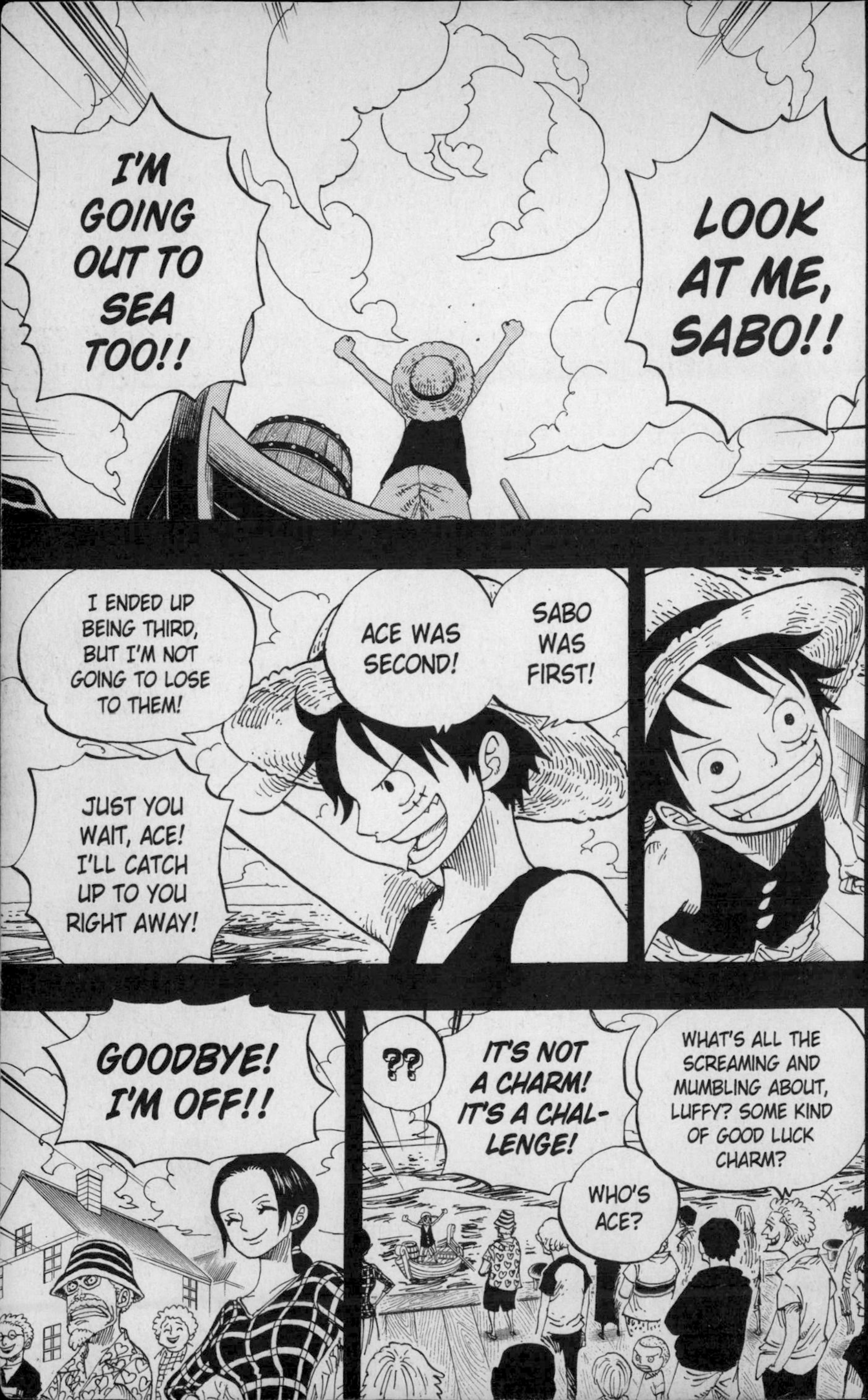
LOOK AT ME, SABO!!
I'M GOING OUT TO SEA TOO!!
SABO WAS FIRST!
ACE WAS SECOND!
I ENDED UP BEING THIRD, BUT I'M NOT GOING TO LOSE TO THEM!
JUST YOU WAIT, ACE! I'LL CATCH UP TO YOU RIGHT AWAY!
WHAT'S ALL THE SCREAMING AND MUMBLING ABOUT, LUFFY? SOME KIND OF GOOD LUCK CHARM?
IT'S NOT A CHARM! IT'S A CHAL-LENGE!
??
WHO'S ACE?
GOODBYE! I'M OFF!!

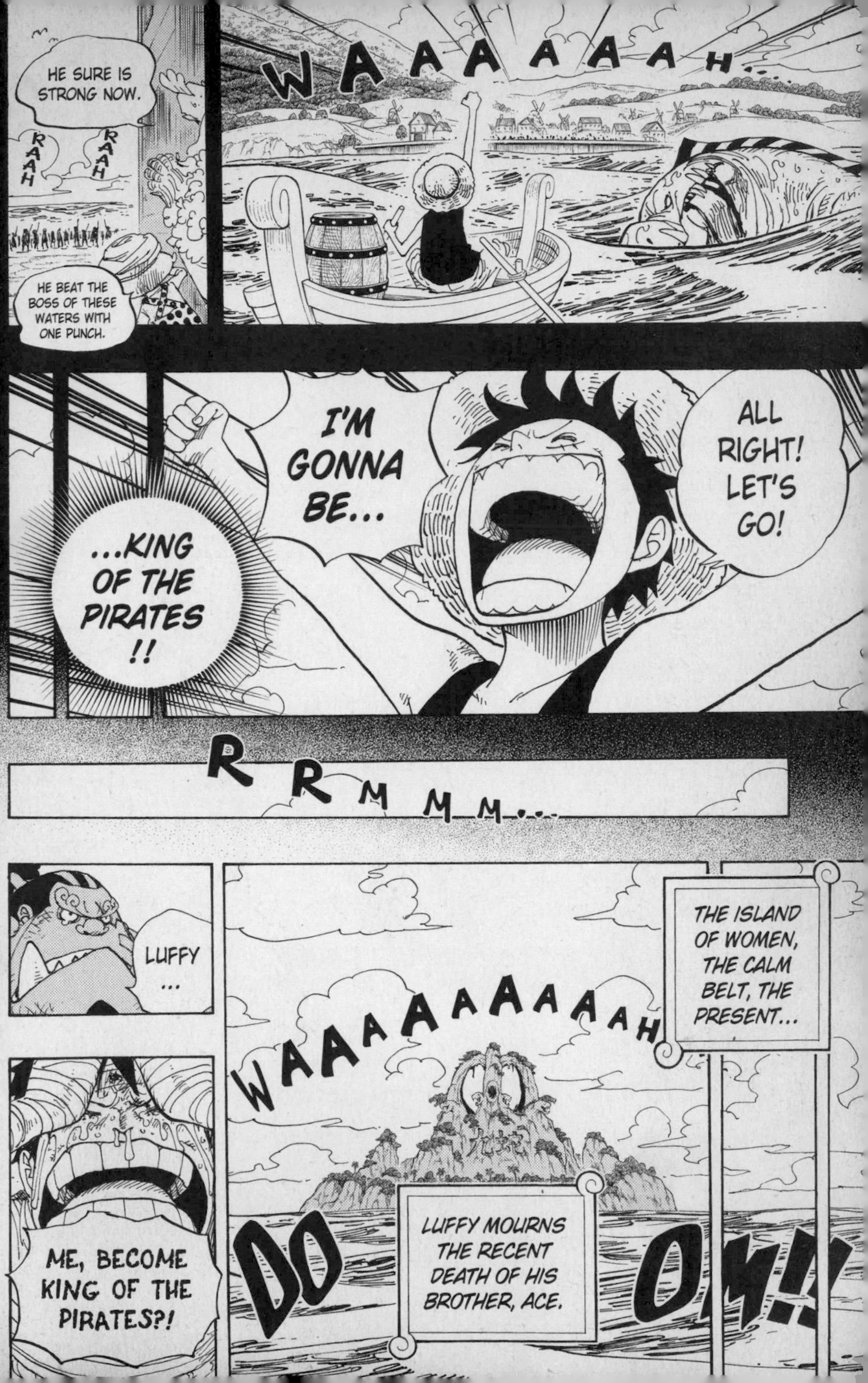
WAAAAAAH...
HE SURE IS STRONG NOW.
RAAH
RAAH
HE BEAT THE BOSS OF THESE WATERS WITH ONE PUNCH.
ALL RIGHT! LET'S GO!
I'M GONNA BE...
...KING OF THE PIRATES!!
RRMMM...
THE ISLAND OF WOMEN, THE CALM BELT, THE PRESENT...
WAAAAAAAAAAH
LUFFY MOURNS THE RECENT DEATH OF HIS BROTHER, ACE.
DOOM!!
LUFFY ...
ME, BECOME KING OF THE PIRATES?!

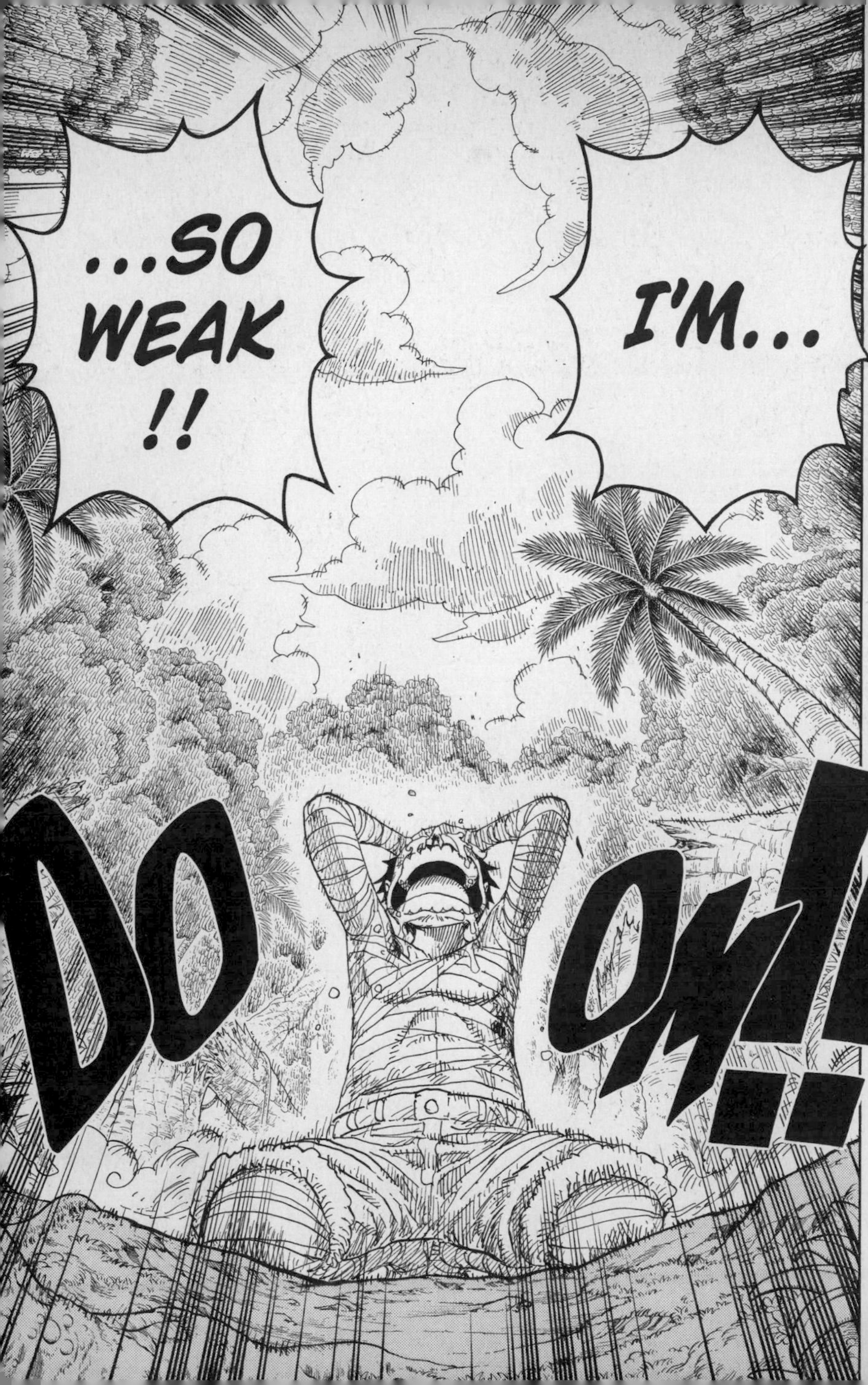
I'M...
...SO WEAK!!
DOON!!

SBS Question Corner

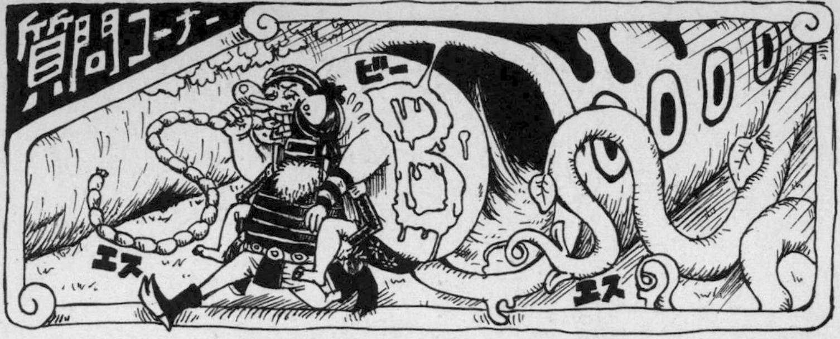
質問コーナー
ビー
エス
エス

(Shamoji, Gifu)

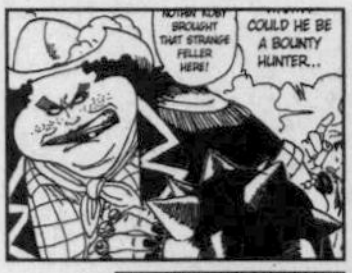
COULD HE BE A BOUNTY HUNTER...

Q: I found a mistake you made, Odacchi! In volume 59, chapter 584, Luffy was bleeding when he got hit by Porchemy's gloves. But in volume 1, chapter 2, Luffy is unharmed by Alvida's club! Are you sure about this?! Now give me something!

--MONIO

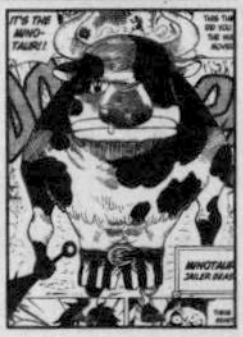

A: I see. Don't worry. It's fine. It might not seem obvious at first, but take a closer look. Don't you see how the spikes are at a different angle?! I added this difference to the jailer beasts of Impel Down too. Even if those weapons all have spikes, I drew it so that you can see which ones can actually hurt Luffy. The sharper ones can puncture rubber. On the other hand, Alvida's club only has a kind of blunt impact on rubber. That's the effect the spikes have. So I didn't mess up! No prize for you!

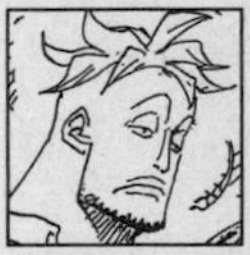

Q: I have a question. Is the thing on Marco's head a banana or is it a pineapple? And is Kid's head a tulip or a chrysanthemum? Which is it? I really want to know.

--Kaho

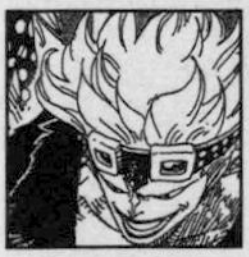

A: You're giving me only two choices?! I guess I'll just have to pick one. Then I guess Marco is a pineapple and Kid is a chrysanthemum. What were we talking about again?!

Q: I was watching *Rocky* the other day and Rocky's pet goldfish is named Moby Dick! Just like Whitebeard's ship! Is that where you got the name from?

--Negishi

A: Wow, *Rocky*, huh? That blockbuster boxing movie sure brings back memories. I thought it was really funny to name his goldfish Moby Dick. Anyway, *Moby Dick* is actually a book written by an American author named Melville. It's a very famous story about a battle between a man and a white whale. In Japan, the book simply goes by the title *White Whale*. I used that name because I thought it was perfect for Whitebeard.

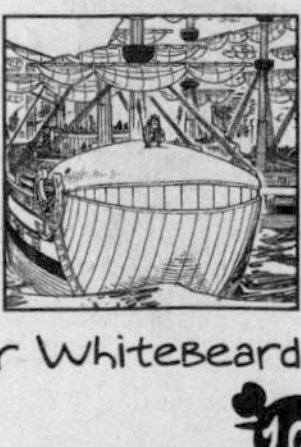

Chapter 590:
MY LITTLE BROTHER

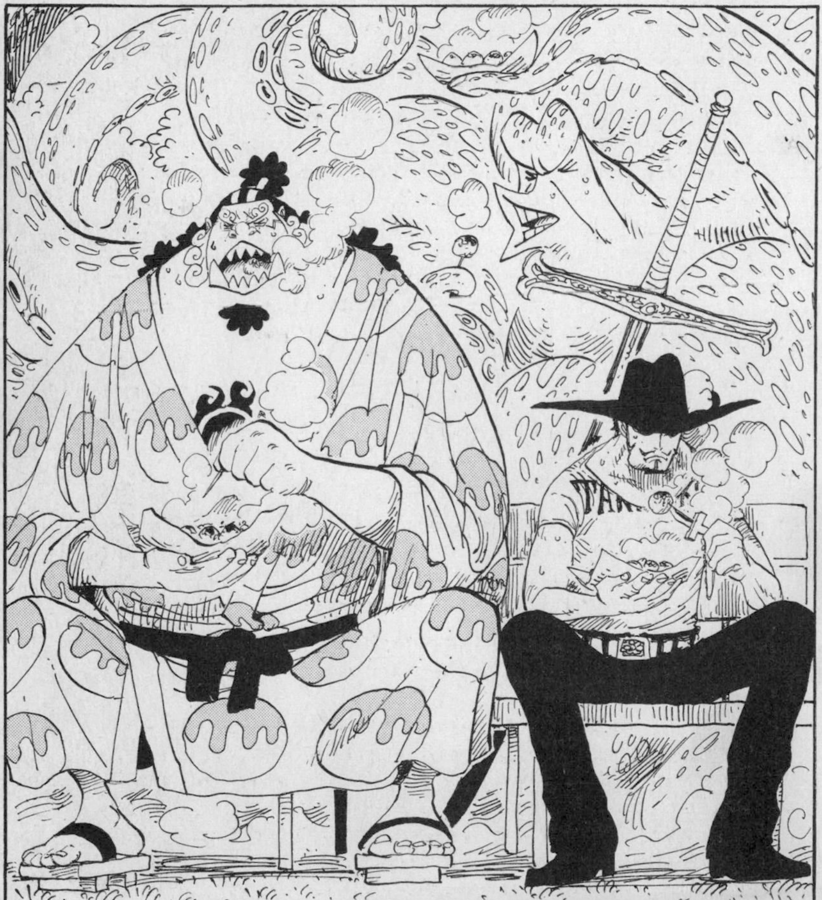

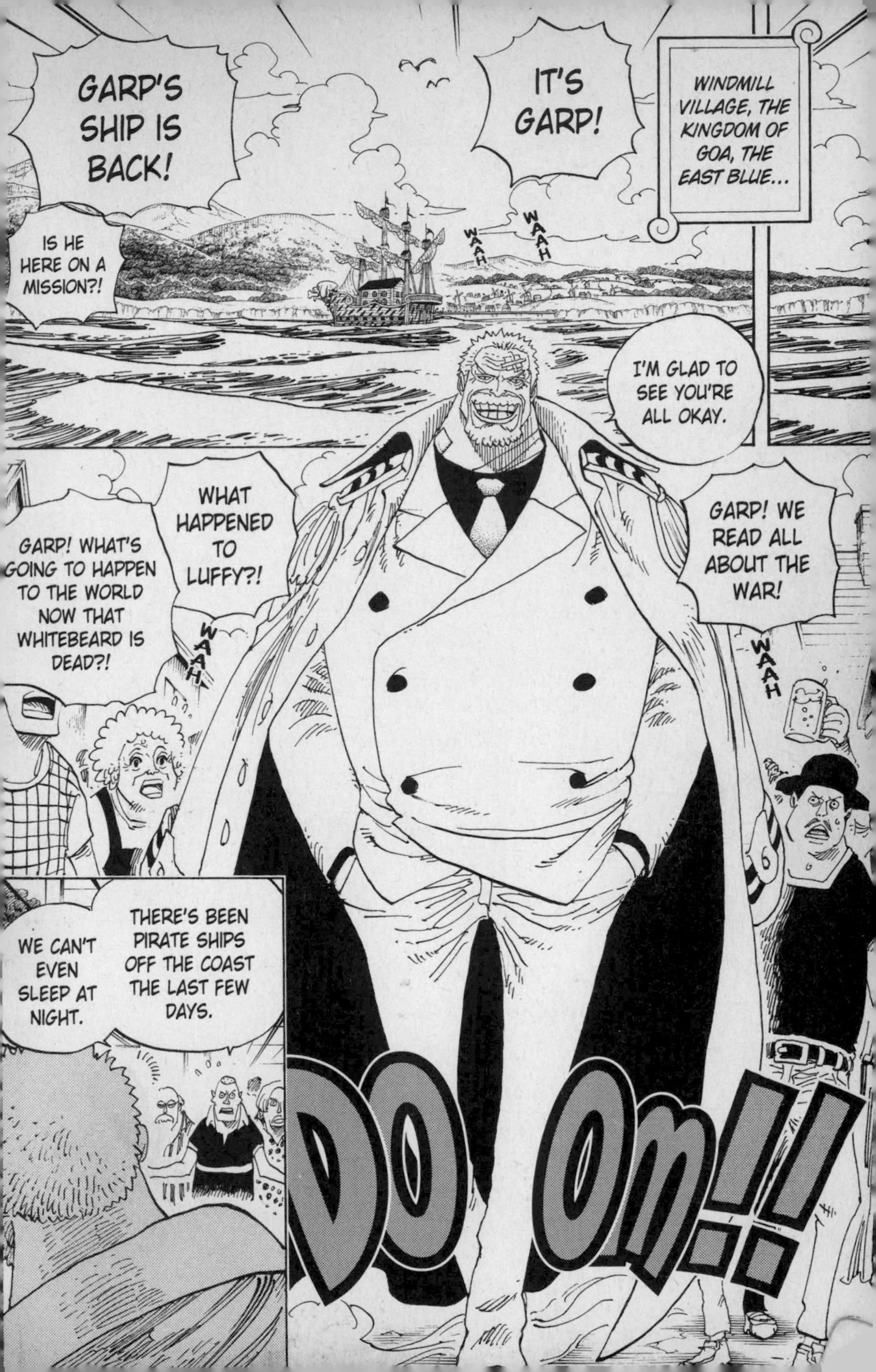
WINDMILL VILLAGE, THE KINGDOM OF GOA, THE EAST BLUE...
IT'S GARP!
WAAH
WAAH
GARP'S SHIP IS BACK!
IS HE HERE ON A MISSION?!
I'M GLAD TO SEE YOU'RE ALL OKAY.
GARP! WE READ ALL ABOUT THE WAR!
WAAH
WHAT HAPPENED TO LUFFY?!
WAAH
GARP! WHAT'S GOING TO HAPPEN TO THE WORLD NOW THAT WHITEBEARD IS DEAD?!
THERE'S BEEN PIRATE SHIPS OFF THE COAST THE LAST FEW DAYS.
WE CAN'T EVEN SLEEP AT NIGHT.
DOOM!!

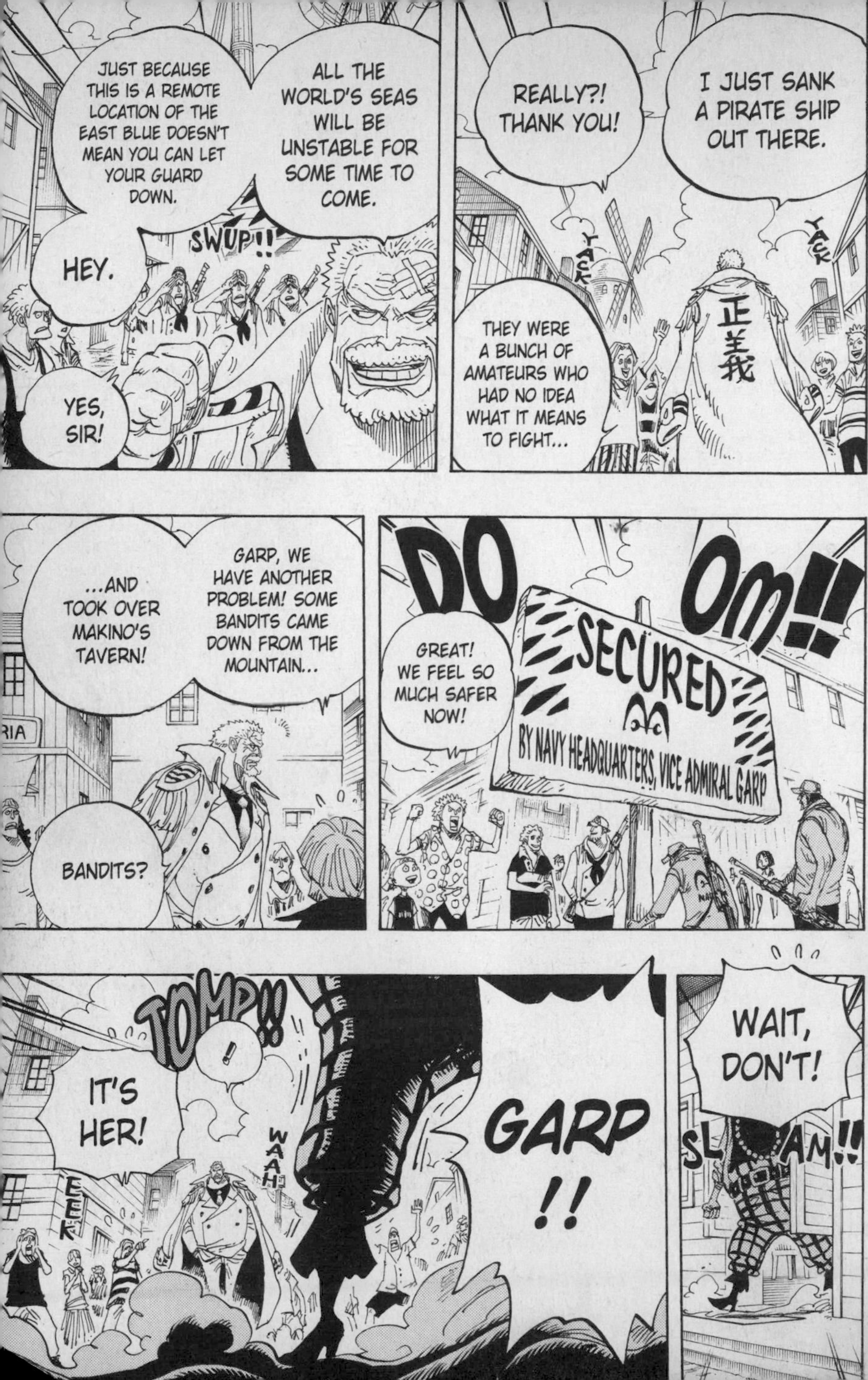

I JUST SANK A PIRATE SHIP OUT THERE.
REALLY?! THANK YOU!
YACK
YACK
THEY WERE A BUNCH OF AMATEURS WHO HAD NO IDEA WHAT IT MEANS TO FIGHT...
正義
ALL THE WORLD'S SEAS WILL BE UNSTABLE FOR SOME TIME TO COME.
JUST BECAUSE THIS IS A REMOTE LOCATION OF THE EAST BLUE DOESN'T MEAN YOU CAN LET YOUR GUARD DOWN.
SWUP!!
HEY.
YES, SIR!
DO OM!!
SECURED
BY NAVY HEADQUARTERS, VICE ADMIRAL GARP
GREAT! WE FEEL SO MUCH SAFER NOW!
GARP, WE HAVE ANOTHER PROBLEM! SOME BANDITS CAME DOWN FROM THE MOUNTAIN...
...AND TOOK OVER MAKINO'S TAVERN!
RIA
BANDITS?
WAIT, DON'T!
SLAM!!
GARP !!
TOMP!!
!
IT'S HER!
WAAAH
EEEK

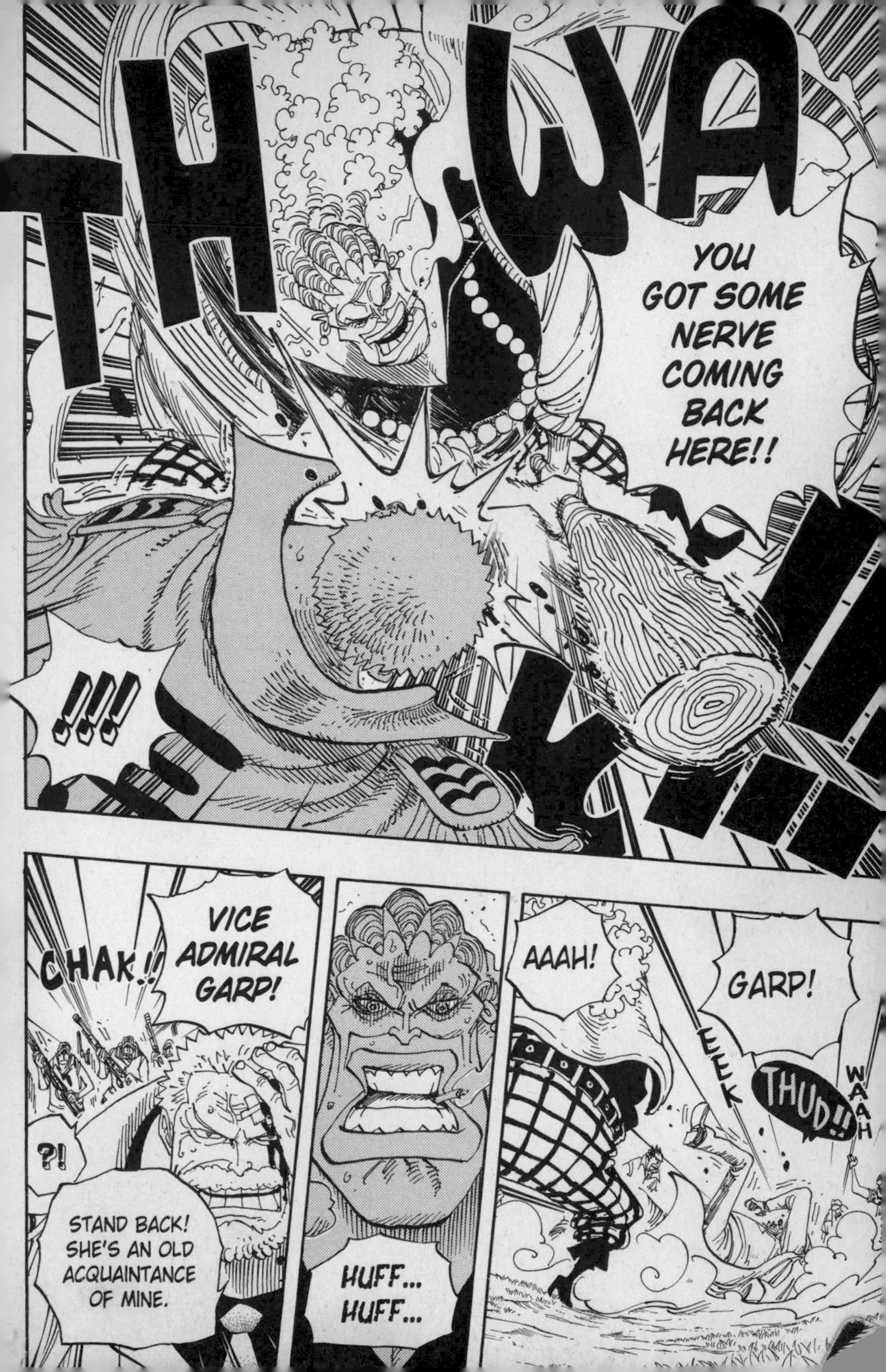
YOU GOT SOME NERVE COMING BACK HERE!!
!!!
GARP!
AAAH!
EEEK
THUD!!
WAAAH
HUFF... HUFF...
VICE ADMIRAL GARP!
CHAK!!
?!
STAND BACK! SHE'S AN OLD ACQUAINTANCE OF MINE.

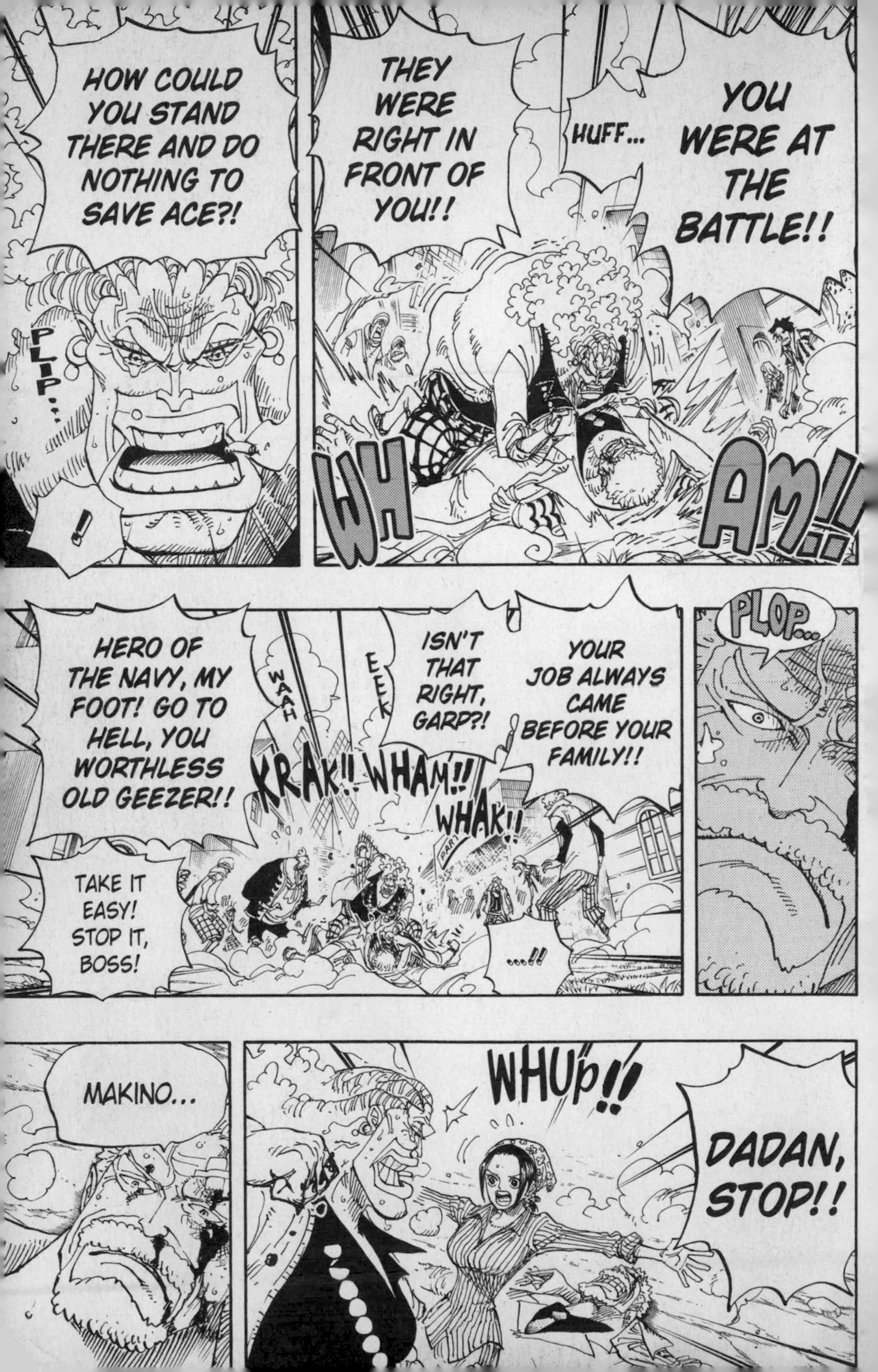
YOU WERE AT THE BATTLE!!
HUFF...
THEY WERE RIGHT IN FRONT OF YOU!!
WHAM!!
HOW COULD YOU STAND THERE AND DO NOTHING TO SAVE ACE?!
PLIP...
!
PLOP...
YOUR JOB ALWAYS CAME BEFORE YOUR FAMILY!!
ISN'T THAT RIGHT, GARP?!
EEEK
WAAAH
HERO OF THE NAVY, MY FOOT! GO TO HELL, YOU WORTHLESS OLD GEEZER!!
KRAK!! WHAM!!
WHAK!!
TAKE IT EASY! STOP IT, BOSS!
...!!
DADAN, STOP!!
WHUP!!
MAKINO...

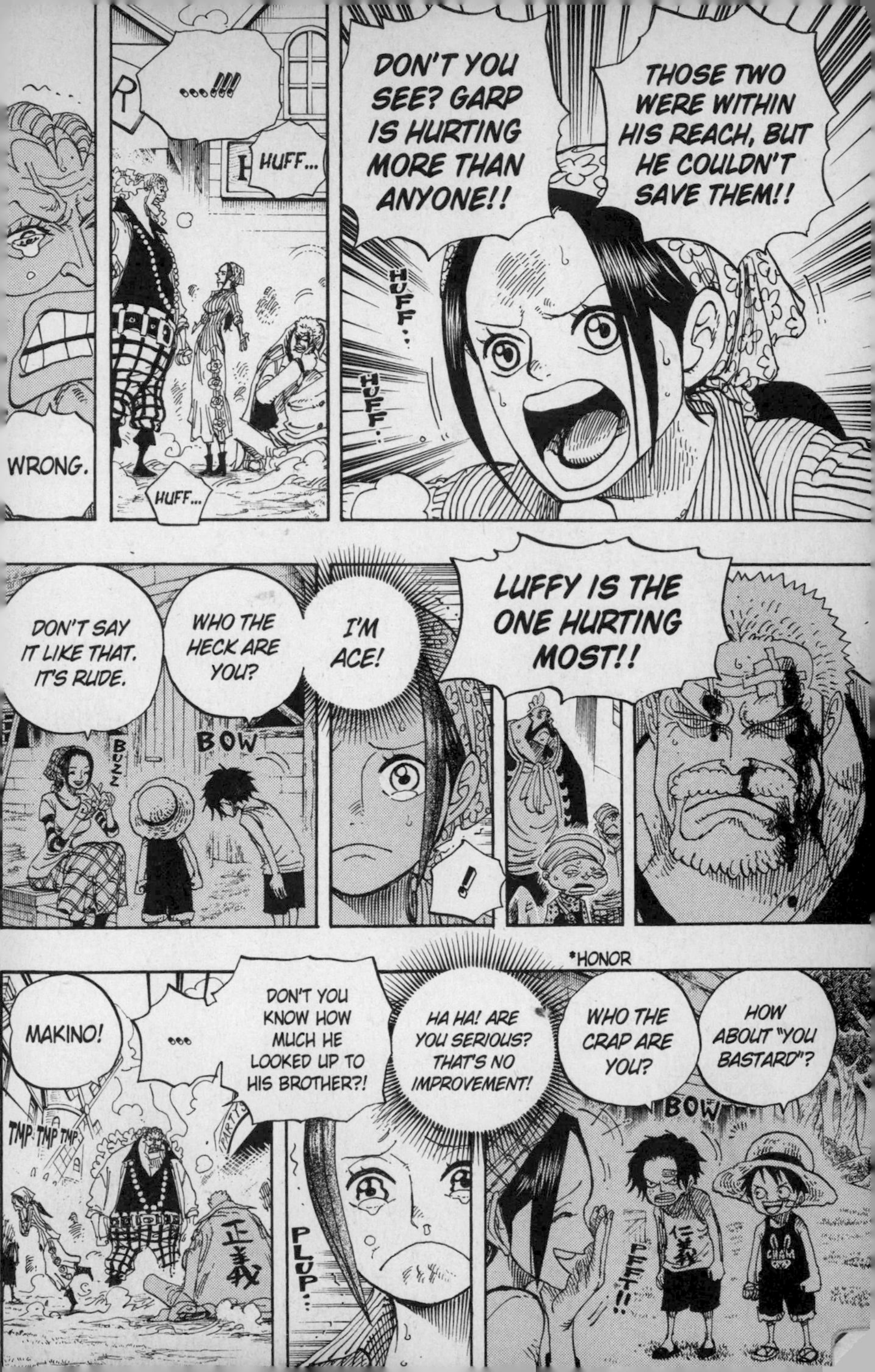
THOSE TWO WERE WITHIN HIS REACH, BUT HE COULDN'T SAVE THEM!!
DON'T YOU SEE? GARP IS HURTING MORE THAN ANYONE!!
HUFF...
HUFF...
...!!!
HUFF...
HUFF...
WRONG.
LUFFY IS THE ONE HURTING MOST!!
!
I'M ACE!
WHO THE HECK ARE YOU?
BOW
DON'T SAY IT LIKE THAT. IT'S RUDE.
BUZZ
*HONOR
HOW ABOUT "YOU BASTARD"?
WHO THE CRAP ARE YOU?
BOW
HA HA! ARE YOU SERIOUS? THAT'S NO IMPROVEMENT!
PFFT!!
DON'T YOU KNOW HOW MUCH HE LOOKED UP TO HIS BROTHER?!
PLUP..
...
MAKINO!
TMP TMP TMP

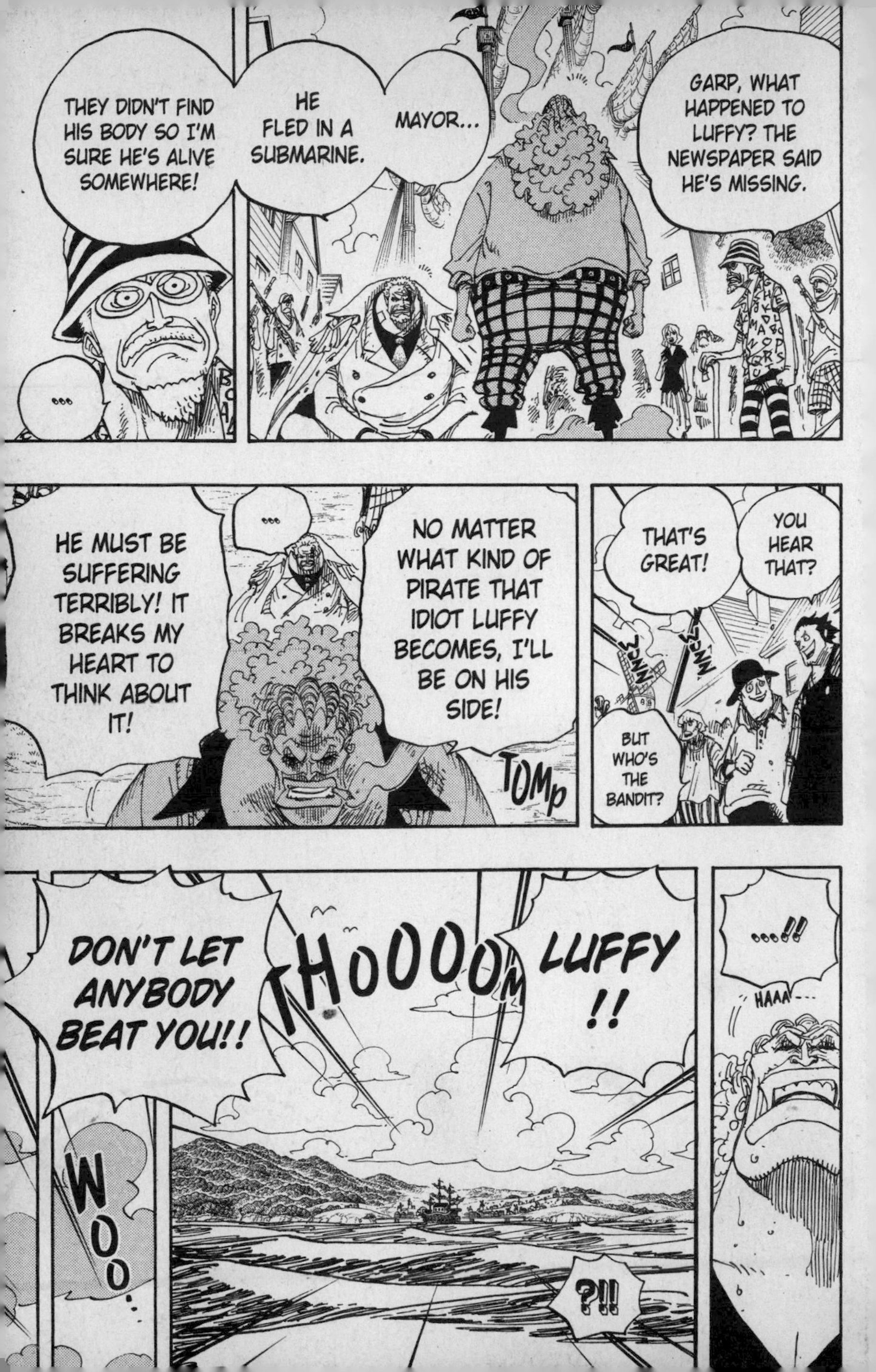
GARP, WHAT HAPPENED TO LUFFY? THE NEWSPAPER SAID HE'S MISSING.
MAYOR...
HE FLED IN A SUBMARINE.
THEY DIDN'T FIND HIS BODY SO I'M SURE HE'S ALIVE SOMEWHERE!
...
YOU HEAR THAT?
THAT'S GREAT!
BUT WHO'S THE BANDIT?
...
NO MATTER WHAT KIND OF PIRATE THAT IDIOT LUFFY BECOMES, I'LL BE ON HIS SIDE!
TOMP
HE MUST BE SUFFERING TERRIBLY! IT BREAKS MY HEART TO THINK ABOUT IT!
...!!
HAAA---
LUFFY!!
THOOOOM
?!!
DON'T LET ANYBODY BEAT YOU!!
WOO

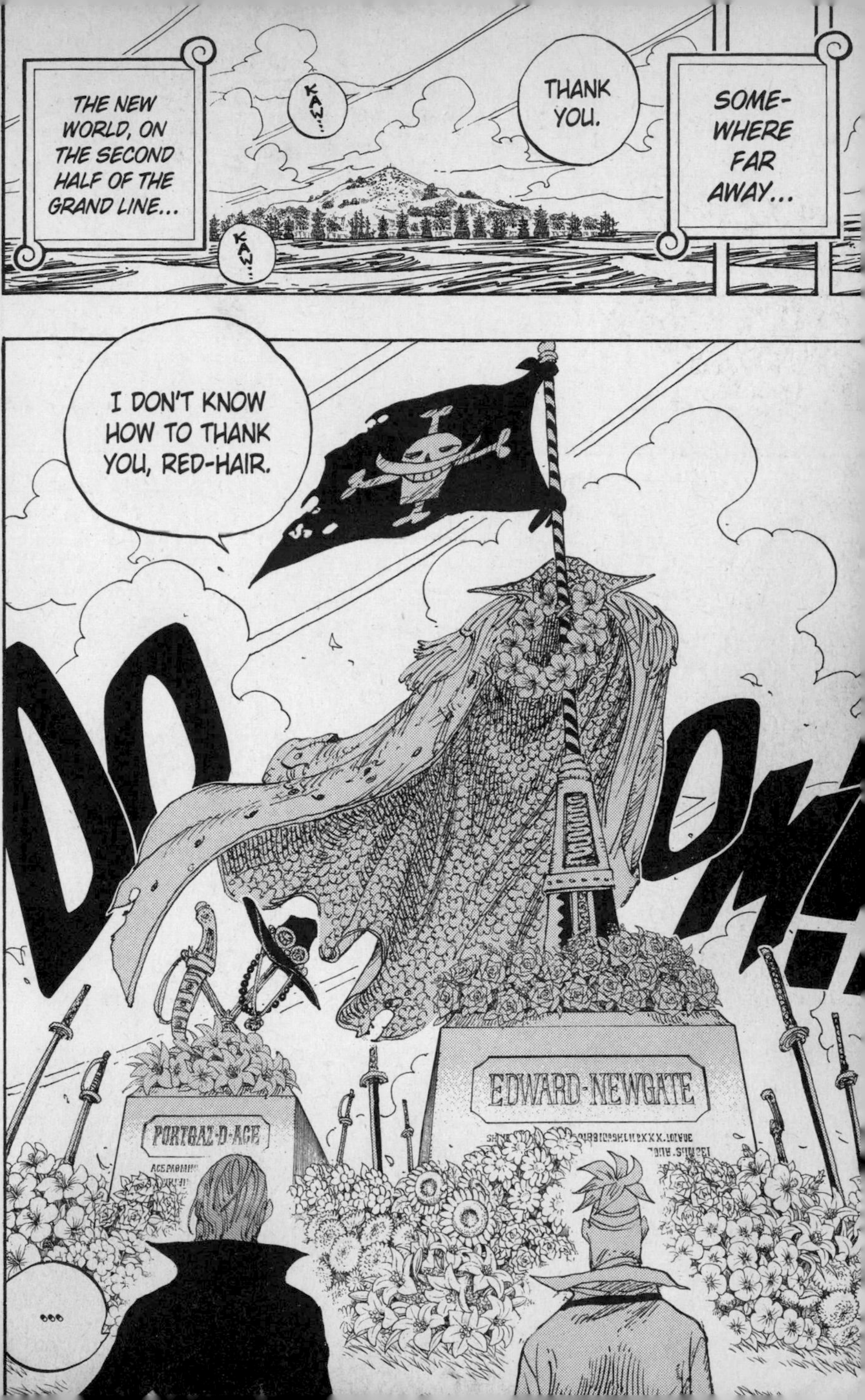

SOME-WHERE FAR AWAY...
THANK YOU.
KAW...
KAW...
THE NEW WORLD, ON THE SECOND HALF OF THE GRAND LINE...
I DON'T KNOW HOW TO THANK YOU, RED-HAIR.
DOOM!!
EDWARD·NEWGATE
PORTGAZ·D·ACE
...

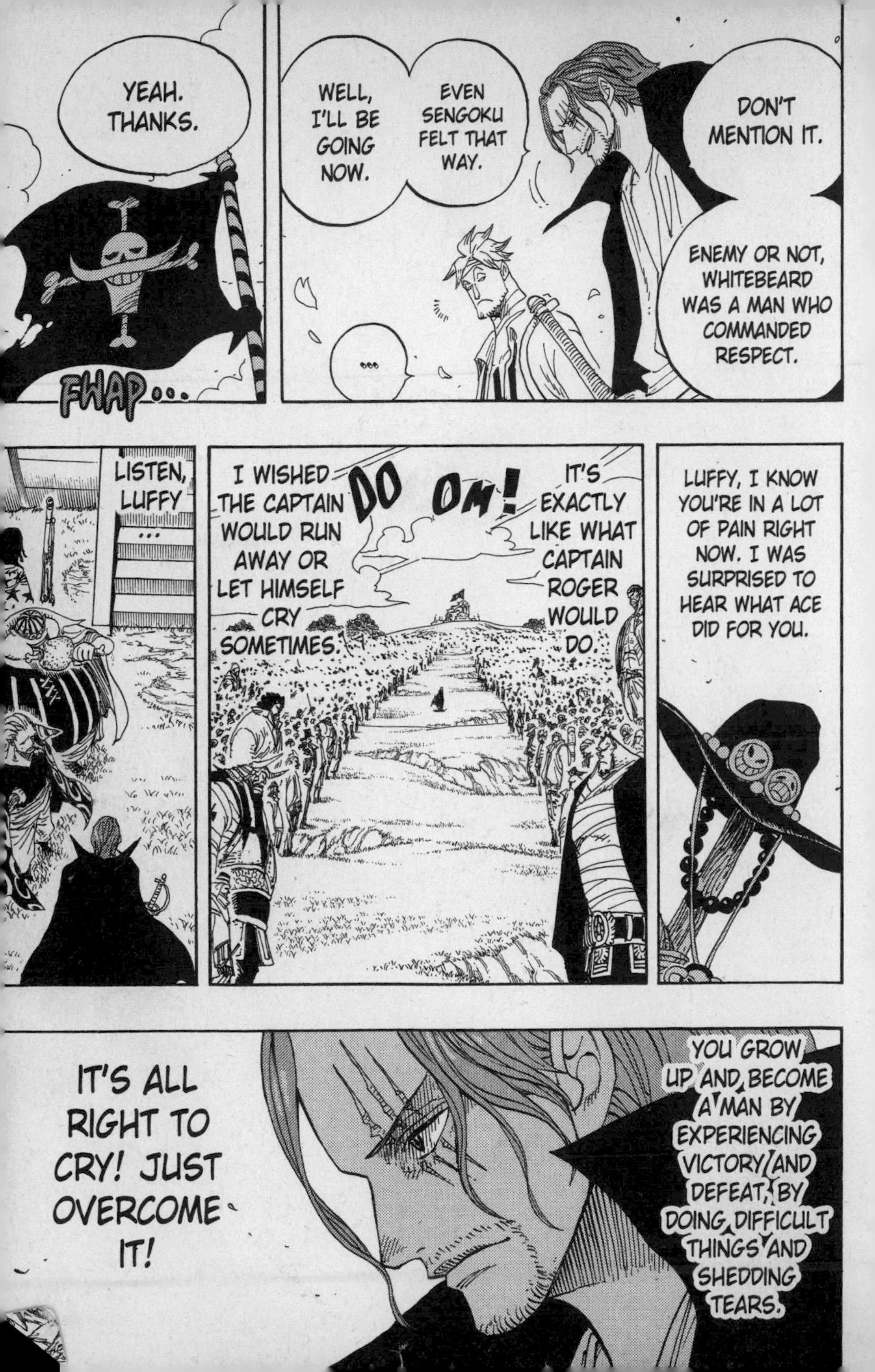
DON'T MENTION IT.
ENEMY OR NOT, WHITEBEARD WAS A MAN WHO COMMANDED RESPECT.
EVEN SENGOKU FELT THAT WAY.
WELL, I'LL BE GOING NOW.
...
YEAH. THANKS.
FWAP...
LUFFY, I KNOW YOU'RE IN A LOT OF PAIN RIGHT NOW. I WAS SURPRISED TO HEAR WHAT ACE DID FOR YOU.
IT'S EXACTLY LIKE WHAT CAPTAIN ROGER WOULD DO.
DOOM!
I WISHED THE CAPTAIN WOULD RUN AWAY OR LET HIMSELF CRY SOMETIMES.
LISTEN, LUFFY...
YOU GROW UP AND BECOME A MAN BY EXPERIENCING VICTORY AND DEFEAT, BY DOING DIFFICULT THINGS AND SHEDDING TEARS.
IT'S ALL RIGHT TO CRY! JUST OVERCOME IT!

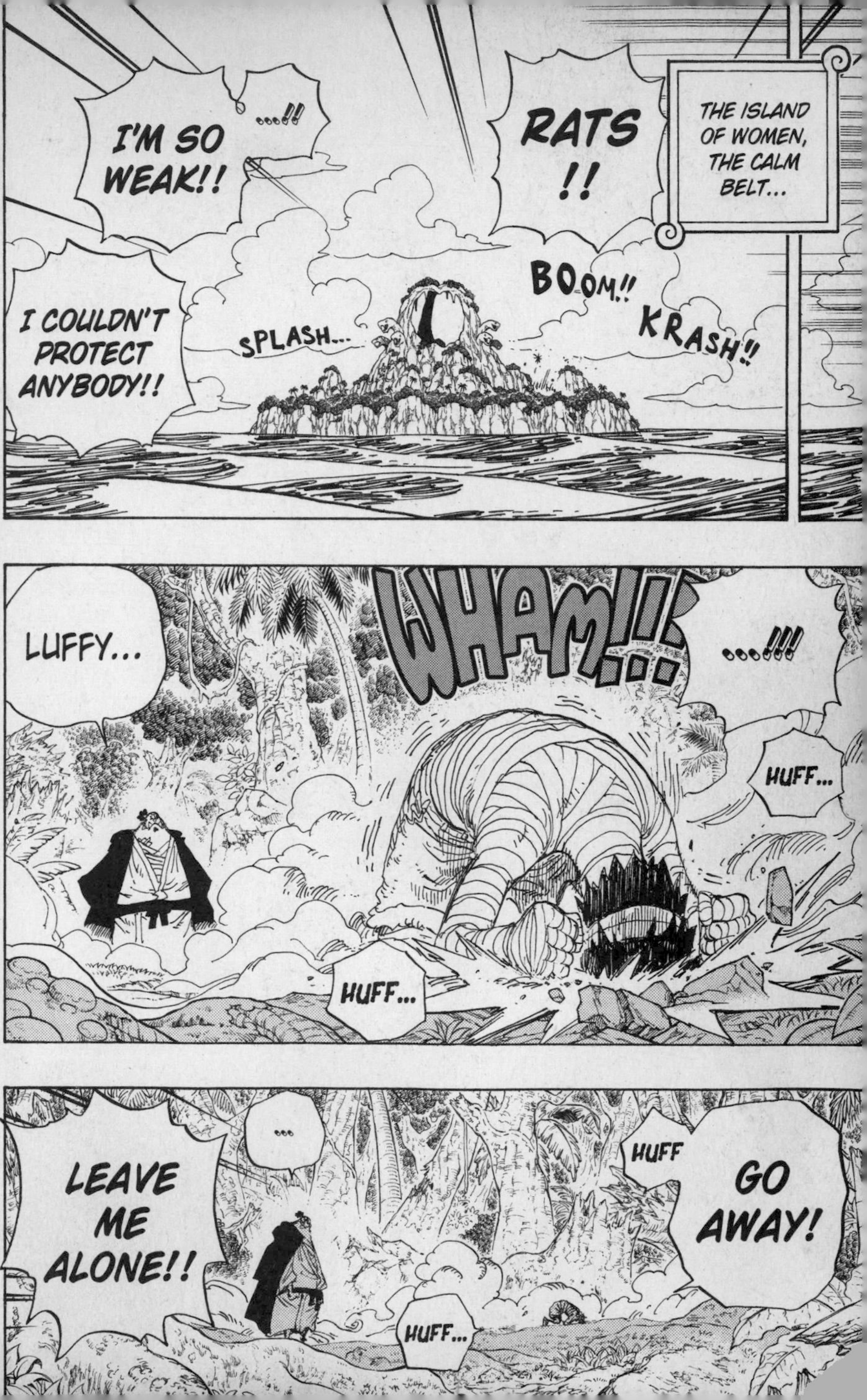
THE ISLAND OF WOMEN, THE CALM BELT...
RATS !!
...!!
I'M SO WEAK!!
I COULDN'T PROTECT ANYBODY!!
BOOM!!
KRASH!!
SPLASH...
WHAM!!!
...!!!
HUFF...
LUFFY...
HUFF...
GO AWAY!
HUFF
...
LEAVE ME ALONE!!
HUFF...

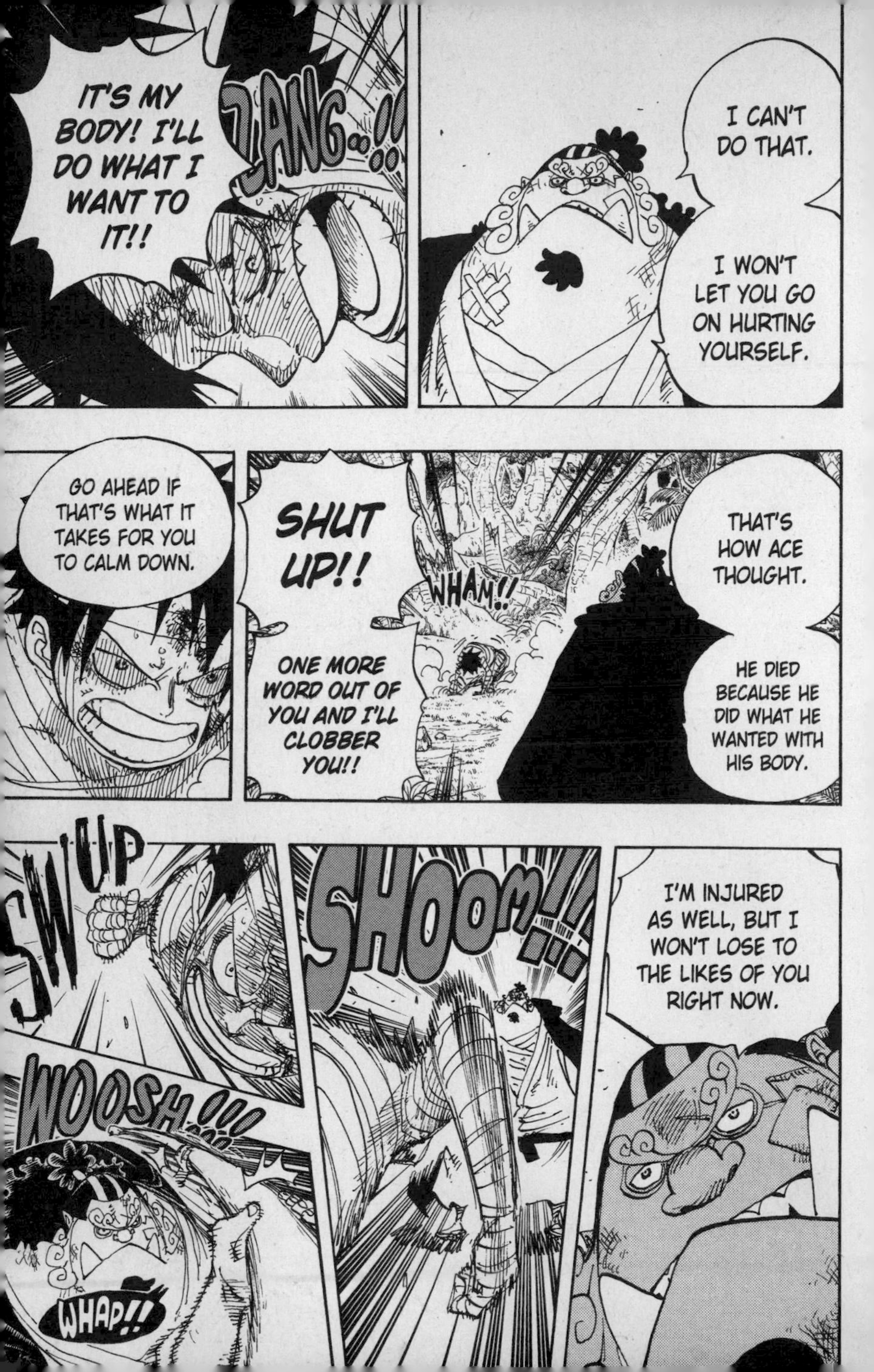
I CAN'T DO THAT.
I WON'T LET YOU GO ON HURTING YOURSELF.
IT'S MY BODY! I'LL DO WHAT I WANT TO IT!!
ZANG..!!
THAT'S HOW ACE THOUGHT.
HE DIED BECAUSE HE DID WHAT HE WANTED WITH HIS BODY.
SHUT UP!!
WHAM!!
ONE MORE WORD OUT OF YOU AND I'LL CLOBBER YOU!!
GO AHEAD IF THAT'S WHAT IT TAKES FOR YOU TO CALM DOWN.
I'M INJURED AS WELL, BUT I WON'T LOSE TO THE LIKES OF YOU RIGHT NOW.
SHOOM!!!
SWUP
WOOSH!!!
WHAP!!

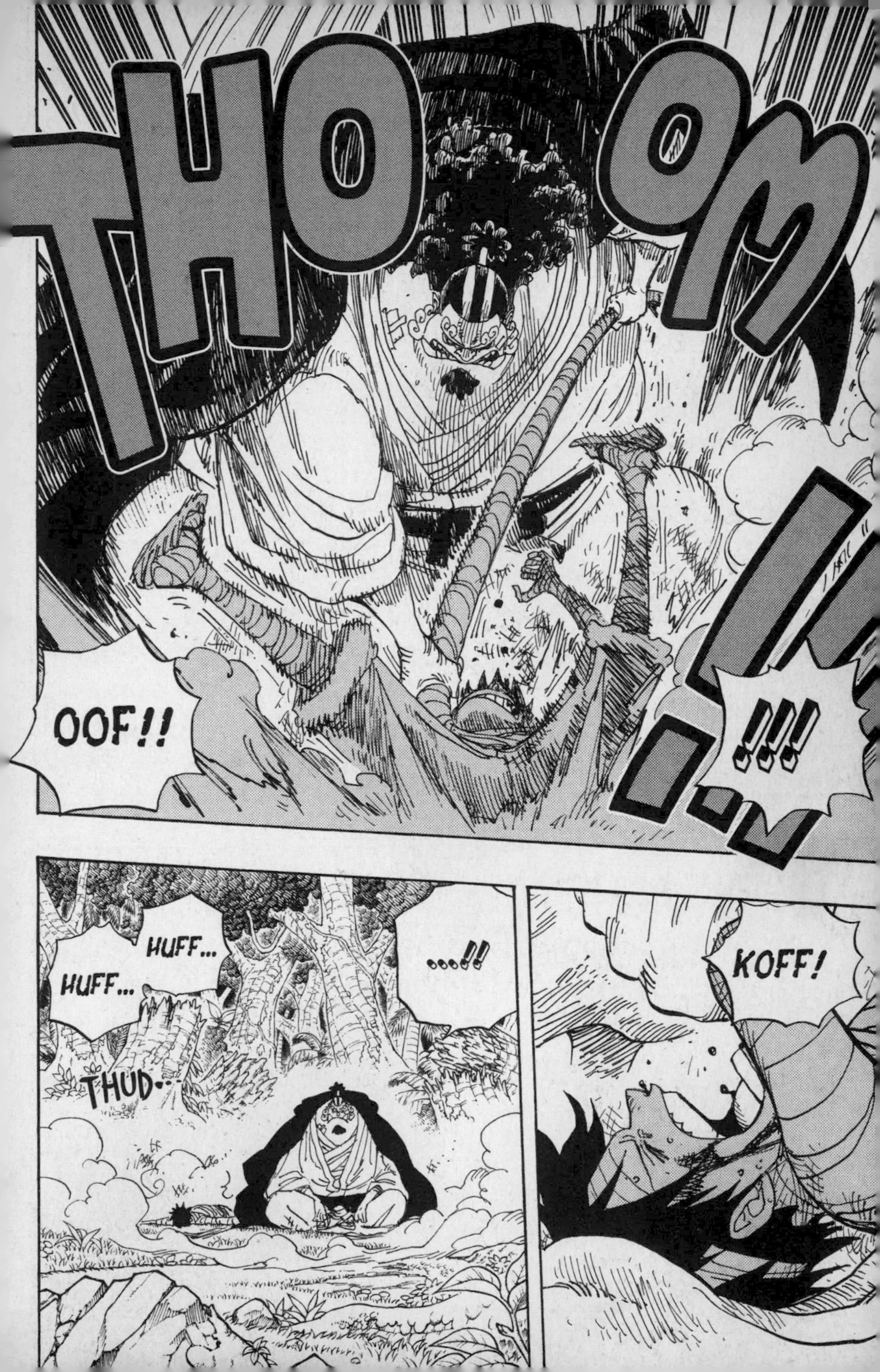
THOOM!!
!!!
OOF!!
KOFF!
...!!
HUFF...
HUFF...
THUD...

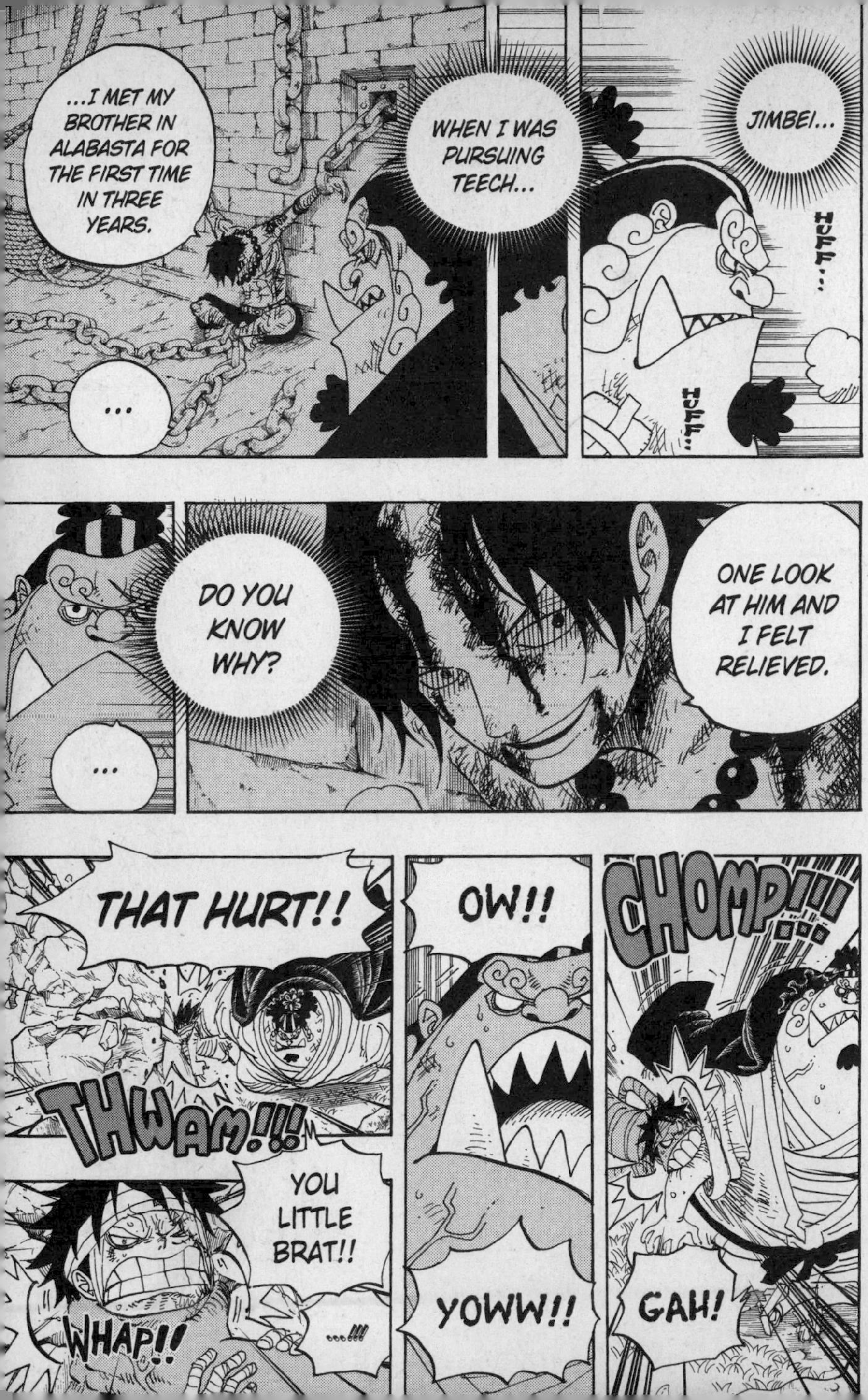
JIMBEI...
HUFF...
HUFF...
WHEN I WAS PURSUING TEECH...
...I MET MY BROTHER IN ALABASTA FOR THE FIRST TIME IN THREE YEARS.
...
ONE LOOK AT HIM AND I FELT RELIEVED.
DO YOU KNOW WHY?
...
CHOMP!!!
GAH!
OW!!
YOWW!!
THAT HURT!!
THWAM!!!
YOU LITTLE BRAT!!
WHAP!!
...!!!

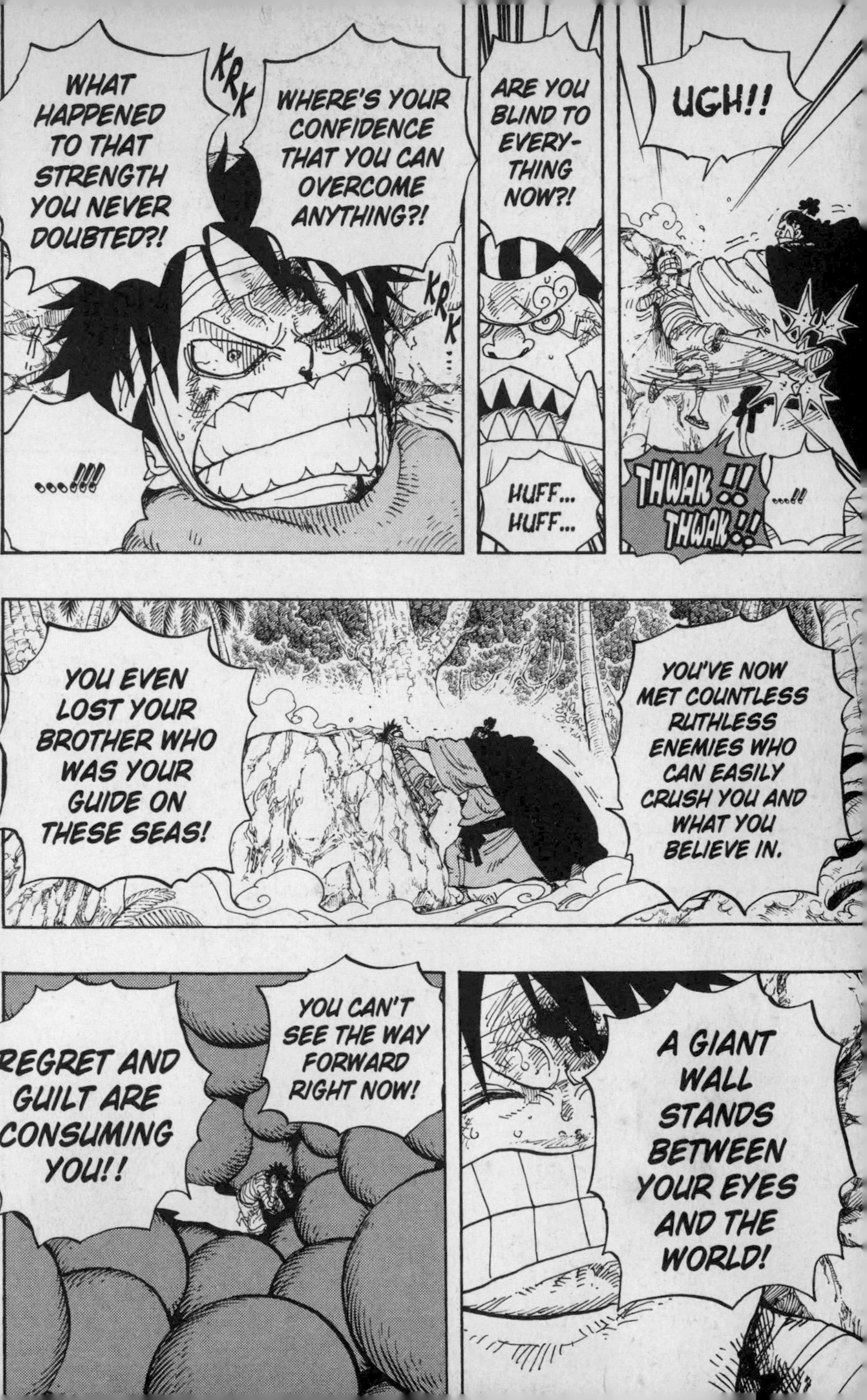
UGH!!
THWAK!! THWAK!!
...!!
ARE YOU BLIND TO EVERY-THING NOW?!
HUFF... HUFF...
KRK
WHERE'S YOUR CONFIDENCE THAT YOU CAN OVERCOME ANYTHING?!
KRK
WHAT HAPPENED TO THAT STRENGTH YOU NEVER DOUBTED?!
...!!!
YOU'VE NOW MET COUNTLESS RUTHLESS ENEMIES WHO CAN EASILY CRUSH YOU AND WHAT YOU BELIEVE IN.
YOU EVEN LOST YOUR BROTHER WHO WAS YOUR GUIDE ON THESE SEAS!
A GIANT WALL STANDS BETWEEN YOUR EYES AND THE WORLD!
YOU CAN'T SEE THE WAY FORWARD RIGHT NOW!
REGRET AND GUILT ARE CONSUMING YOU!!

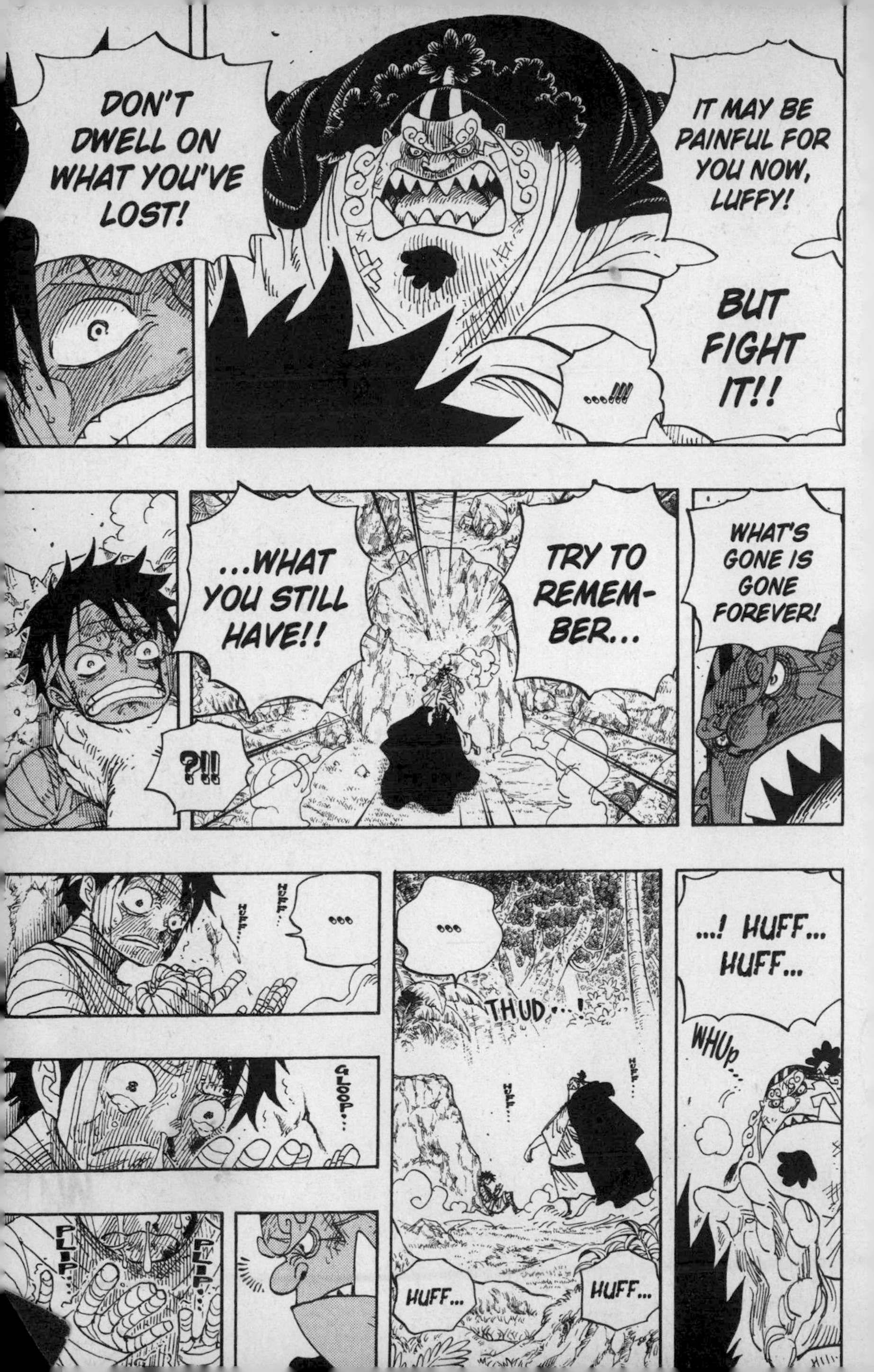
IT MAY BE PAINFUL FOR YOU NOW, LUFFY!
BUT FIGHT IT!!
...!!!
DON'T DWELL ON WHAT YOU'VE LOST!
WHAT'S GONE IS GONE FOREVER!
TRY TO REMEMBER...
...WHAT YOU STILL HAVE!!
?!!
...! HUFF... HUFF...
WHUP...
...
THUD...!
HUFF...
HUFF...
HUFF...
HUFF...
...
HUFF... HUFF...
GLOOP...
PLIP...
PLIP...

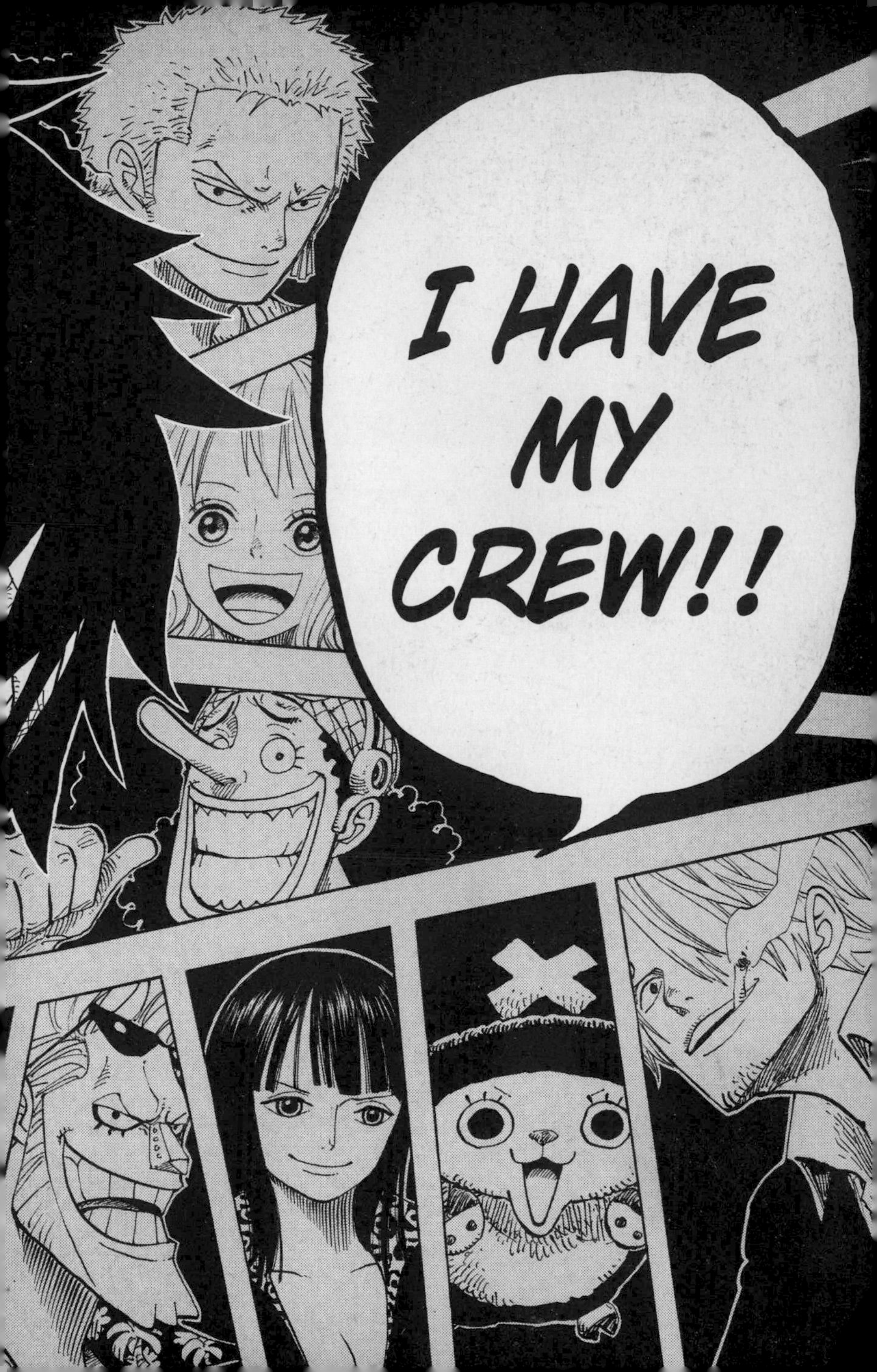
I HAVE MY CREW!!

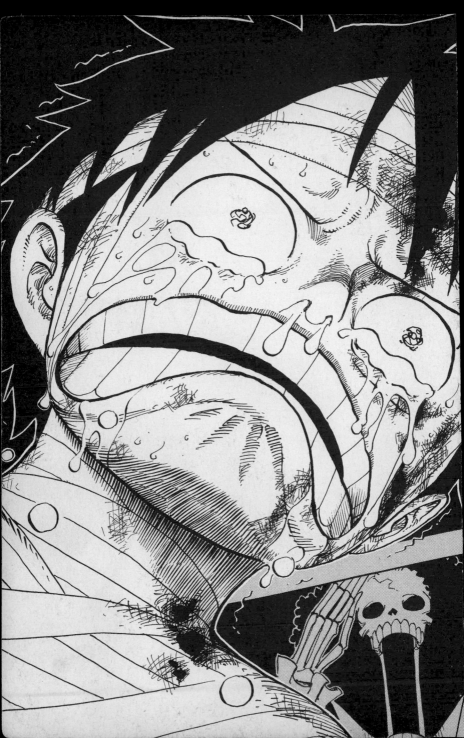

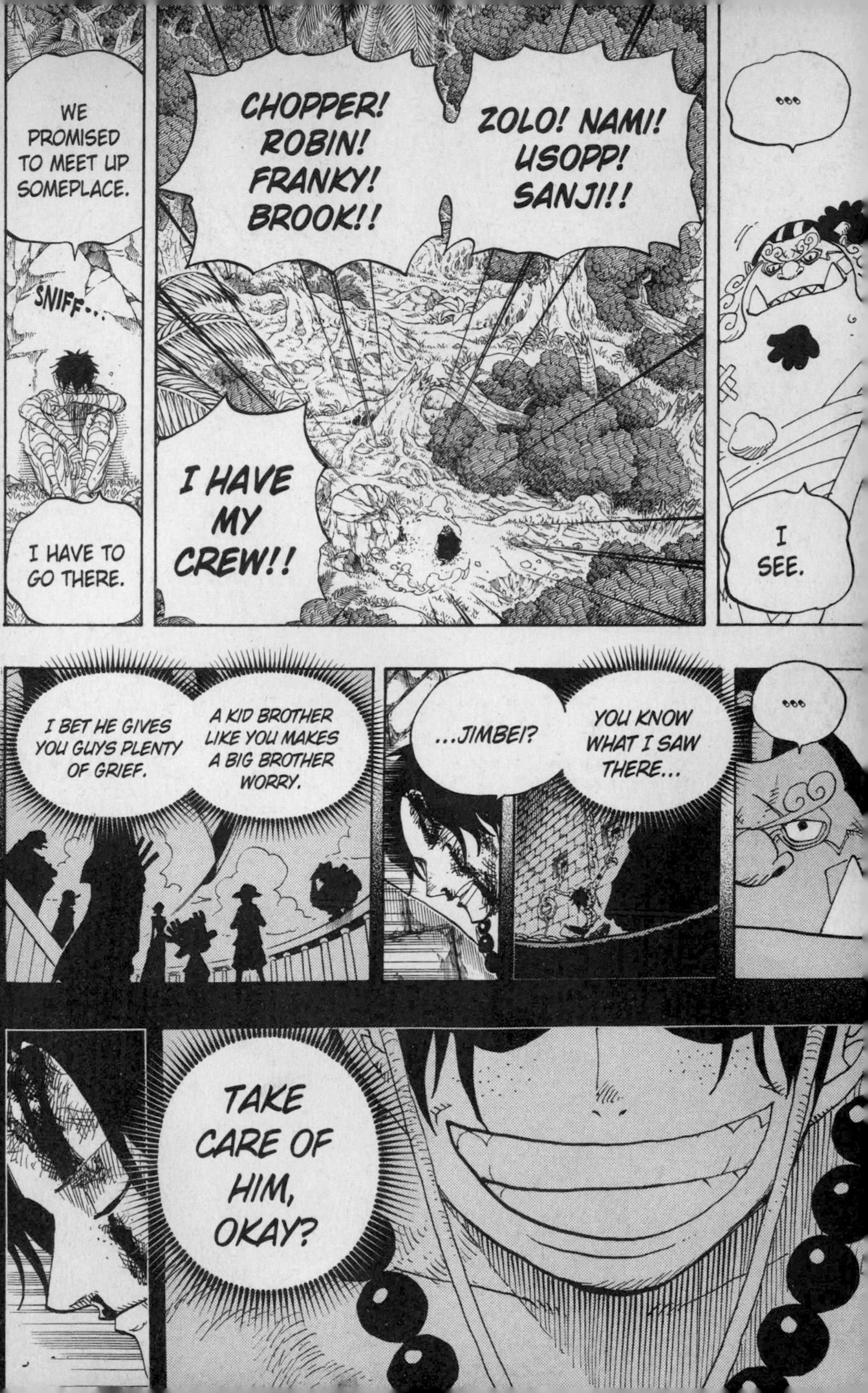
...
I SEE.
ZOLO! NAMI! USOPP! SANJI!!
CHOPPER! ROBIN! FRANKY! BROOK!!
I HAVE MY CREW!!
WE PROMISED TO MEET UP SOMEPLACE.
SNIFF...
I HAVE TO GO THERE.
...
YOU KNOW WHAT I SAW THERE...
...JIMBEI?
A KID BROTHER LIKE YOU MAKES A BIG BROTHER WORRY.
I BET HE GIVES YOU GUYS PLENTY OF GRIEF.
TAKE CARE OF HIM, OKAY?

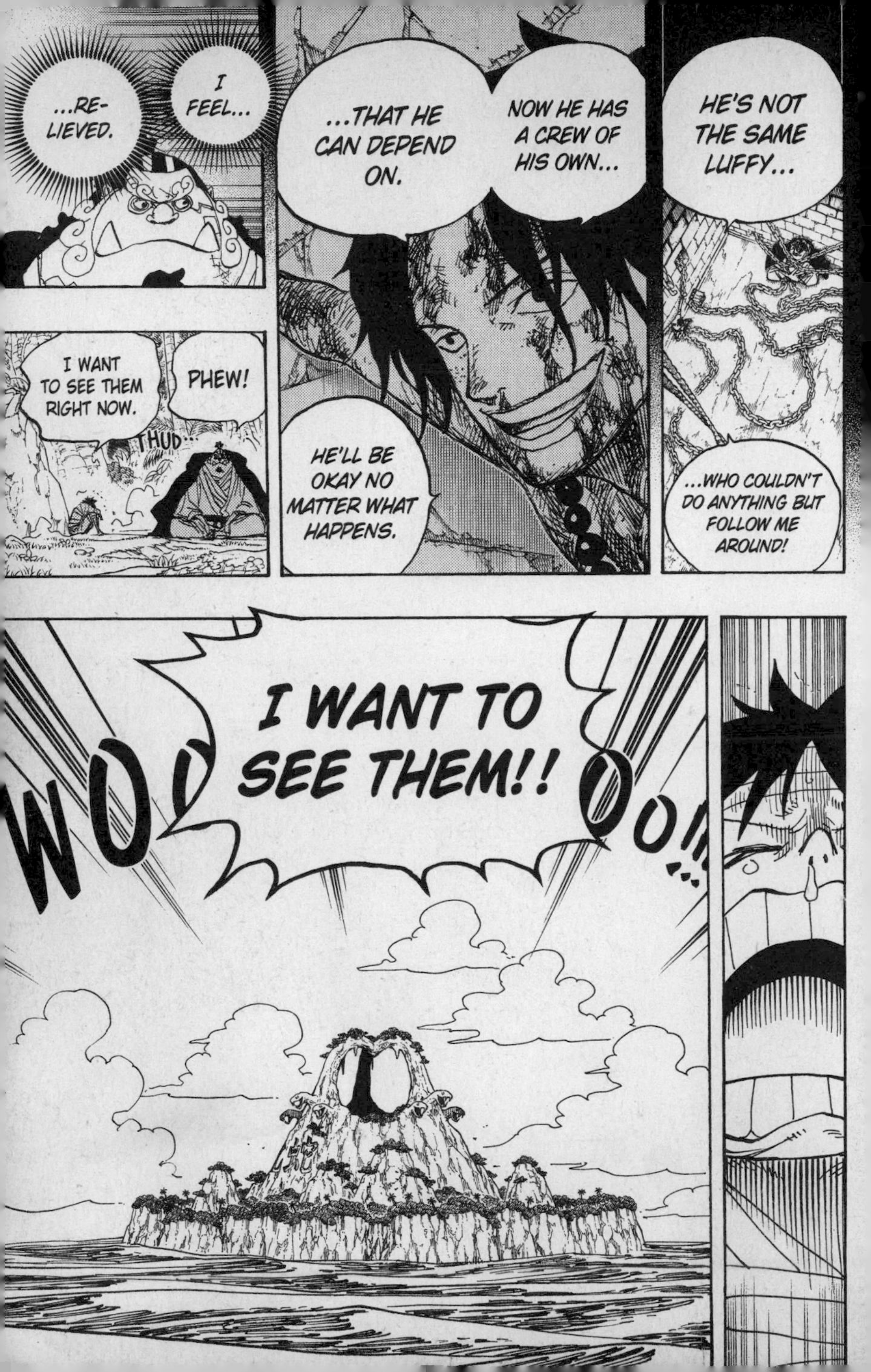
HE'S NOT THE SAME LUFFY...
...WHO COULDN'T DO ANYTHING BUT FOLLOW ME AROUND!
NOW HE HAS A CREW OF HIS OWN...
...THAT HE CAN DEPEND ON.
HE'LL BE OKAY NO MATTER WHAT HAPPENS.
I FEEL...
...RE-LIEVED.
PHEW!
I WANT TO SEE THEM RIGHT NOW.
THUD...
I WANT TO SEE THEM!!
WOOOO!!

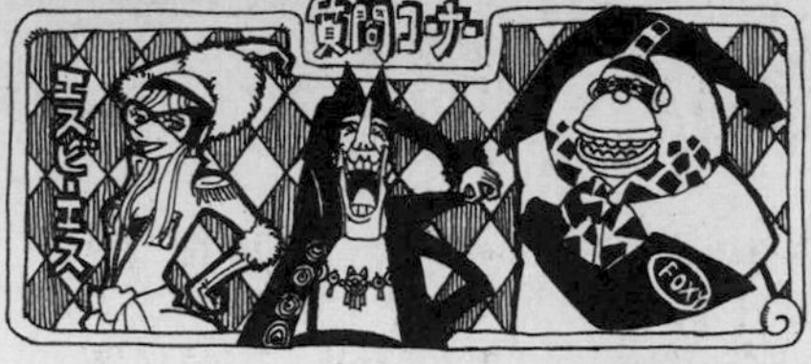
質問コーナー
エスビーエス
FOXY

(Yukiko Nakai, Osaka)

Oda: BIO--(B)ring (I)t (O)n! Come on! Here we go! I did this in the last volume too, because so many people wanted to choose the birthdays of the characters, so I decided to set this section up to make it as hard as possible! I'm going to stop all of you! Bring it on!

Q: Hello, Mr. Oda. I'm a huge fan of yours.☆ This may be sudden, but can Buggy's birthday be August 8th? And how about making Mr. 3's birthday March 3rd? Is that okay?

--Omanju

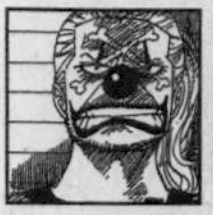

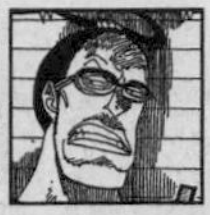

A: Okay! (・▽・)/

Q: Hi, Odacchi! This may be sudden, but I thought of a good day for Rayleigh's birthday!☆ Since he's the Dark King, make it May 13! It gets kind of dark in May and the king is the number 13 in playing cards. What do you think?

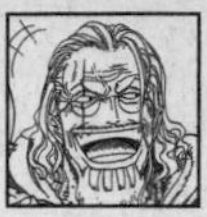

--Azuma

A: Okay! (≧▽≦)/

Q: About Sabo's birthday, how about making it March 20?! Because it just feels right!

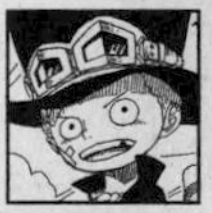

--Seii Taishogun

A: Sure thing! (・▽<)b

Q: Nice to meet you! I've been a fan of *One Piece* ever since it began!♥ By the way, Mr. Oda, those new guys that appeared on the Sabaody Archipelago are really awesome. Please tell me their profiles! By the way, can you use the birthdays I came up with?

--Cat Lover ♥

Eustass "Captain" Kid
January 10

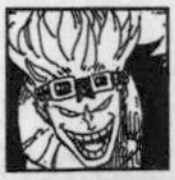

"Murder Machine" Killer
February 2

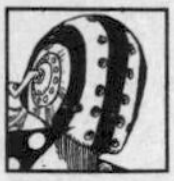

Basil Hawkins
September 9
(Fortune-telling Day)

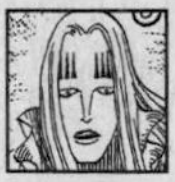

"Mad Monk" Urouge
August 1

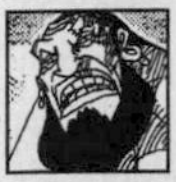

"Glutton" Jewelry Bonney
September 1

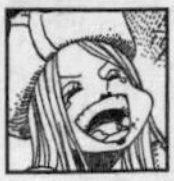

Bepo
November 20

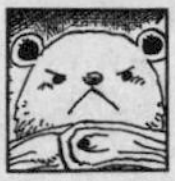

Scratchmen Apoo
March 19
"Day of Music"

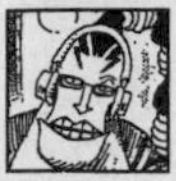

Oda: Okay! (・▽・)/ But I removed Drake and Bege because they were too much of a stretch. I'm waiting for someone else to suggest some good ideas. By the way, Kuro from Chiba Prefecture sent me over 50 postcards asking to set Marco's birthday as October 5, but it looks like Marunyamu already set the same date in the last volume. It's great to see your enthusiasm for this. I'm glad it was the same day.

Chapter 591:
ARE YOU SURE ABOUT THAT?

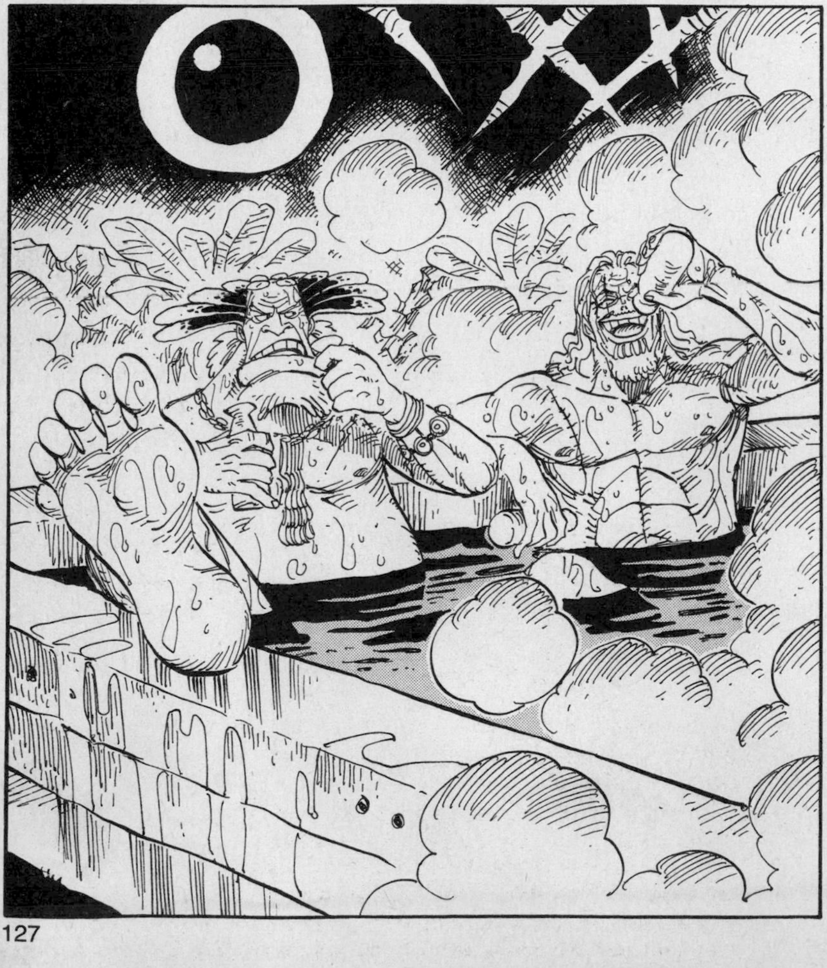

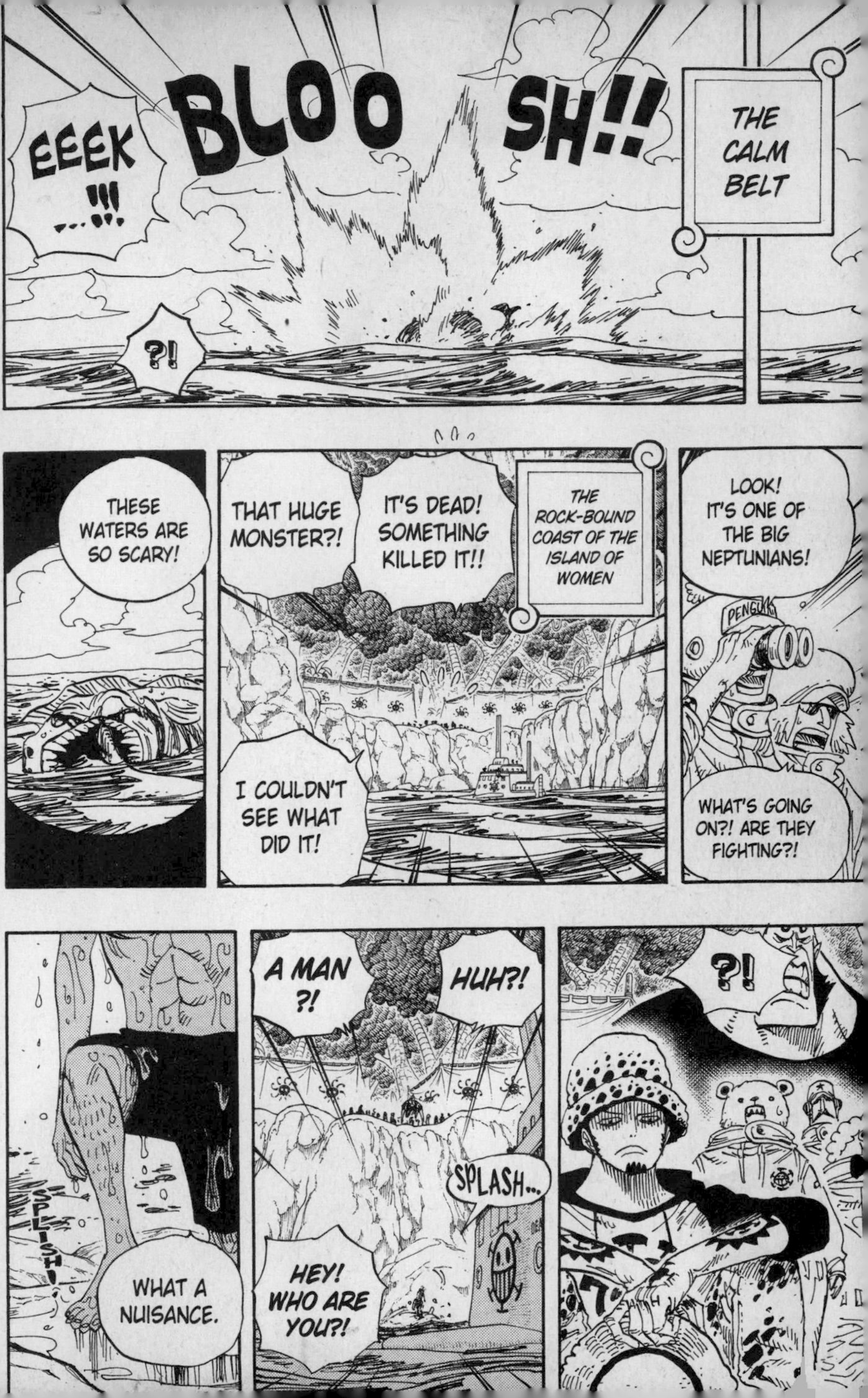

THE CALM BELT
BLOO SH!!
EEEK !!! ...!!
?!
LOOK! IT'S ONE OF THE BIG NEPTUNIANS!
WHAT'S GOING ON?! ARE THEY FIGHTING?!
THE ROCK-BOUND COAST OF THE ISLAND OF WOMEN
IT'S DEAD! SOMETHING KILLED IT!!
THAT HUGE MONSTER?!
I COULDN'T SEE WHAT DID IT!
THESE WATERS ARE SO SCARY!
?!
HUH?!
A MAN ?!
SPLASH...
HEY! WHO ARE YOU?!
SPLISH...
WHAT A NUISANCE.

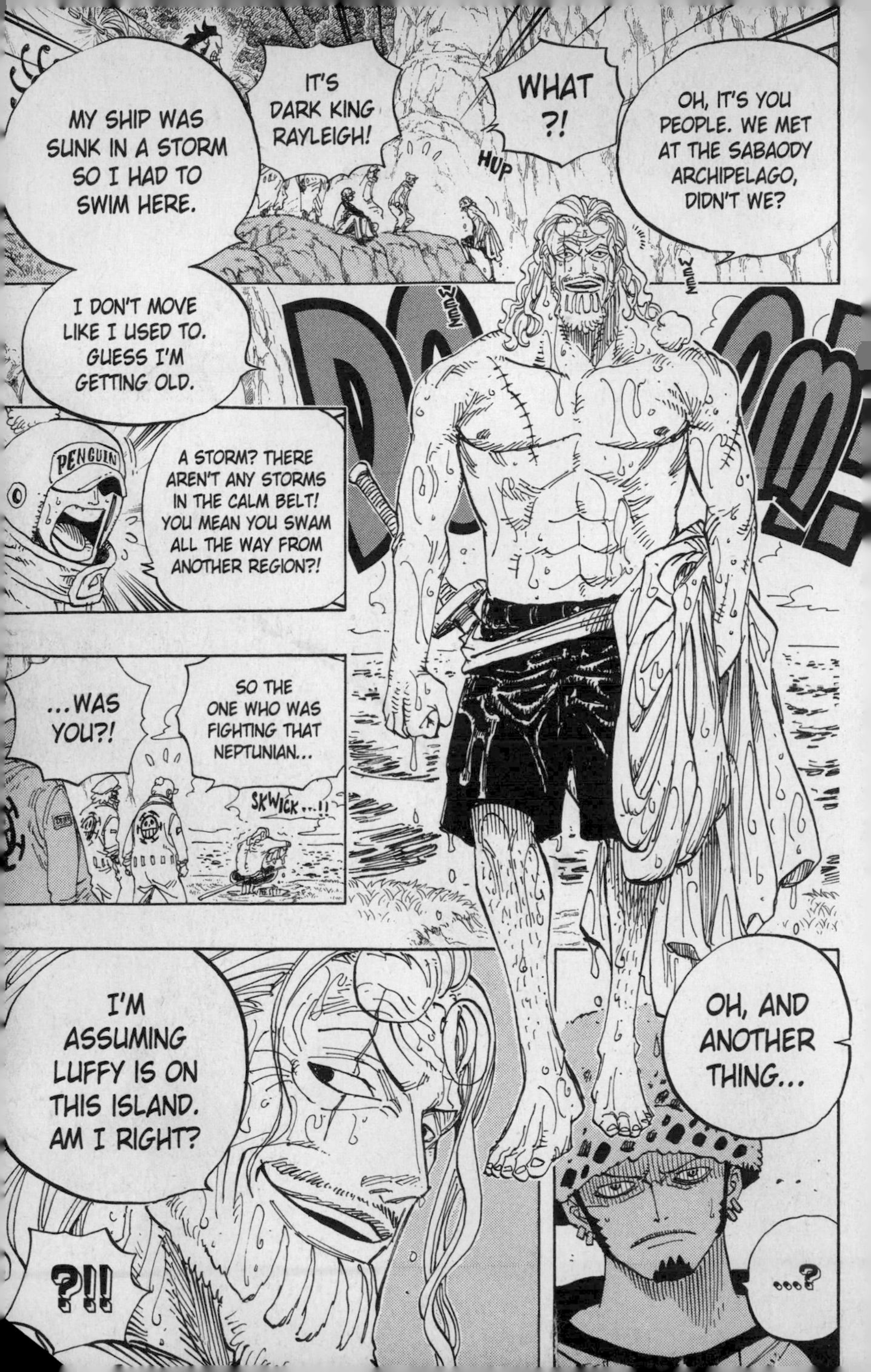
WHAT ?!
OH, IT'S YOU PEOPLE. WE MET AT THE SABAODY ARCHIPELAGO, DIDN'T WE?
IT'S DARK KING RAYLEIGH!
HUP
MY SHIP WAS SUNK IN A STORM SO I HAD TO SWIM HERE.
WEEN
WEEN
I DON'T MOVE LIKE I USED TO. GUESS I'M GETTING OLD.
PENGUIN
A STORM? THERE AREN'T ANY STORMS IN THE CALM BELT! YOU MEAN YOU SWAM ALL THE WAY FROM ANOTHER REGION?!
SO THE ONE WHO WAS FIGHTING THAT NEPTUNIAN...
SKWICK...!!
...WAS YOU?!
OH, AND ANOTHER THING...
...?
I'M ASSUMING LUFFY IS ON THIS ISLAND. AM I RIGHT?
?!!

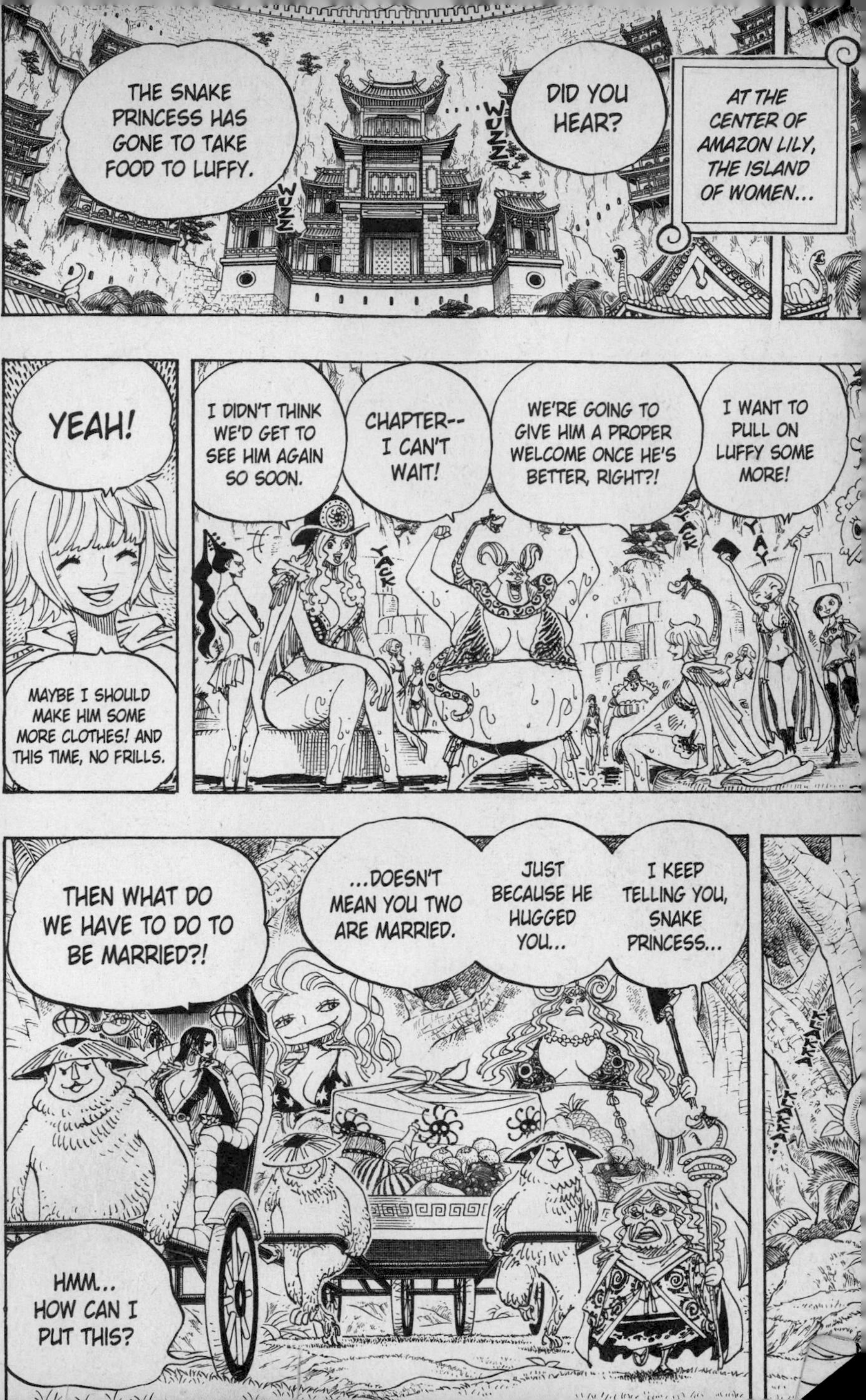
AT THE CENTER OF AMAZON LILY, THE ISLAND OF WOMEN...
WUZZ
DID YOU HEAR?
WUZZ
THE SNAKE PRINCESS HAS GONE TO TAKE FOOD TO LUFFY.
I WANT TO PULL ON LUFFY SOME MORE!
YAY
YACK
WE'RE GOING TO GIVE HIM A PROPER WELCOME ONCE HE'S BETTER, RIGHT?!
CHAPTER-- I CAN'T WAIT!
YACK
I DIDN'T THINK WE'D GET TO SEE HIM AGAIN SO SOON.
YEAH!
MAYBE I SHOULD MAKE HIM SOME MORE CLOTHES! AND THIS TIME, NO FRILLS.
KLAKA
KLAKA
I KEEP TELLING YOU, SNAKE PRINCESS...
JUST BECAUSE HE HUGGED YOU...
...DOESN'T MEAN YOU TWO ARE MARRIED.
THEN WHAT DO WE HAVE TO DO TO BE MARRIED?!
HMM.. HOW CAN I PUT THIS?

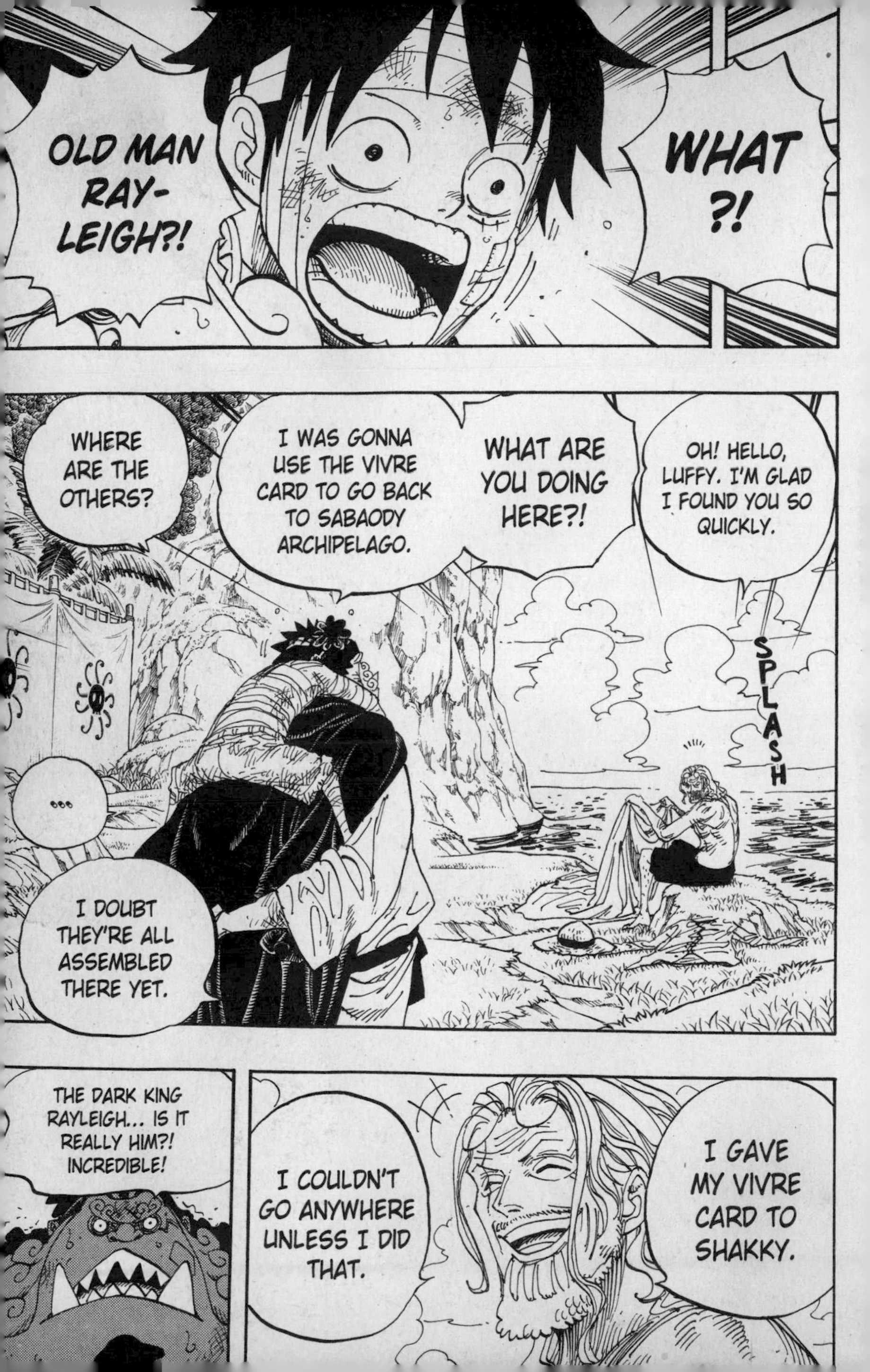
WHAT ?!
OLD MAN RAY-LEIGH?!
SPLASH
OH! HELLO, LUFFY. I'M GLAD I FOUND YOU SO QUICKLY.
WHAT ARE YOU DOING HERE?!
I WAS GONNA USE THE VIVRE CARD TO GO BACK TO SABAODY ARCHIPELAGO.
WHERE ARE THE OTHERS?
...
I DOUBT THEY'RE ALL ASSEMBLED THERE YET.
I GAVE MY VIVRE CARD TO SHAKKY.
I COULDN'T GO ANYWHERE UNLESS I DID THAT.
THE DARK KING RAYLEIGH... IS IT REALLY HIM?! INCREDIBLE!

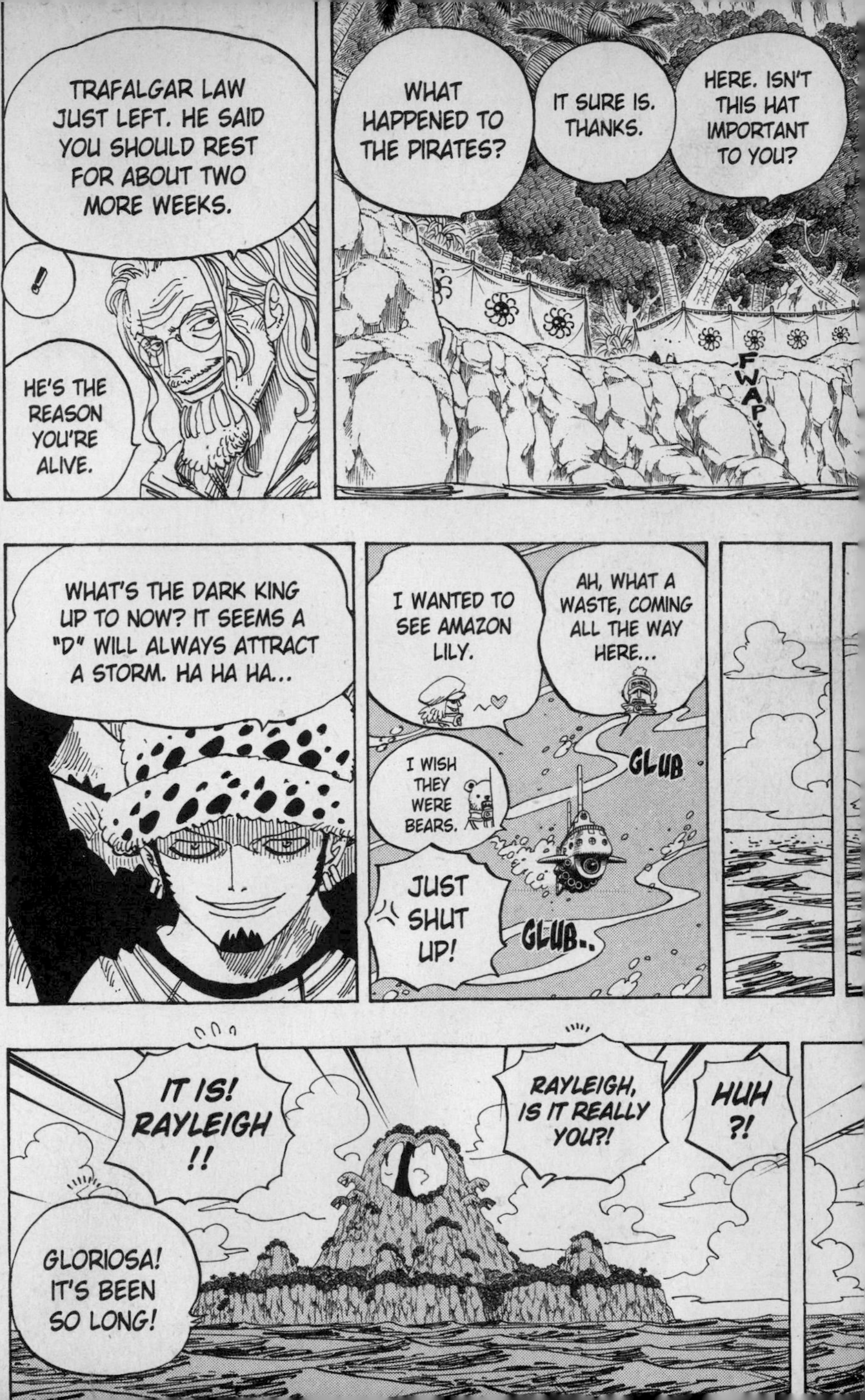
HERE. ISN'T THIS HAT IMPORTANT TO YOU?
IT SURE IS. THANKS.
WHAT HAPPENED TO THE PIRATES?
FWAP...
TRAFALGAR LAW JUST LEFT. HE SAID YOU SHOULD REST FOR ABOUT TWO MORE WEEKS.
!
HE'S THE REASON YOU'RE ALIVE.
AH, WHAT A WASTE, COMING ALL THE WAY HERE...
I WANTED TO SEE AMAZON LILY.
GLUB
I WISH THEY WERE BEARS.
JUST SHUT UP!
GLUB..
WHAT'S THE DARK KING UP TO NOW? IT SEEMS A "D" WILL ALWAYS ATTRACT A STORM. HA HA HA...
HUH ?!
RAYLEIGH, IS IT REALLY YOU?!
IT IS! RAYLEIGH !!
GLORIOSA! IT'S BEEN SO LONG!

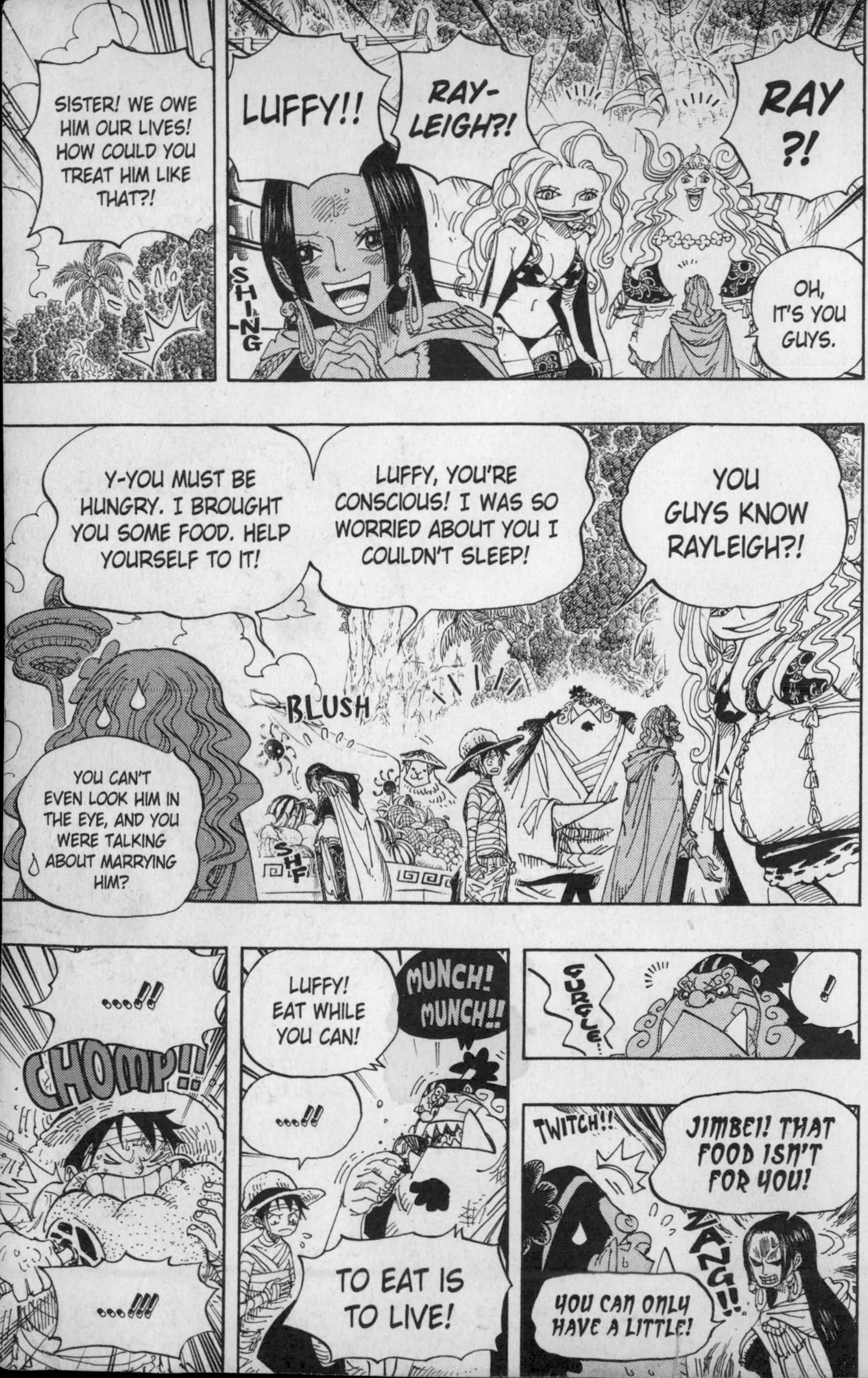
RAY ?!
RAY-LEIGH?!
LUFFY!!
OH, IT'S YOU GUYS.
SHING
SISTER! WE OWE HIM OUR LIVES! HOW COULD YOU TREAT HIM LIKE THAT?!
YOU GUYS KNOW RAYLEIGH?!
LUFFY, YOU'RE CONSCIOUS! I WAS SO WORRIED ABOUT YOU I COULDN'T SLEEP!
Y-YOU MUST BE HUNGRY. I BROUGHT YOU SOME FOOD. HELP YOURSELF TO IT!
BLUSH
SHF
YOU CAN'T EVEN LOOK HIM IN THE EYE, AND YOU WERE TALKING ABOUT MARRYING HIM?
!
GURGLE...
JIMBEI! THAT FOOD ISN'T FOR YOU!
TWITCH!!
ZANG!!
YOU CAN ONLY HAVE A LITTLE!
MUNCH! MUNCH!!
LUFFY! EAT WHILE YOU CAN!
...!!
TO EAT IS TO LIVE!
...!!
CHOMP!!
...!!!

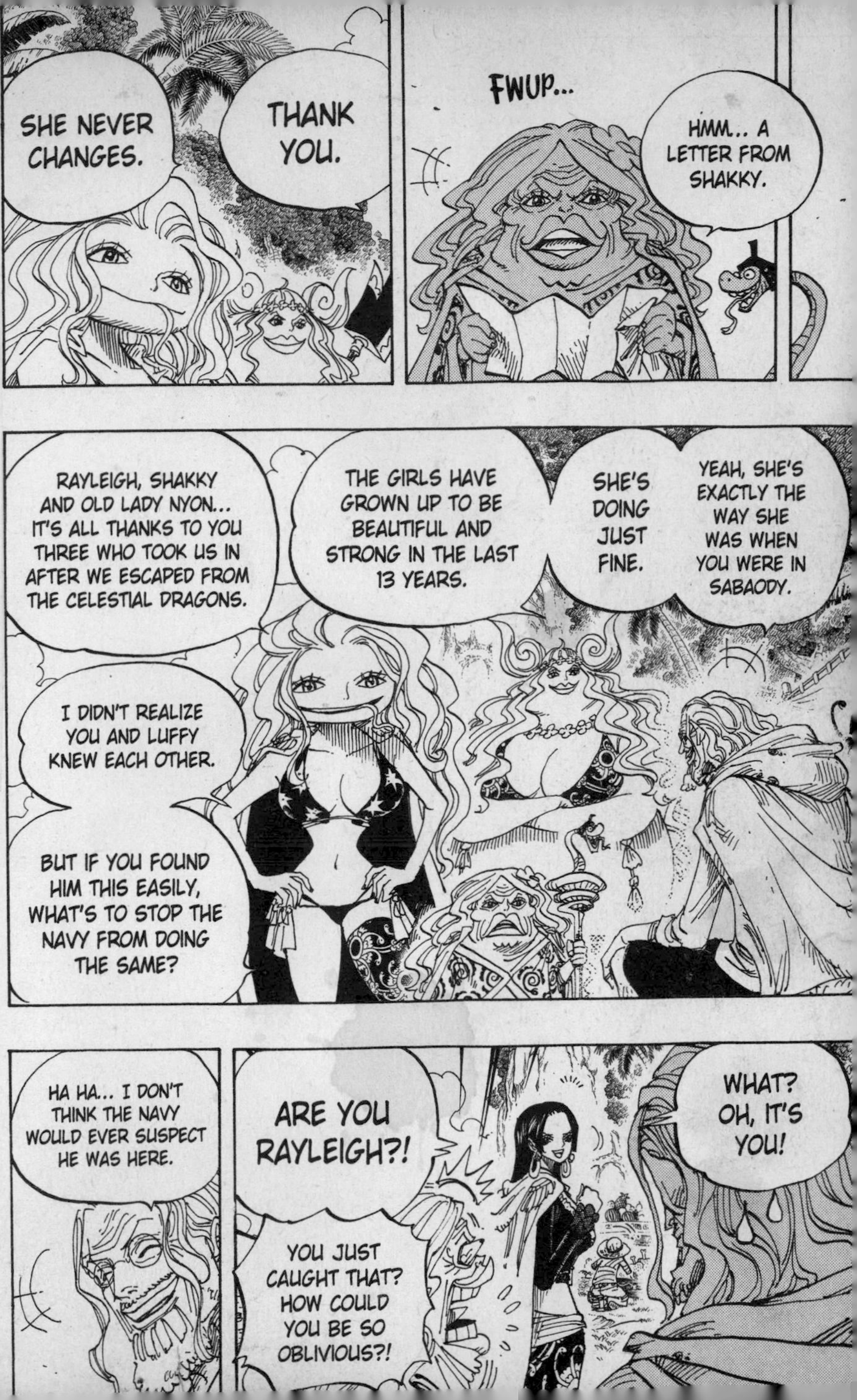
FWUP...
HMM... A LETTER FROM SHAKKY.
THANK YOU.
SHE NEVER CHANGES.
YEAH, SHE'S EXACTLY THE WAY SHE WAS WHEN YOU WERE IN SABAODY.
SHE'S DOING JUST FINE.
THE GIRLS HAVE GROWN UP TO BE BEAUTIFUL AND STRONG IN THE LAST 13 YEARS.
RAYLEIGH, SHAKKY AND OLD LADY NYON... IT'S ALL THANKS TO YOU THREE WHO TOOK US IN AFTER WE ESCAPED FROM THE CELESTIAL DRAGONS.
I DIDN'T REALIZE YOU AND LUFFY KNEW EACH OTHER.
BUT IF YOU FOUND HIM THIS EASILY, WHAT'S TO STOP THE NAVY FROM DOING THE SAME?
WHAT? OH, IT'S YOU!
ARE YOU RAYLEIGH?!
YOU JUST CAUGHT THAT? HOW COULD YOU BE SO OBLIVIOUS?!
HA HA... I DON'T THINK THE NAVY WOULD EVER SUSPECT HE WAS HERE.

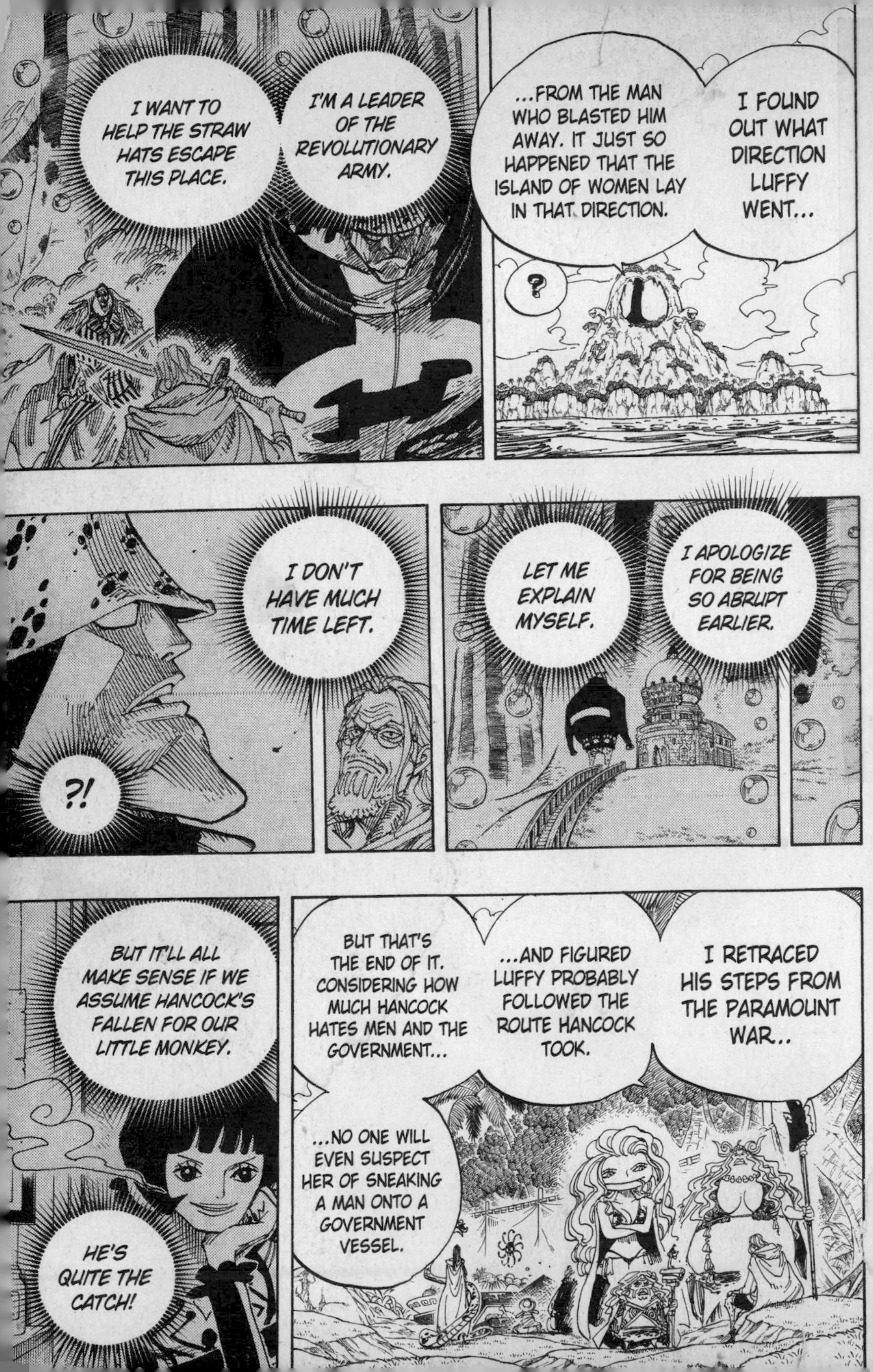
I FOUND OUT WHAT DIRECTION LUFFY WENT...
...FROM THE MAN WHO BLASTED HIM AWAY. IT JUST SO HAPPENED THAT THE ISLAND OF WOMEN LAY IN THAT DIRECTION.
?
I'M A LEADER OF THE REVOLUTIONARY ARMY.
I WANT TO HELP THE STRAW HATS ESCAPE THIS PLACE.
I APOLOGIZE FOR BEING SO ABRUPT EARLIER.
LET ME EXPLAIN MYSELF.
I DON'T HAVE MUCH TIME LEFT.
?!
I RETRACED HIS STEPS FROM THE PARAMOUNT WAR..
...AND FIGURED LUFFY PROBABLY FOLLOWED THE ROUTE HANCOCK TOOK.
BUT THAT'S THE END OF IT. CONSIDERING HOW MUCH HANCOCK HATES MEN AND THE GOVERNMENT...
...NO ONE WILL EVEN SUSPECT HER OF SNEAKING A MAN ONTO A GOVERNMENT VESSEL.
BUT IT'LL ALL MAKE SENSE IF WE ASSUME HANCOCK'S FALLEN FOR OUR LITTLE MONKEY.
HE'S QUITE THE CATCH!

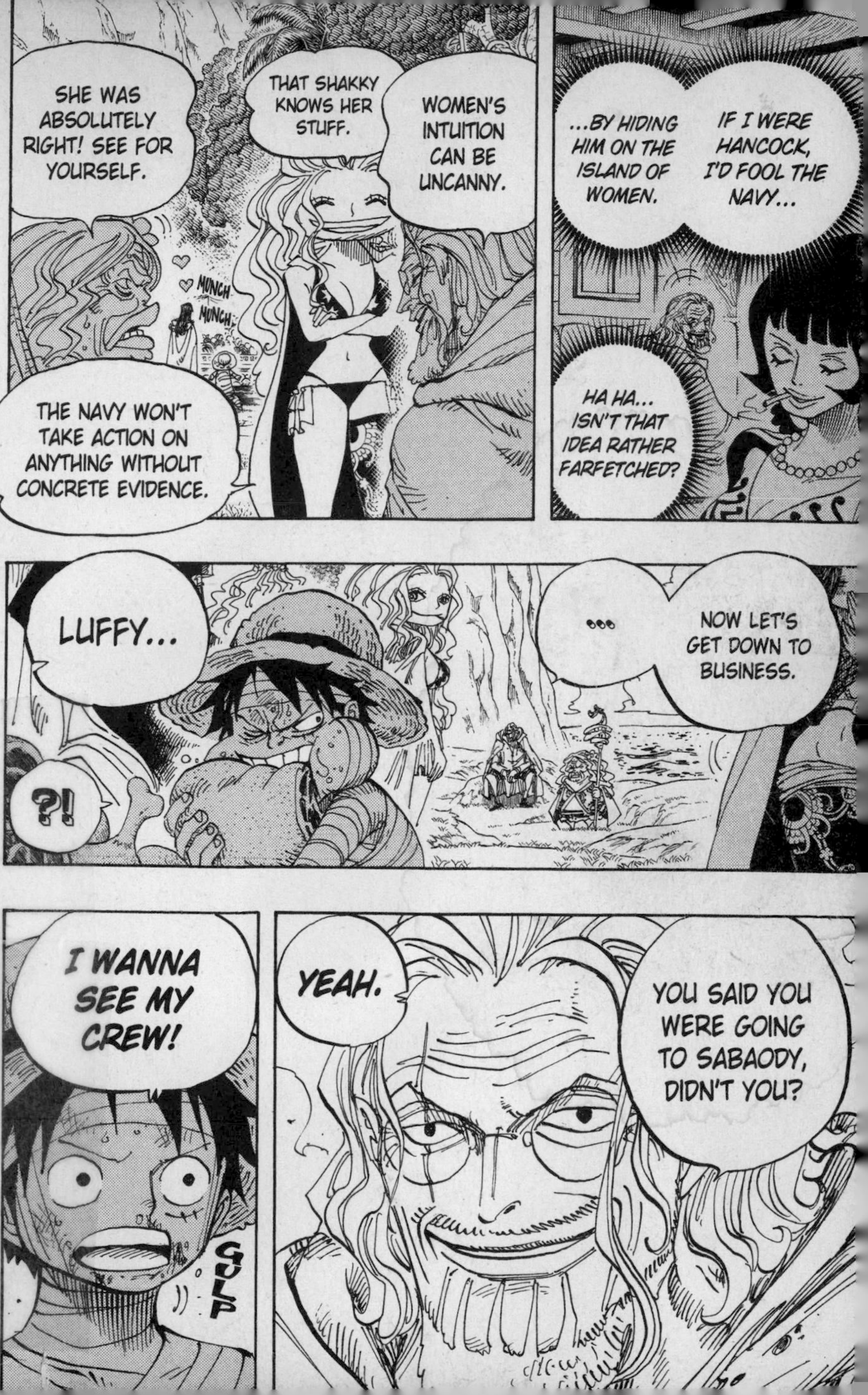
IF I WERE HANCOCK, I'D FOOL THE NAVY...
...BY HIDING HIM ON THE ISLAND OF WOMEN.
HA HA... ISN'T THAT IDEA RATHER FARFETCHED?
WOMEN'S INTUITION CAN BE UNCANNY.
THAT SHAKKY KNOWS HER STUFF.
SHE WAS ABSOLUTELY RIGHT! SEE FOR YOURSELF.
MUNCH
MUNCH
THE NAVY WON'T TAKE ACTION ON ANYTHING WITHOUT CONCRETE EVIDENCE.
NOW LET'S GET DOWN TO BUSINESS.
...
LUFFY...
?!
YOU SAID YOU WERE GOING TO SABAODY, DIDN'T YOU?
YEAH.
I WANNA SEE MY CREW!
GULP

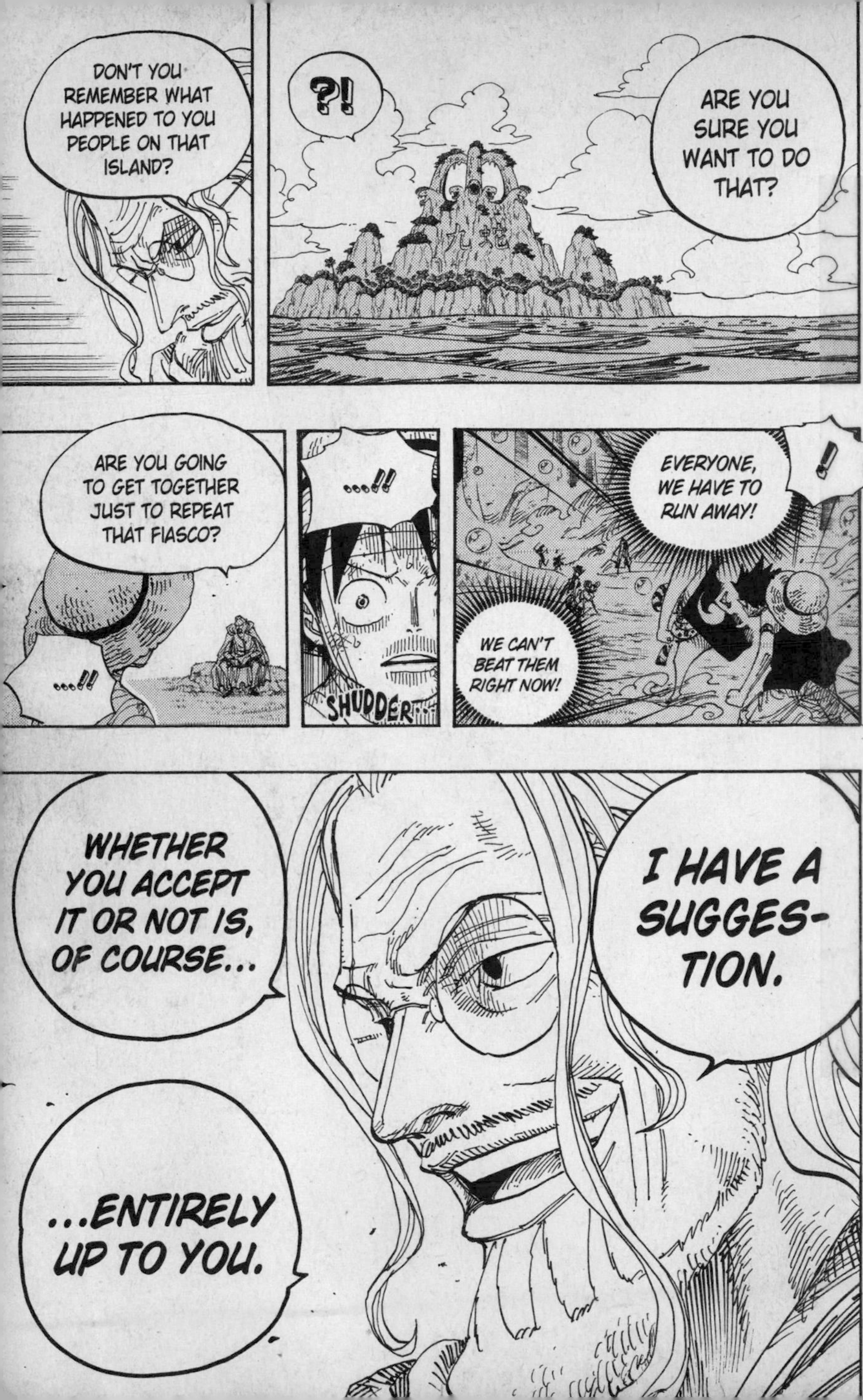
ARE YOU SURE YOU WANT TO DO THAT?
?!
DON'T YOU REMEMBER WHAT HAPPENED TO YOU PEOPLE ON THAT ISLAND?
!
EVERYONE, WE HAVE TO RUN AWAY!
WE CAN'T BEAT THEM RIGHT NOW!
...!!
SHUDDER...
ARE YOU GOING TO GET TOGETHER JUST TO REPEAT THAT FIASCO?
...!!
I HAVE A SUGGES-TION.
WHETHER YOU ACCEPT IT OR NOT IS, OF COURSE...
...ENTIRELY UP TO YOU.

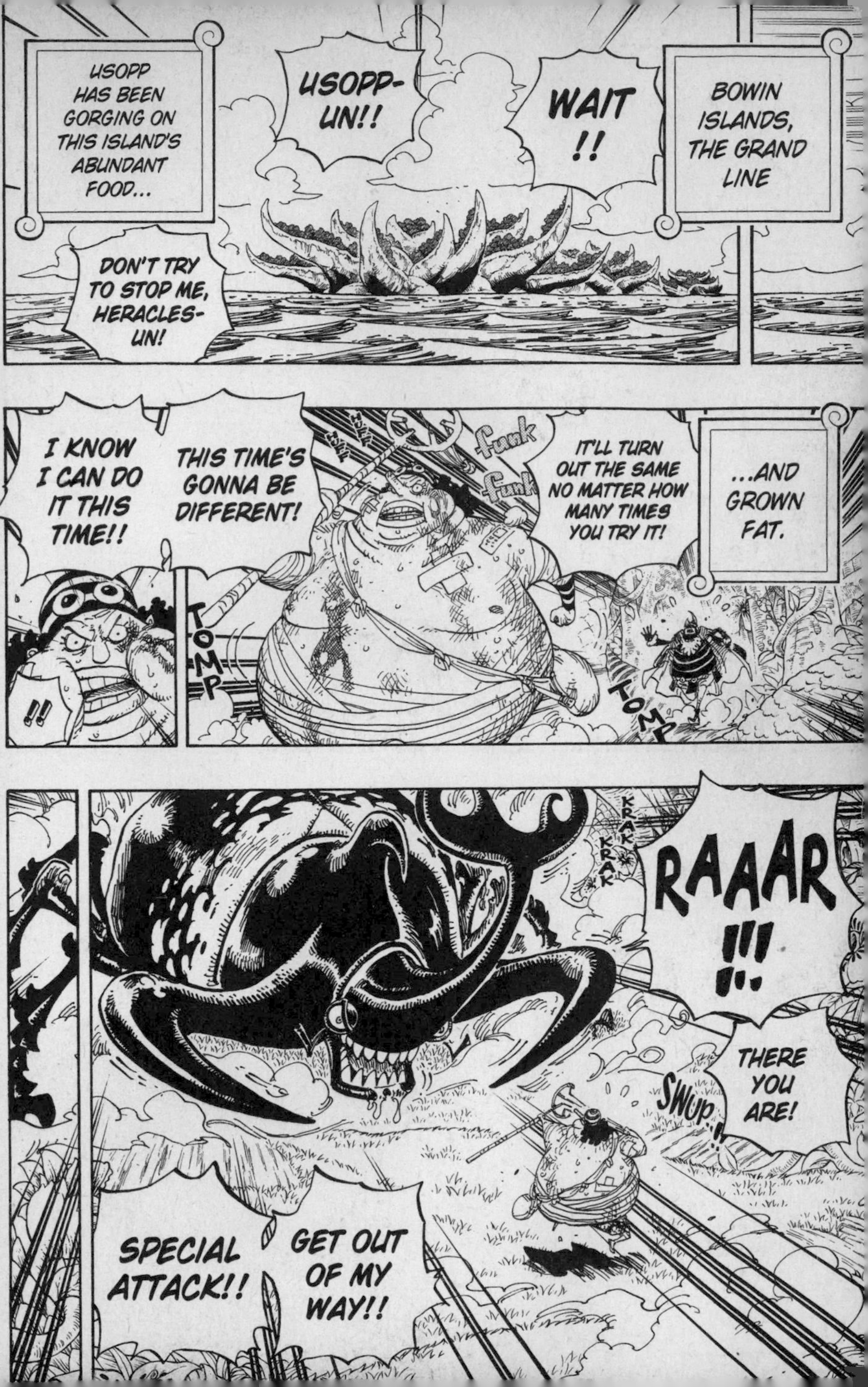
BOWIN ISLANDS, THE GRAND LINE
WAIT!!
USOPP-UN!!
USOPP HAS BEEN GORGING ON THIS ISLAND'S ABUNDANT FOOD...
DON'T TRY TO STOP ME, HERACLES-UN!
...AND GROWN FAT.
IT'LL TURN OUT THE SAME NO MATTER HOW MANY TIMES YOU TRY IT!
funk
funk
TOMP
THIS TIME'S GONNA BE DIFFERENT!
TOMP
I KNOW I CAN DO IT THIS TIME!!
!!
KRAK
KRAK
KRAK
RAAAR!!!
THERE YOU ARE!
SWUP
GET OUT OF MY WAY!!
SPECIAL ATTACK!!

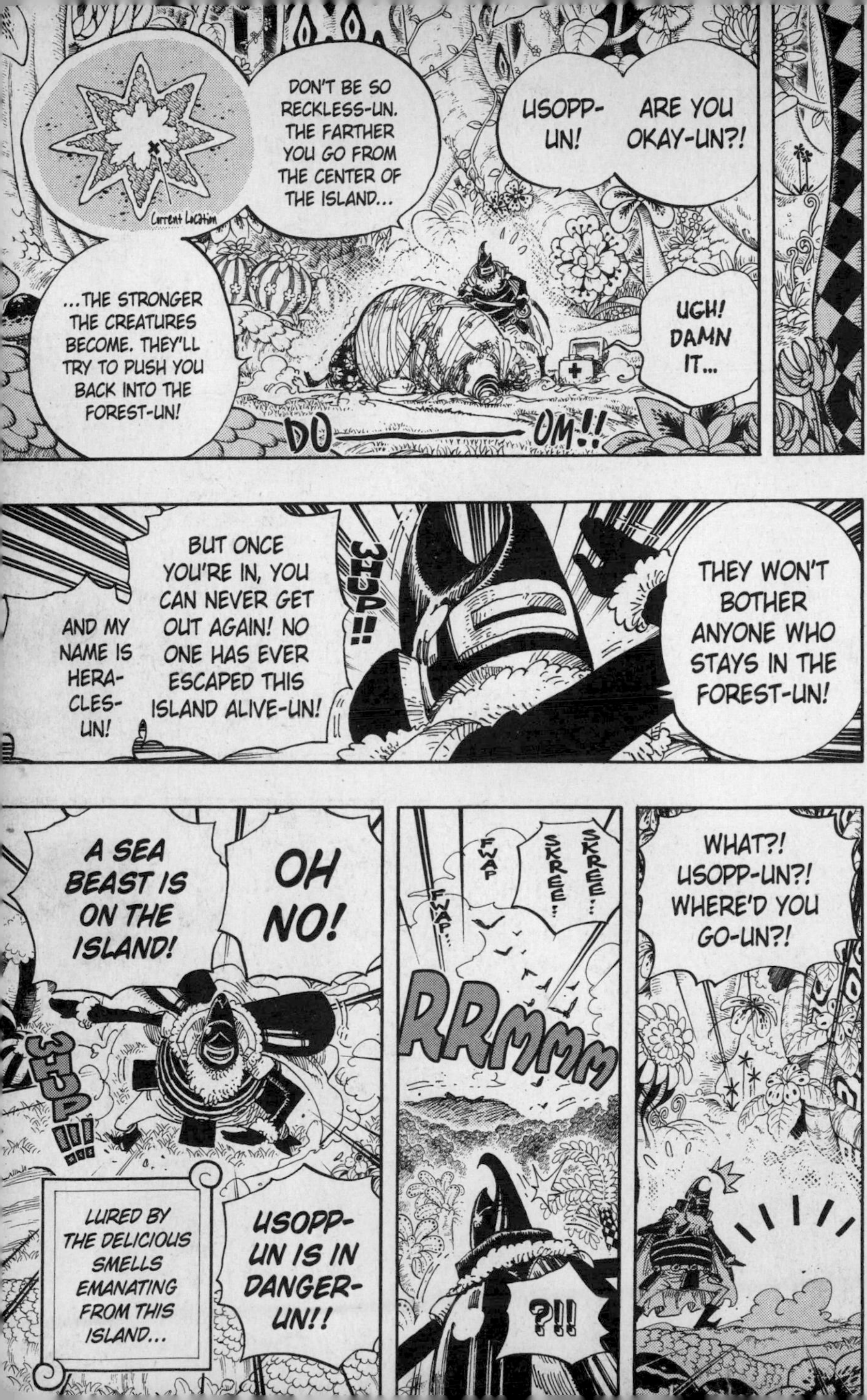
USOPP-UN! ARE YOU OKAY-UN?!
UGH! DAMN IT...
DON'T BE SO RECKLESS-UN. THE FARTHER YOU GO FROM THE CENTER OF THE ISLAND...
Current Location
...THE STRONGER THE CREATURES BECOME. THEY'LL TRY TO PUSH YOU BACK INTO THE FOREST-UN!
DO———OM!!
THEY WON'T BOTHER ANYONE WHO STAYS IN THE FOREST-UN!
WHUP!!
BUT ONCE YOU'RE IN, YOU CAN NEVER GET OUT AGAIN! NO ONE HAS EVER ESCAPED THIS ISLAND ALIVE-UN!
AND MY NAME IS HERA-CLES-UN!
WHAT?! USOPP-UN?! WHERE'D YOU GO-UN?!
SKREE...
SKREE...
FWAP
FWAP...
RRMMMM
?!!
OH NO!
A SEA BEAST IS ON THE ISLAND!
WHUP!!!
USOPP-UN IS IN DANGER-UN!!
LURED BY THE DELICIOUS SMELLS EMANATING FROM THIS ISLAND...

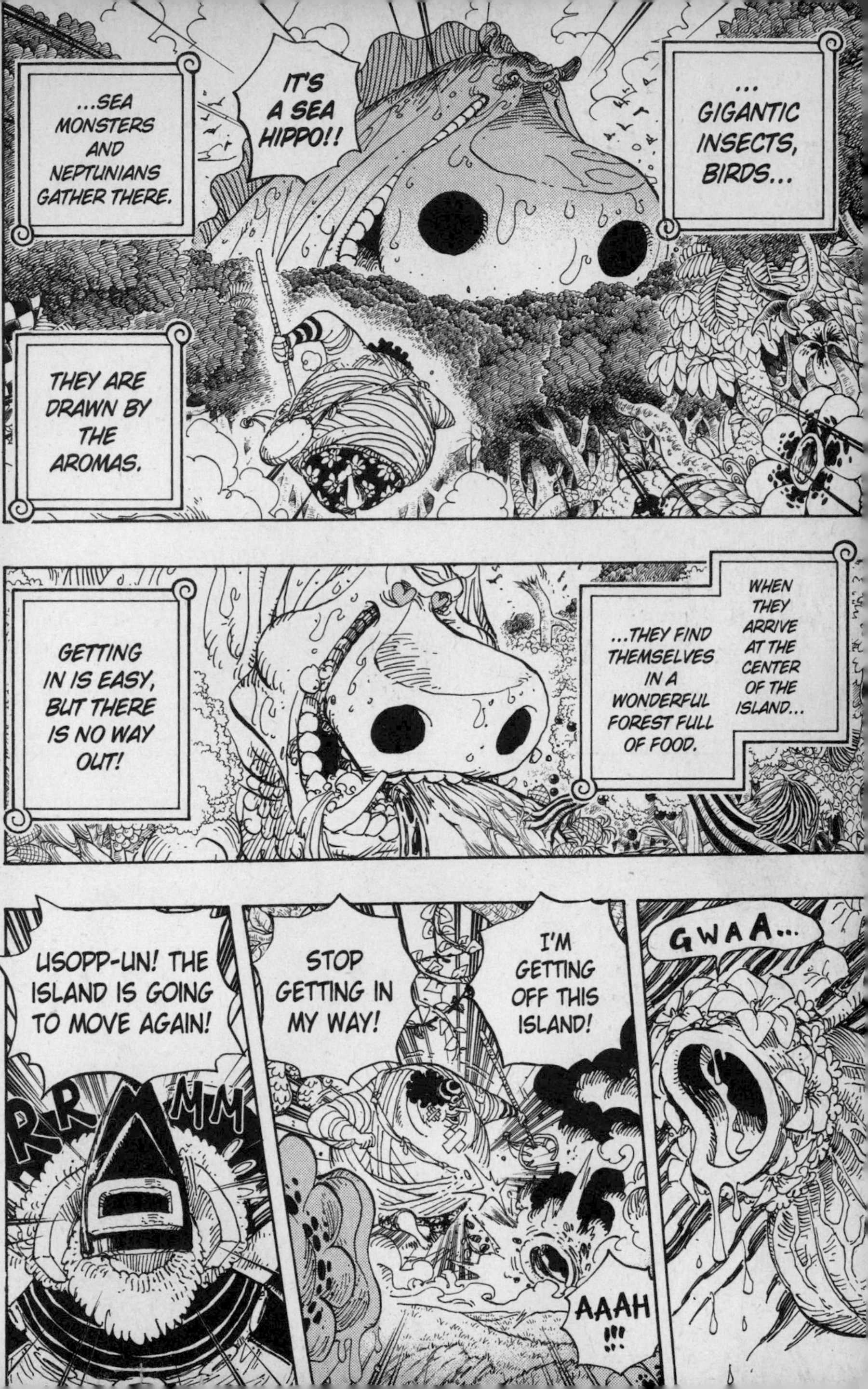
...GIGANTIC INSECTS, BIRDS...
IT'S A SEA HIPPO!!
...SEA MONSTERS AND NEPTUNIANS GATHER THERE.
THEY ARE DRAWN BY THE AROMAS.
WHEN THEY ARRIVE AT THE CENTER OF THE ISLAND...
...THEY FIND THEMSELVES IN A WONDERFUL FOREST FULL OF FOOD.
GETTING IN IS EASY, BUT THERE IS NO WAY OUT!
GWAA...
I'M GETTING OFF THIS ISLAND!
STOP GETTING IN MY WAY!
AAAH!!!
USOPP-UN! THE ISLAND IS GOING TO MOVE AGAIN!
RRMM

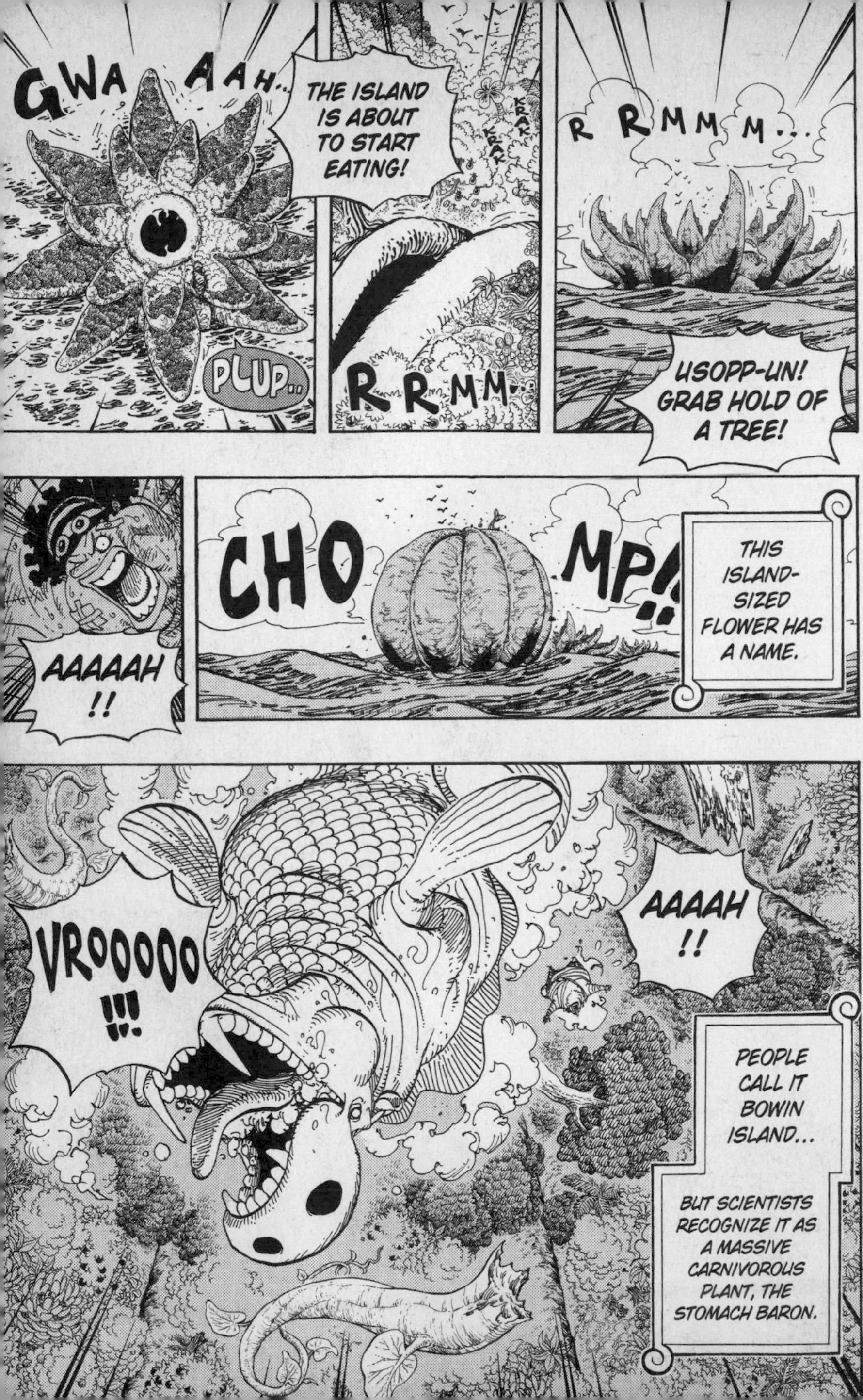

R RMMM M...
USOPP-UN! GRAB HOLD OF A TREE!
THE ISLAND IS ABOUT TO START EATING!
KRAK
KRAK
R R MM...
GWA AAH...
PLUP..
THIS ISLAND-SIZED FLOWER HAS A NAME.
CHO MP!!
AAAAAH !!
AAAAH !!
PEOPLE CALL IT BOWIN ISLAND...
BUT SCIENTISTS RECOGNIZE IT AS A MASSIVE CARNIVOROUS PLANT, THE STOMACH BARON.
VROOOOO !!!

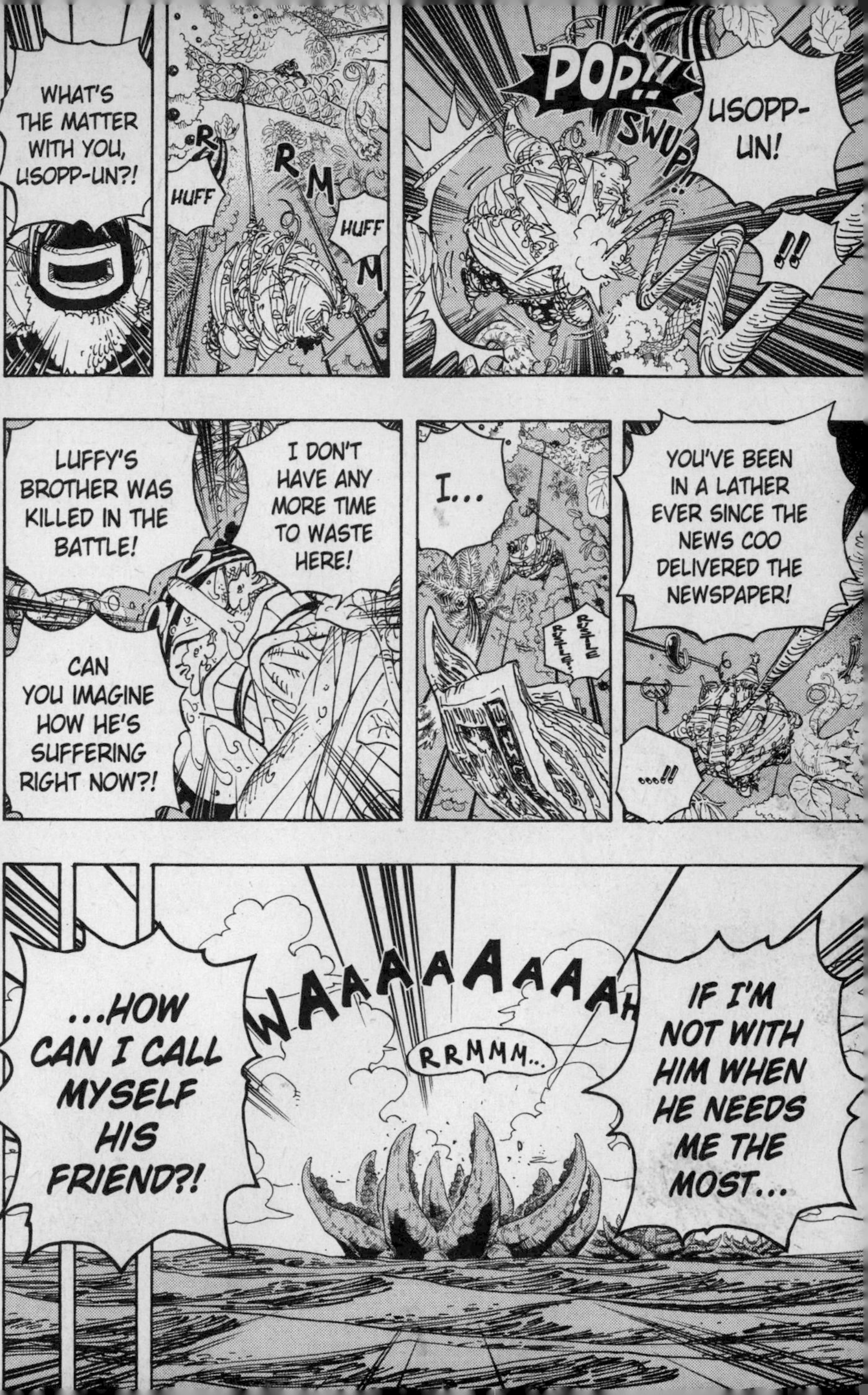
POP!!
SWUP!!
USOPP-UN!
!!
R R M M
HUFF
HUFF
WHAT'S THE MATTER WITH YOU, USOPP-UN?!
YOU'VE BEEN IN A LATHER EVER SINCE THE NEWS COO DELIVERED THE NEWSPAPER!
...!!
I...
I DON'T HAVE ANY MORE TIME TO WASTE HERE!
LUFFY'S BROTHER WAS KILLED IN THE BATTLE!
CAN YOU IMAGINE HOW HE'S SUFFERING RIGHT NOW?!
IF I'M NOT WITH HIM WHEN HE NEEDS ME THE MOST...
WAAAAAAAAAH
RRMMM...
...HOW CAN I CALL MYSELF HIS FRIEND?!

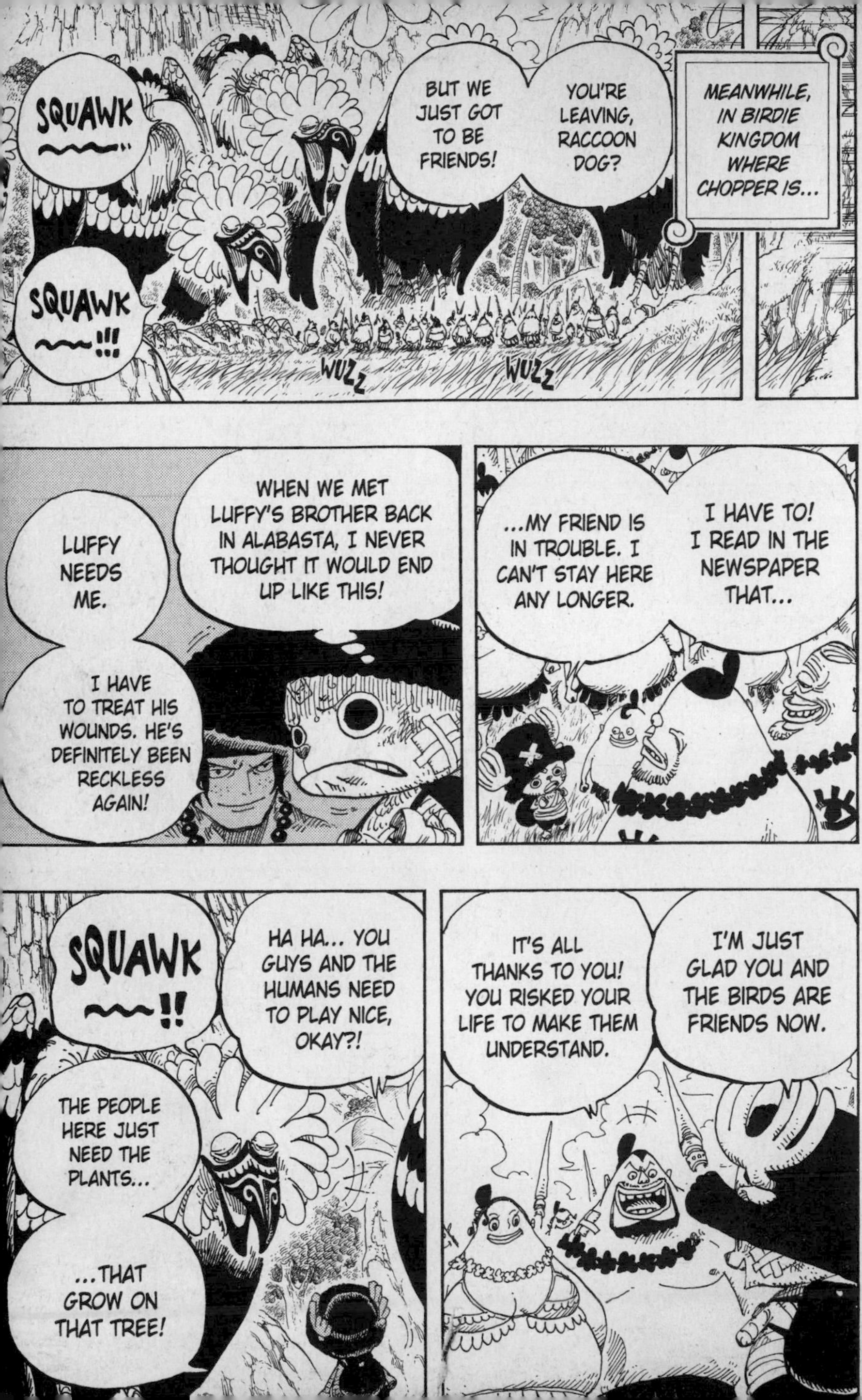
MEANWHILE, IN BIRDIE KINGDOM WHERE CHOPPER IS...
YOU'RE LEAVING, RACCOON DOG?
BUT WE JUST GOT TO BE FRIENDS!
SQUAWK ~~~!!
SQUAWK ~~~!!!
WUZZ
WUZZ
I HAVE TO! I READ IN THE NEWSPAPER THAT...
...MY FRIEND IS IN TROUBLE. I CAN'T STAY HERE ANY LONGER.
WHEN WE MET LUFFY'S BROTHER BACK IN ALABASTA, I NEVER THOUGHT IT WOULD END UP LIKE THIS!
LUFFY NEEDS ME.
I HAVE TO TREAT HIS WOUNDS. HE'S DEFINITELY BEEN RECKLESS AGAIN!
I'M JUST GLAD YOU AND THE BIRDS ARE FRIENDS NOW.
IT'S ALL THANKS TO YOU! YOU RISKED YOUR LIFE TO MAKE THEM UNDERSTAND.
HA HA... YOU GUYS AND THE HUMANS NEED TO PLAY NICE, OKAY?!
SQUAWK ~~~!!
THE PEOPLE HERE JUST NEED THE PLANTS...
...THAT GROW ON THAT TREE!

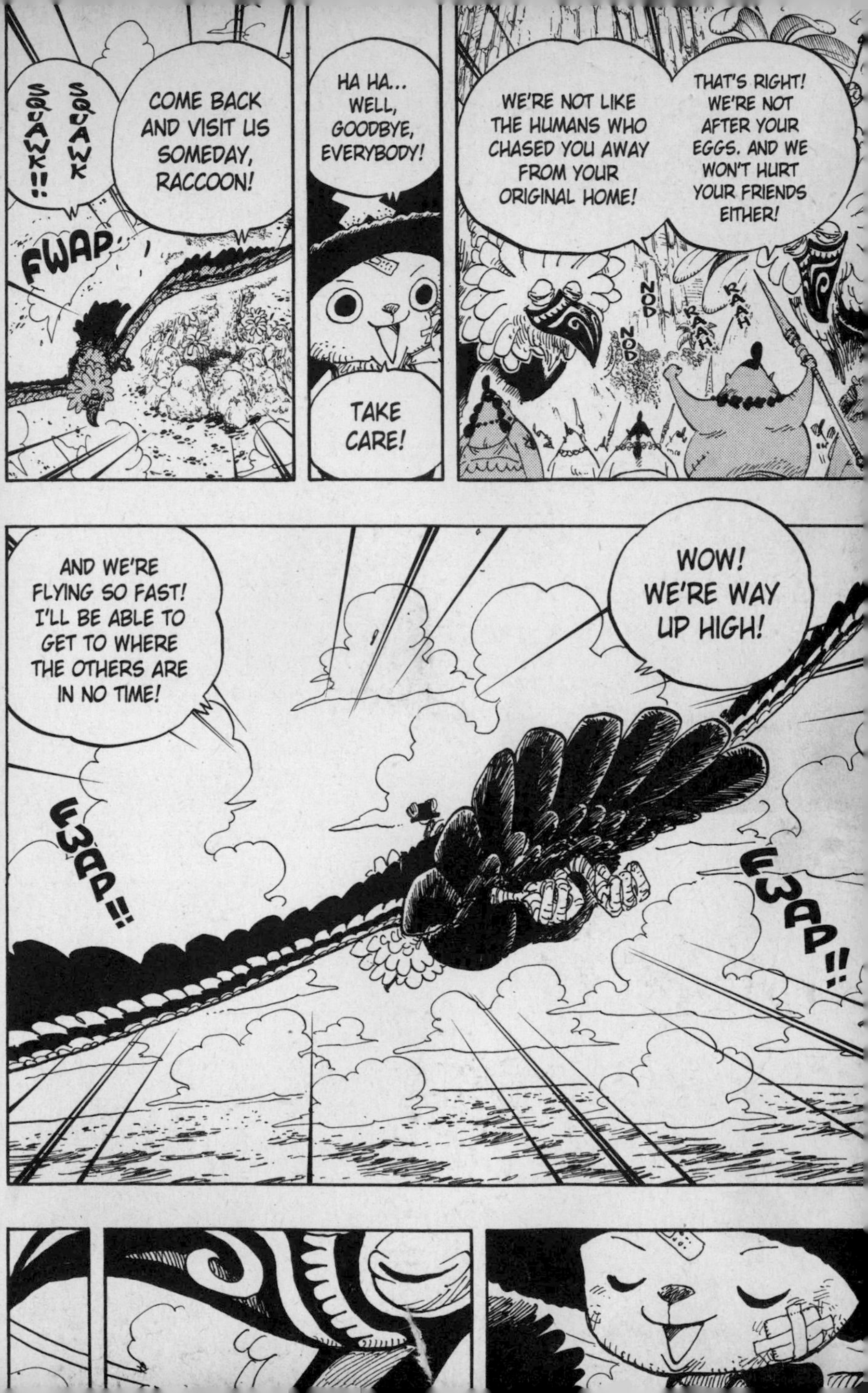
THAT'S RIGHT! WE'RE NOT AFTER YOUR EGGS. AND WE WON'T HURT YOUR FRIENDS EITHER!
WE'RE NOT LIKE THE HUMANS WHO CHASED YOU AWAY FROM YOUR ORIGINAL HOME!
RAAH RAAH
NOD NOD
HA HA... WELL, GOODBYE, EVERYBODY!
TAKE CARE!
COME BACK AND VISIT US SOMEDAY, RACCOON!
SQUAWK SQUAWK!!
FWAP
WOW! WE'RE WAY UP HIGH!
AND WE'RE FLYING SO FAST! I'LL BE ABLE TO GET TO WHERE THE OTHERS ARE IN NO TIME!
FWAP!!
FWAP!!

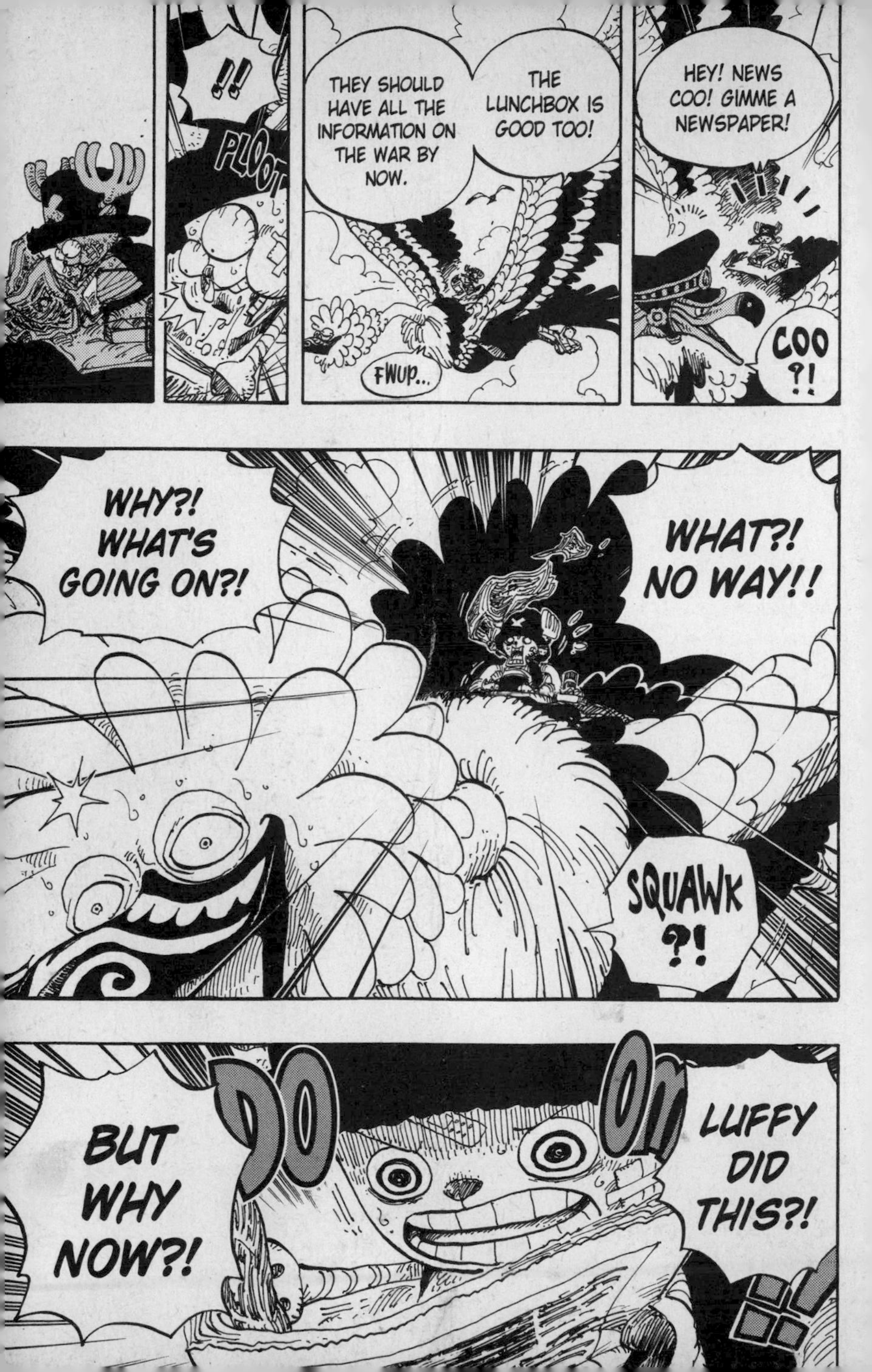
HEY! NEWS COO! GIMME A NEWSPAPER!
COO ?!
THE LUNCHBOX IS GOOD TOO!
THEY SHOULD HAVE ALL THE INFORMATION ON THE WAR BY NOW.
FWUP...
!!
PLOOT
WHAT?! NO WAY!!
SQUAWK ?!
WHY?! WHAT'S GOING ON?!
DOON
LUFFY DID THIS?!
BUT WHY NOW?!

SBS Question Corner

質問コーナー
エス
ビー
エス

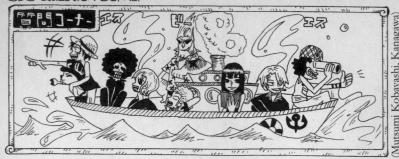

(Mutsumi Kobayashi, Kanagawa)

Q: Mr. Oda! Hello! This may be sudden, but give my wooper looper (gender unknown) a name! Please!
--Uaaaauoooo

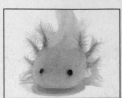

A: A wooper looper? Those used to be really popular. They're really cute salamanders from Mexico, right? And their official name is axolotl. I came up with a name you can use: Axoaxo-Axoboy. Please take good care of it.

Q: Hello, Mr. Oda! This is just a guess, but in chapter 558 (volume 57), there's a shadow on the left edge in the third panel of page 11. Is it Sabo's cup?
--Saito Ryo

FROM NOW ON...
PLUP PLUP PLUP
...WE'RE BROTHERS!

A: Wow, you guys really pick up on the details. The answer to that is revealed in chapter 585 of this volume. If you read that, you'll see the same scene there. You can tell it's Sabo's cup. But back in chapter 558, revealing Sabo's existence would've complicated things way too much. That's why when lots of people asked me, "What's that shadow there?!" I was really surprised and nervous. What's with you people?! You were right!

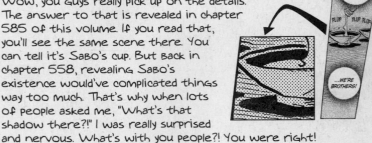

Q: I noticed while reading *One Piece* that, except for the character introductions and Question Corners, you never recycle old pictures for flashbacks and stuff. Is that a personal policy of yours?
--Soramame

A: You noticed that? The answer is yes. I never copy and paste any of my old drawings. Shueisha (Publishing Company) pays us a manuscript fee and it's by the page. So since we're getting paid by the page, I thought it would be kind of cheap to recycle stuff I'd drawn in the past. (Ha!) But this is by no means a shot at other comic authors. This is just something I do because it's in my nature to do it. It lets me keep drawing comics with all of my heart. Yes, I know, I sound like a sucker. I think it just shows that I'm an earnest-minded person who's not at all lewd. Seriously.

Chapter 592:
CHEER

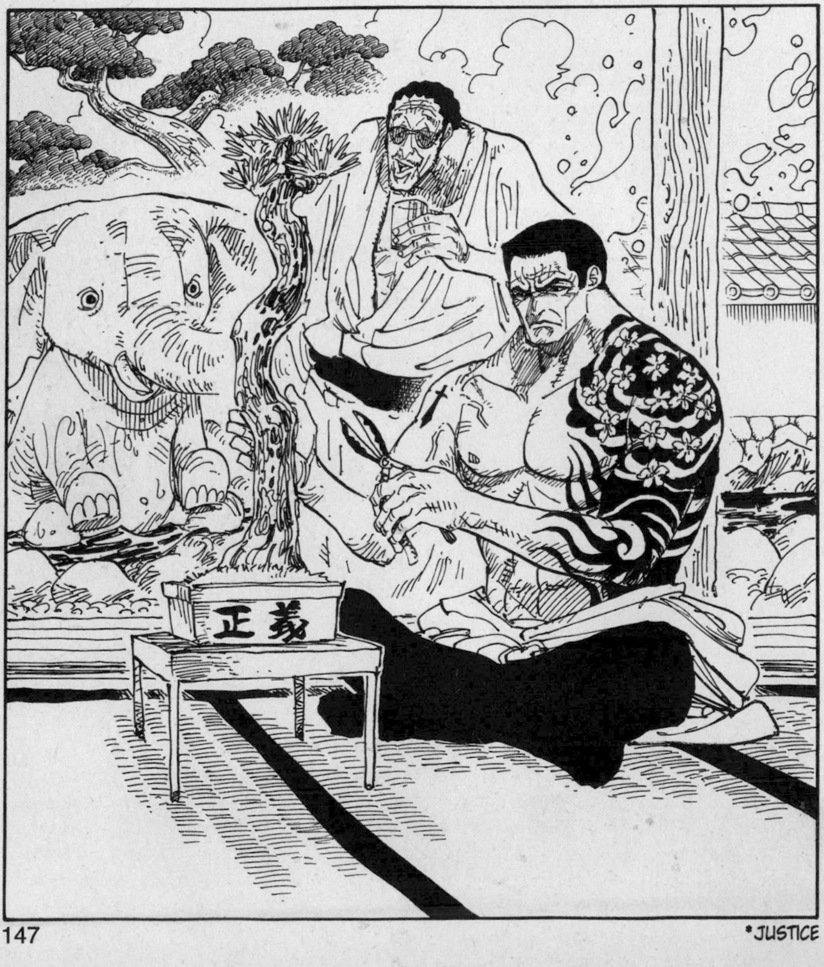
正義

*JUSTICE

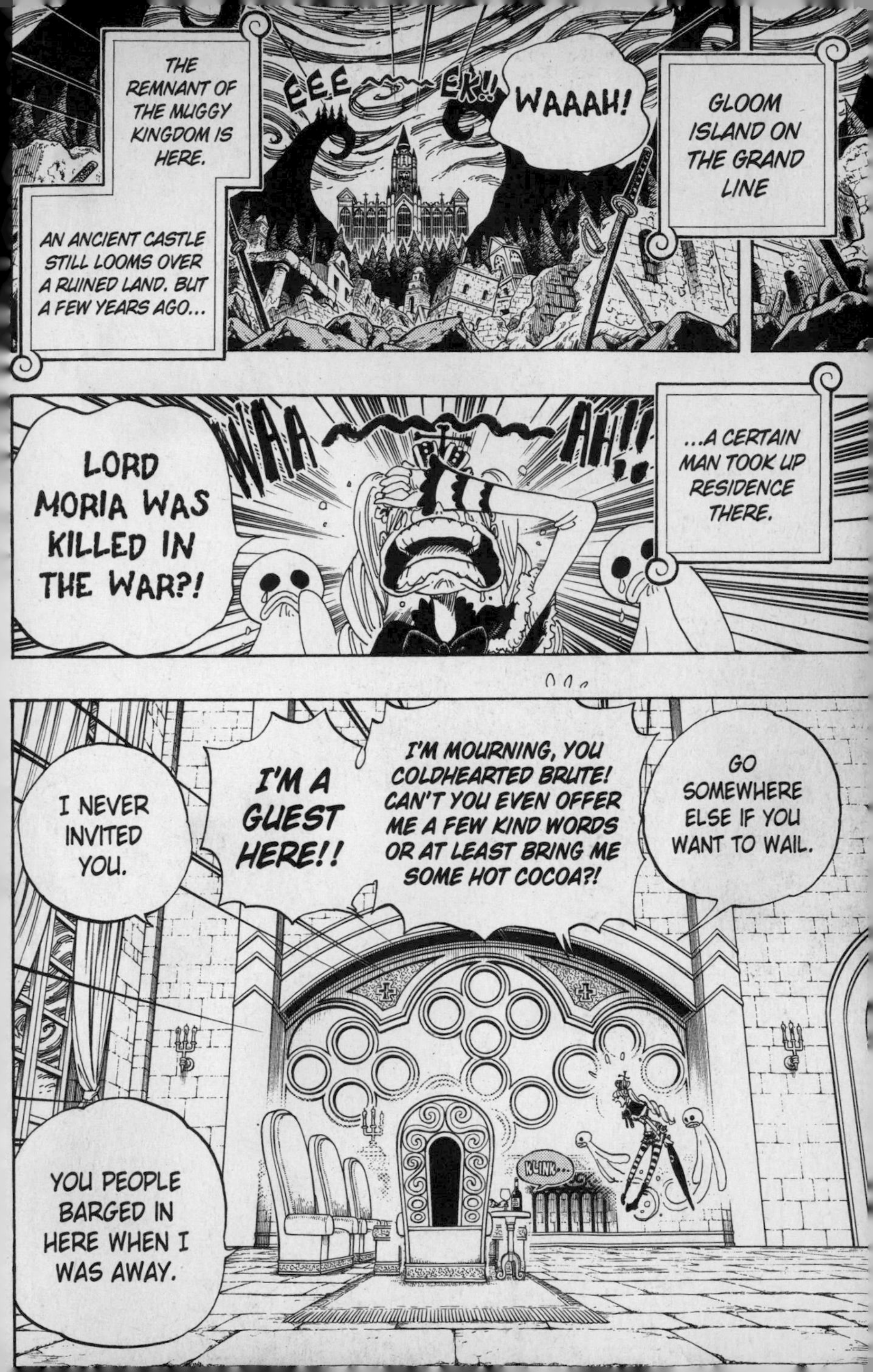

GLOOM ISLAND ON THE GRAND LINE
WAAAH!
EEE~EK!!
THE REMNANT OF THE MUGGY KINGDOM IS HERE.
AN ANCIENT CASTLE STILL LOOMS OVER A RUINED LAND. BUT A FEW YEARS AGO...
...A CERTAIN MAN TOOK UP RESIDENCE THERE.
WAA~AH!!
LORD MORIA WAS KILLED IN THE WAR?!
GO SOMEWHERE ELSE IF YOU WANT TO WAIL.
I'M MOURNING, YOU COLDHEARTED BRUTE! CAN'T YOU EVEN OFFER ME A FEW KIND WORDS OR AT LEAST BRING ME SOME HOT COCOA?!
I'M A GUEST HERE!!
I NEVER INVITED YOU.
KLINK...
YOU PEOPLE BARGED IN HERE WHEN I WAS AWAY.

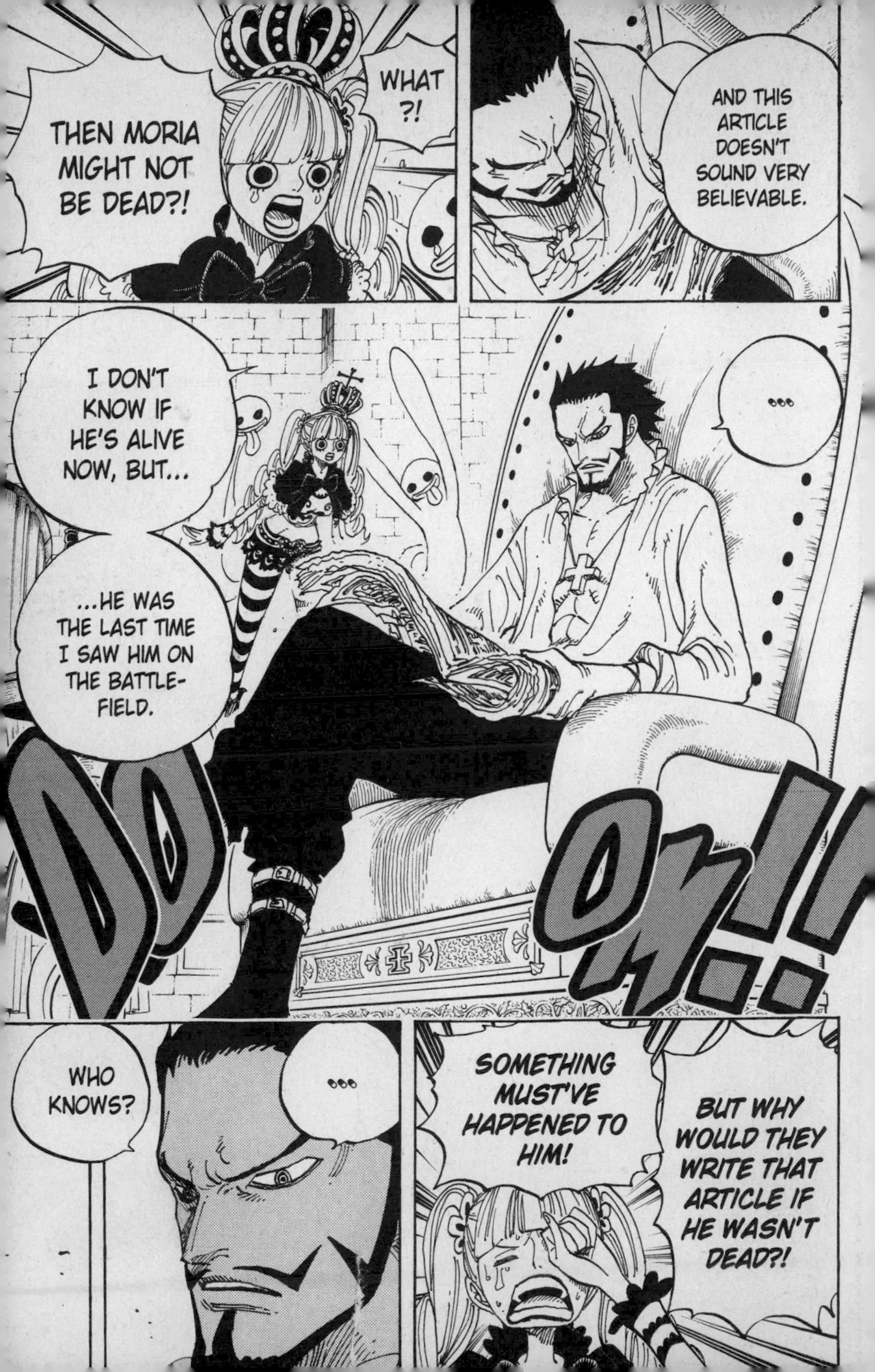
AND THIS ARTICLE DOESN'T SOUND VERY BELIEVABLE.
WHAT ?!
THEN MORIA MIGHT NOT BE DEAD?!
...
I DON'T KNOW IF HE'S ALIVE NOW, BUT...
...HE WAS THE LAST TIME I SAW HIM ON THE BATTLE-FIELD.
DOOn!!
BUT WHY WOULD THEY WRITE THAT ARTICLE IF HE WASN'T DEAD?!
SOMETHING MUST'VE HAPPENED TO HIM!
...
WHO KNOWS?

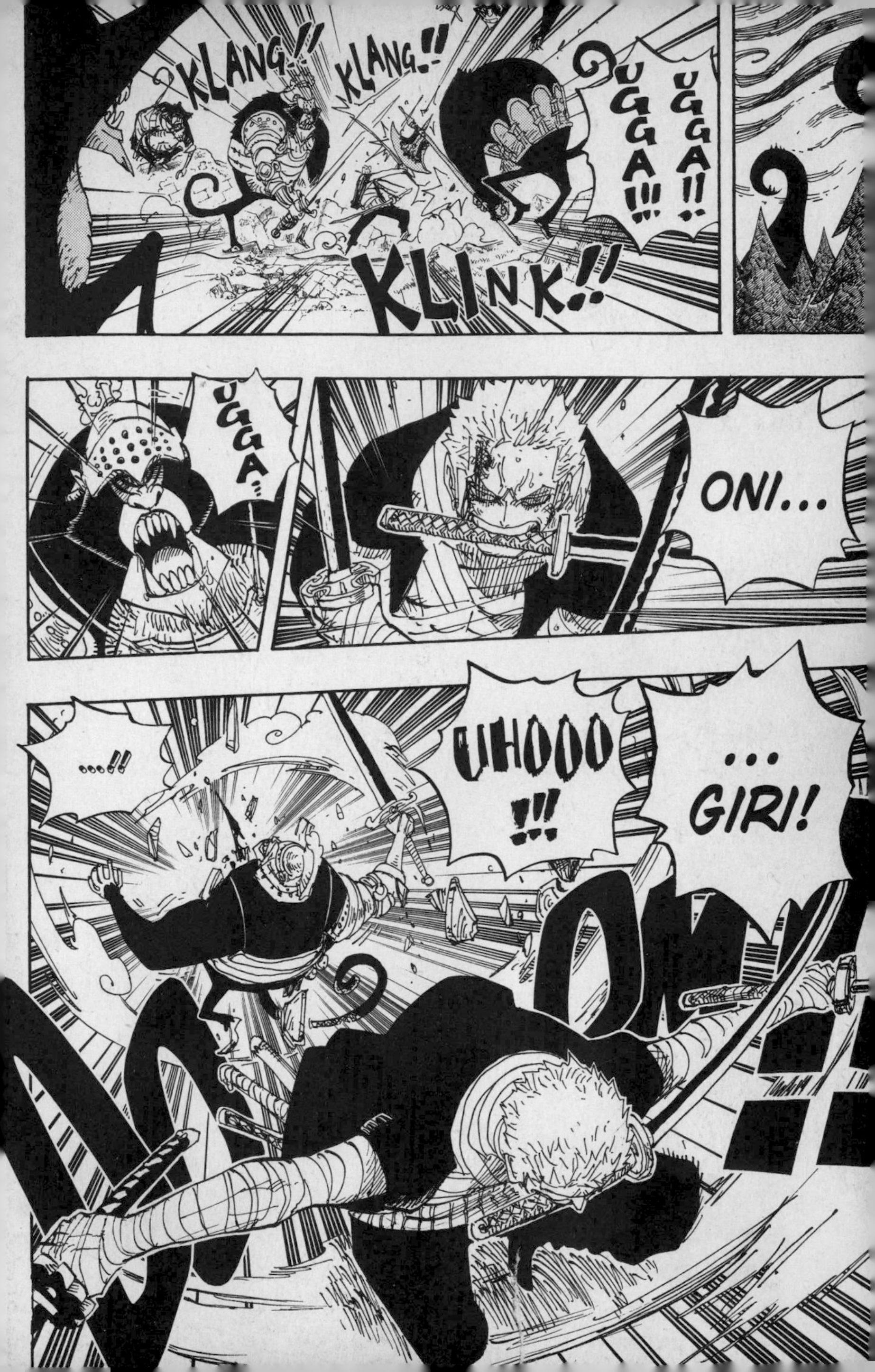
UGGA!!
UGGA!!!
KLANG!!
KLANG!!
KLINK!!
ONI...
UGGA...
...GIRI!
UHOOO!!!
...!!

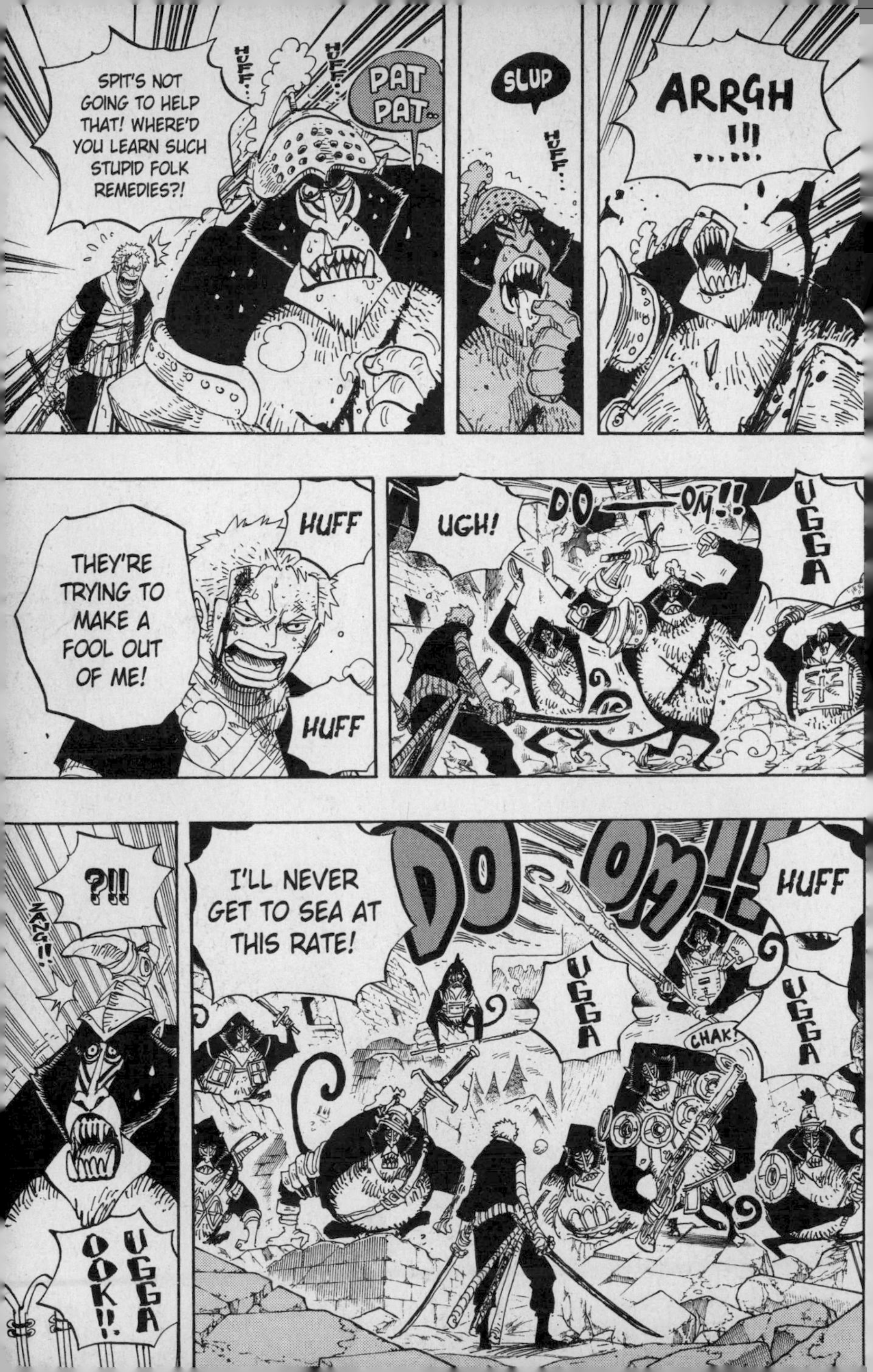
ARRGH
!!!
......
SLUP
HUFF...
PAT PAT..
HUFF...
HUFF...
SPIT'S NOT GOING TO HELP THAT! WHERE'D YOU LEARN SUCH STUPID FOLK REMEDIES?!
DO—OM!!
UGGA
UGH!
HUFF
THEY'RE TRYING TO MAKE A FOOL OUT OF ME!
HUFF
DO—OM!!
HUFF
I'LL NEVER GET TO SEA AT THIS RATE!
UGGA
UGGA
CHAK!
?!!
ZANG!!
UGGA
OOK!!

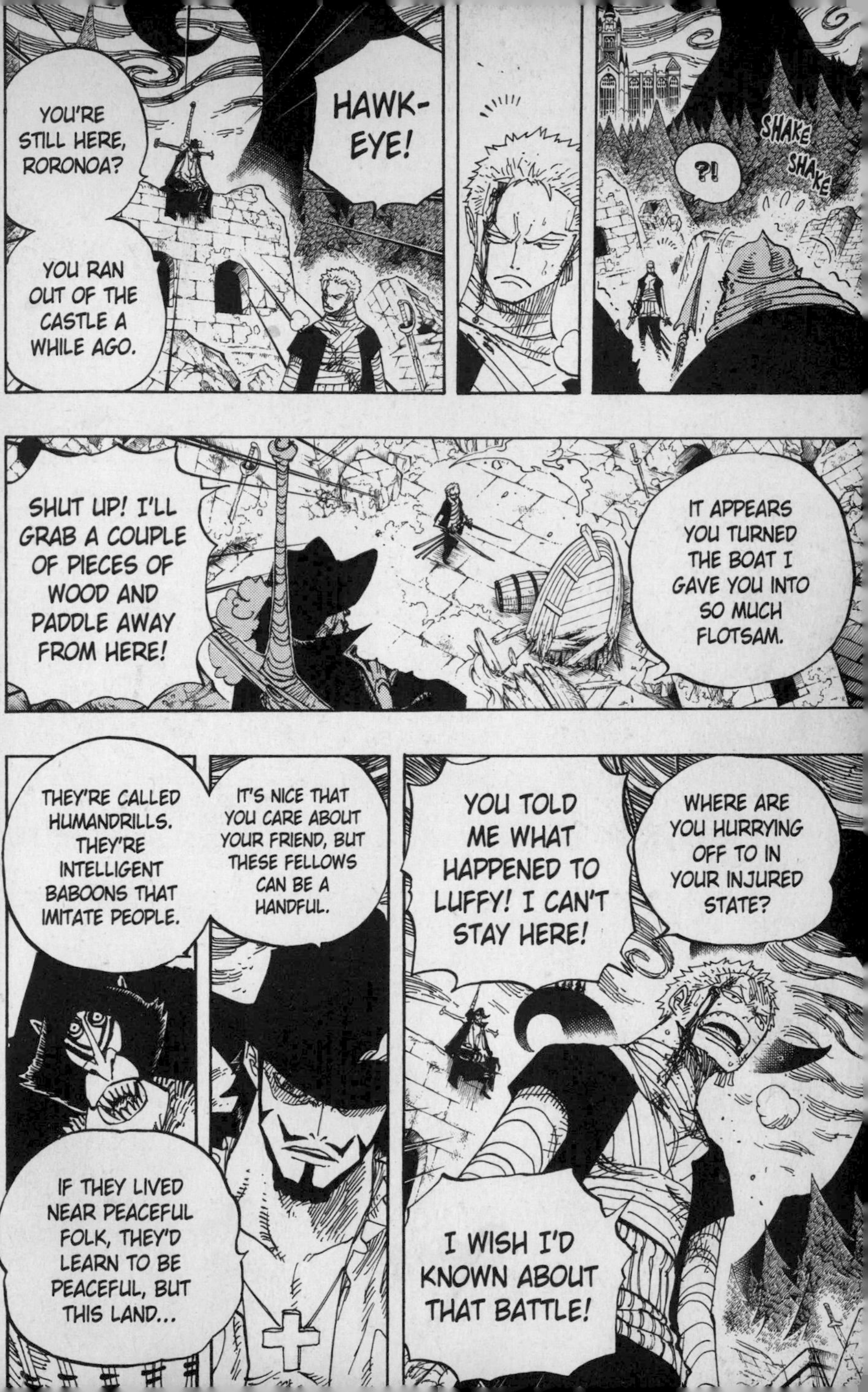
SHAKE
SHAKE
?!
HAWK-EYE!
YOU'RE STILL HERE, RORONOA?
YOU RAN OUT OF THE CASTLE A WHILE AGO.
IT APPEARS YOU TURNED THE BOAT I GAVE YOU INTO SO MUCH FLOTSAM.
SHUT UP! I'LL GRAB A COUPLE OF PIECES OF WOOD AND PADDLE AWAY FROM HERE!
WHERE ARE YOU HURRYING OFF TO IN YOUR INJURED STATE?
YOU TOLD ME WHAT HAPPENED TO LUFFY! I CAN'T STAY HERE!
I WISH I'D KNOWN ABOUT THAT BATTLE!
IT'S NICE THAT YOU CARE ABOUT YOUR FRIEND, BUT THESE FELLOWS CAN BE A HANDFUL.
THEY'RE CALLED HUMANDRILLS. THEY'RE INTELLIGENT BABOONS THAT IMITATE PEOPLE.
IF THEY LIVED NEAR PEACEFUL FOLK, THEY'D LEARN TO BE PEACEFUL, BUT THIS LAND...

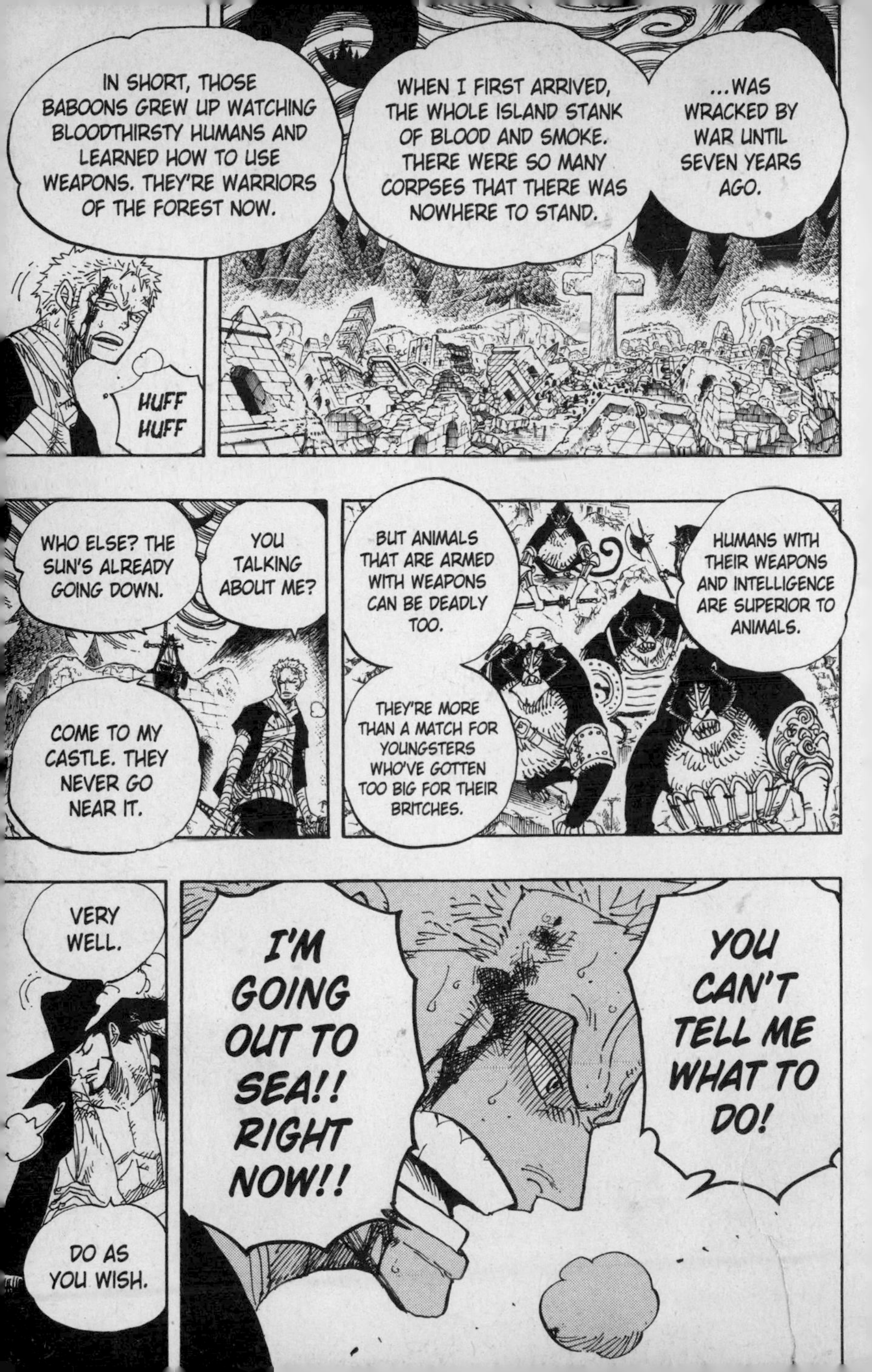
...WAS WRACKED BY WAR UNTIL SEVEN YEARS AGO.
WHEN I FIRST ARRIVED, THE WHOLE ISLAND STANK OF BLOOD AND SMOKE. THERE WERE SO MANY CORPSES THAT THERE WAS NOWHERE TO STAND.
IN SHORT, THOSE BABOONS GREW UP WATCHING BLOODTHIRSTY HUMANS AND LEARNED HOW TO USE WEAPONS. THEY'RE WARRIORS OF THE FOREST NOW.
HUFF HUFF
HUMANS WITH THEIR WEAPONS AND INTELLIGENCE ARE SUPERIOR TO ANIMALS.
BUT ANIMALS THAT ARE ARMED WITH WEAPONS CAN BE DEADLY TOO.
THEY'RE MORE THAN A MATCH FOR YOUNGSTERS WHO'VE GOTTEN TOO BIG FOR THEIR BRITCHES.
YOU TALKING ABOUT ME?
WHO ELSE? THE SUN'S ALREADY GOING DOWN.
COME TO MY CASTLE. THEY NEVER GO NEAR IT.
YOU CAN'T TELL ME WHAT TO DO!
I'M GOING OUT TO SEA!! RIGHT NOW!!
VERY WELL.
DO AS YOU WISH.

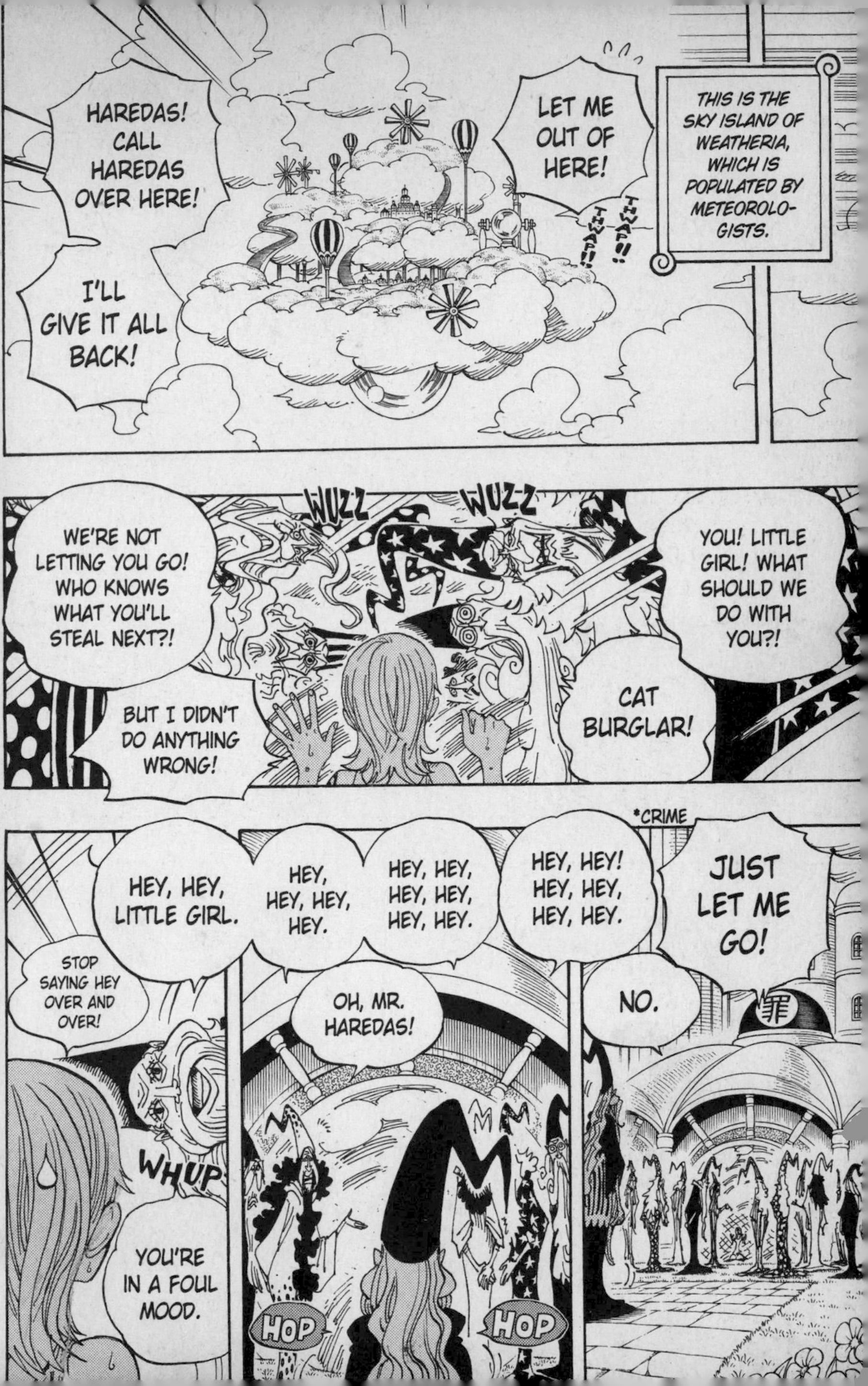
THIS IS THE SKY ISLAND OF WEATHERIA, WHICH IS POPULATED BY METEOROLOGISTS.
LET ME OUT OF HERE!
THWAP!!
THWAP!!
HAREDAS! CALL HAREDAS OVER HERE!
I'LL GIVE IT ALL BACK!
YOU! LITTLE GIRL! WHAT SHOULD WE DO WITH YOU?!
CAT BURGLAR!
WUZZ
WUZZ
WE'RE NOT LETTING YOU GO! WHO KNOWS WHAT YOU'LL STEAL NEXT?!
BUT I DIDN'T DO ANYTHING WRONG!
*CRIME
JUST LET ME GO!
罪
NO.
HEY, HEY! HEY, HEY, HEY, HEY.
HEY, HEY, HEY, HEY, HEY, HEY.
HEY, HEY, HEY, HEY.
OH, MR. HAREDAS!
HOP
HOP
HEY, HEY, LITTLE GIRL.
STOP SAYING HEY OVER AND OVER!
WHUP
YOU'RE IN A FOUL MOOD.

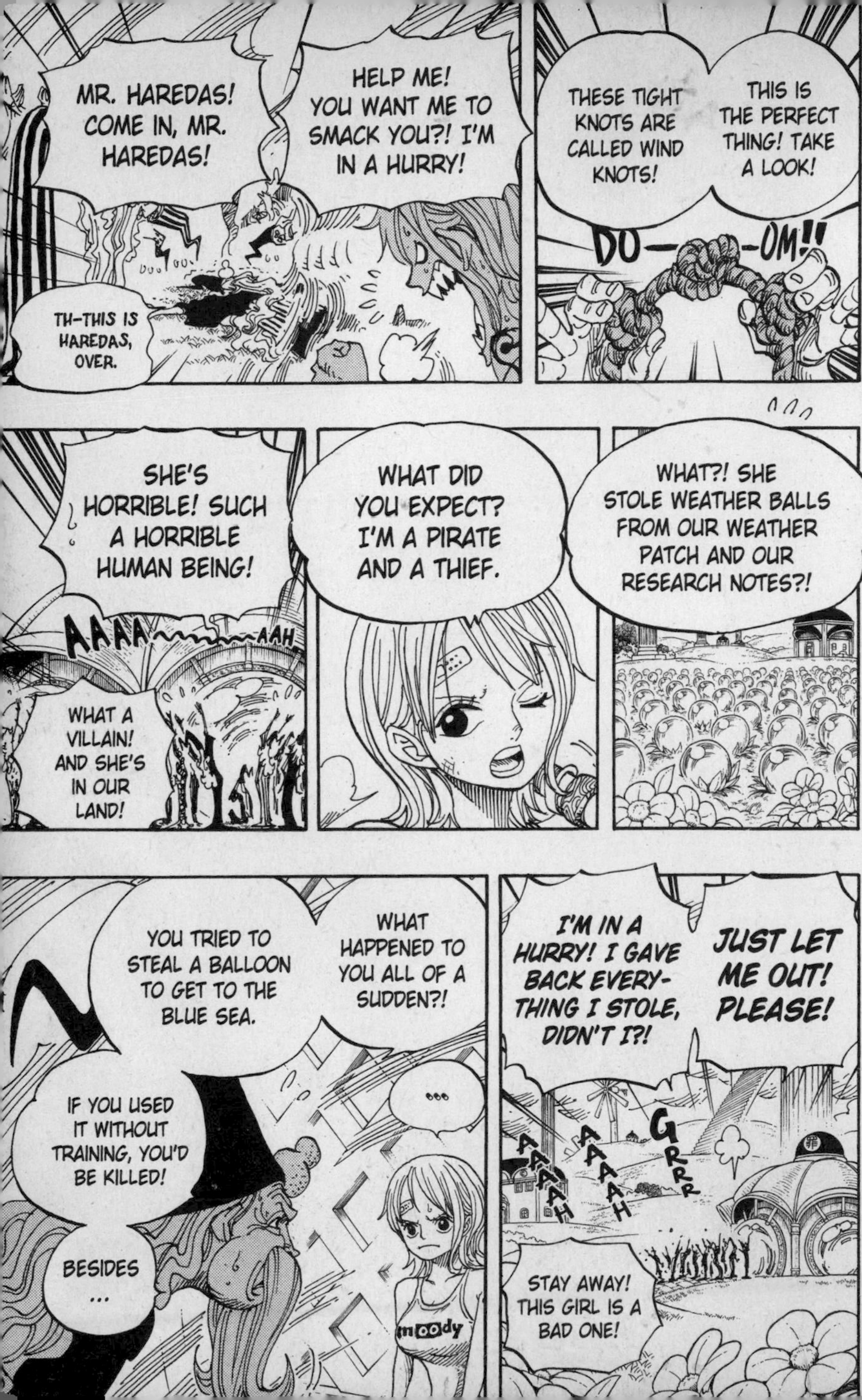
THIS IS THE PERFECT THING! TAKE A LOOK!
THESE TIGHT KNOTS ARE CALLED WIND KNOTS!
DO—-OM!!
HELP ME! YOU WANT ME TO SMACK YOU?! I'M IN A HURRY!
MR. HAREDAS! COME IN, MR. HAREDAS!
TH-THIS IS HAREDAS, OVER.
WHAT?! SHE STOLE WEATHER BALLS FROM OUR WEATHER PATCH AND OUR RESEARCH NOTES?!
WHAT DID YOU EXPECT? I'M A PIRATE AND A THIEF.
SHE'S HORRIBLE! SUCH A HORRIBLE HUMAN BEING!
AAAA~AAH
WHAT A VILLAIN! AND SHE'S IN OUR LAND!
JUST LET ME OUT! PLEASE!
I'M IN A HURRY! I GAVE BACK EVERY-THING I STOLE, DIDN'T I?!
AAAAH
AAAAH
GRRR
STAY AWAY! THIS GIRL IS A BAD ONE!
WHAT HAPPENED TO YOU ALL OF A SUDDEN?!
YOU TRIED TO STEAL A BALLOON TO GET TO THE BLUE SEA.
...
IF YOU USED IT WITHOUT TRAINING, YOU'D BE KILLED!
BESIDES ...
moody

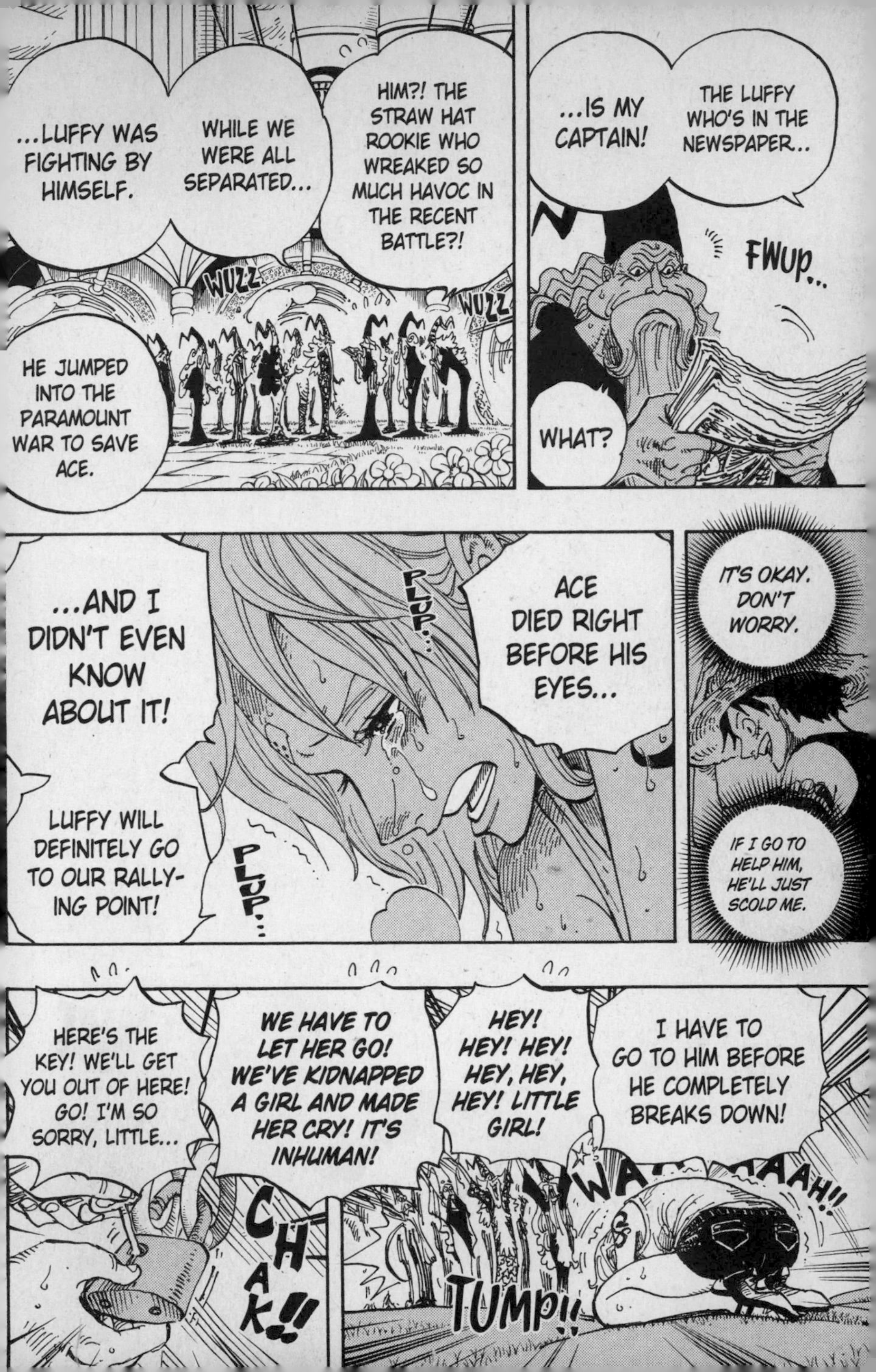
THE LUFFY WHO'S IN THE NEWSPAPER...
...IS MY CAPTAIN!
FWUP...
WHAT?
HIM?! THE STRAW HAT ROOKIE WHO WREAKED SO MUCH HAVOC IN THE RECENT BATTLE?!
WHILE WE WERE ALL SEPARATED...
...LUFFY WAS FIGHTING BY HIMSELF.
WUZZ
WUZZ
HE JUMPED INTO THE PARAMOUNT WAR TO SAVE ACE.
IT'S OKAY. DON'T WORRY.
IF I GO TO HELP HIM, HE'LL JUST SCOLD ME.
ACE DIED RIGHT BEFORE HIS EYES...
PLUP...
...AND I DIDN'T EVEN KNOW ABOUT IT!
PLUP...
LUFFY WILL DEFINITELY GO TO OUR RALLY-ING POINT!
I HAVE TO GO TO HIM BEFORE HE COMPLETELY BREAKS DOWN!
HEY! HEY! HEY! HEY, HEY, HEY! LITTLE GIRL!
WE HAVE TO LET HER GO! WE'VE KIDNAPPED A GIRL AND MADE HER CRY! IT'S INHUMAN!
HERE'S THE KEY! WE'LL GET YOU OUT OF HERE! GO! I'M SO SORRY, LITTLE...
TUMP!!
CHAK!!

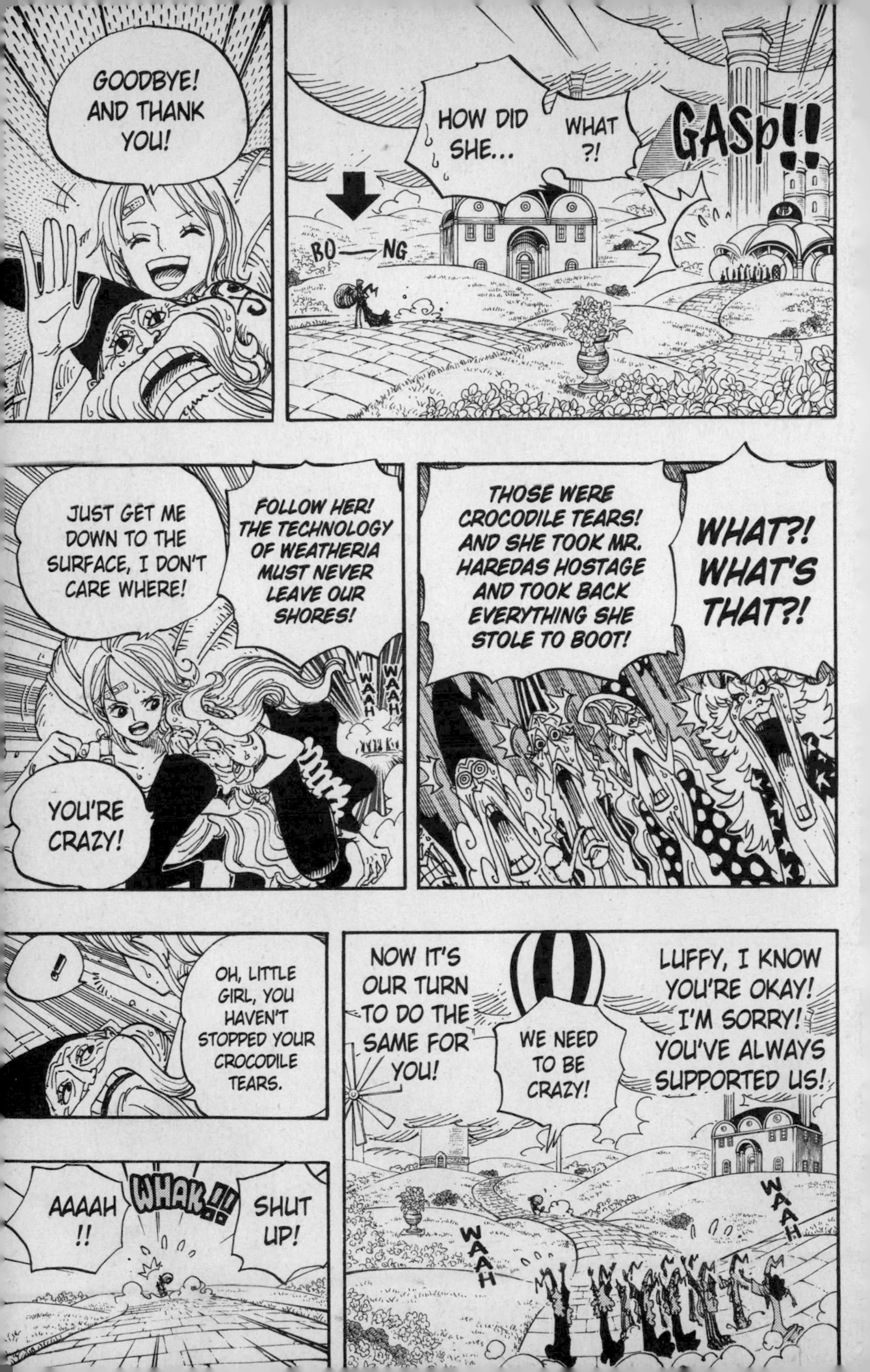
GASp!!
WHAT ?!
HOW DID SHE...
BO—NG
GOODBYE! AND THANK YOU!
WHAT?! WHAT'S THAT?!
THOSE WERE CROCODILE TEARS! AND SHE TOOK MR. HAREDAS HOSTAGE AND TOOK BACK EVERYTHING SHE STOLE TO BOOT!
FOLLOW HER! THE TECHNOLOGY OF WEATHERIA MUST NEVER LEAVE OUR SHORES!
WAAH
WAAH
JUST GET ME DOWN TO THE SURFACE, I DON'T CARE WHERE!
YOU'RE CRAZY!
LUFFY, I KNOW YOU'RE OKAY! I'M SORRY! YOU'VE ALWAYS SUPPORTED US!
WE NEED TO BE CRAZY!
NOW IT'S OUR TURN TO DO THE SAME FOR YOU!
WAAH
WAAH
OH, LITTLE GIRL, YOU HAVEN'T STOPPED YOUR CROCODILE TEARS.
!
SHUT UP!
WHAK!!
AAAAH !!

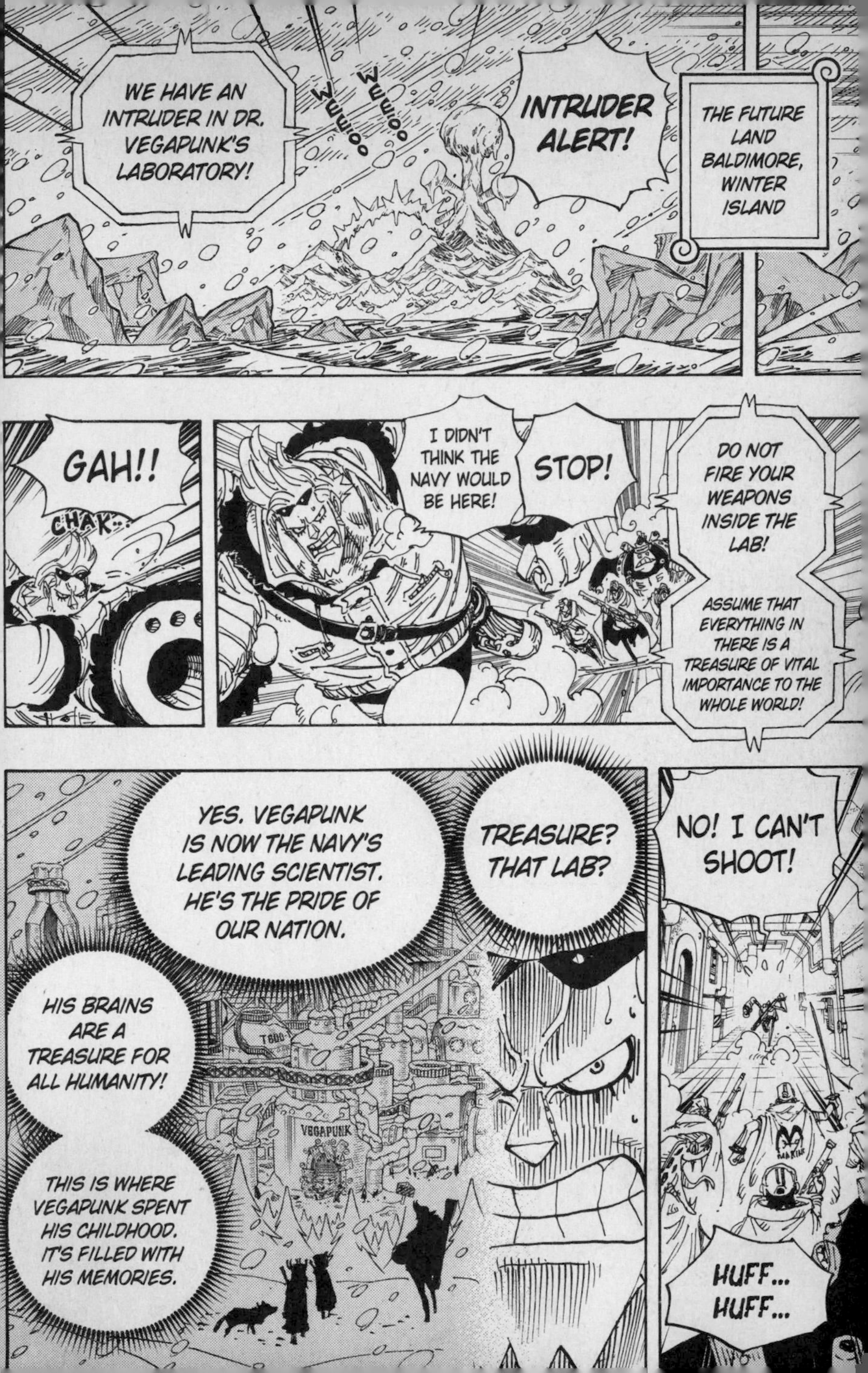
THE FUTURE LAND BALDIMORE, WINTER ISLAND
INTRUDER ALERT!
WEEOO
WEEOO
WE HAVE AN INTRUDER IN DR. VEGAPUNK'S LABORATORY!
DO NOT FIRE YOUR WEAPONS INSIDE THE LAB!
ASSUME THAT EVERYTHING IN THERE IS A TREASURE OF VITAL IMPORTANCE TO THE WHOLE WORLD!
STOP!
I DIDN'T THINK THE NAVY WOULD BE HERE!
GAH!!
CHAK...
NO! I CAN'T SHOOT!
HUFF... HUFF...
TREASURE? THAT LAB?
YES. VEGAPUNK IS NOW THE NAVY'S LEADING SCIENTIST. HE'S THE PRIDE OF OUR NATION.
HIS BRAINS ARE A TREASURE FOR ALL HUMANITY!
VEGAPUNK
THIS IS WHERE VEGAPUNK SPENT HIS CHILDHOOD. IT'S FILLED WITH HIS MEMORIES.

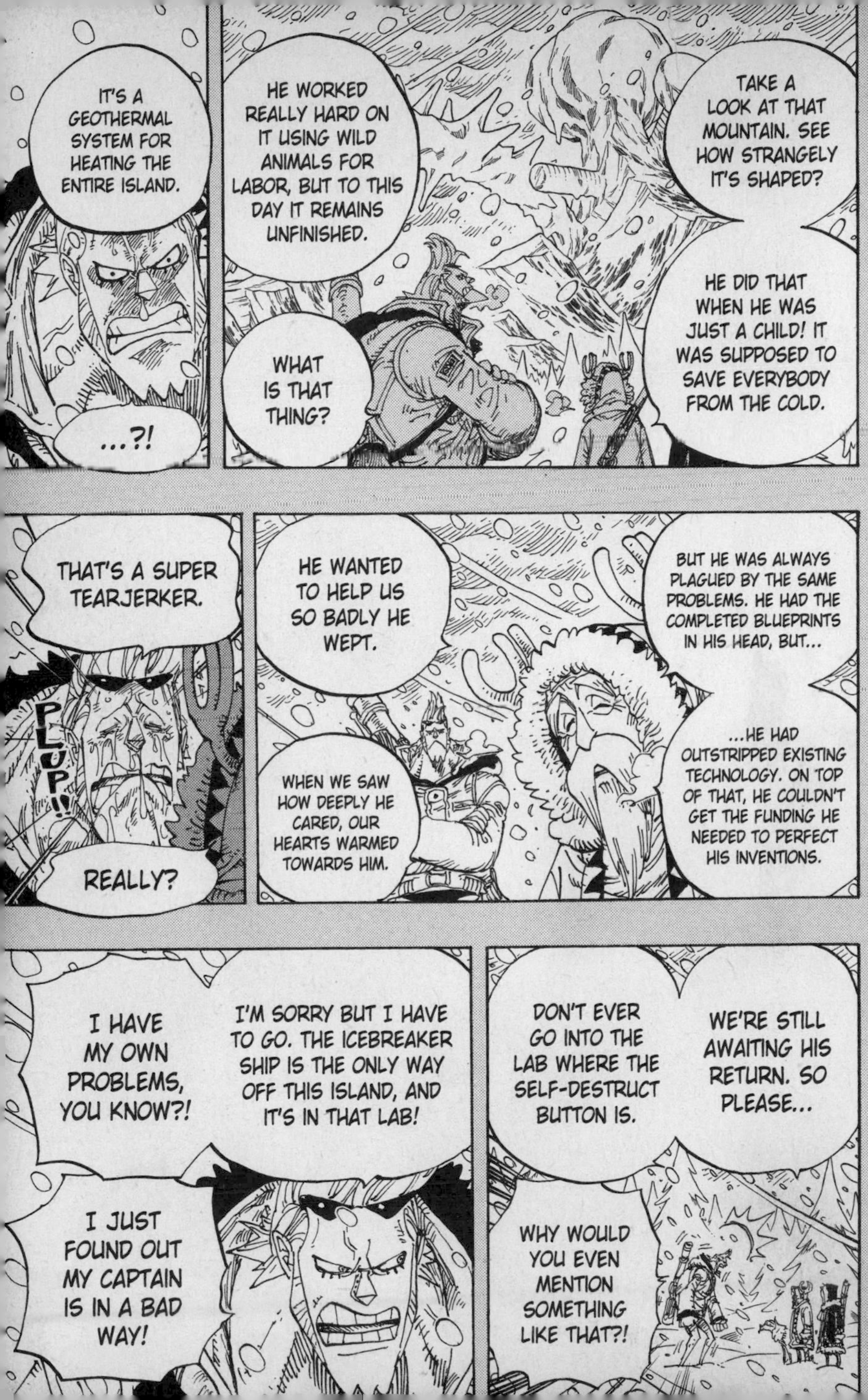
TAKE A LOOK AT THAT MOUNTAIN. SEE HOW STRANGELY IT'S SHAPED?
HE DID THAT WHEN HE WAS JUST A CHILD! IT WAS SUPPOSED TO SAVE EVERYBODY FROM THE COLD.
HE WORKED REALLY HARD ON IT USING WILD ANIMALS FOR LABOR, BUT TO THIS DAY IT REMAINS UNFINISHED.
WHAT IS THAT THING?
IT'S A GEOTHERMAL SYSTEM FOR HEATING THE ENTIRE ISLAND.
...?!
BUT HE WAS ALWAYS PLAGUED BY THE SAME PROBLEMS. HE HAD THE COMPLETED BLUEPRINTS IN HIS HEAD, BUT...
...HE HAD OUTSTRIPPED EXISTING TECHNOLOGY. ON TOP OF THAT, HE COULDN'T GET THE FUNDING HE NEEDED TO PERFECT HIS INVENTIONS.
HE WANTED TO HELP US SO BADLY HE WEPT.
WHEN WE SAW HOW DEEPLY HE CARED, OUR HEARTS WARMED TOWARDS HIM.
THAT'S A SUPER TEARJERKER.
PLUP!!
REALLY?
WE'RE STILL AWAITING HIS RETURN. SO PLEASE...
DON'T EVER GO INTO THE LAB WHERE THE SELF-DESTRUCT BUTTON IS.
WHY WOULD YOU EVEN MENTION SOMETHING LIKE THAT?!
I'M SORRY BUT I HAVE TO GO. THE ICEBREAKER SHIP IS THE ONLY WAY OFF THIS ISLAND, AND IT'S IN THAT LAB!
I HAVE MY OWN PROBLEMS, YOU KNOW?!
I JUST FOUND OUT MY CAPTAIN IS IN A BAD WAY!

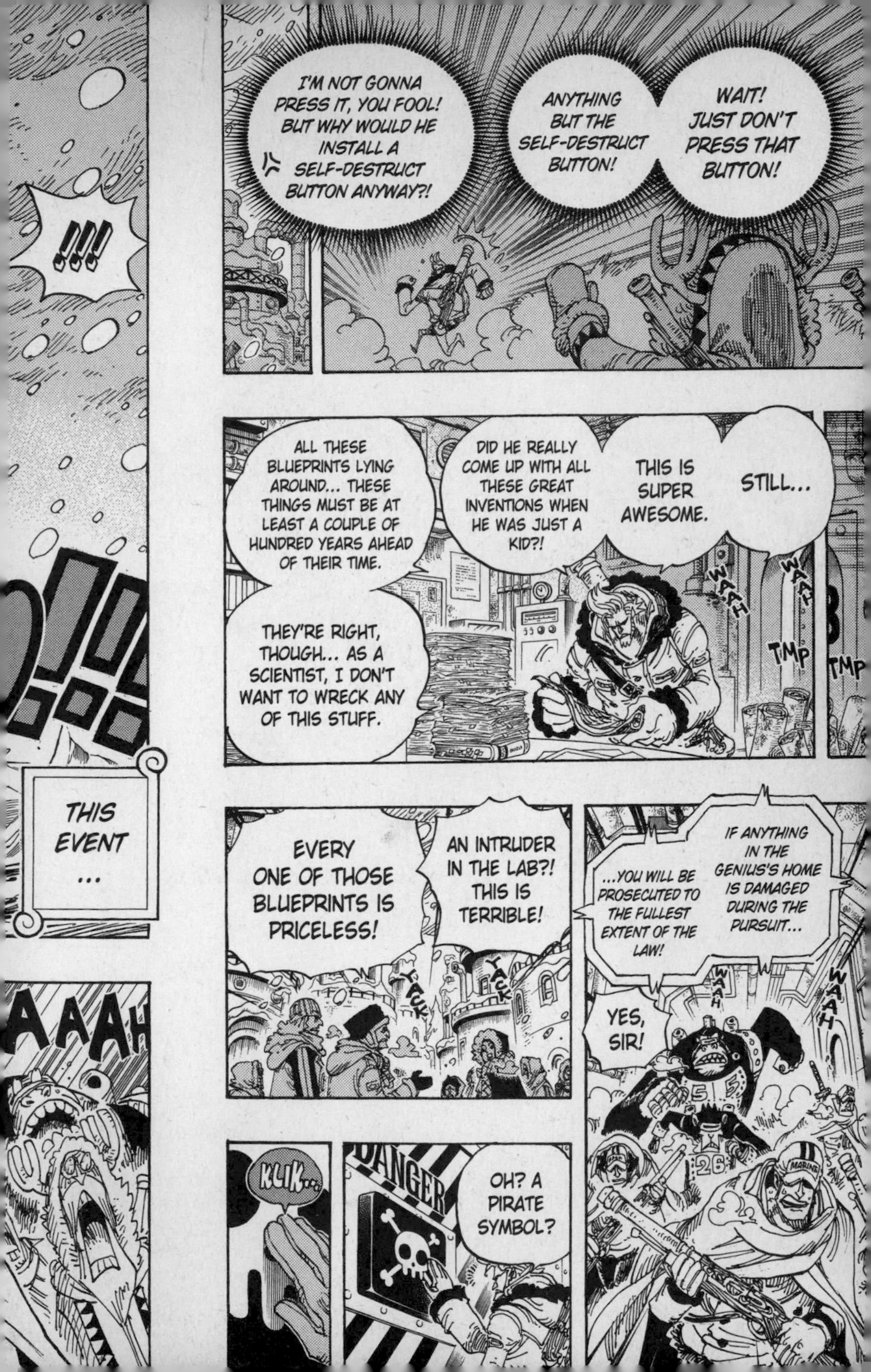
WAIT! JUST DON'T PRESS THAT BUTTON!
ANYTHING BUT THE SELF-DESTRUCT BUTTON!
I'M NOT GONNA PRESS IT, YOU FOOL! BUT WHY WOULD HE INSTALL A SELF-DESTRUCT BUTTON ANYWAY?!
STILL...
THIS IS SUPER AWESOME.
DID HE REALLY COME UP WITH ALL THESE GREAT INVENTIONS WHEN HE WAS JUST A KID?!
ALL THESE BLUEPRINTS LYING AROUND... THESE THINGS MUST BE AT LEAST A COUPLE OF HUNDRED YEARS AHEAD OF THEIR TIME.
THEY'RE RIGHT, THOUGH... AS A SCIENTIST, I DON'T WANT TO WRECK ANY OF THIS STUFF.
WAAH
WAAH
TMP
TMP
IF ANYTHING IN THE GENIUS'S HOME IS DAMAGED DURING THE PURSUIT...
...YOU WILL BE PROSECUTED TO THE FULLEST EXTENT OF THE LAW!
WAAH
WAAH
YES, SIR!
AN INTRUDER IN THE LAB?! THIS IS TERRIBLE!
EVERY ONE OF THOSE BLUEPRINTS IS PRICELESS!
YACK
YACK
OH? A PIRATE SYMBOL?
DANGER
DANGER
KLIK...
!!!
THIS EVENT ...
AAAAH

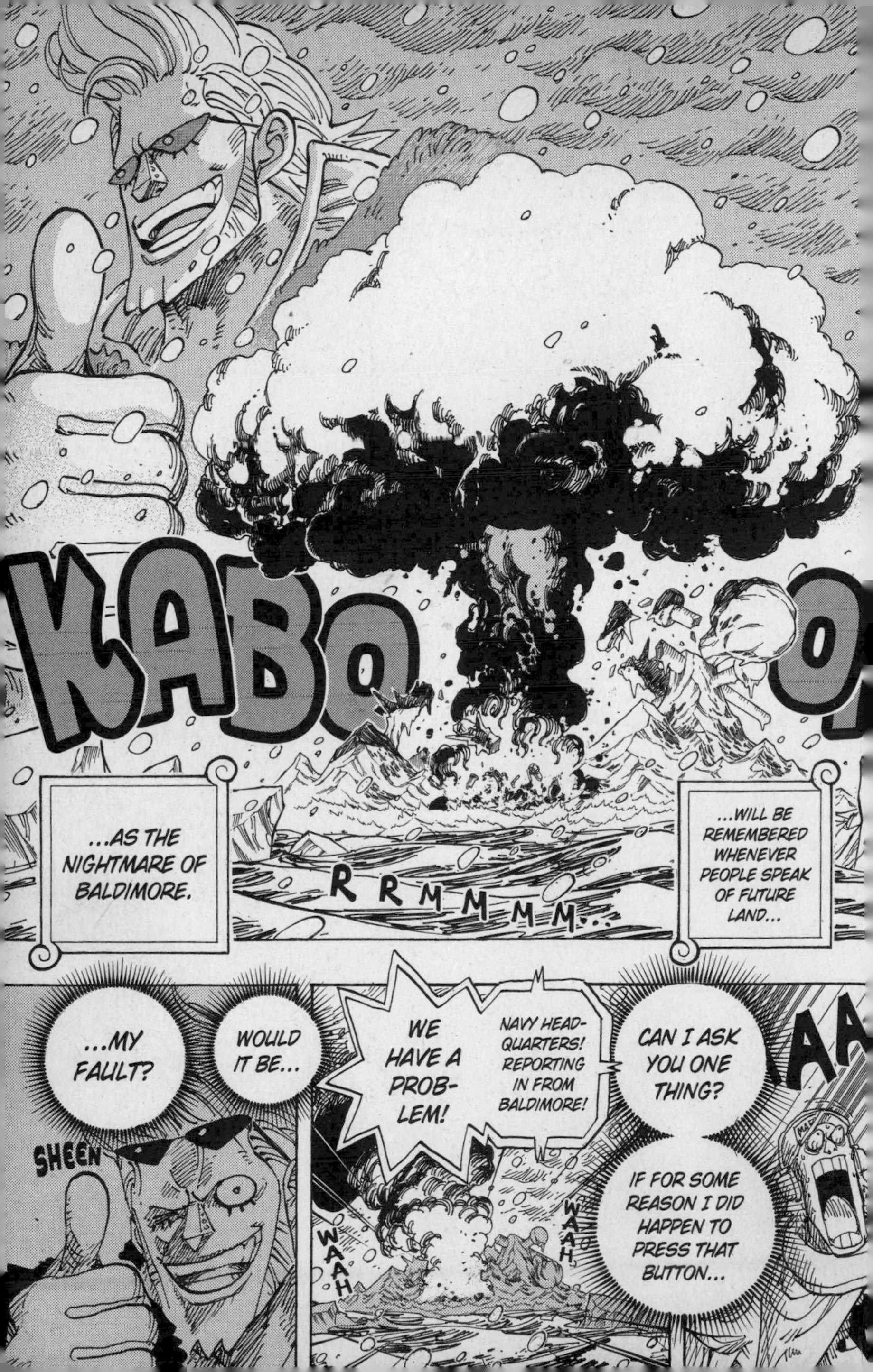

KABOO
...WILL BE REMEMBERED WHENEVER PEOPLE SPEAK OF FUTURE LAND...
...AS THE NIGHTMARE OF BALDIMORE.
RRMMMMM..
AA
CAN I ASK YOU ONE THING?
IF FOR SOME REASON I DID HAPPEN TO PRESS THAT BUTTON...
NAVY HEAD-QUARTERS! REPORTING IN FROM BALDIMORE!
WE HAVE A PROB-LEM!
WAAH
WAAH
WOULD IT BE...
...MY FAULT?
SHEEN

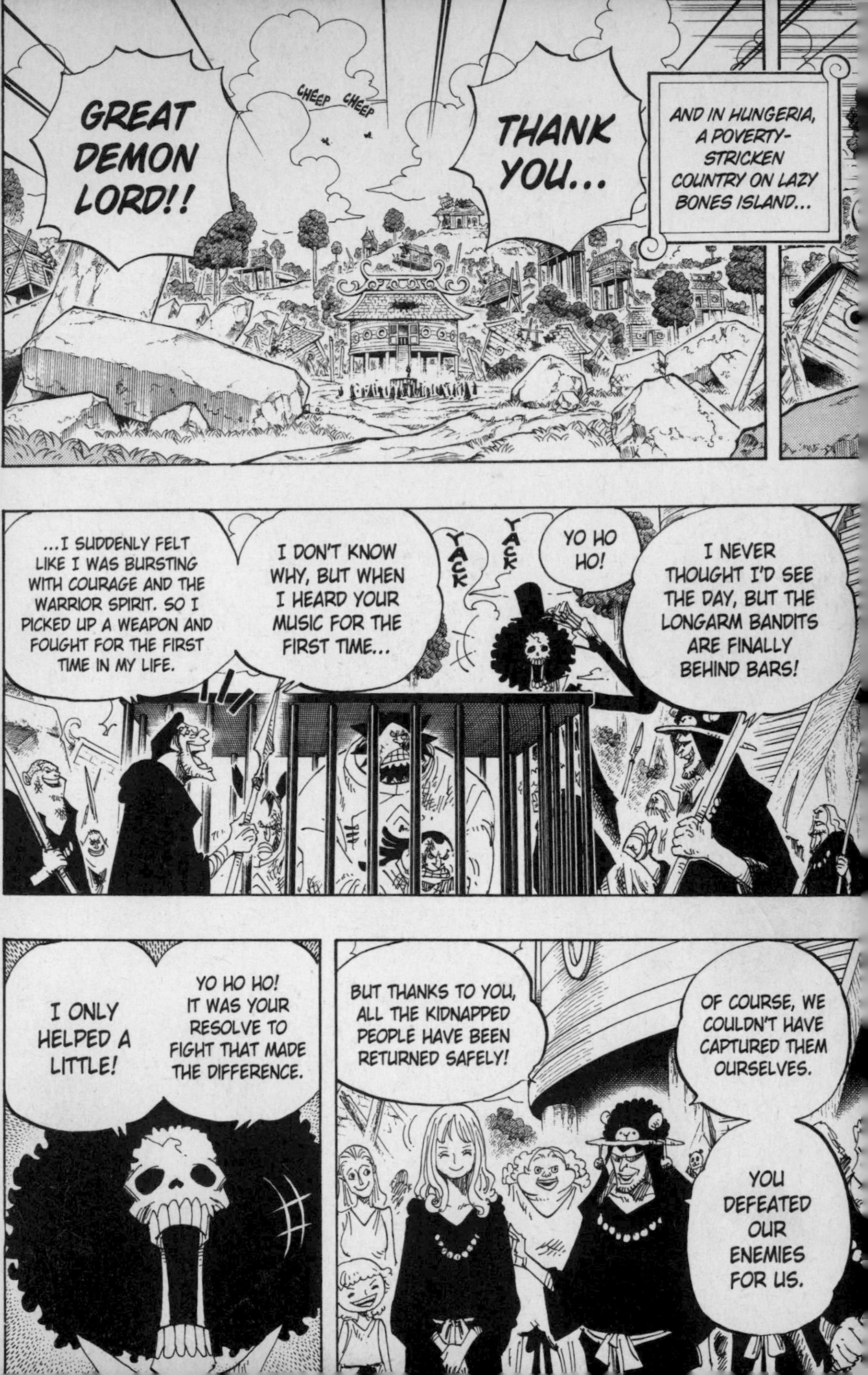
AND IN HUNGERIA, A POVERTY-STRICKEN COUNTRY ON LAZY BONES ISLAND...
THANK YOU...
CHEEP CHEEP
GREAT DEMON LORD!!
I NEVER THOUGHT I'D SEE THE DAY, BUT THE LONGARM BANDITS ARE FINALLY BEHIND BARS!
YO HO HO!
YACK
YACK
I DON'T KNOW WHY, BUT WHEN I HEARD YOUR MUSIC FOR THE FIRST TIME...
...I SUDDENLY FELT LIKE I WAS BURSTING WITH COURAGE AND THE WARRIOR SPIRIT. SO I PICKED UP A WEAPON AND FOUGHT FOR THE FIRST TIME IN MY LIFE.
OF COURSE, WE COULDN'T HAVE CAPTURED THEM OURSELVES.
YOU DEFEATED OUR ENEMIES FOR US.
BUT THANKS TO YOU, ALL THE KIDNAPPED PEOPLE HAVE BEEN RETURNED SAFELY!
YO HO HO! IT WAS YOUR RESOLVE TO FIGHT THAT MADE THE DIFFERENCE.
I ONLY HELPED A LITTLE!

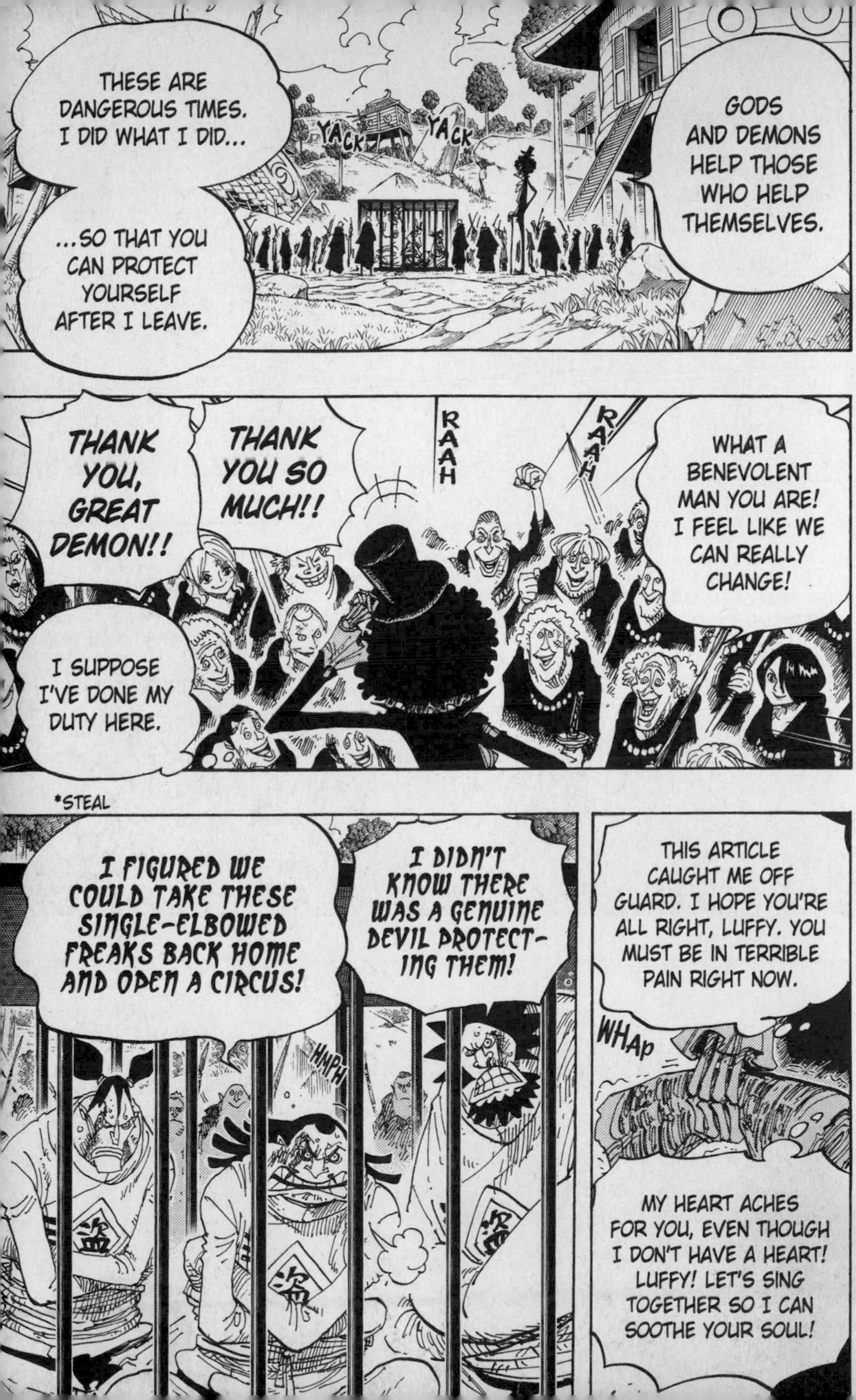
GODS AND DEMONS HELP THOSE WHO HELP THEMSELVES.
YACK
YACK
THESE ARE DANGEROUS TIMES. I DID WHAT I DID...
...SO THAT YOU CAN PROTECT YOURSELF AFTER I LEAVE.
WHAT A BENEVOLENT MAN YOU ARE! I FEEL LIKE WE CAN REALLY CHANGE!
RAAAH
RAAH
THANK YOU SO MUCH!!
THANK YOU, GREAT DEMON!!
I SUPPOSE I'VE DONE MY DUTY HERE.
*STEAL
THIS ARTICLE CAUGHT ME OFF GUARD. I HOPE YOU'RE ALL RIGHT, LUFFY. YOU MUST BE IN TERRIBLE PAIN RIGHT NOW.
WHAp
MY HEART ACHES FOR YOU, EVEN THOUGH I DON'T HAVE A HEART! LUFFY! LET'S SING TOGETHER SO I CAN SOOTHE YOUR SOUL!
I DIDN'T KNOW THERE WAS A GENUINE DEVIL PROTECTING THEM!
I FIGURED WE COULD TAKE THESE SINGLE-ELBOWED FREAKS BACK HOME AND OPEN A CIRCUS!
HMPH

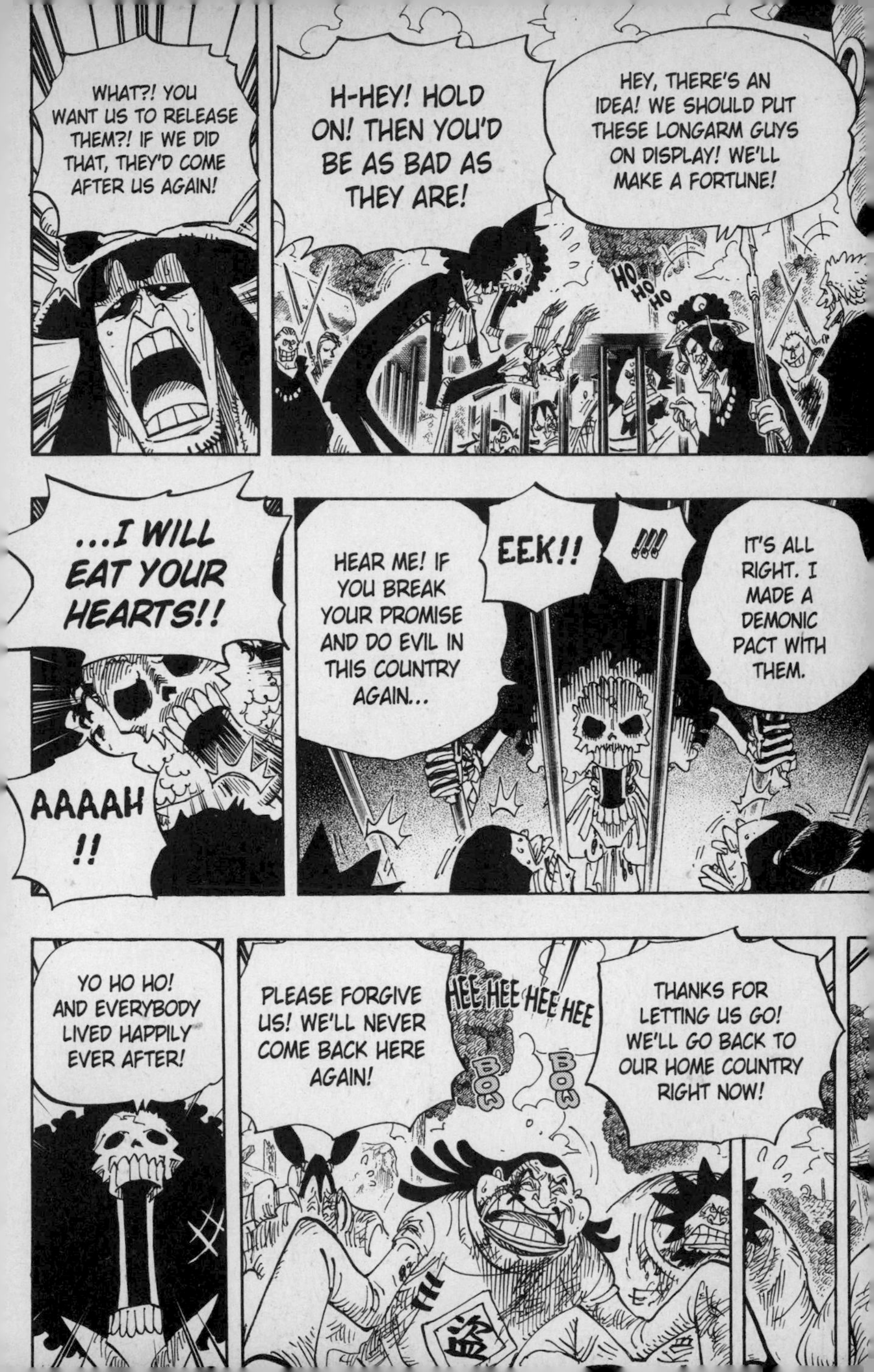
HEY, THERE'S AN IDEA! WE SHOULD PUT THESE LONGARM GUYS ON DISPLAY! WE'LL MAKE A FORTUNE!
H-HEY! HOLD ON! THEN YOU'D BE AS BAD AS THEY ARE!
HO HO HO
WHAT?! YOU WANT US TO RELEASE THEM?! IF WE DID THAT, THEY'D COME AFTER US AGAIN!
IT'S ALL RIGHT. I MADE A DEMONIC PACT WITH THEM.
!!!
EEK!!
HEAR ME! IF YOU BREAK YOUR PROMISE AND DO EVIL IN THIS COUNTRY AGAIN...
...I WILL EAT YOUR HEARTS!!
AAAAH !!
THANKS FOR LETTING US GO! WE'LL GO BACK TO OUR HOME COUNTRY RIGHT NOW!
HEE HEE HEE HEE
BOW
BOW
PLEASE FORGIVE US! WE'LL NEVER COME BACK HERE AGAIN!
盗
YO HO HO! AND EVERYBODY LIVED HAPPILY EVER AFTER!

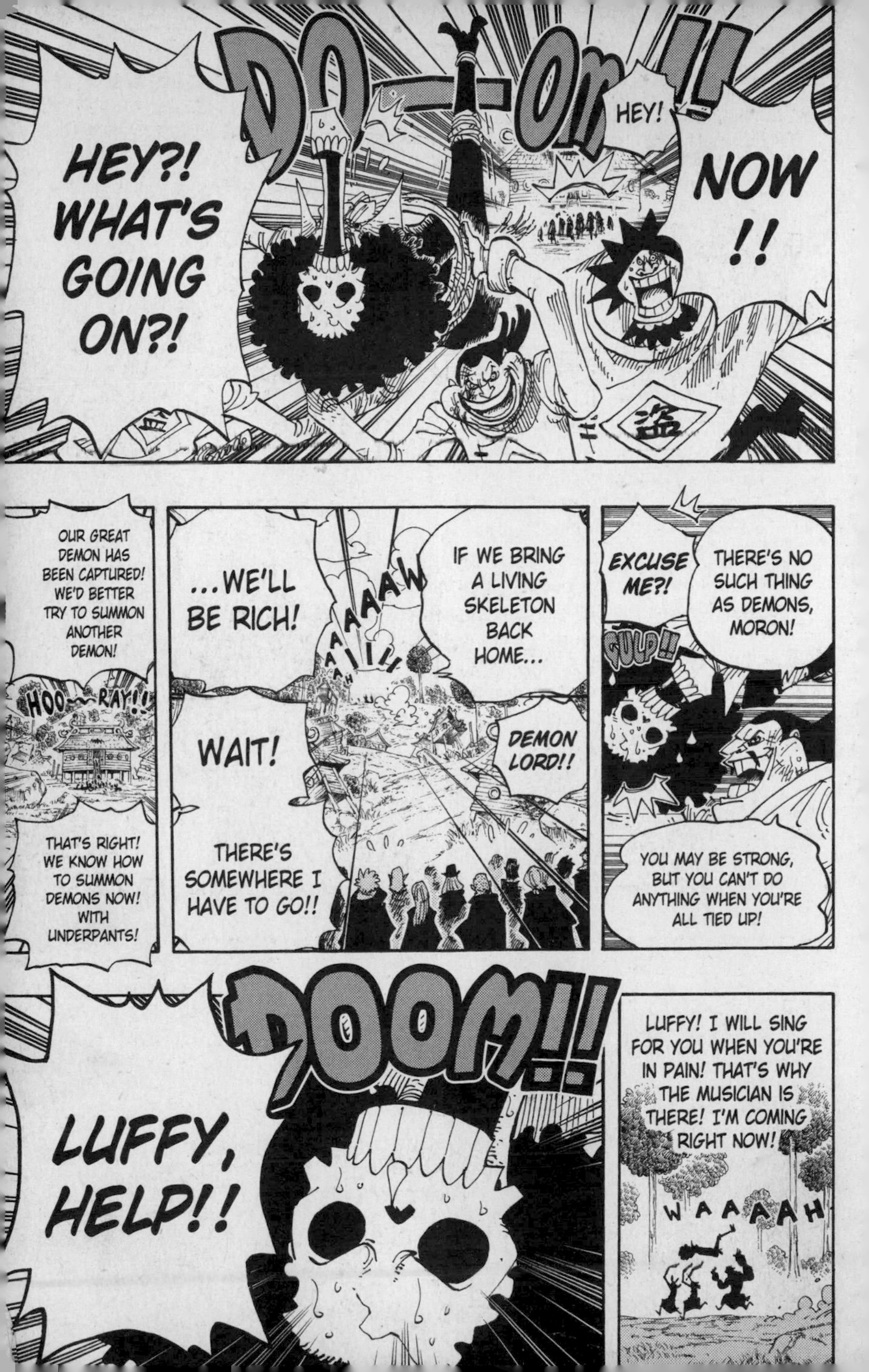
DO—ON!!
HEY!
NOW!!
HEY?! WHAT'S GOING ON?!
THERE'S NO SUCH THING AS DEMONS, MORON!
EXCUSE ME?!
GULP!!
YOU MAY BE STRONG, BUT YOU CAN'T DO ANYTHING WHEN YOU'RE ALL TIED UP!
IF WE BRING A LIVING SKELETON BACK HOME...
...WE'LL BE RICH!
AAAAAW
DEMON LORD!!
WAIT!
THERE'S SOMEWHERE I HAVE TO GO!!
OUR GREAT DEMON HAS BEEN CAPTURED! WE'D BETTER TRY TO SUMMON ANOTHER DEMON!
HOO~RAY!!
THAT'S RIGHT! WE KNOW HOW TO SUMMON DEMONS NOW! WITH UNDERPANTS!
LUFFY! I WILL SING FOR YOU WHEN YOU'RE IN PAIN! THAT'S WHY THE MUSICIAN IS THERE! I'M COMING RIGHT NOW!
WAAAAH
DOOM!!
LUFFY, HELP!!

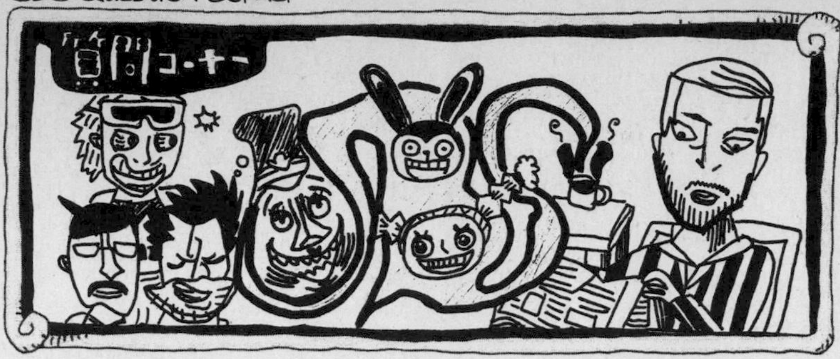

(Honoka Yoshioka, Shiga)

Q: Good afternoon, Mr. Oda. In chapter 589, in the fourth panel on page 4, Luffy's shirt says "Noodle Maker." On the fifth panel of page 8, it says "Morning Glory." In the ninth panel of page 10, it says "Eskimo." In the third panel of page 11, it says "Change up." In the fourth panel of page 12, it says "Tapioca." Isn't that right? My sister found them all.

--Harusame Soup

A: You actually got one wrong. I got a lot of comments about the words on Ace and Luffy's shirts, so I'll list them all here. Let's start with Ace's shirt. Then we'll do Luffy's. (Chapters 585-589)

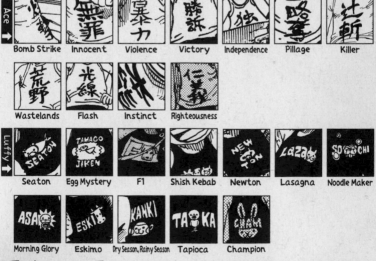

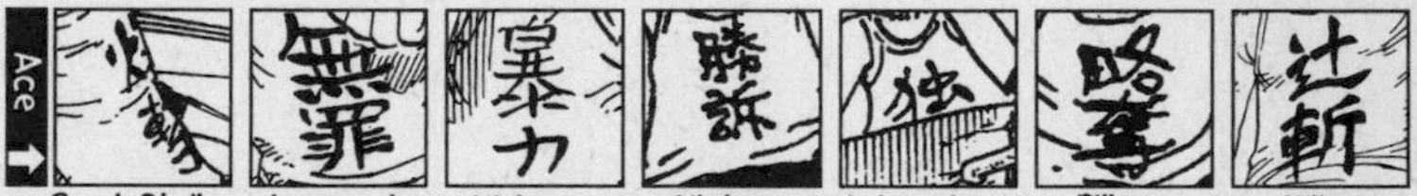
Ace
Bomb Strike
Innocent
Violence
Victory
Independence
Pillage
Killer
Wastelands
Flash
Instinct
Righteousness
Luffy
Seaton
Egg Mystery
F1
Shish Kebab
Newton
Lasagna
Noodle Maker
Morning Glory
Eskimo
Dry Season, Rainy Season
Tapioca
Champion

That's about it. The one thing I regret is in chapter 589. Even I can't read what's there! (Ha!) It really says "(something)NO" and it's some kind of animal. I just can't remember. Oh, well. Anyway, I wanted to show that they're not always wearing the same clothes all the time, so I came up with this. Anyway, that's it for the Question Corner! Starting on page 186 is the voice actor SBS!

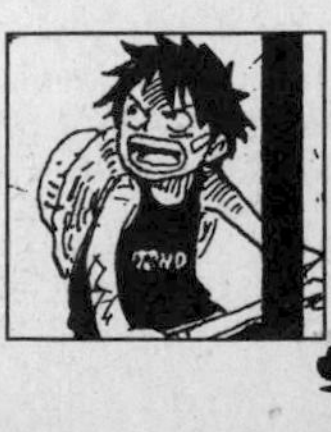

Chapter 593: NEWS

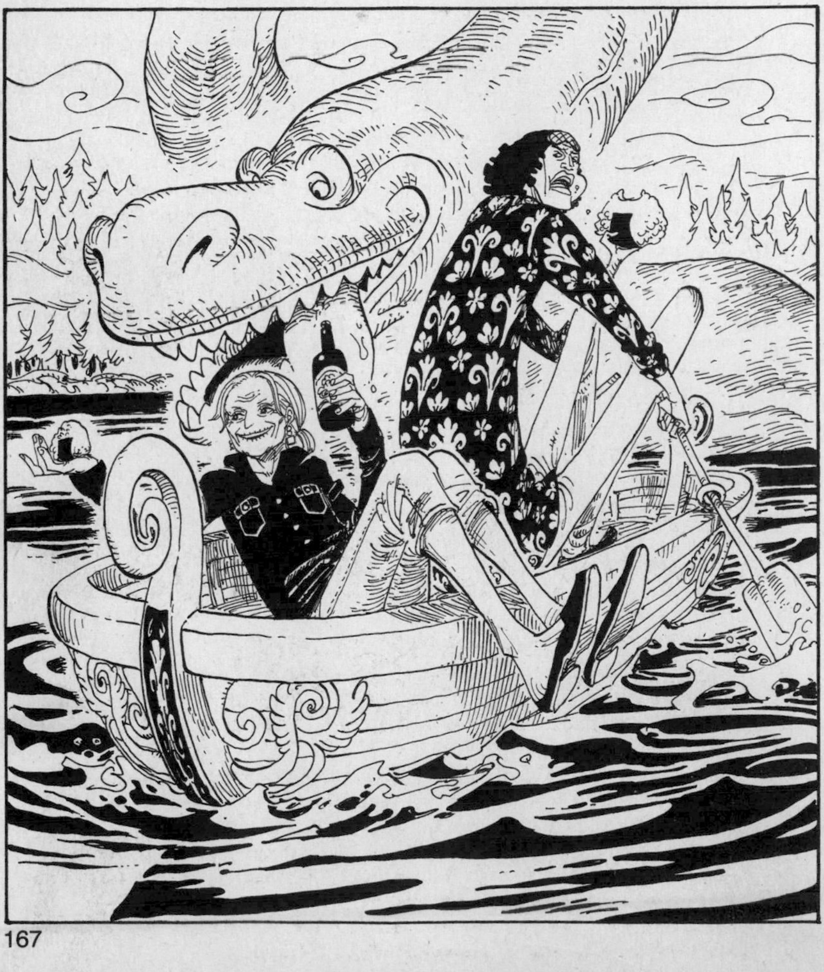

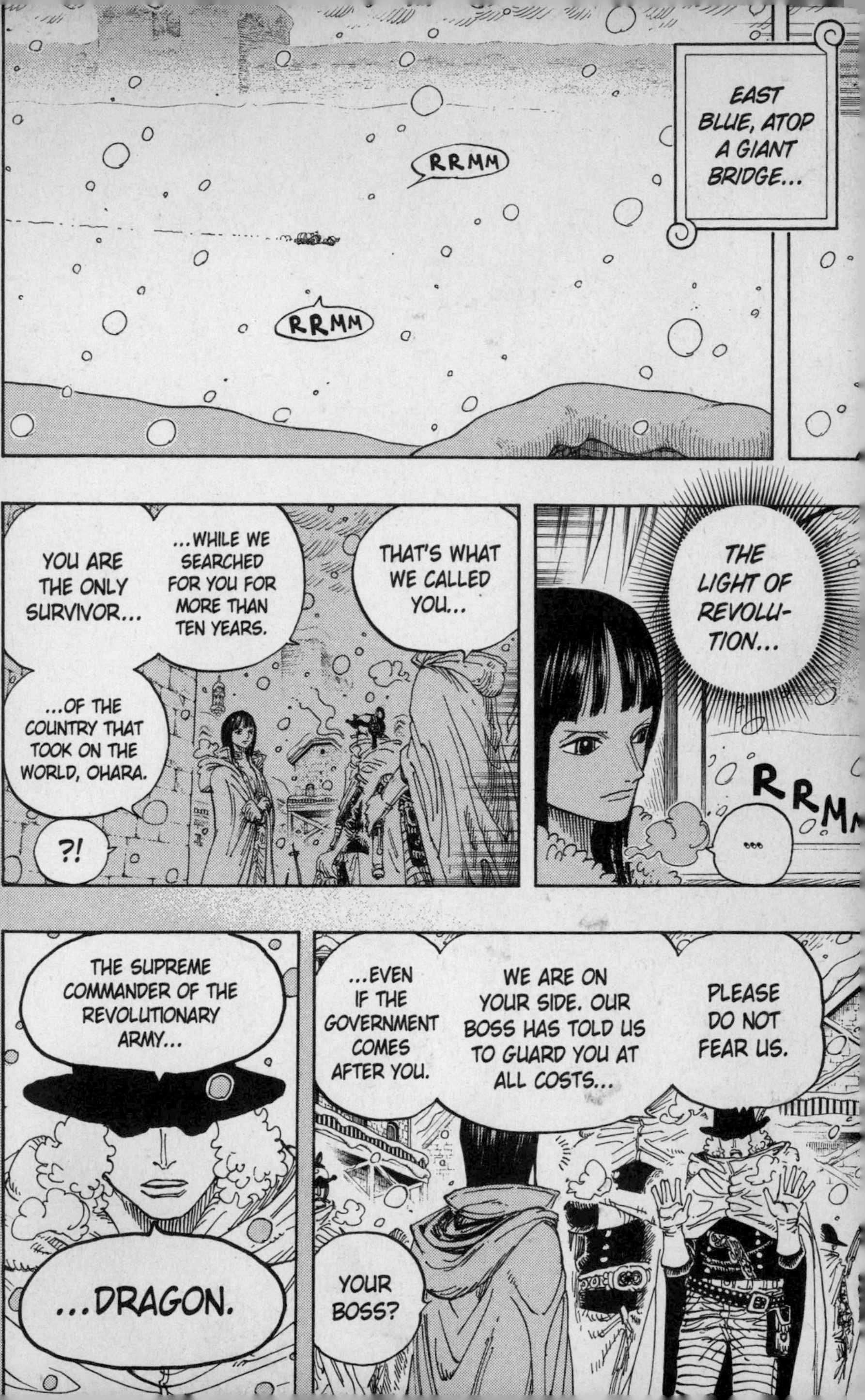
EAST BLUE, ATOP A GIANT BRIDGE...
RRMM
RRMM
THE LIGHT OF REVOLUTION...
RRMM
...
THAT'S WHAT WE CALLED YOU...
...WHILE WE SEARCHED FOR YOU FOR MORE THAN TEN YEARS.
YOU ARE THE ONLY SURVIVOR...
...OF THE COUNTRY THAT TOOK ON THE WORLD, OHARA.
?!
PLEASE DO NOT FEAR US.
WE ARE ON YOUR SIDE. OUR BOSS HAS TOLD US TO GUARD YOU AT ALL COSTS...
...EVEN IF THE GOVERNMENT COMES AFTER YOU.
YOUR BOSS?
THE SUPREME COMMANDER OF THE REVOLUTIONARY ARMY...
...DRAGON.

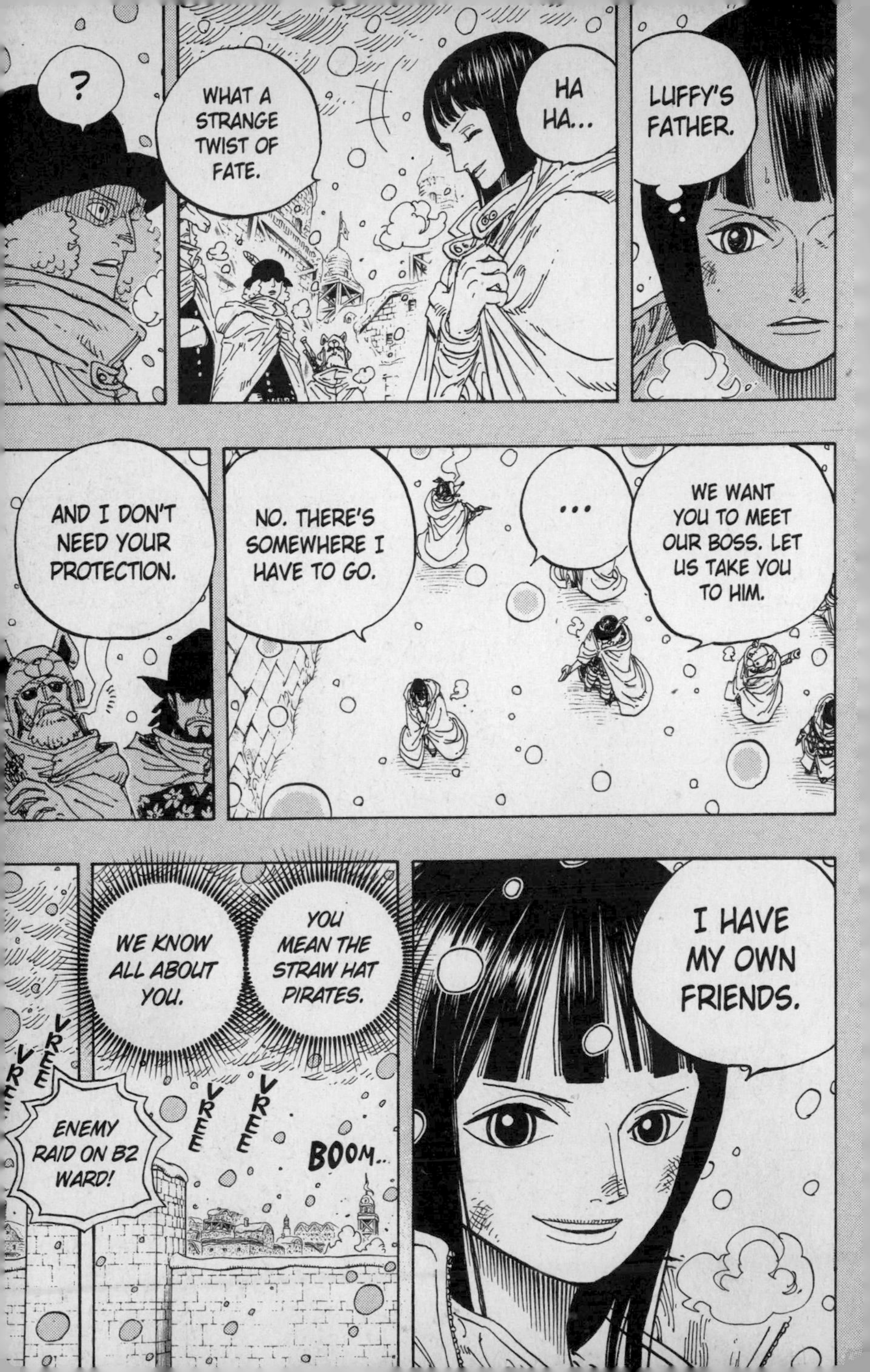
LUFFY'S FATHER.
HA HA...
WHAT A STRANGE TWIST OF FATE.
?
WE WANT YOU TO MEET OUR BOSS. LET US TAKE YOU TO HIM.
...
NO. THERE'S SOMEWHERE I HAVE TO GO.
AND I DON'T NEED YOUR PROTECTION.
I HAVE MY OWN FRIENDS.
YOU MEAN THE STRAW HAT PIRATES.
WE KNOW ALL ABOUT YOU.
VREE
VREE
BOOM..
ENEMY RAID ON B2 WARD!
VREE
VREE

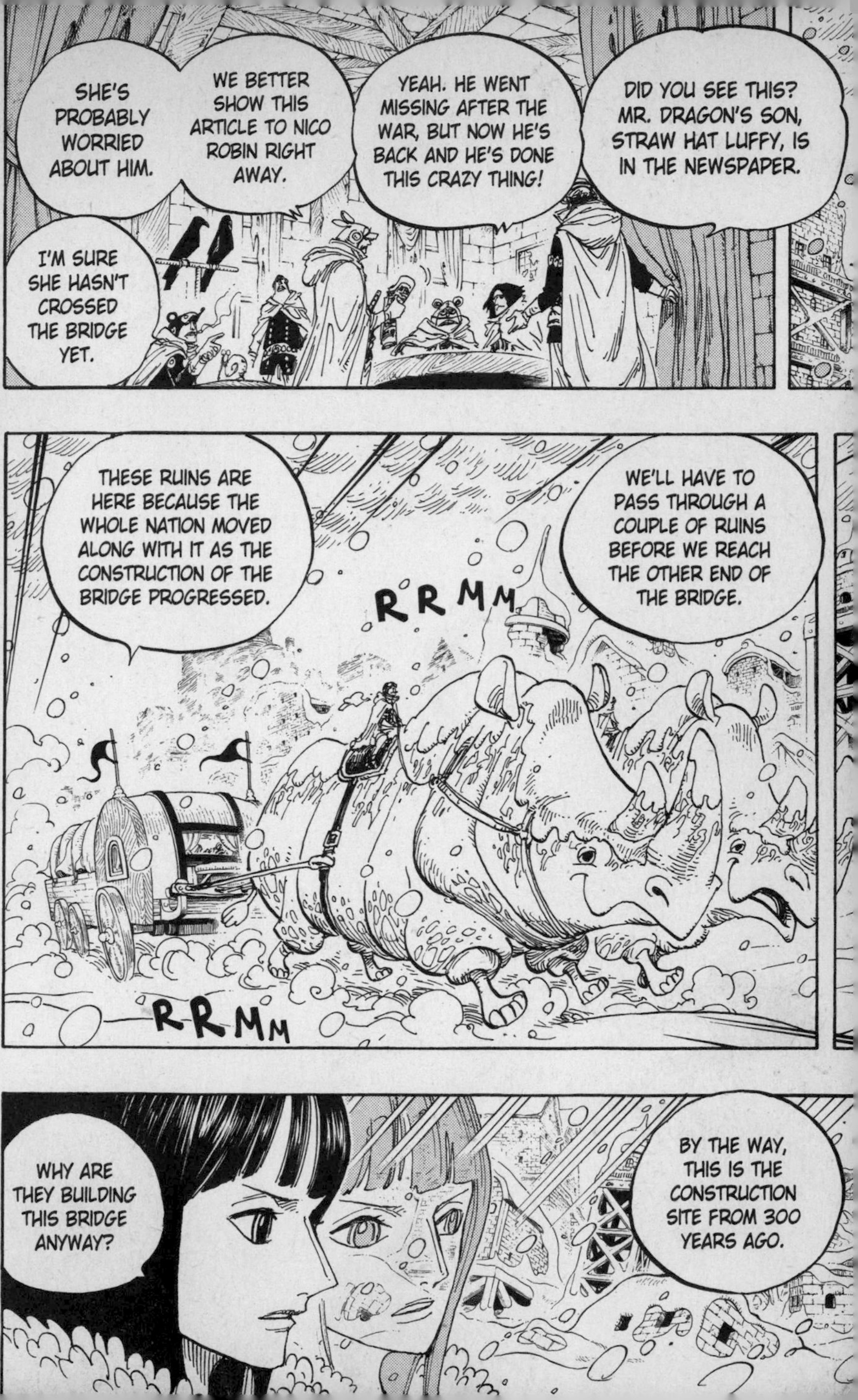
DID YOU SEE THIS? MR. DRAGON'S SON, STRAW HAT LUFFY, IS IN THE NEWSPAPER.
YEAH. HE WENT MISSING AFTER THE WAR, BUT NOW HE'S BACK AND HE'S DONE THIS CRAZY THING!
WE BETTER SHOW THIS ARTICLE TO NICO ROBIN RIGHT AWAY.
SHE'S PROBABLY WORRIED ABOUT HIM.
I'M SURE SHE HASN'T CROSSED THE BRIDGE YET.
WE'LL HAVE TO PASS THROUGH A COUPLE OF RUINS BEFORE WE REACH THE OTHER END OF THE BRIDGE.
RRMM
THESE RUINS ARE HERE BECAUSE THE WHOLE NATION MOVED ALONG WITH IT AS THE CONSTRUCTION OF THE BRIDGE PROGRESSED.
RRMM
BY THE WAY, THIS IS THE CONSTRUCTION SITE FROM 300 YEARS AGO.
WHY ARE THEY BUILDING THIS BRIDGE ANYWAY?

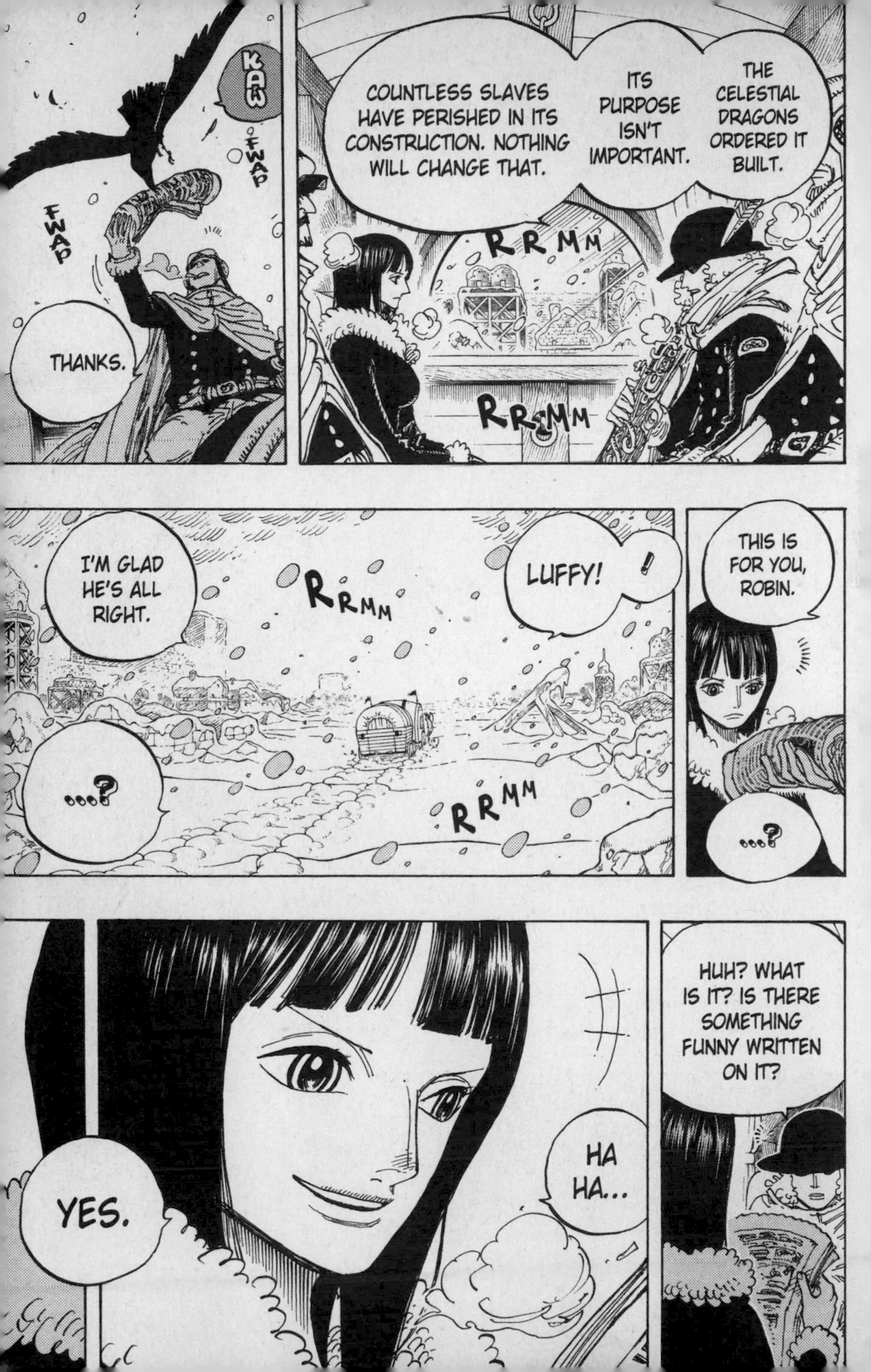
THE CELESTIAL DRAGONS ORDERED IT BUILT.
ITS PURPOSE ISN'T IMPORTANT.
COUNTLESS SLAVES HAVE PERISHED IN ITS CONSTRUCTION. NOTHING WILL CHANGE THAT.
RRMM
RRMM
KAW
FWAP
FWAP
THANKS.
THIS IS FOR YOU, ROBIN.
...?
!
LUFFY!
RRMM
I'M GLAD HE'S ALL RIGHT.
...?
RRMM
HUH? WHAT IS IT? IS THERE SOMETHING FUNNY WRITTEN ON IT?
HA HA...
YES.

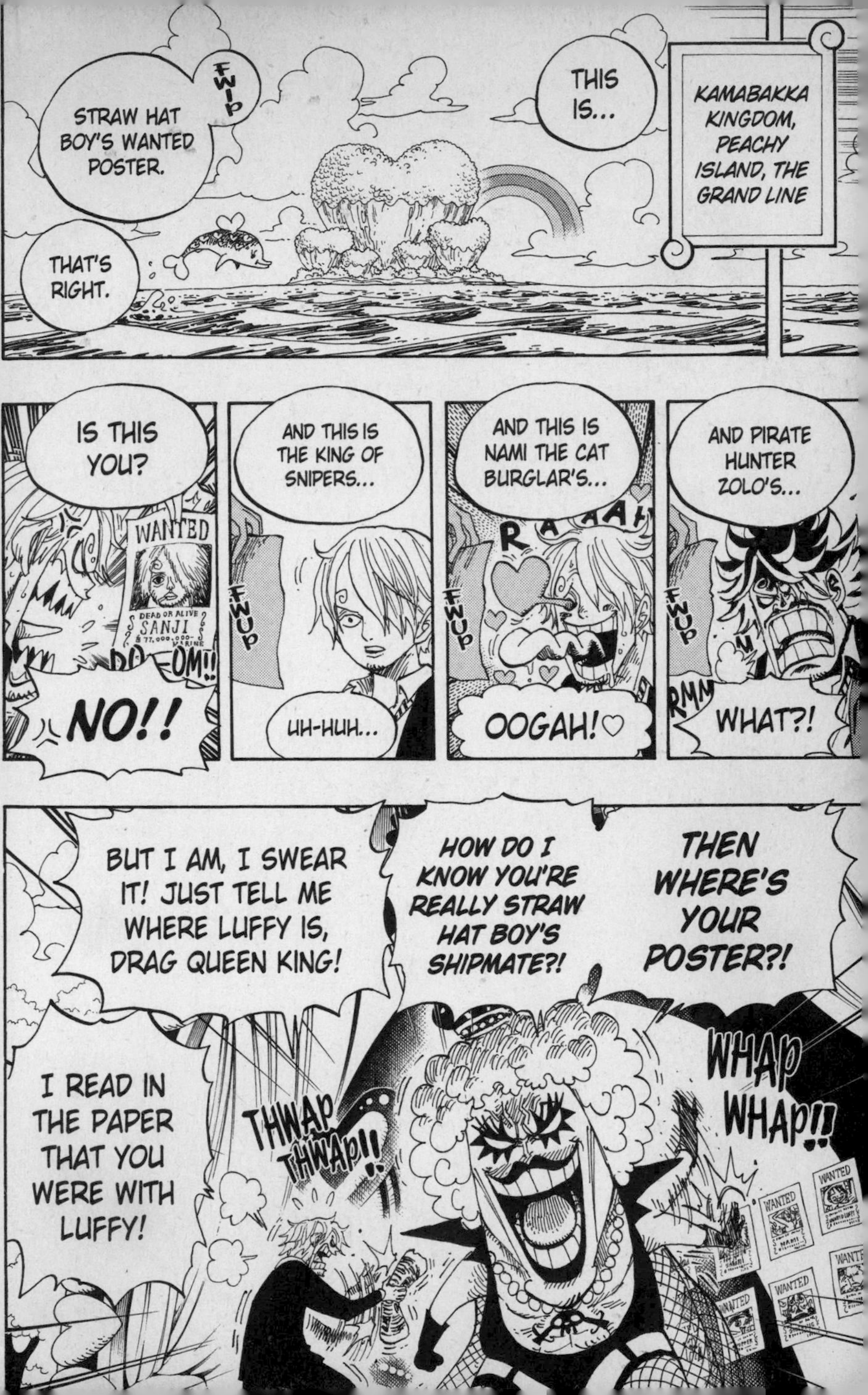
KAMABAKKA KINGDOM, PEACHY ISLAND, THE GRAND LINE
THIS IS...
FWIP
STRAW HAT BOY'S WANTED POSTER.
THAT'S RIGHT.
AND PIRATE HUNTER ZOLO'S...
FWUP
WHAT?!
AND THIS IS NAMI THE CAT BURGLAR'S...
FWUP
OOGAH!♡
AND THIS IS THE KING OF SNIPERS...
FWUP
UH-HUH...
IS THIS YOU?
WANTED
DEAD OR ALIVE
SANJI
NO!!
THEN WHERE'S YOUR POSTER?!
HOW DO I KNOW YOU'RE REALLY STRAW HAT BOY'S SHIPMATE?!
BUT I AM, I SWEAR IT! JUST TELL ME WHERE LUFFY IS, DRAG QUEEN KING!
WHAP WHAP!!
THWAP THWAP!!
I READ IN THE PAPER THAT YOU WERE WITH LUFFY!

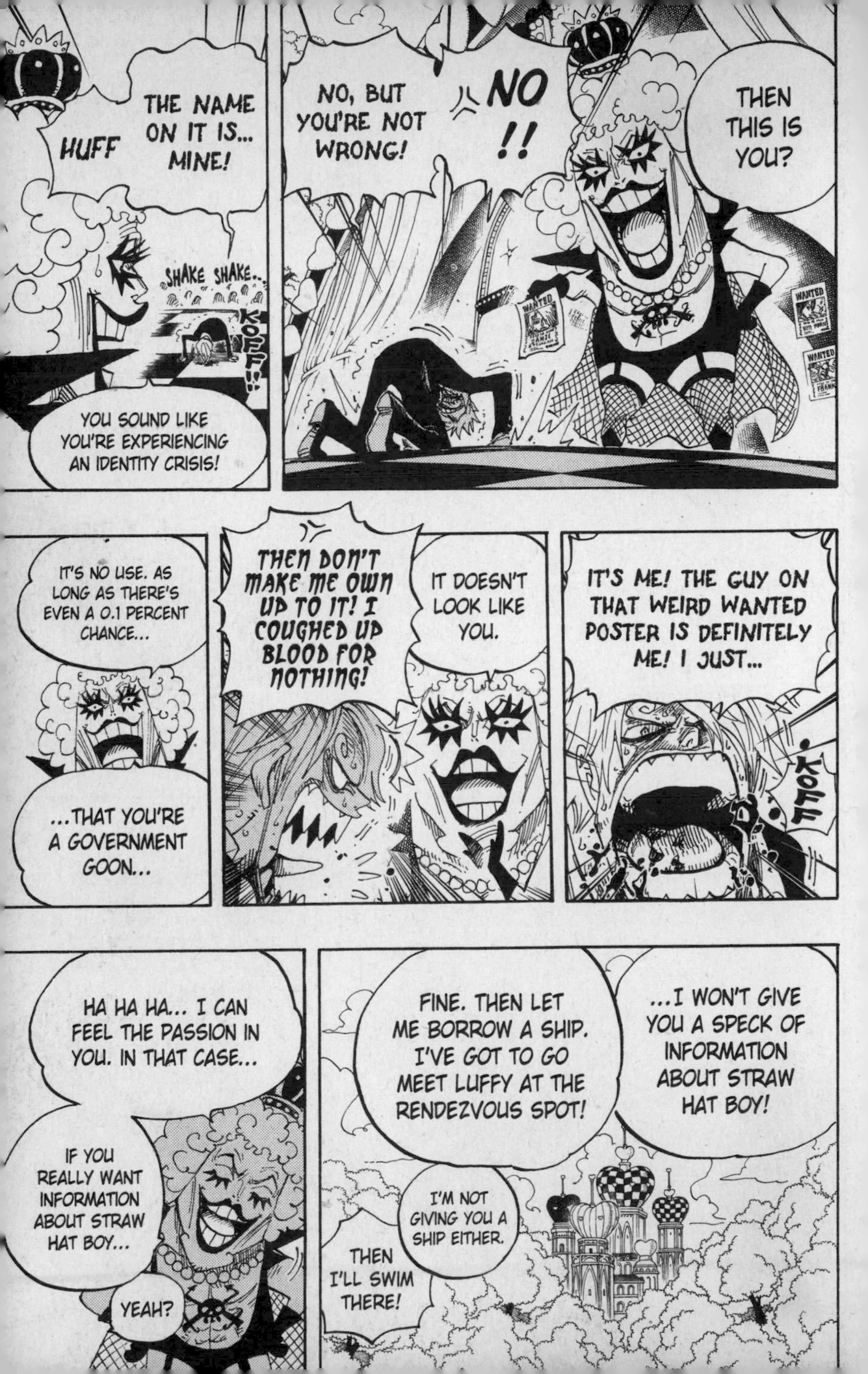
THEN THIS IS YOU?
NO!!
NO, BUT YOU'RE NOT WRONG!
THE NAME ON IT IS... MINE!
HUFF
SHAKE SHAKE...
KOFF!!
YOU SOUND LIKE YOU'RE EXPERIENCING AN IDENTITY CRISIS!
IT'S ME! THE GUY ON THAT WEIRD WANTED POSTER IS DEFINITELY ME! I JUST...
KOFF
IT DOESN'T LOOK LIKE YOU.
THEN DON'T MAKE ME OWN UP TO IT! I COUGHED UP BLOOD FOR NOTHING!
IT'S NO USE. AS LONG AS THERE'S EVEN A 0.1 PERCENT CHANCE...
...THAT YOU'RE A GOVERNMENT GOON...
...I WON'T GIVE YOU A SPECK OF INFORMATION ABOUT STRAW HAT BOY!
FINE. THEN LET ME BORROW A SHIP. I'VE GOT TO GO MEET LUFFY AT THE RENDEZVOUS SPOT!
I'M NOT GIVING YOU A SHIP EITHER.
THEN I'LL SWIM THERE!
HA HA HA... I CAN FEEL THE PASSION IN YOU. IN THAT CASE...
IF YOU REALLY WANT INFORMATION ABOUT STRAW HAT BOY...
YEAH?

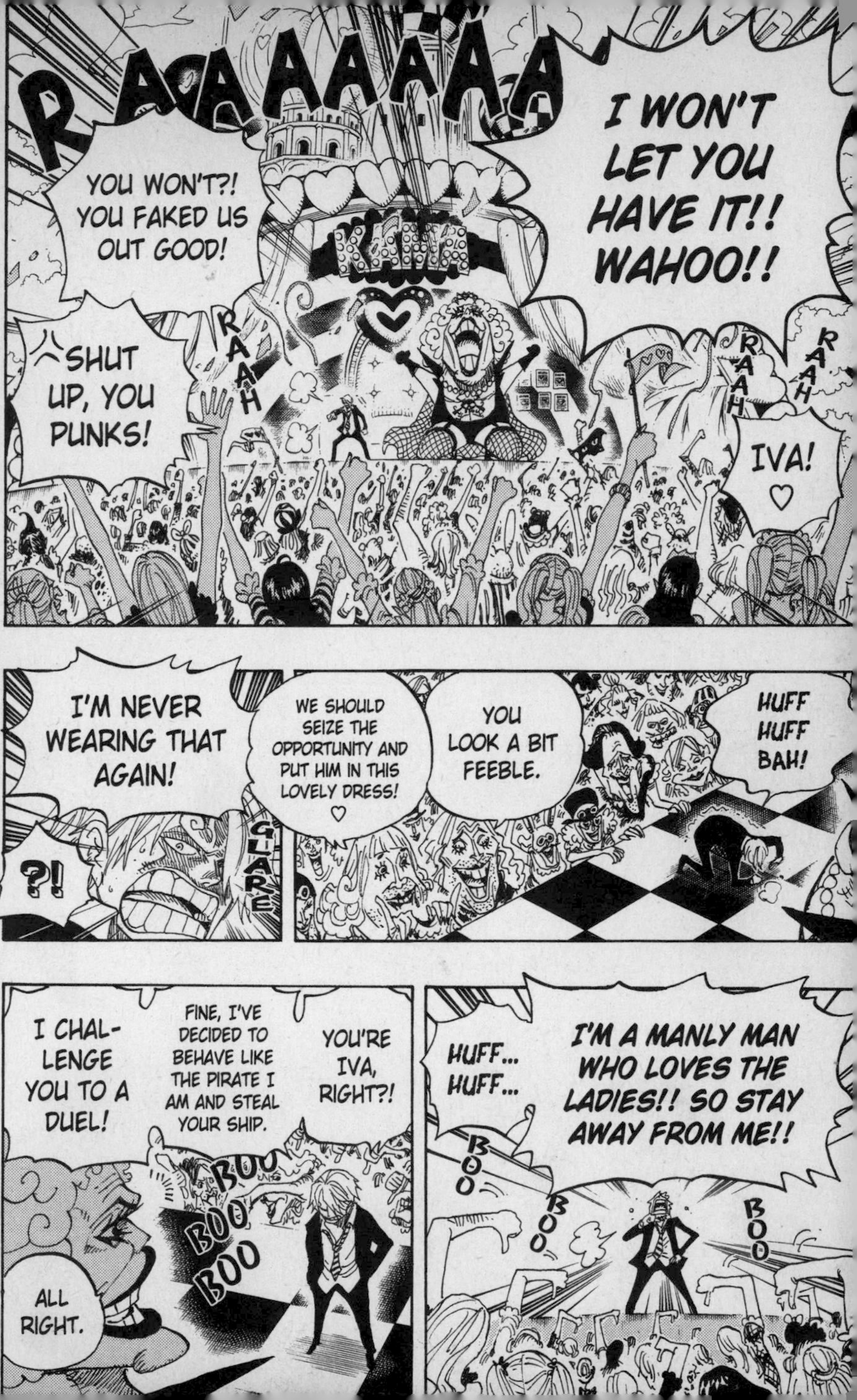
RAAAAAAAA
I WON'T LET YOU HAVE IT!! WAHOO!!
YOU WON'T?! YOU FAKED US OUT GOOD!
RAAH
RAAH
IVA! ♡
RAAH
SHUT UP, YOU PUNKS!
HUFF HUFF BAH!
YOU LOOK A BIT FEEBLE.
WE SHOULD SEIZE THE OPPORTUNITY AND PUT HIM IN THIS LOVELY DRESS! ♡
I'M NEVER WEARING THAT AGAIN!
GLARE
?!
I'M A MANLY MAN WHO LOVES THE LADIES!! SO STAY AWAY FROM ME!!
HUFF... HUFF...
BOO
BOO
BOO
YOU'RE IVA, RIGHT?!
FINE, I'VE DECIDED TO BEHAVE LIKE THE PIRATE I AM AND STEAL YOUR SHIP.
I CHAL-LENGE YOU TO A DUEL!
BOO
BOO
BOO
ALL RIGHT.

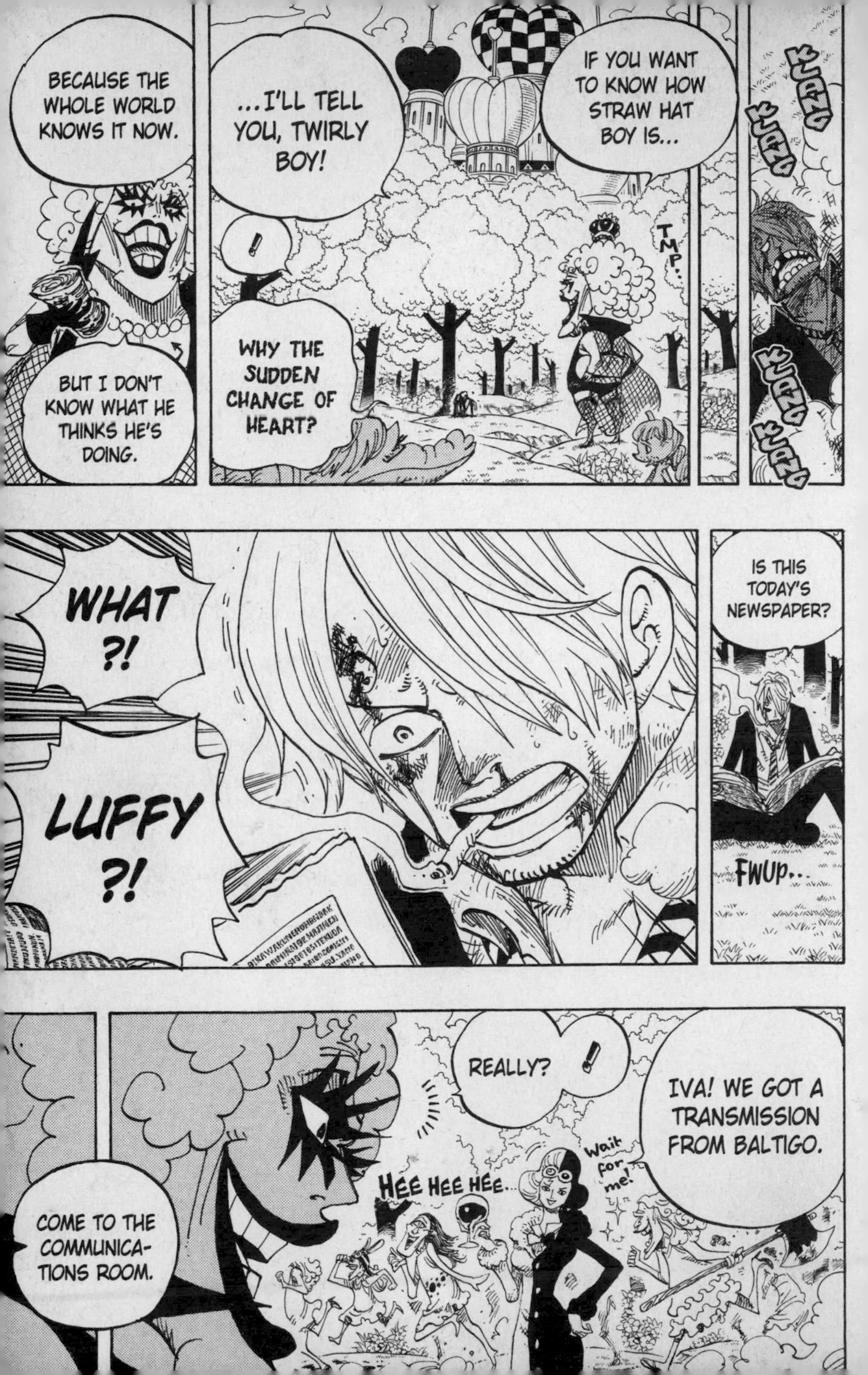
KLANG
KLANG
KLANG
KLANG
IF YOU WANT TO KNOW HOW STRAW HAT BOY IS...
TMP...
...I'LL TELL YOU, TWIRLY BOY!
!
WHY THE SUDDEN CHANGE OF HEART?
BECAUSE THE WHOLE WORLD KNOWS IT NOW.
BUT I DON'T KNOW WHAT HE THINKS HE'S DOING.
IS THIS TODAY'S NEWSPAPER?
FWUP...
WHAT?!
LUFFY?!
IVA! WE GOT A TRANSMISSION FROM BALTIGO.
!
REALLY?
Wait for me!
HEE HEE HEE...
COME TO THE COMMUNICATIONS ROOM.

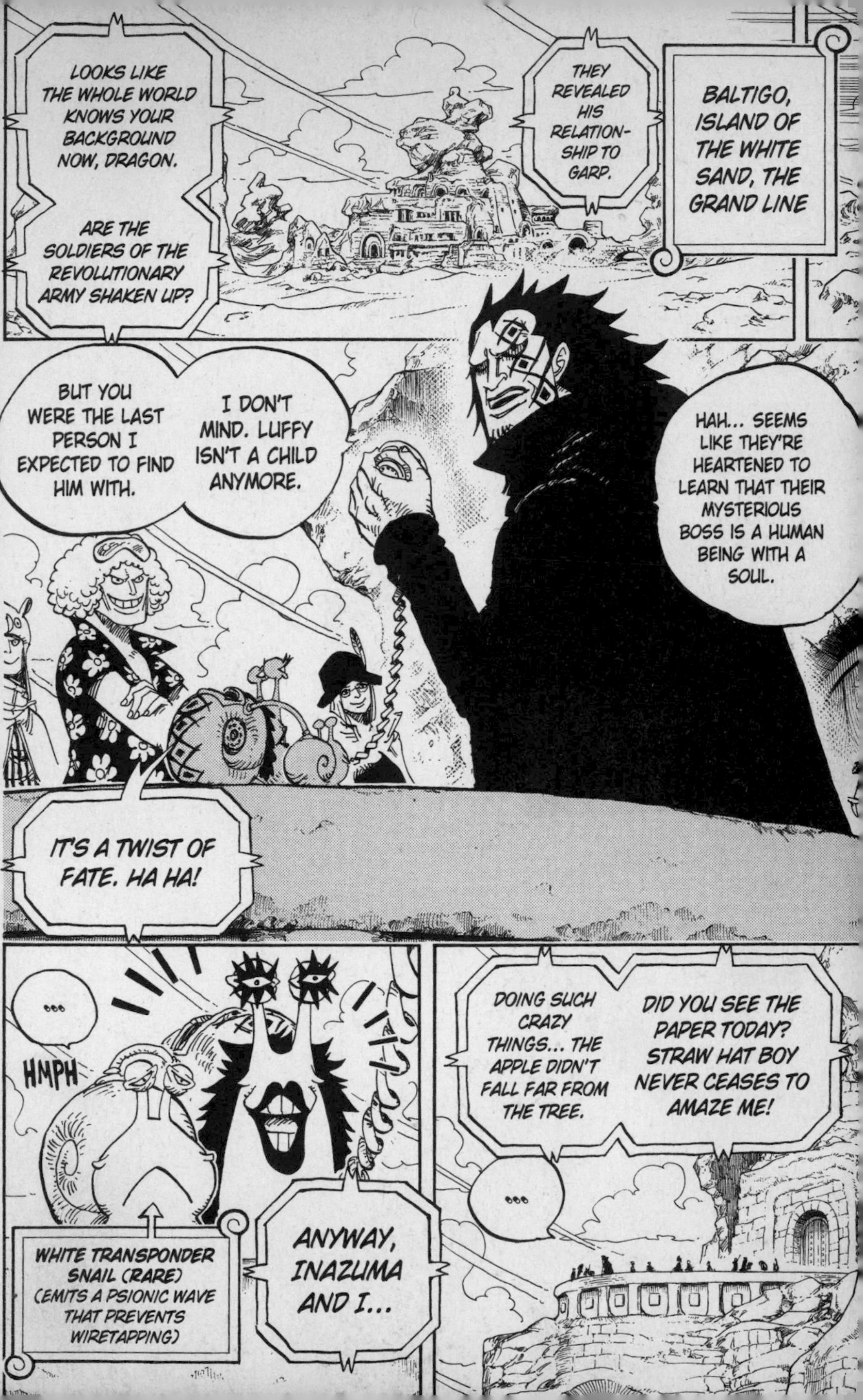
BALTIGO, ISLAND OF THE WHITE SAND, THE GRAND LINE
THEY REVEALED HIS RELATIONSHIP TO GARP.
LOOKS LIKE THE WHOLE WORLD KNOWS YOUR BACKGROUND NOW, DRAGON.
ARE THE SOLDIERS OF THE REVOLUTIONARY ARMY SHAKEN UP?
HAH... SEEMS LIKE THEY'RE HEARTENED TO LEARN THAT THEIR MYSTERIOUS BOSS IS A HUMAN BEING WITH A SOUL.
I DON'T MIND. LUFFY ISN'T A CHILD ANYMORE.
BUT YOU WERE THE LAST PERSON I EXPECTED TO FIND HIM WITH.
IT'S A TWIST OF FATE. HA HA!
DID YOU SEE THE PAPER TODAY? STRAW HAT BOY NEVER CEASES TO AMAZE ME!
DOING SUCH CRAZY THINGS... THE APPLE DIDN'T FALL FAR FROM THE TREE.
...
...
HMPH
ANYWAY, INAZUMA AND I...
WHITE TRANSPONDER SNAIL (RARE) (EMITS A PSIONIC WAVE THAT PREVENTS WIRETAPPING)

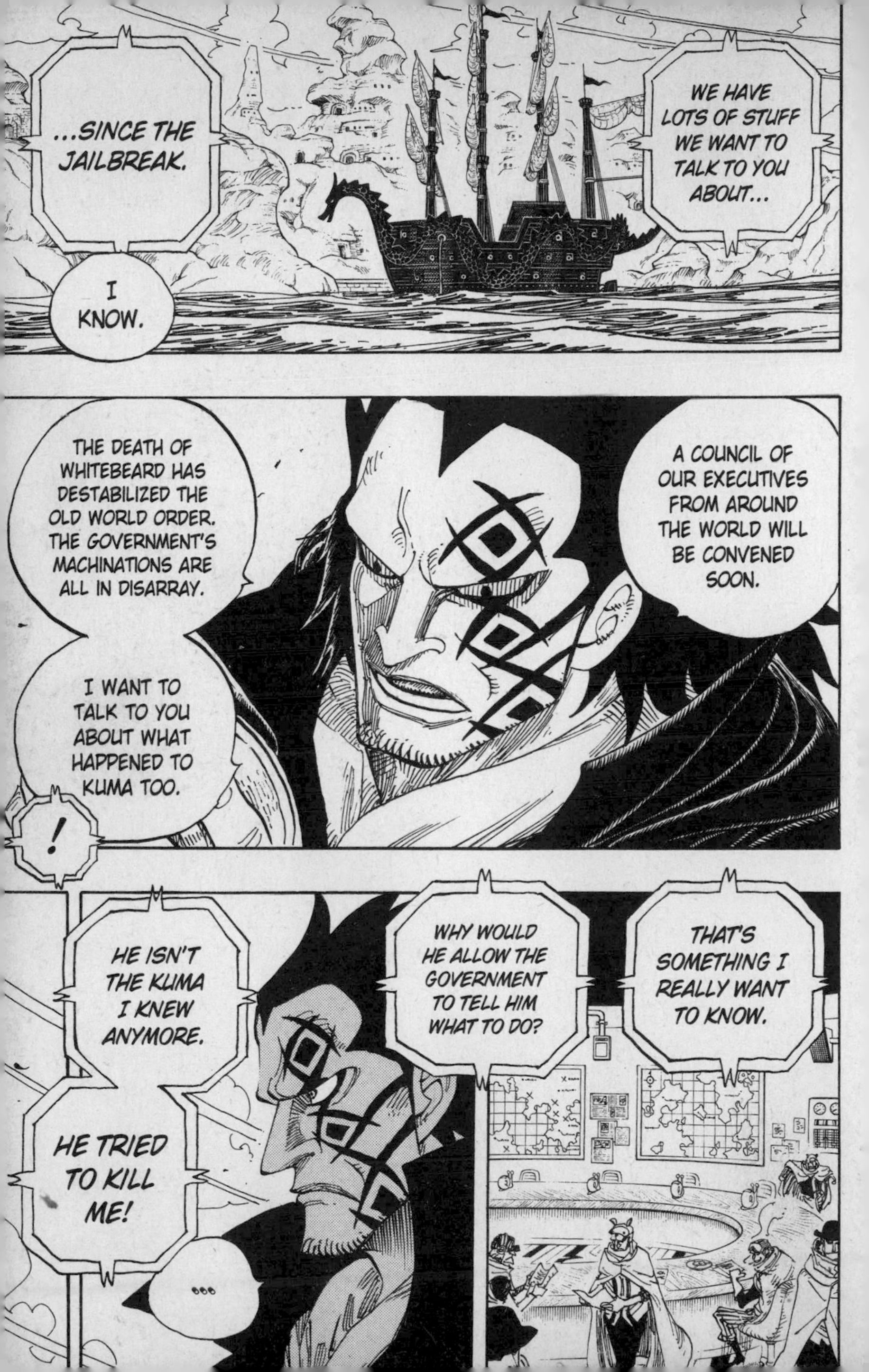
WE HAVE LOTS OF STUFF WE WANT TO TALK TO YOU ABOUT...
...SINCE THE JAILBREAK.
I KNOW.
A COUNCIL OF OUR EXECUTIVES FROM AROUND THE WORLD WILL BE CONVENED SOON.
THE DEATH OF WHITEBEARD HAS DESTABILIZED THE OLD WORLD ORDER. THE GOVERNMENT'S MACHINATIONS ARE ALL IN DISARRAY.
I WANT TO TALK TO YOU ABOUT WHAT HAPPENED TO KUMA TOO.
!
HE ISN'T THE KUMA I KNEW ANYMORE.
WHY WOULD HE ALLOW THE GOVERNMENT TO TELL HIM WHAT TO DO?
THAT'S SOMETHING I REALLY WANT TO KNOW.
HE TRIED TO KILL ME!
...

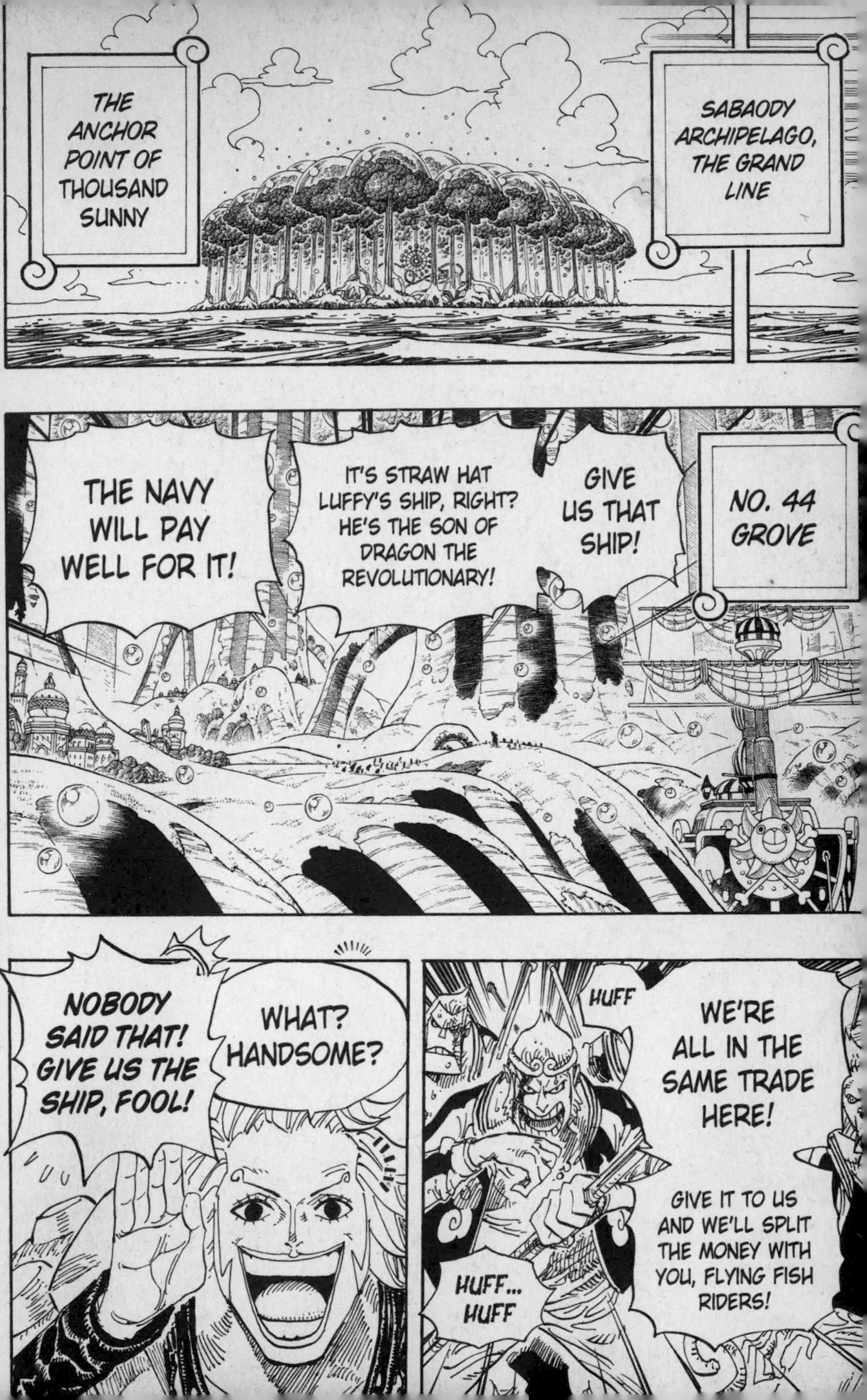
SABAODY ARCHIPELAGO, THE GRAND LINE
THE ANCHOR POINT OF THOUSAND SUNNY
NO. 44 GROVE
GIVE US THAT SHIP!
IT'S STRAW HAT LUFFY'S SHIP, RIGHT? HE'S THE SON OF DRAGON THE REVOLUTIONARY!
THE NAVY WILL PAY WELL FOR IT!
HUFF
WE'RE ALL IN THE SAME TRADE HERE!
GIVE IT TO US AND WE'LL SPLIT THE MONEY WITH YOU, FLYING FISH RIDERS!
HUFF... HUFF
WHAT? HANDSOME?
NOBODY SAID THAT! GIVE US THE SHIP, FOOL!

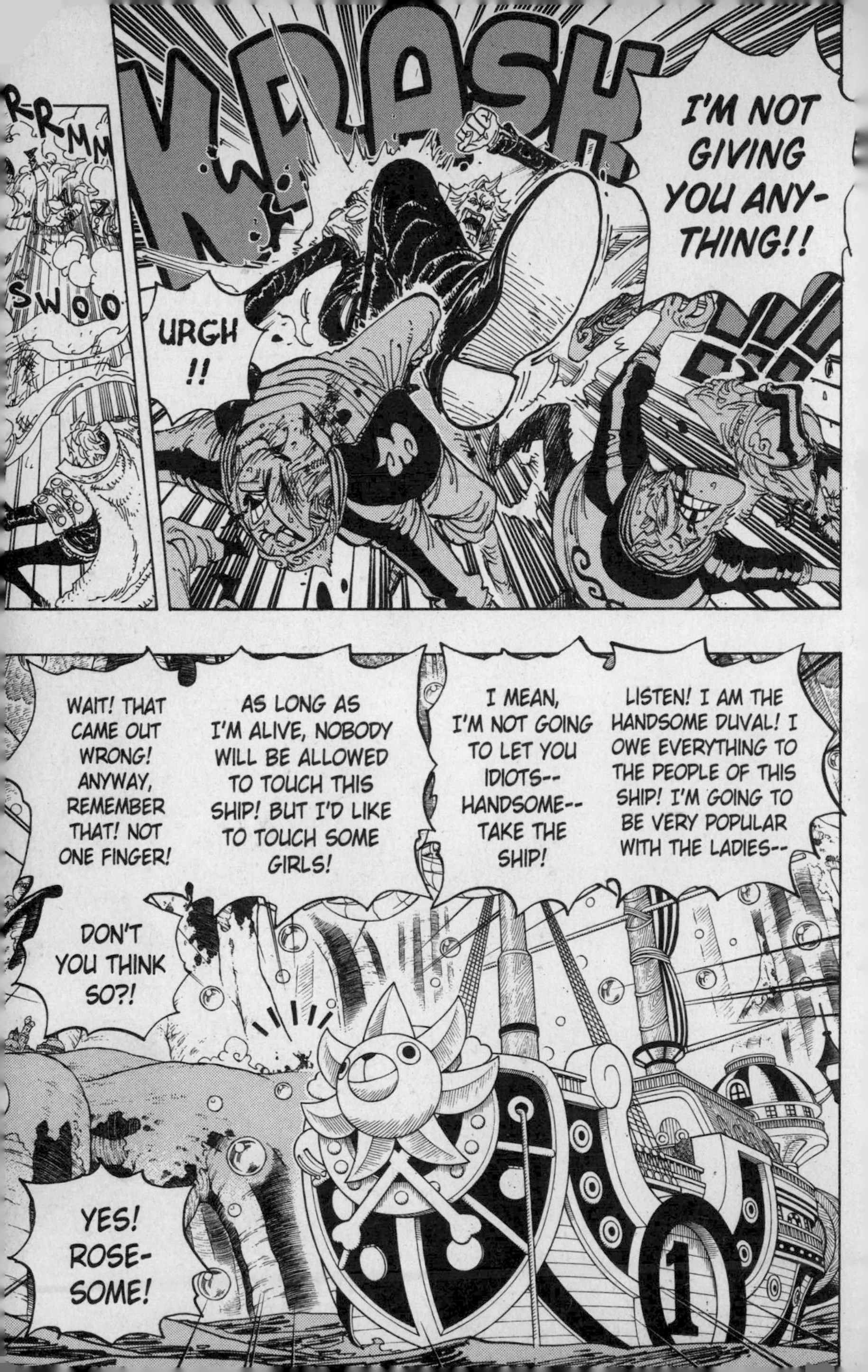
I'M NOT GIVING YOU ANY-THING!!
WRASH
URGH !!
R-R-MN
SWOO
LISTEN! I AM THE HANDSOME DUVAL! I OWE EVERYTHING TO THE PEOPLE OF THIS SHIP! I'M GOING TO BE VERY POPULAR WITH THE LADIES--
I MEAN, I'M NOT GOING TO LET YOU IDIOTS-- HANDSOME-- TAKE THE SHIP!
AS LONG AS I'M ALIVE, NOBODY WILL BE ALLOWED TO TOUCH THIS SHIP! BUT I'D LIKE TO TOUCH SOME GIRLS!
WAIT! THAT CAME OUT WRONG! ANYWAY, REMEMBER THAT! NOT ONE FINGER!
DON'T YOU THINK SO?!
YES! ROSE-SOME!
1

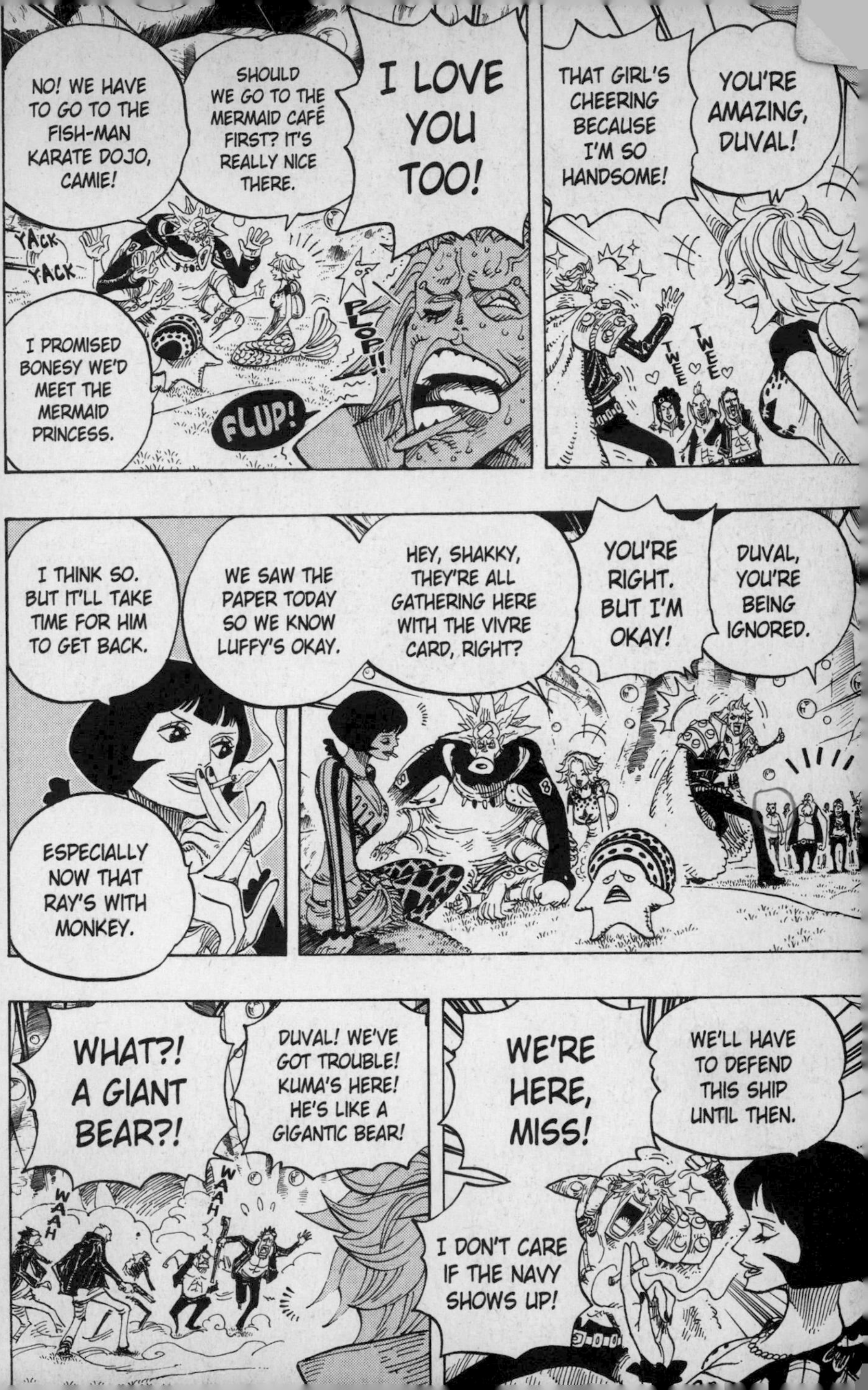
YOU'RE AMAZING, DUVAL!
THAT GIRL'S CHEERING BECAUSE I'M SO HANDSOME!
TWEE
TWEE
I LOVE YOU TOO!
SHOULD WE GO TO THE MERMAID CAFÉ FIRST? IT'S REALLY NICE THERE.
NO! WE HAVE TO GO TO THE FISH-MAN KARATE DOJO, CAMIE!
YACK
YACK
PLOP!!
I PROMISED BONESY WE'D MEET THE MERMAID PRINCESS.
FLUP!
DUVAL, YOU'RE BEING IGNORED.
YOU'RE RIGHT. BUT I'M OKAY!
HEY, SHAKKY, THEY'RE ALL GATHERING HERE WITH THE VIVRE CARD, RIGHT?
WE SAW THE PAPER TODAY SO WE KNOW LUFFY'S OKAY.
I THINK SO. BUT IT'LL TAKE TIME FOR HIM TO GET BACK.
ESPECIALLY NOW THAT RAY'S WITH MONKEY.
WE'LL HAVE TO DEFEND THIS SHIP UNTIL THEN.
WE'RE HERE, MISS!
I DON'T CARE IF THE NAVY SHOWS UP!
DUVAL! WE'VE GOT TROUBLE! KUMA'S HERE! HE'S LIKE A GIGANTIC BEAR!
WHAT?! A GIANT BEAR?!
WAAH
WAAH

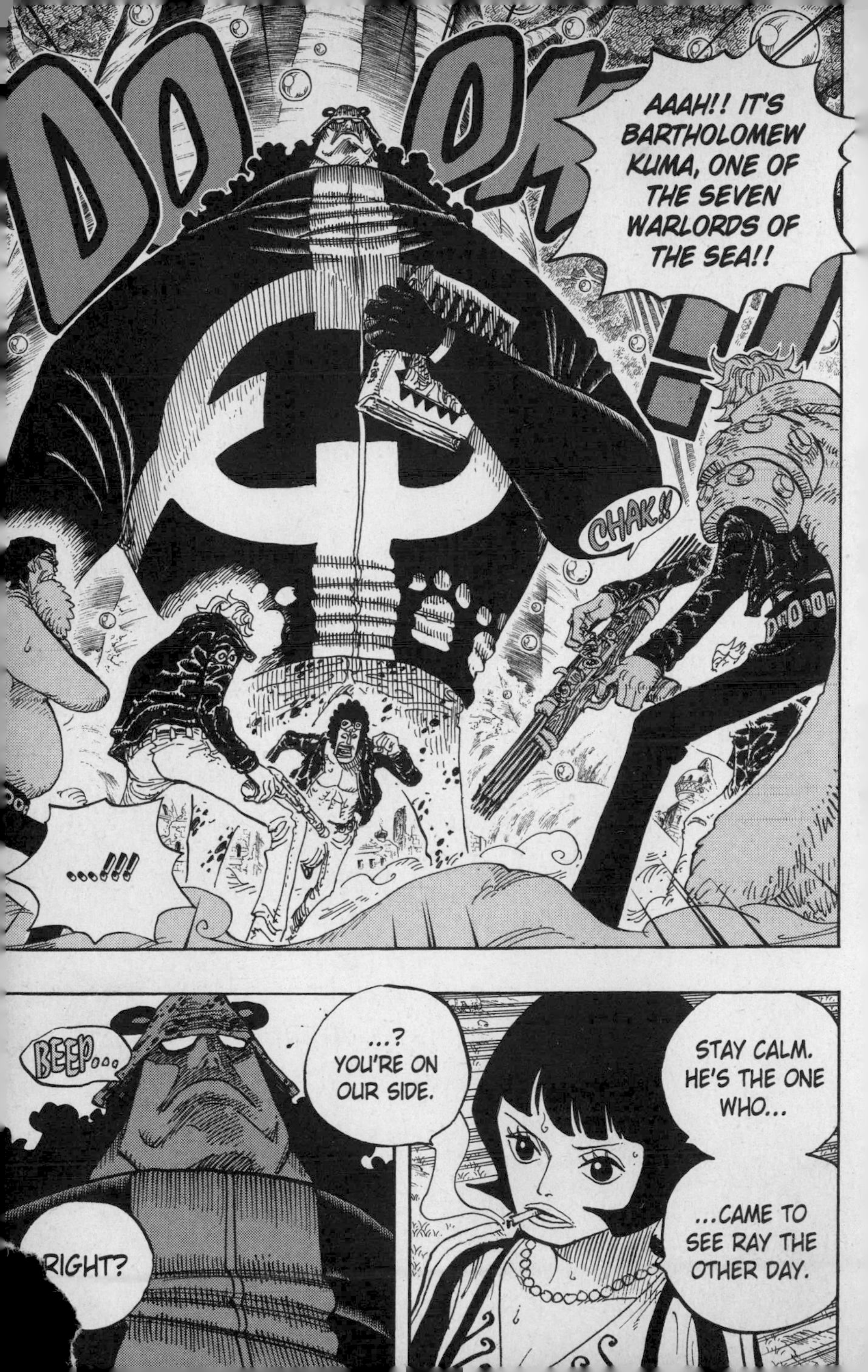
AAAH!! IT'S BARTHOLOMEW KUMA, ONE OF THE SEVEN WARLORDS OF THE SEA!!
CHAK!!
...!!!
STAY CALM. HE'S THE ONE WHO...
...CAME TO SEE RAY THE OTHER DAY.
...? YOU'RE ON OUR SIDE.
BEEP...
RIGHT?

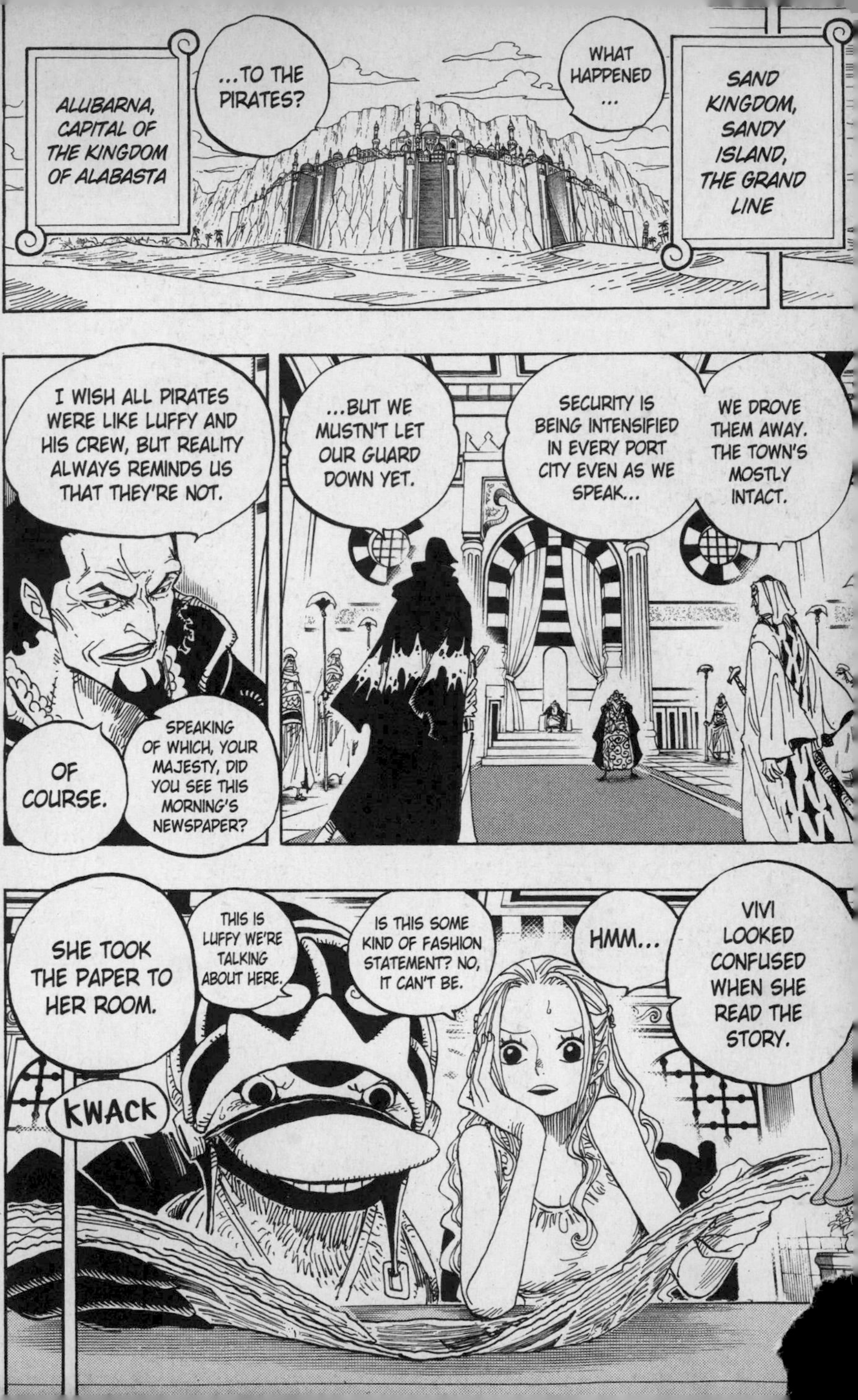
SAND KINGDOM, SANDY ISLAND, THE GRAND LINE
WHAT HAPPENED ...
...TO THE PIRATES?
ALUBARNA, CAPITAL OF THE KINGDOM OF ALABASTA
WE DROVE THEM AWAY. THE TOWN'S MOSTLY INTACT.
SECURITY IS BEING INTENSIFIED IN EVERY PORT CITY EVEN AS WE SPEAK...
...BUT WE MUSTN'T LET OUR GUARD DOWN YET.
I WISH ALL PIRATES WERE LIKE LUFFY AND HIS CREW, BUT REALITY ALWAYS REMINDS US THAT THEY'RE NOT.
SPEAKING OF WHICH, YOUR MAJESTY, DID YOU SEE THIS MORNING'S NEWSPAPER?
OF COURSE.
VIVI LOOKED CONFUSED WHEN SHE READ THE STORY.
HMM...
IS THIS SOME KIND OF FASHION STATEMENT? NO, IT CAN'T BE.
THIS IS LUFFY WE'RE TALKING ABOUT HERE.
SHE TOOK THE PAPER TO HER ROOM.
KWACK

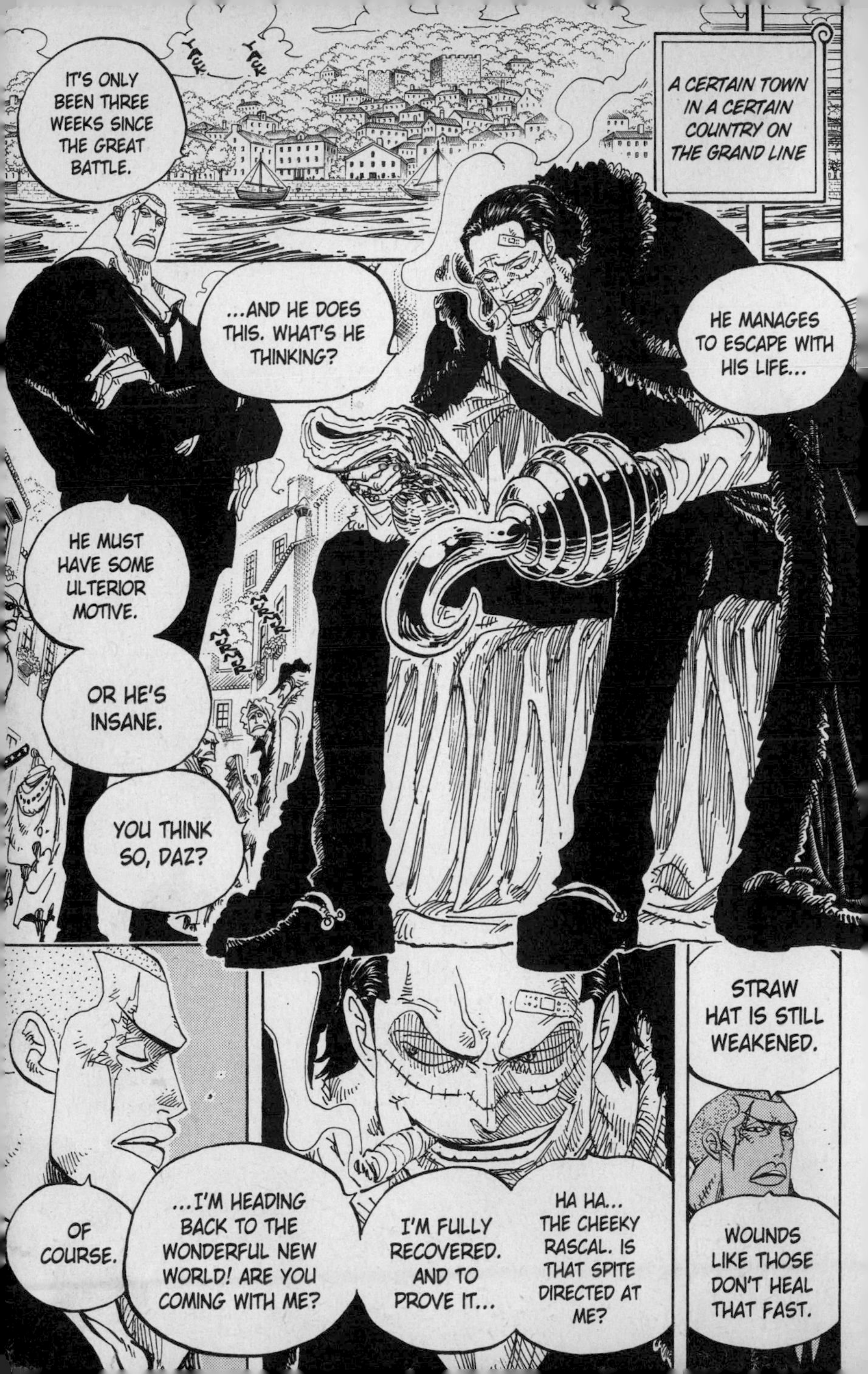
A CERTAIN TOWN IN A CERTAIN COUNTRY ON THE GRAND LINE
YACK YACK
IT'S ONLY BEEN THREE WEEKS SINCE THE GREAT BATTLE.
HE MANAGES TO ESCAPE WITH HIS LIFE...
...AND HE DOES THIS. WHAT'S HE THINKING?
HE MUST HAVE SOME ULTERIOR MOTIVE.
OR HE'S INSANE.
YOU THINK SO, DAZ?
STRAW HAT IS STILL WEAKENED.
WOUNDS LIKE THOSE DON'T HEAL THAT FAST.
HA HA... THE CHEEKY RASCAL. IS THAT SPITE DIRECTED AT ME?
I'M FULLY RECOVERED. AND TO PROVE IT...
...I'M HEADING BACK TO THE WONDERFUL NEW WORLD! ARE YOU COMING WITH ME?
OF COURSE.

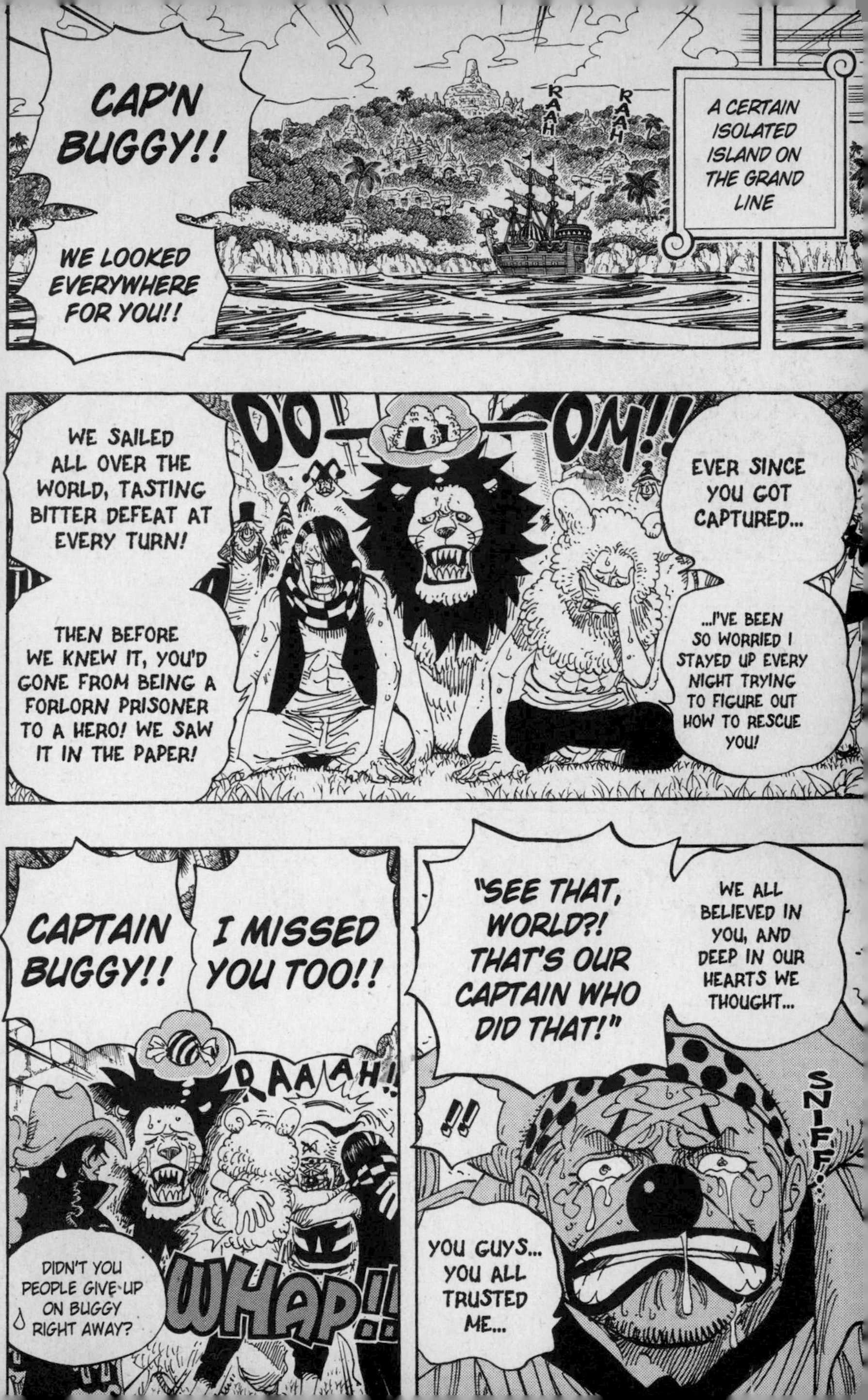
A CERTAIN ISOLATED ISLAND ON THE GRAND LINE
RAAH
RAAH
CAP'N BUGGY!!
WE LOOKED EVERYWHERE FOR YOU!!
DO—OM!!
EVER SINCE YOU GOT CAPTURED...
...I'VE BEEN SO WORRIED I STAYED UP EVERY NIGHT TRYING TO FIGURE OUT HOW TO RESCUE YOU!
WE SAILED ALL OVER THE WORLD, TASTING BITTER DEFEAT AT EVERY TURN!
THEN BEFORE WE KNEW IT, YOU'D GONE FROM BEING A FORLORN PRISONER TO A HERO! WE SAW IT IN THE PAPER!
WE ALL BELIEVED IN YOU, AND DEEP IN OUR HEARTS WE THOUGHT...
"SEE THAT, WORLD?! THAT'S OUR CAPTAIN WHO DID THAT!"
!!
SNIFF...
YOU GUYS... YOU ALL TRUSTED ME...
I MISSED YOU TOO!!
CAPTAIN BUGGY!!
RAAAH!!
WHAP!!
DIDN'T YOU PEOPLE GIVE UP ON BUGGY RIGHT AWAY?

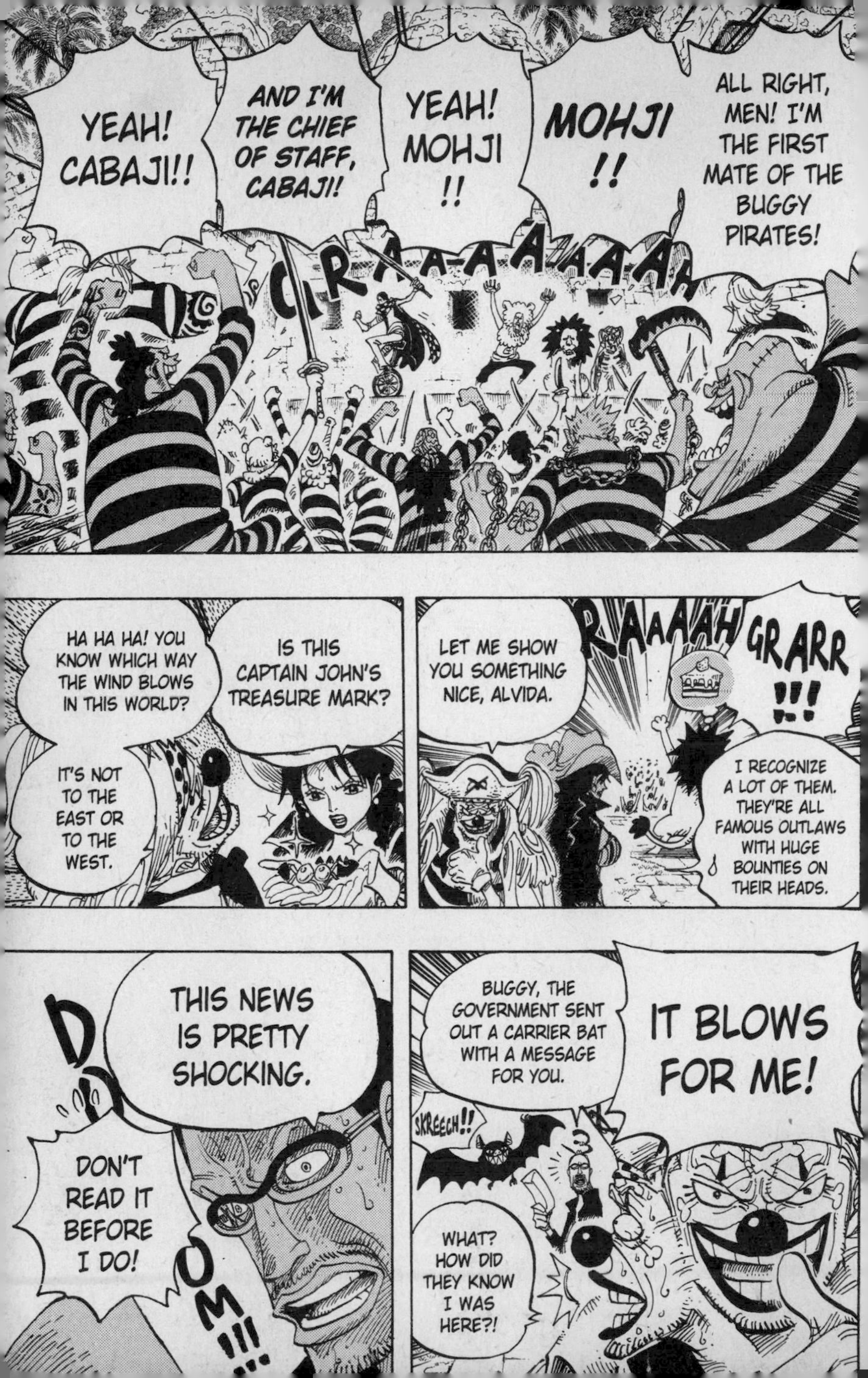
ALL RIGHT, MEN! I'M THE FIRST MATE OF THE BUGGY PIRATES!
MOHJI!!
YEAH! MOHJI!!
AND I'M THE CHIEF OF STAFF, CABAJI!
YEAH! CABAJI!!
GRAAAAAAAAH
RAAAAH
GRARR!!!
LET ME SHOW YOU SOMETHING NICE, ALVIDA.
I RECOGNIZE A LOT OF THEM. THEY'RE ALL FAMOUS OUTLAWS WITH HUGE BOUNTIES ON THEIR HEADS.
IS THIS CAPTAIN JOHN'S TREASURE MARK?
HA HA HA! YOU KNOW WHICH WAY THE WIND BLOWS IN THIS WORLD?
IT'S NOT TO THE EAST OR TO THE WEST.
IT BLOWS FOR ME!
BUGGY, THE GOVERNMENT SENT OUT A CARRIER BAT WITH A MESSAGE FOR YOU.
SKREECH!!
WHAT? HOW DID THEY KNOW I WAS HERE?!
THIS NEWS IS PRETTY SHOCKING.
DOOM!!!
DON'T READ IT BEFORE I DO!

IT'S NICO ROBIN'S VOICE ACTRESS, YURIKO YAMAGUCHI!!

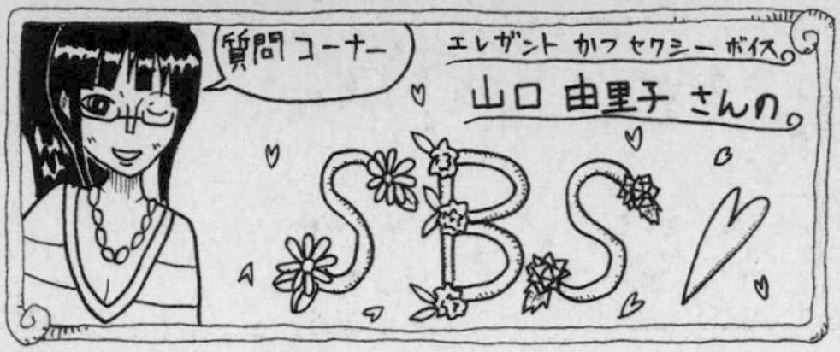
質問コーナー
エレガント かつ セクシー ボイス。
山口 由里子 さんの
SBS

(Yoshiko, Miyagi Prefecture)

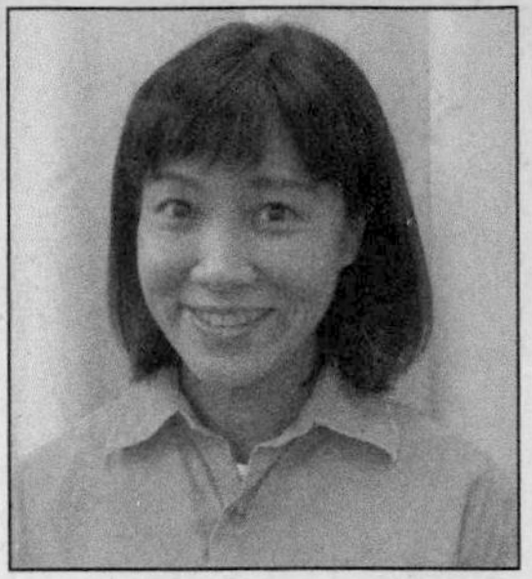

SBS Question Corner

HDYD! (How Do You Do!)
This is our...seventh! Our seventh Voice Actor Question Corner! Our guest today isn't like the other Straw Hat voice actors! She is Nico Robin, the mysterious woman who never lets down her guard! But the actress who voices her always has her guard down! Allow me to introduce Yuriko Yamaguchi! In the house!

Oda(O): Hi, Yuriko, or as I like to call you, Softie. Please introduce yourself.

Yamaguchi(Y): I'm Nico Robin!♡

O: That's just the character you portray, but whatever. If I push back now, we'll never get anywhere. But once you get into character, you look just like...

Y: This is delicious.

O: Hey! Those rice crackers were a gift! Why did you start eating them now?! Hey! Hey! No, thank you! Don't mind me! I don't need any tea! Now let's start! Oh yeah, do you know what SBS stands for?

Y: (S)hoot, (B)rook got (S)tabbed by me!

O: Don't stab him! Geez!

Y: Hey, Odacchi, want some tea?

O: I said I'm good!

Y: Oh, I get it. SBS stands for (S)houldn't we take a (B)reak (S)oon?

O: Not yet! Geez! Can you please do it right?!

Yamaguchi's Question Corner will continue on page 206! ☞

PREVIEW FOR NEXT VOICE ACTOR'S SBS

The next Voice Actor SBS will be for these two! Send in your questions! Ask whatever you want so you won't regret it later!

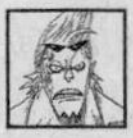

Franky (Kazuki Yao)

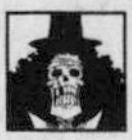

Brook (Cho)

Weirdos are coming out of the woodwork! So ask Franky your weird questions! Ask Brook even weirder questions!

Chapter 594: MESSAGE

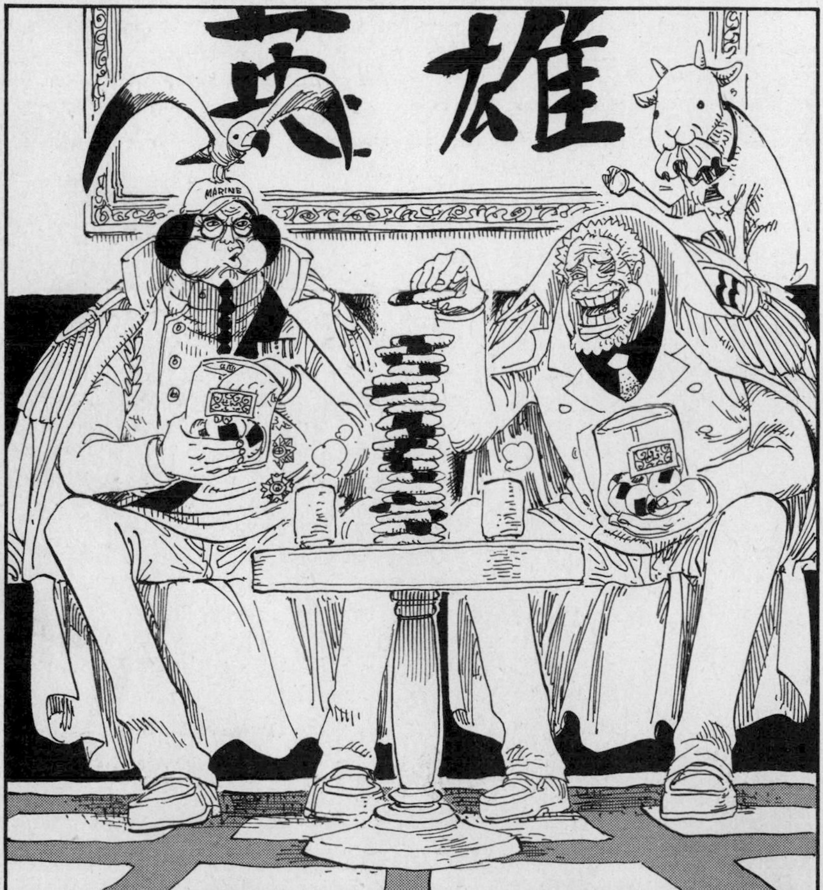
英雄
MARINE

*HERO

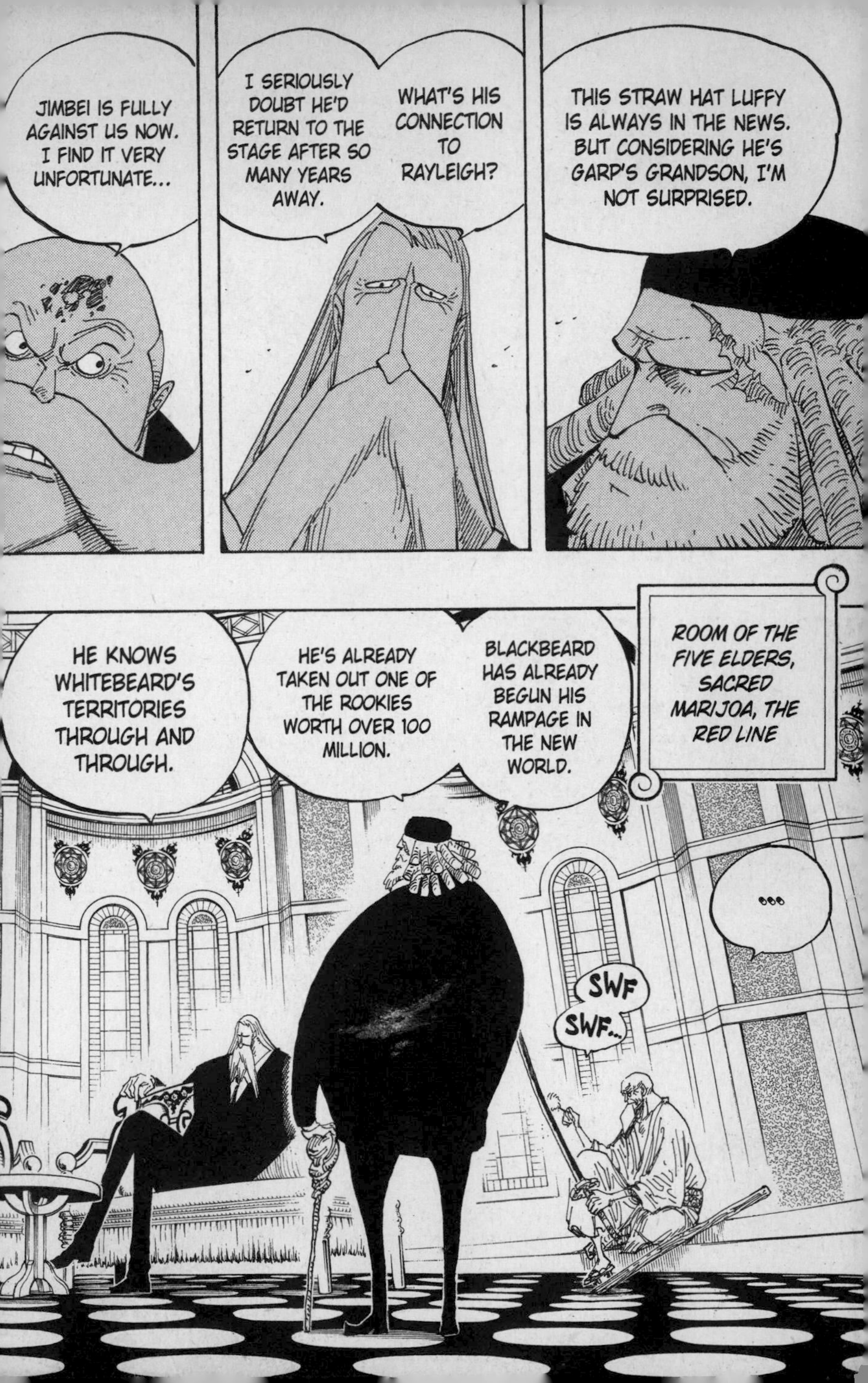
THIS STRAW HAT LUFFY IS ALWAYS IN THE NEWS. BUT CONSIDERING HE'S GARP'S GRANDSON, I'M NOT SURPRISED.
WHAT'S HIS CONNECTION TO RAYLEIGH?
I SERIOUSLY DOUBT HE'D RETURN TO THE STAGE AFTER SO MANY YEARS AWAY.
JIMBEI IS FULLY AGAINST US NOW. I FIND IT VERY UNFORTUNATE...
ROOM OF THE FIVE ELDERS, SACRED MARIJOA, THE RED LINE
BLACKBEARD HAS ALREADY BEGUN HIS RAMPAGE IN THE NEW WORLD.
HE'S ALREADY TAKEN OUT ONE OF THE ROOKIES WORTH OVER 100 MILLION.
HE KNOWS WHITEBEARD'S TERRITORIES THROUGH AND THROUGH.
...
SWF
SWF...

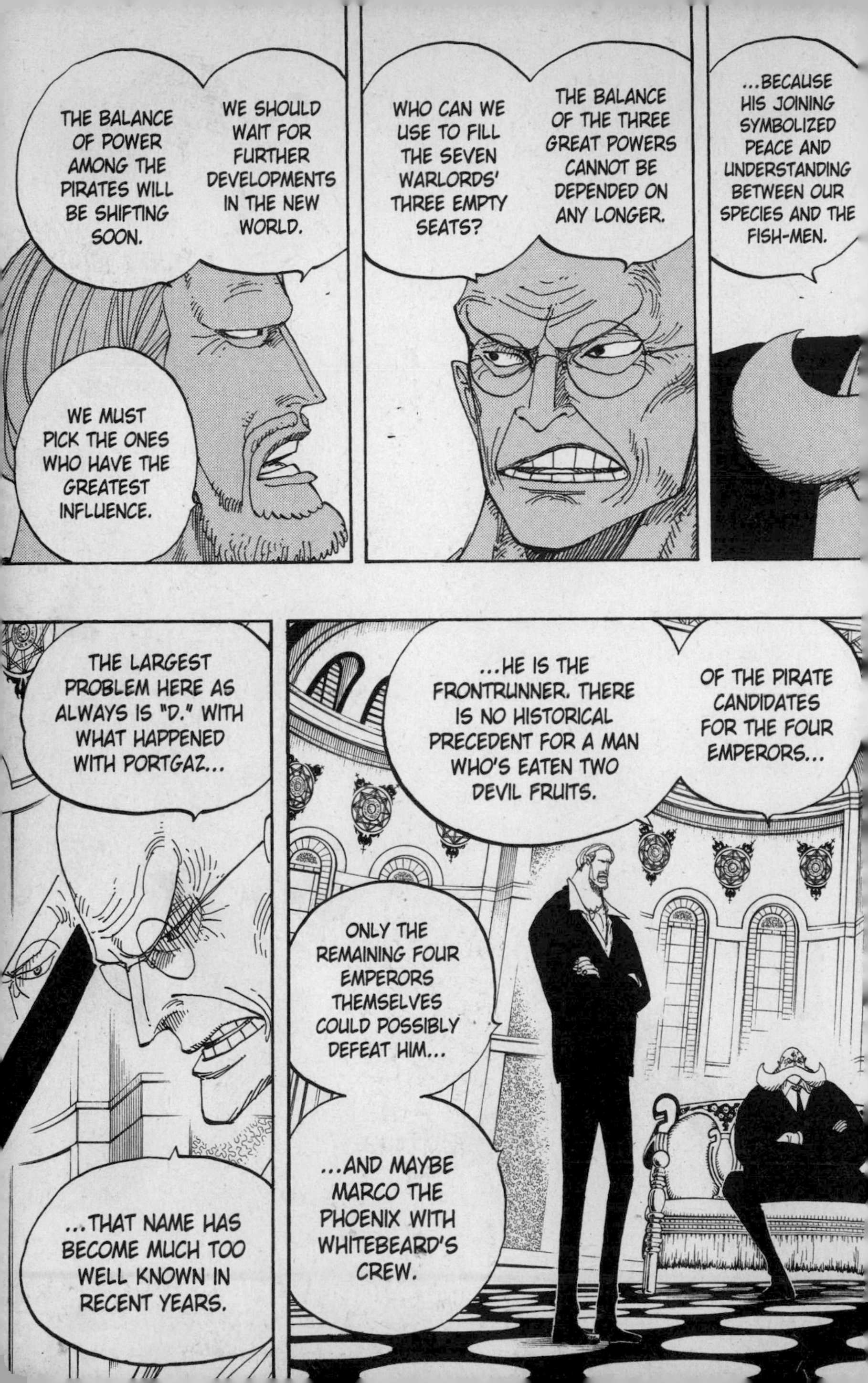
...BECAUSE HIS JOINING SYMBOLIZED PEACE AND UNDERSTANDING BETWEEN OUR SPECIES AND THE FISH-MEN.
THE BALANCE OF THE THREE GREAT POWERS CANNOT BE DEPENDED ON ANY LONGER.
WHO CAN WE USE TO FILL THE SEVEN WARLORDS' THREE EMPTY SEATS?
WE SHOULD WAIT FOR FURTHER DEVELOPMENTS IN THE NEW WORLD.
THE BALANCE OF POWER AMONG THE PIRATES WILL BE SHIFTING SOON.
WE MUST PICK THE ONES WHO HAVE THE GREATEST INFLUENCE.
OF THE PIRATE CANDIDATES FOR THE FOUR EMPERORS...
...HE IS THE FRONTRUNNER. THERE IS NO HISTORICAL PRECEDENT FOR A MAN WHO'S EATEN TWO DEVIL FRUITS.
ONLY THE REMAINING FOUR EMPERORS THEMSELVES COULD POSSIBLY DEFEAT HIM...
...AND MAYBE MARCO THE PHOENIX WITH WHITEBEARD'S CREW.
THE LARGEST PROBLEM HERE AS ALWAYS IS "D." WITH WHAT HAPPENED WITH PORTGAZ...
...THAT NAME HAS BECOME MUCH TOO WELL KNOWN IN RECENT YEARS.

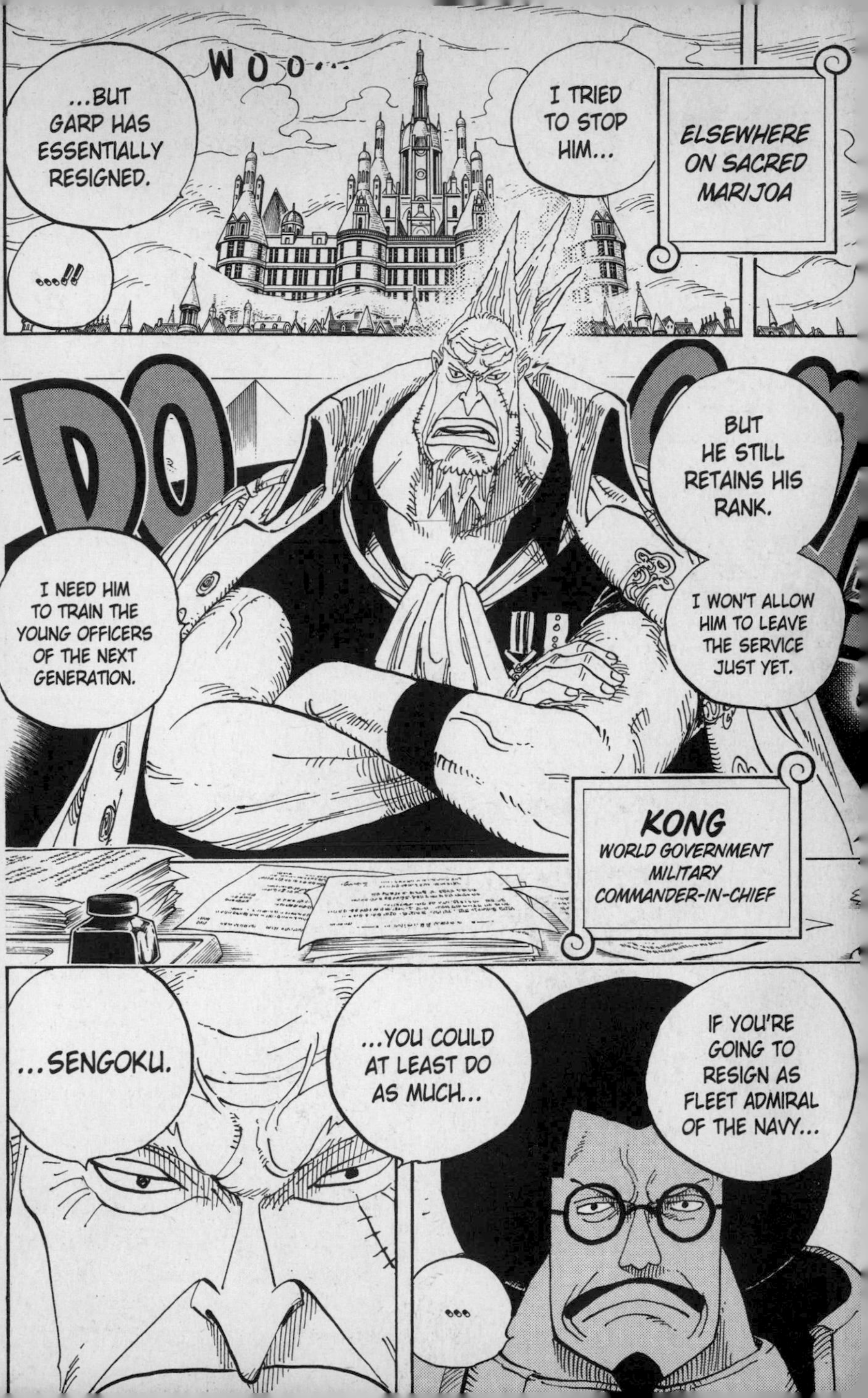
ELSEWHERE ON SACRED MARIJOA
I TRIED TO STOP HIM...
WOO...
...BUT GARP HAS ESSENTIALLY RESIGNED.
...!!
DO
BUT HE STILL RETAINS HIS RANK.
I WON'T ALLOW HIM TO LEAVE THE SERVICE JUST YET.
I NEED HIM TO TRAIN THE YOUNG OFFICERS OF THE NEXT GENERATION.
KONG
WORLD GOVERNMENT MILITARY COMMANDER-IN-CHIEF
IF YOU'RE GOING TO RESIGN AS FLEET ADMIRAL OF THE NAVY...
...YOU COULD AT LEAST DO AS MUCH...
...
...SENGOKU.

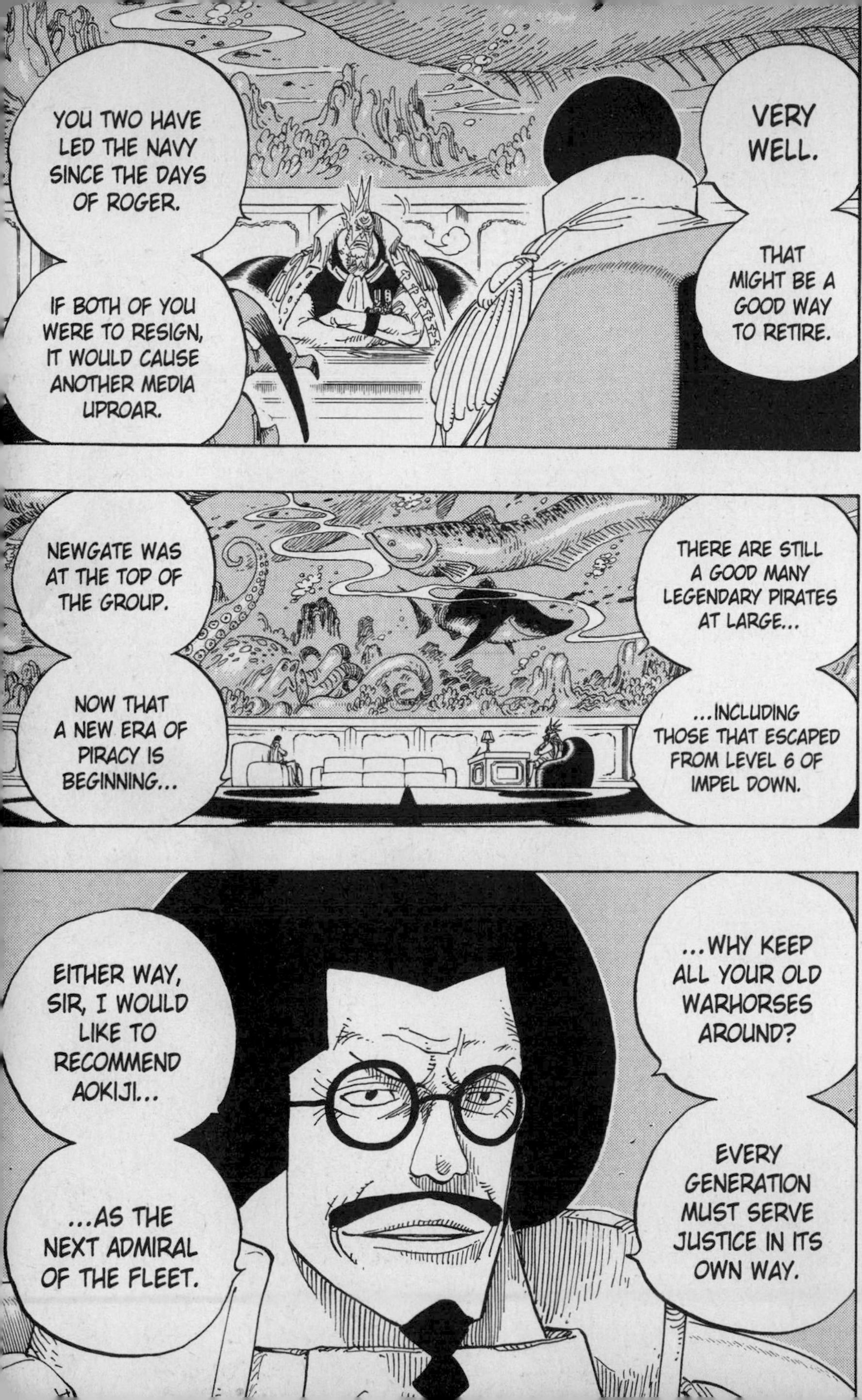
VERY WELL.
THAT MIGHT BE A GOOD WAY TO RETIRE.
YOU TWO HAVE LED THE NAVY SINCE THE DAYS OF ROGER.
IF BOTH OF YOU WERE TO RESIGN, IT WOULD CAUSE ANOTHER MEDIA UPROAR.
THERE ARE STILL A GOOD MANY LEGENDARY PIRATES AT LARGE...
...INCLUDING THOSE THAT ESCAPED FROM LEVEL 6 OF IMPEL DOWN.
NEWGATE WAS AT THE TOP OF THE GROUP.
NOW THAT A NEW ERA OF PIRACY IS BEGINNING...
...WHY KEEP ALL YOUR OLD WARHORSES AROUND?
EVERY GENERATION MUST SERVE JUSTICE IN ITS OWN WAY.
EITHER WAY, SIR, I WOULD LIKE TO RECOMMEND AOKIJI...
...AS THE NEXT ADMIRAL OF THE FLEET.

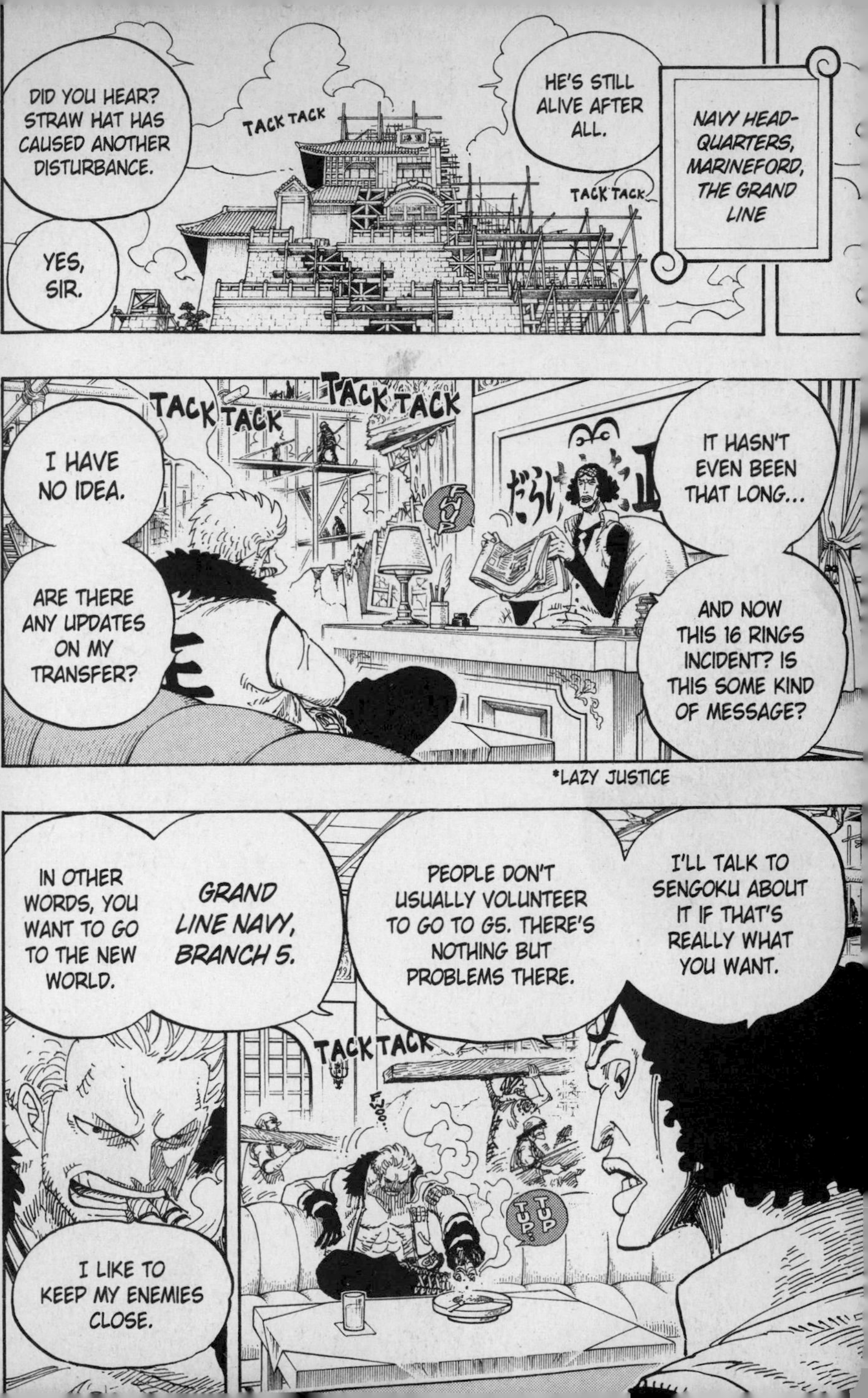
NAVY HEAD-QUARTERS, MARINEFORD, THE GRAND LINE
HE'S STILL ALIVE AFTER ALL.
TACK TACK
DID YOU HEAR? STRAW HAT HAS CAUSED ANOTHER DISTURBANCE.
TACK TACK
YES, SIR.
IT HASN'T EVEN BEEN THAT LONG...
AND NOW THIS 16 RINGS INCIDENT? IS THIS SOME KIND OF MESSAGE?
TACK TACK
TACK TACK
I HAVE NO IDEA.
ARE THERE ANY UPDATES ON MY TRANSFER?
*LAZY JUSTICE
I'LL TALK TO SENGOKU ABOUT IT IF THAT'S REALLY WHAT YOU WANT.
PEOPLE DON'T USUALLY VOLUNTEER TO GO TO G5. THERE'S NOTHING BUT PROBLEMS THERE.
GRAND LINE NAVY, BRANCH 5.
IN OTHER WORDS, YOU WANT TO GO TO THE NEW WORLD.
TACK TACK
TUP TUP
FZOO...
I LIKE TO KEEP MY ENEMIES CLOSE.

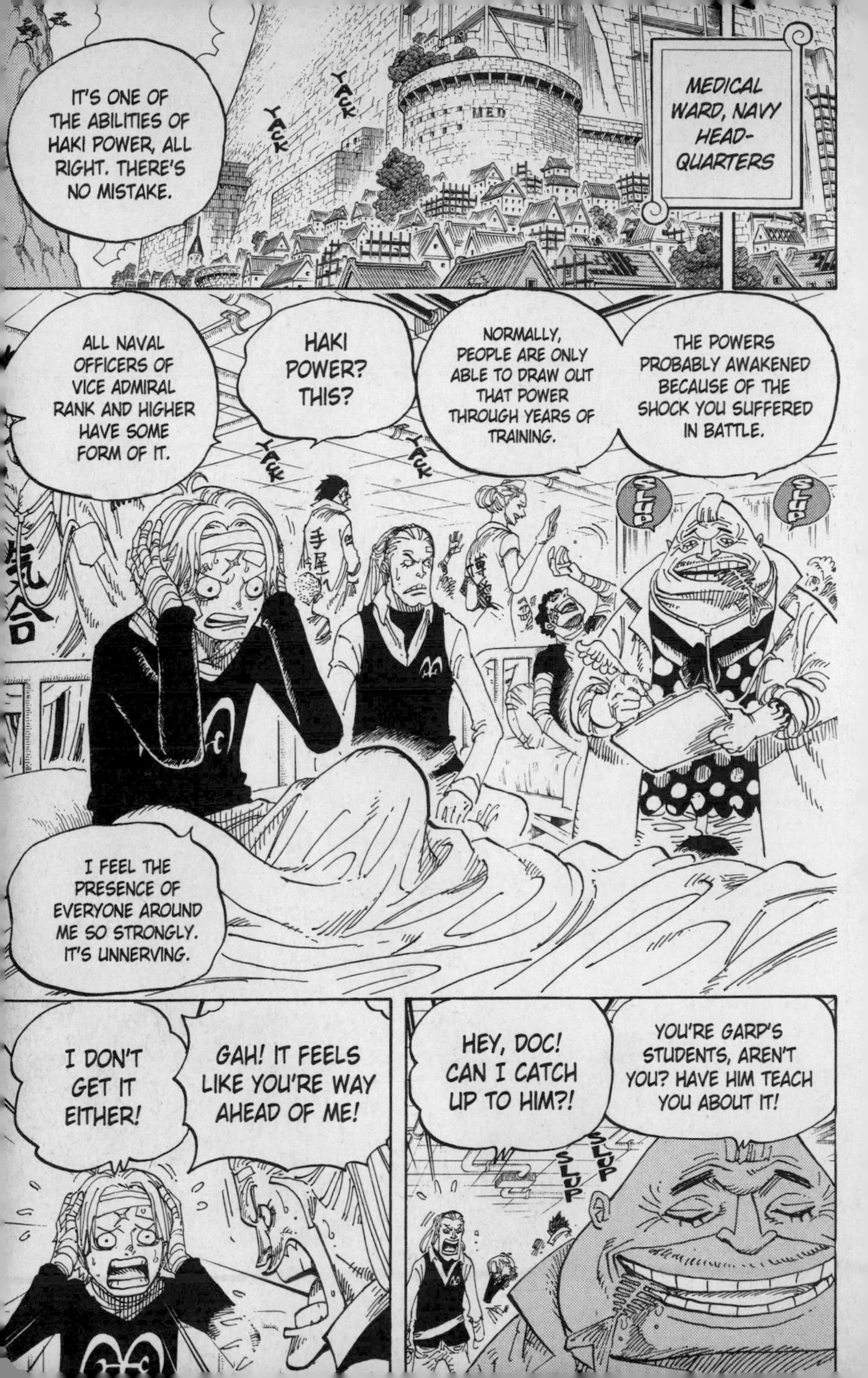
MEDICAL WARD, NAVY HEAD-QUARTERS
YACK
YACK
IT'S ONE OF THE ABILITIES OF HAKI POWER, ALL RIGHT. THERE'S NO MISTAKE.
THE POWERS PROBABLY AWAKENED BECAUSE OF THE SHOCK YOU SUFFERED IN BATTLE.
NORMALLY, PEOPLE ARE ONLY ABLE TO DRAW OUT THAT POWER THROUGH YEARS OF TRAINING.
HAKI POWER? THIS?
ALL NAVAL OFFICERS OF VICE ADMIRAL RANK AND HIGHER HAVE SOME FORM OF IT.
SLUP
SLUP
YACK
YACK
I FEEL THE PRESENCE OF EVERYONE AROUND ME SO STRONGLY. IT'S UNNERVING.
YOU'RE GARP'S STUDENTS, AREN'T YOU? HAVE HIM TEACH YOU ABOUT IT!
HEY, DOC! CAN I CATCH UP TO HIM?!
SLUP
SLUP
GAH! IT FEELS LIKE YOU'RE WAY AHEAD OF ME!
I DON'T GET IT EITHER!

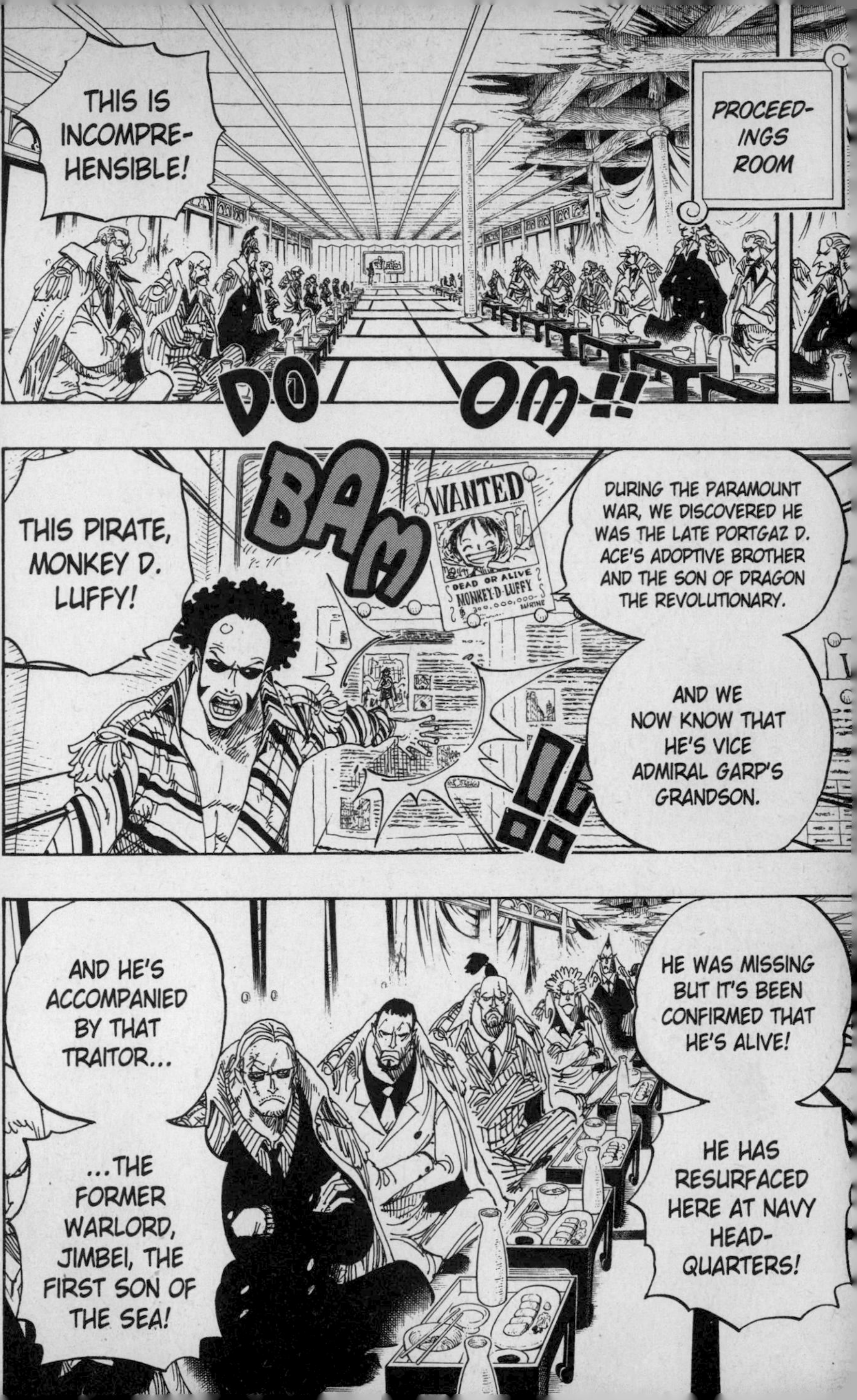
PROCEEDINGS ROOM
THIS IS INCOMPREHENSIBLE!
DOOM!!
DURING THE PARAMOUNT WAR, WE DISCOVERED HE WAS THE LATE PORTGAZ D. ACE'S ADOPTIVE BROTHER AND THE SON OF DRAGON THE REVOLUTIONARY.
WANTED
DEAD OR ALIVE
MONKEY·D·LUFFY
MARINE
BAM
THIS PIRATE, MONKEY D. LUFFY!
AND WE NOW KNOW THAT HE'S VICE ADMIRAL GARP'S GRANDSON.
!!
HE WAS MISSING BUT IT'S BEEN CONFIRMED THAT HE'S ALIVE!
HE HAS RESURFACED HERE AT NAVY HEADQUARTERS!
AND HE'S ACCOMPANIED BY THAT TRAITOR...
...THE FORMER WARLORD, JIMBEI, THE FIRST SON OF THE SEA!

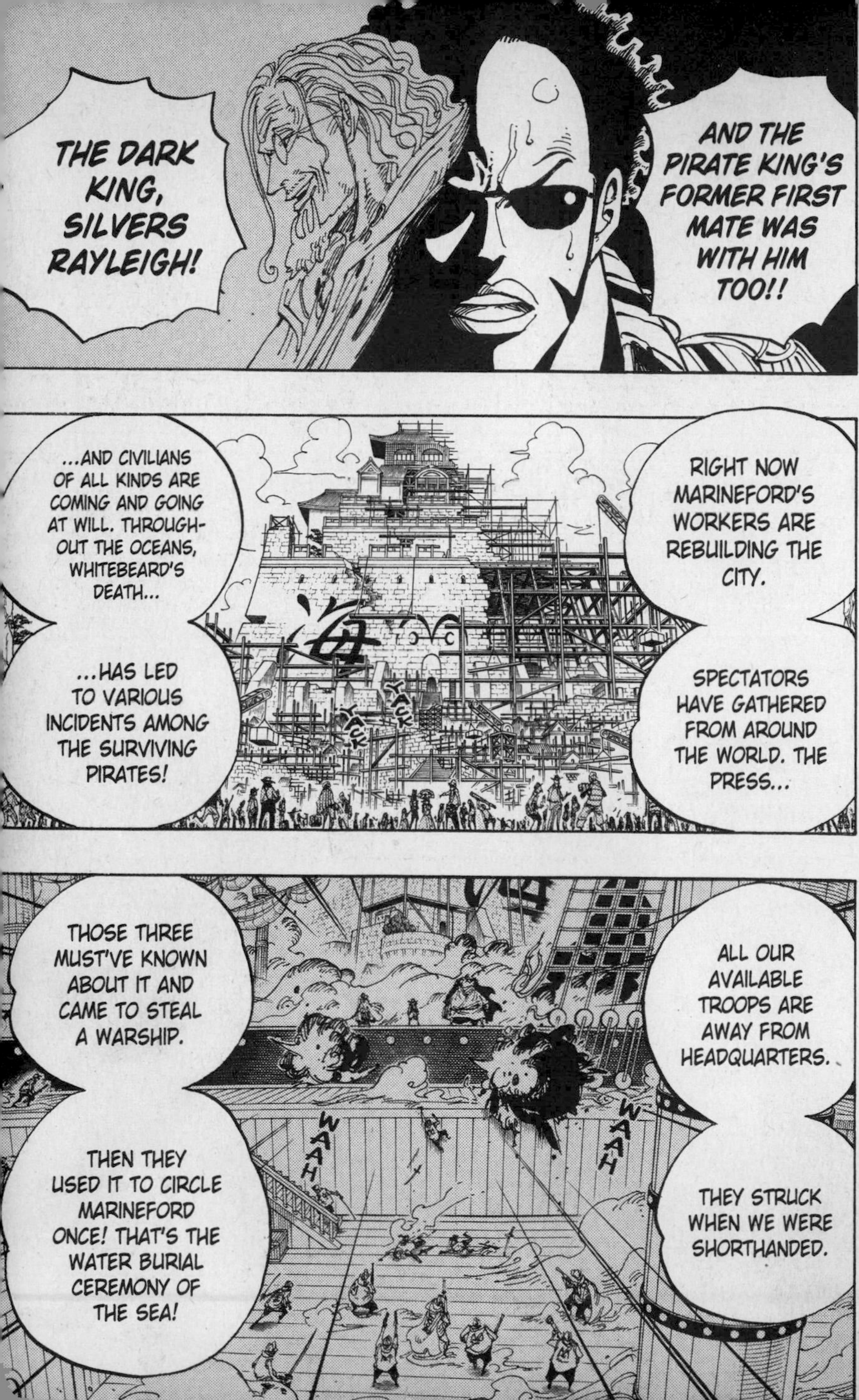
AND THE PIRATE KING'S FORMER FIRST MATE WAS WITH HIM TOO!!
THE DARK KING, SILVERS RAYLEIGH!
RIGHT NOW MARINEFORD'S WORKERS ARE REBUILDING THE CITY.
SPECTATORS HAVE GATHERED FROM AROUND THE WORLD. THE PRESS...
...AND CIVILIANS OF ALL KINDS ARE COMING AND GOING AT WILL. THROUGH-OUT THE OCEANS, WHITEBEARD'S DEATH...
...HAS LED TO VARIOUS INCIDENTS AMONG THE SURVIVING PIRATES!
YACK
YACK
ALL OUR AVAILABLE TROOPS ARE AWAY FROM HEADQUARTERS.
THEY STRUCK WHEN WE WERE SHORTHANDED.
WAAH
WAAH
THOSE THREE MUST'VE KNOWN ABOUT IT AND CAME TO STEAL A WARSHIP.
THEN THEY USED IT TO CIRCLE MARINEFORD ONCE! THAT'S THE WATER BURIAL CEREMONY OF THE SEA!

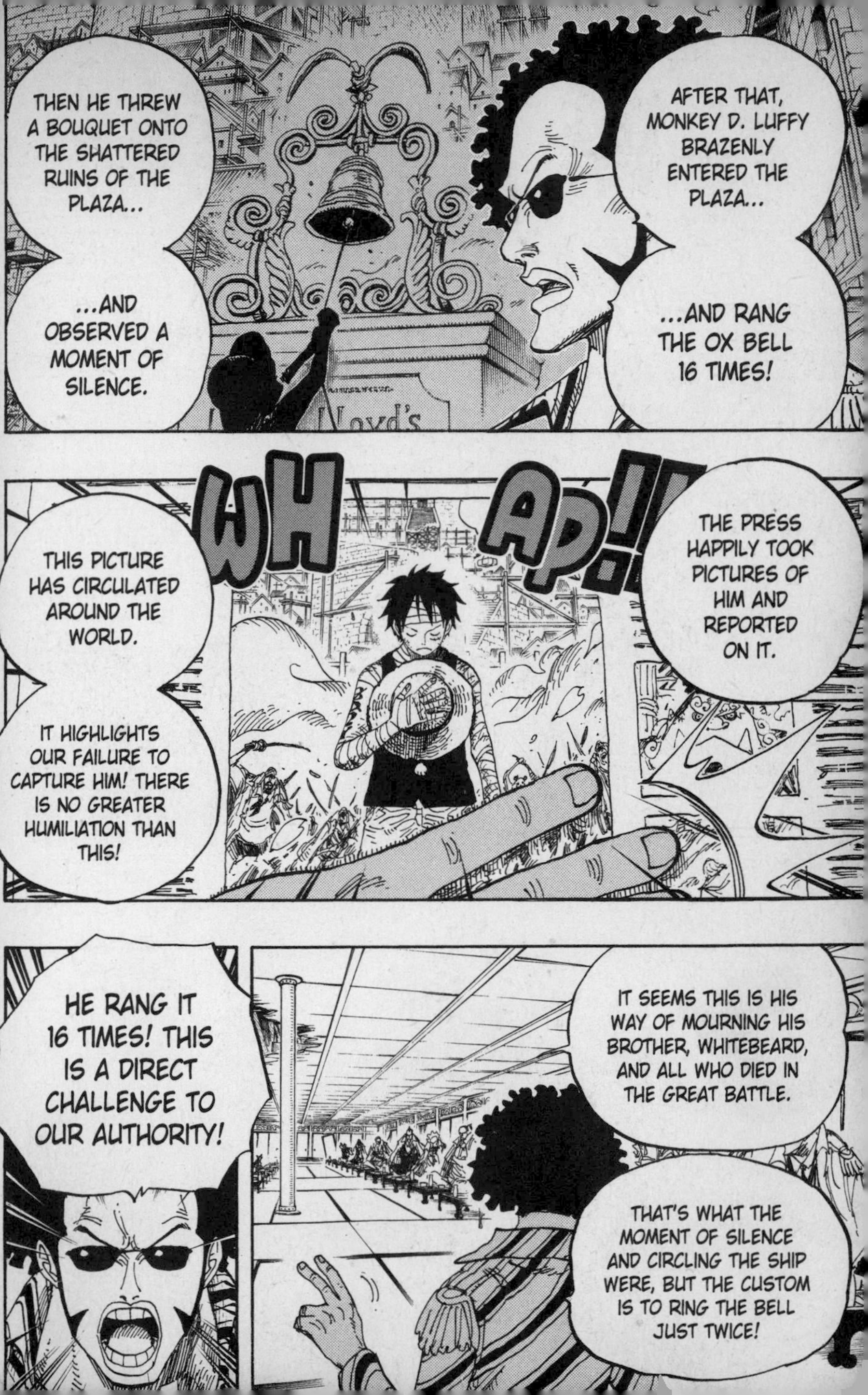
AFTER THAT, MONKEY D. LUFFY BRAZENLY ENTERED THE PLAZA...
...AND RANG THE OX BELL 16 TIMES!
THEN HE THREW A BOUQUET ONTO THE SHATTERED RUINS OF THE PLAZA...
...AND OBSERVED A MOMENT OF SILENCE.
WHAP!!
THE PRESS HAPPILY TOOK PICTURES OF HIM AND REPORTED ON IT.
THIS PICTURE HAS CIRCULATED AROUND THE WORLD.
IT HIGHLIGHTS OUR FAILURE TO CAPTURE HIM! THERE IS NO GREATER HUMILIATION THAN THIS!
IT SEEMS THIS IS HIS WAY OF MOURNING HIS BROTHER, WHITEBEARD, AND ALL WHO DIED IN THE GREAT BATTLE.
THAT'S WHAT THE MOMENT OF SILENCE AND CIRCLING THE SHIP WERE, BUT THE CUSTOM IS TO RING THE BELL JUST TWICE!
HE RANG IT 16 TIMES! THIS IS A DIRECT CHALLENGE TO OUR AUTHORITY!

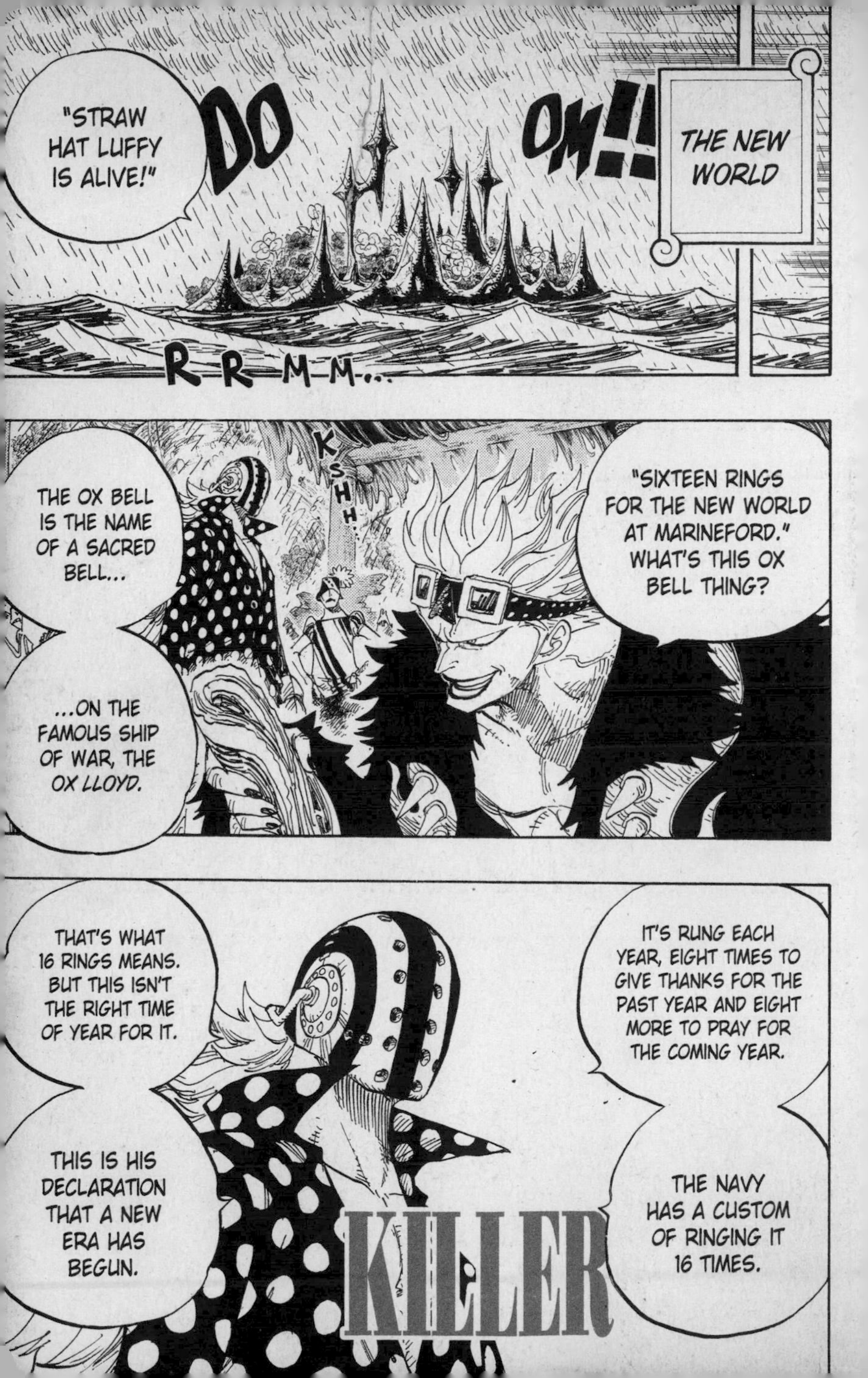
THE NEW WORLD
DO OM!!
"STRAW HAT LUFFY IS ALIVE!"
R R M M...
"SIXTEEN RINGS FOR THE NEW WORLD AT MARINEFORD." WHAT'S THIS OX BELL THING?
KSHH...
THE OX BELL IS THE NAME OF A SACRED BELL...
...ON THE FAMOUS SHIP OF WAR, THE OX LLOYD.
IT'S RUNG EACH YEAR, EIGHT TIMES TO GIVE THANKS FOR THE PAST YEAR AND EIGHT MORE TO PRAY FOR THE COMING YEAR.
THE NAVY HAS A CUSTOM OF RINGING IT 16 TIMES.
THAT'S WHAT 16 RINGS MEANS. BUT THIS ISN'T THE RIGHT TIME OF YEAR FOR IT.
THIS IS HIS DECLARATION THAT A NEW ERA HAS BEGUN.
KILLER

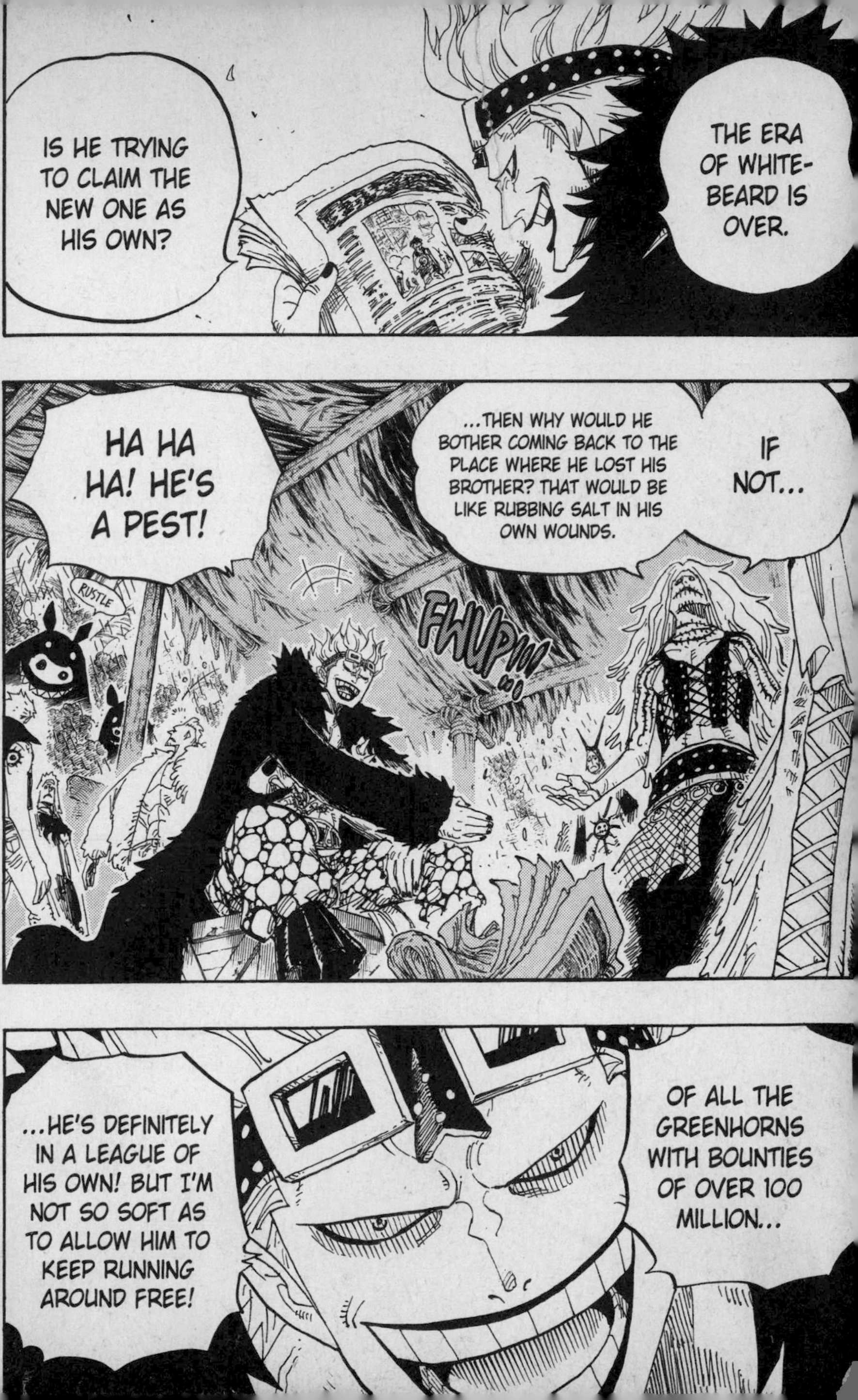
THE ERA OF WHITE-BEARD IS OVER.
IS HE TRYING TO CLAIM THE NEW ONE AS HIS OWN?
IF NOT...
...THEN WHY WOULD HE BOTHER COMING BACK TO THE PLACE WHERE HE LOST HIS BROTHER? THAT WOULD BE LIKE RUBBING SALT IN HIS OWN WOUNDS.
FWUP!!!
HA HA HA! HE'S A PEST!
RUSTLE
OF ALL THE GREENHORNS WITH BOUNTIES OF OVER 100 MILLION...
...HE'S DEFINITELY IN A LEAGUE OF HIS OWN! BUT I'M NOT SO SOFT AS TO ALLOW HIM TO KEEP RUNNING AROUND FREE!

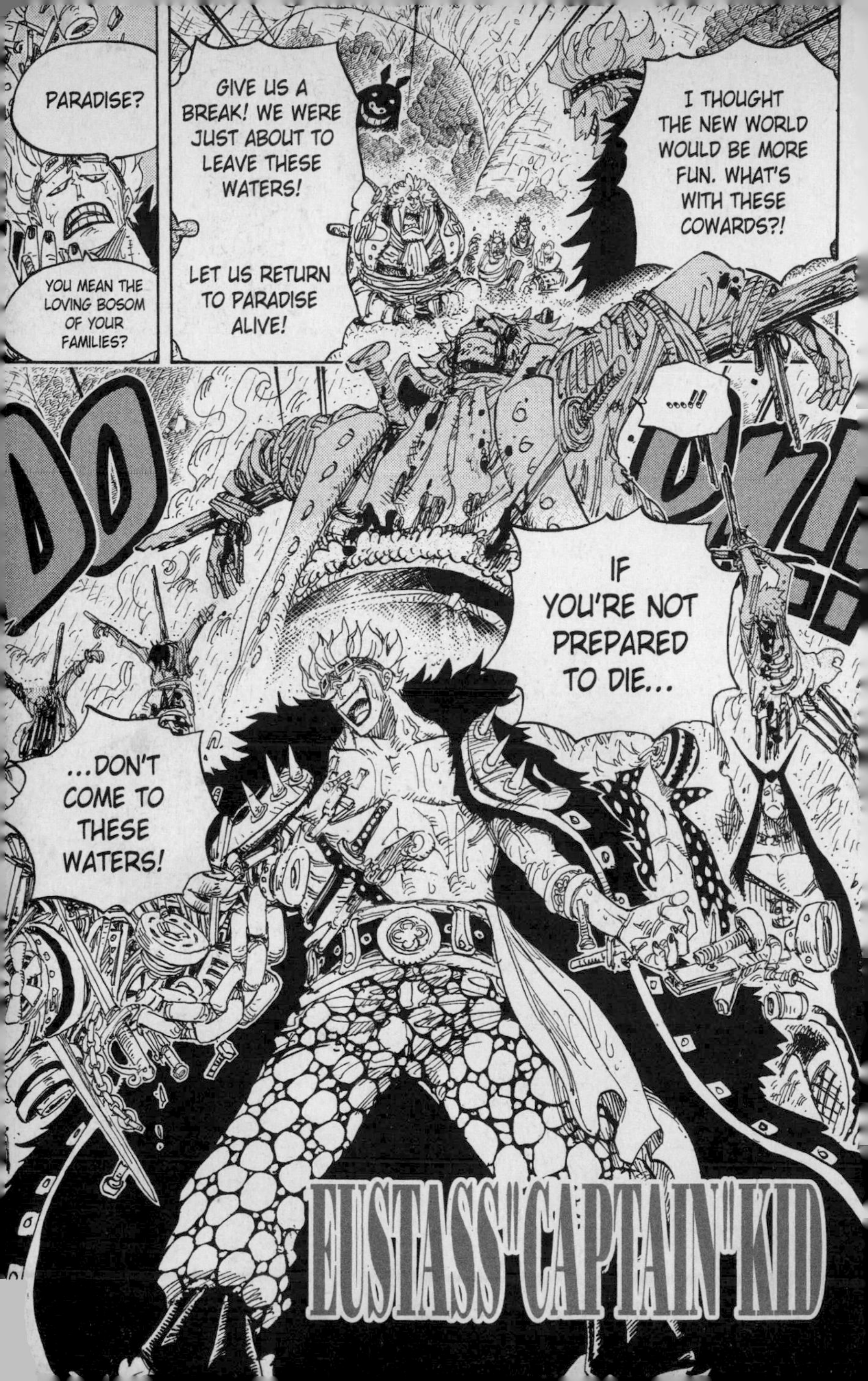
I THOUGHT THE NEW WORLD WOULD BE MORE FUN. WHAT'S WITH THESE COWARDS?!
GIVE US A BREAK! WE WERE JUST ABOUT TO LEAVE THESE WATERS!
LET US RETURN TO PARADISE ALIVE!
PARADISE?
YOU MEAN THE LOVING BOSOM OF YOUR FAMILIES?
....!!
IF YOU'RE NOT PREPARED TO DIE...
...DON'T COME TO THESE WATERS!
EUSTASS "CAPTAIN" KID

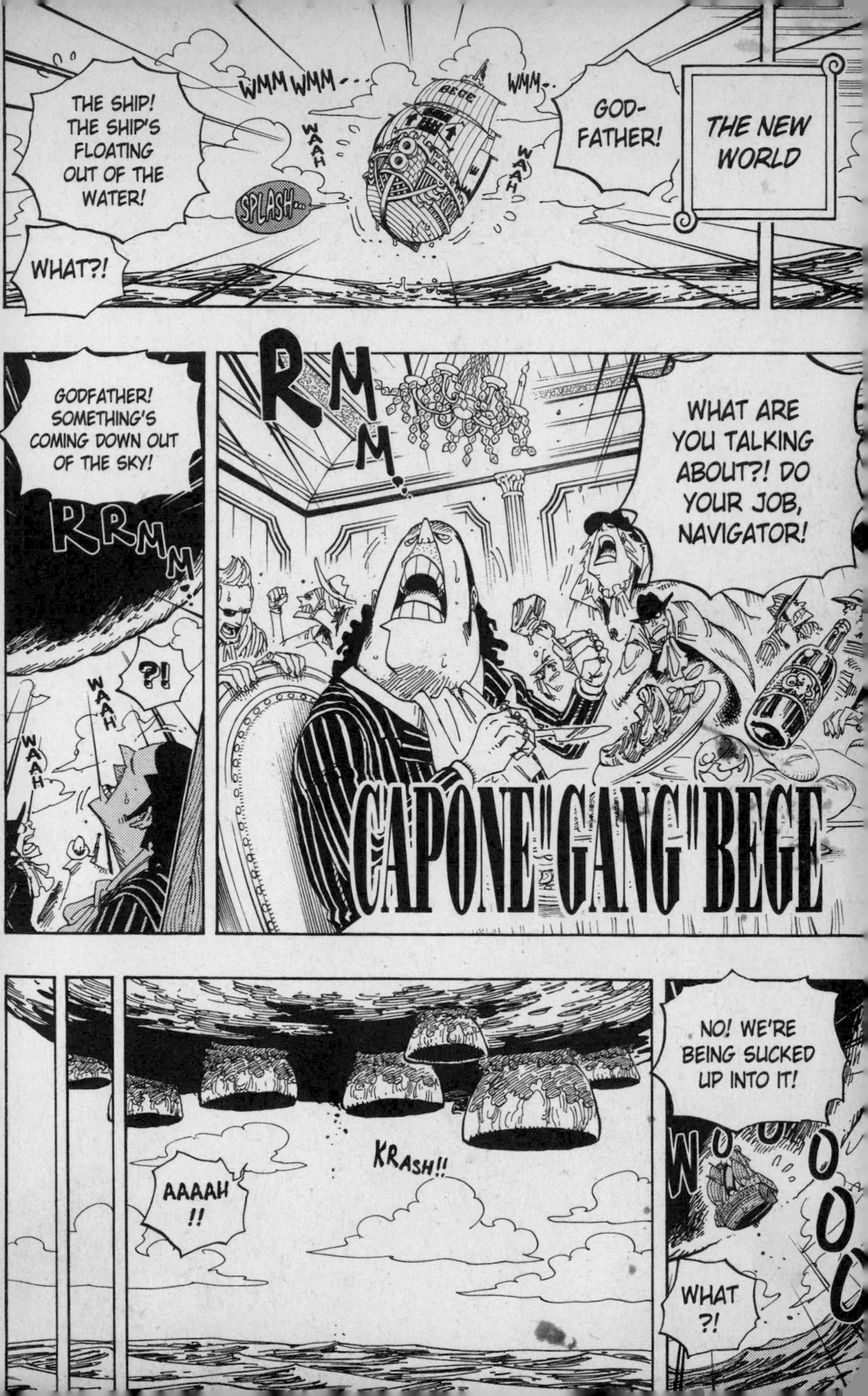

THE NEW WORLD
GOD-FATHER!
WMM-
WMM WMM...
WAAH
WAAH
SPLASH...
THE SHIP! THE SHIP'S FLOATING OUT OF THE WATER!
WHAT?!
RMM
WHAT ARE YOU TALKING ABOUT?! DO YOUR JOB, NAVIGATOR!
CAPONE "GANG" BEGE
GODFATHER! SOMETHING'S COMING DOWN OUT OF THE SKY!
RRMM
?!
WAAH
WAAH
NO! WE'RE BEING SUCKED UP INTO IT!
WHAT ?!
KRASH!!
AAAAH !!

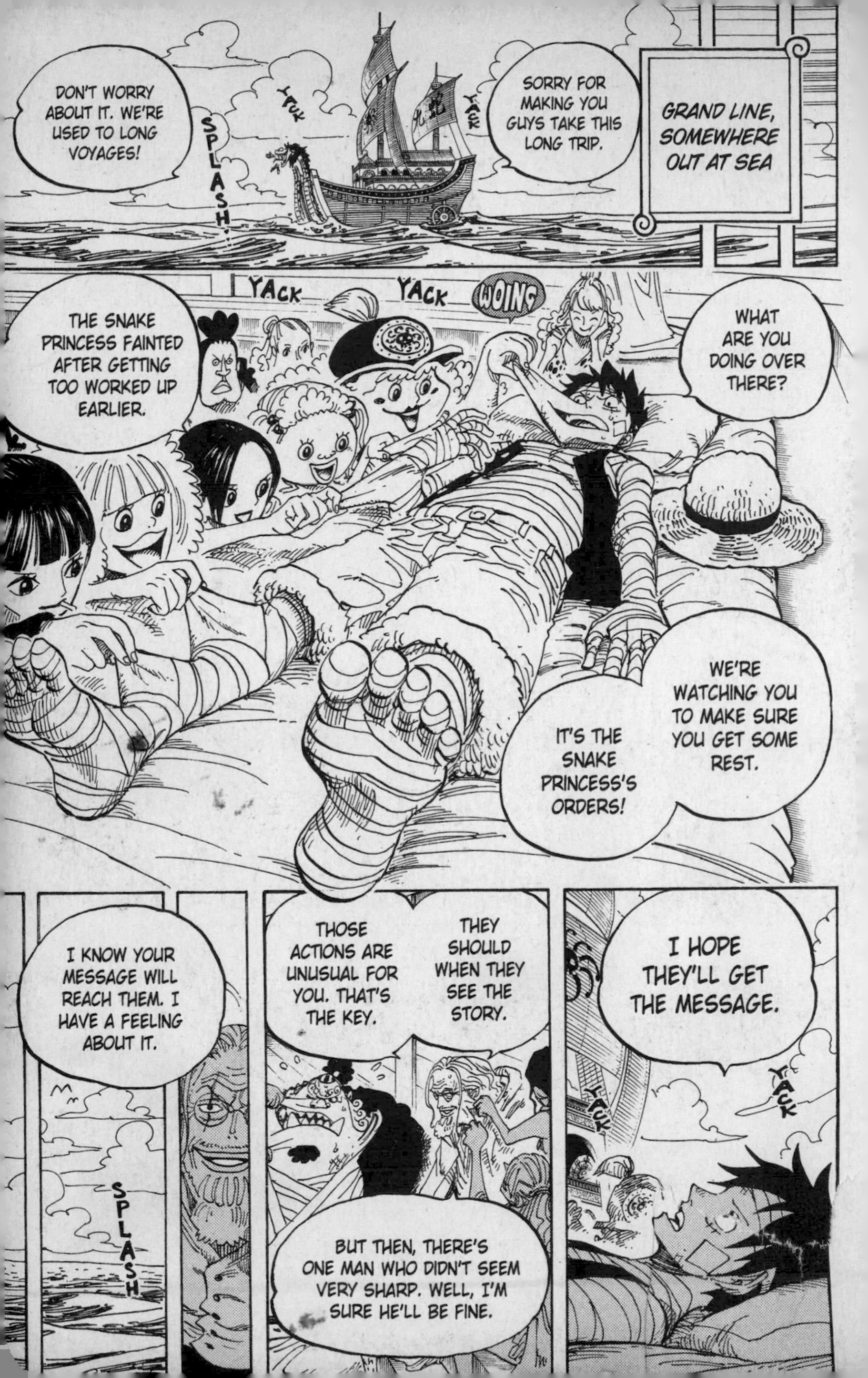
GRAND LINE, SOMEWHERE OUT AT SEA
SORRY FOR MAKING YOU GUYS TAKE THIS LONG TRIP.
YACK
YACK
DON'T WORRY ABOUT IT. WE'RE USED TO LONG VOYAGES!
SPLASH
WHAT ARE YOU DOING OVER THERE?
WOING
YACK
YACK
THE SNAKE PRINCESS FAINTED AFTER GETTING TOO WORKED UP EARLIER.
WE'RE WATCHING YOU TO MAKE SURE YOU GET SOME REST.
IT'S THE SNAKE PRINCESS'S ORDERS!
I HOPE THEY'LL GET THE MESSAGE.
YACK
YACK
THEY SHOULD WHEN THEY SEE THE STORY.
THOSE ACTIONS ARE UNUSUAL FOR YOU. THAT'S THE KEY.
BUT THEN, THERE'S ONE MAN WHO DIDN'T SEEM VERY SHARP. WELL, I'M SURE HE'LL BE FINE.
I KNOW YOUR MESSAGE WILL REACH THEM. I HAVE A FEELING ABOUT IT.
SPLASH

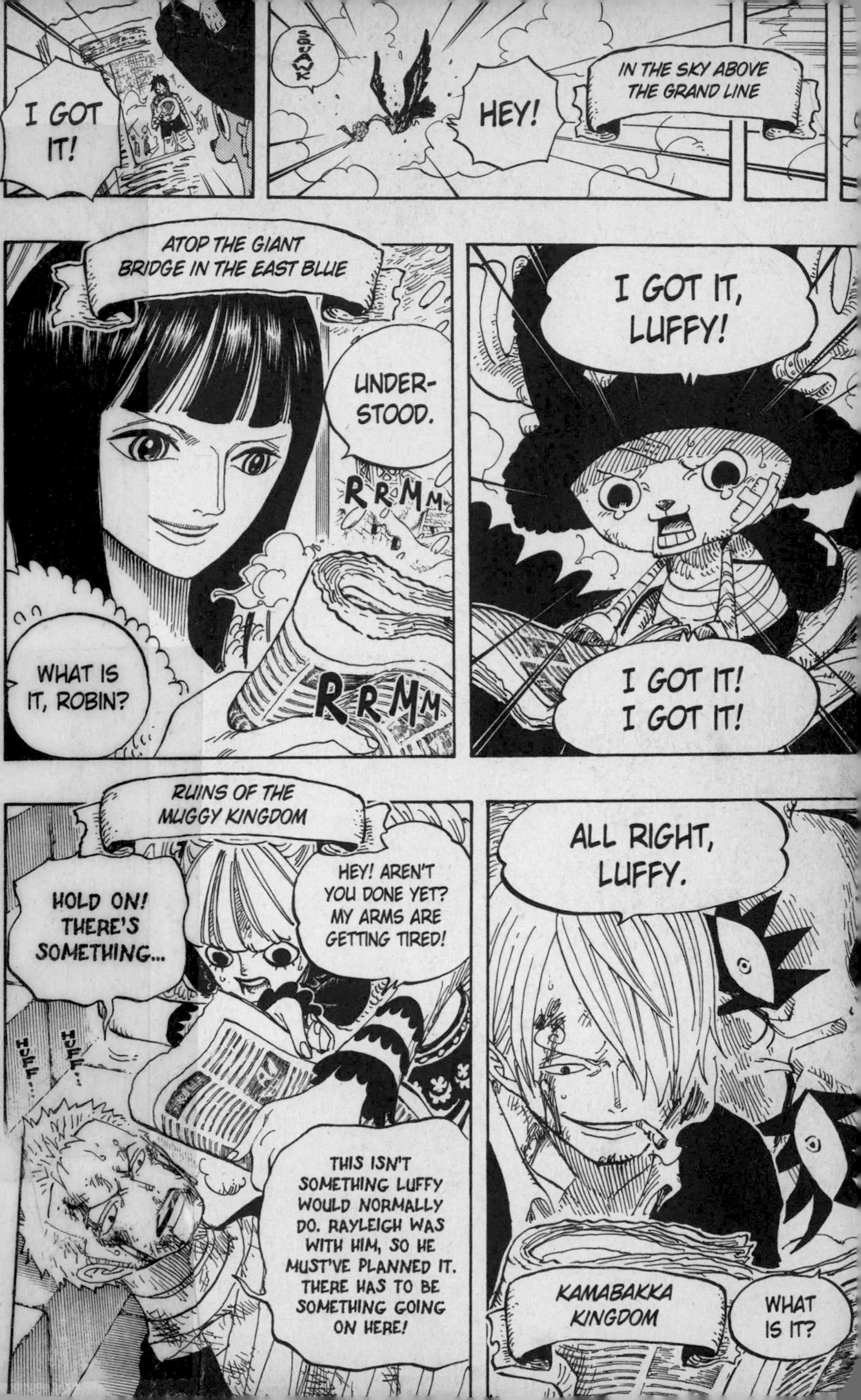
IN THE SKY ABOVE THE GRAND LINE
HEY!
SQUAWK
I GOT IT!
I GOT IT, LUFFY!
I GOT IT! I GOT IT!
ATOP THE GIANT BRIDGE IN THE EAST BLUE
UNDER-STOOD.
RRMM
WHAT IS IT, ROBIN?
RRMM
ALL RIGHT, LUFFY.
KAMABAKKA KINGDOM
WHAT IS IT?
RUINS OF THE MUGGY KINGDOM
HEY! AREN'T YOU DONE YET? MY ARMS ARE GETTING TIRED!
HOLD ON! THERE'S SOMETHING...
HUFF... HUFF...
THIS ISN'T SOMETHING LUFFY WOULD NORMALLY DO. RAYLEIGH WAS WITH HIM, SO HE MUST'VE PLANNED IT. THERE HAS TO BE SOMETHING GOING ON HERE!

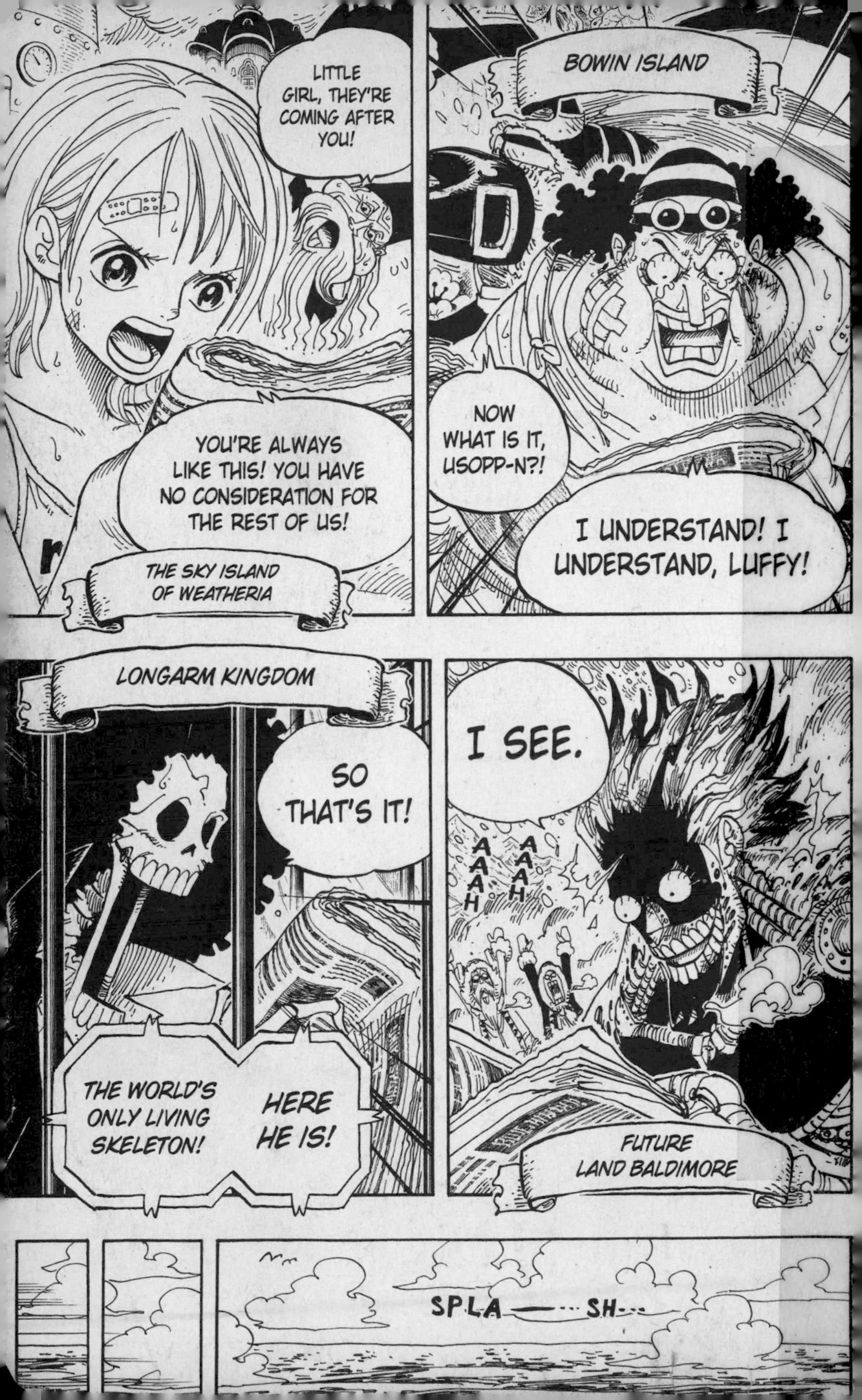
BOWIN ISLAND
NOW WHAT IS IT, USOPP-N?!
I UNDERSTAND! I UNDERSTAND, LUFFY!
LITTLE GIRL, THEY'RE COMING AFTER YOU!
YOU'RE ALWAYS LIKE THIS! YOU HAVE NO CONSIDERATION FOR THE REST OF US!
THE SKY ISLAND OF WEATHERIA
I SEE.
AAAH
AAAH
FUTURE LAND BALDIMORE
LONGARM KINGDOM
SO THAT'S IT!
HERE HE IS!
THE WORLD'S ONLY LIVING SKELETON!
SPLA——···SH···

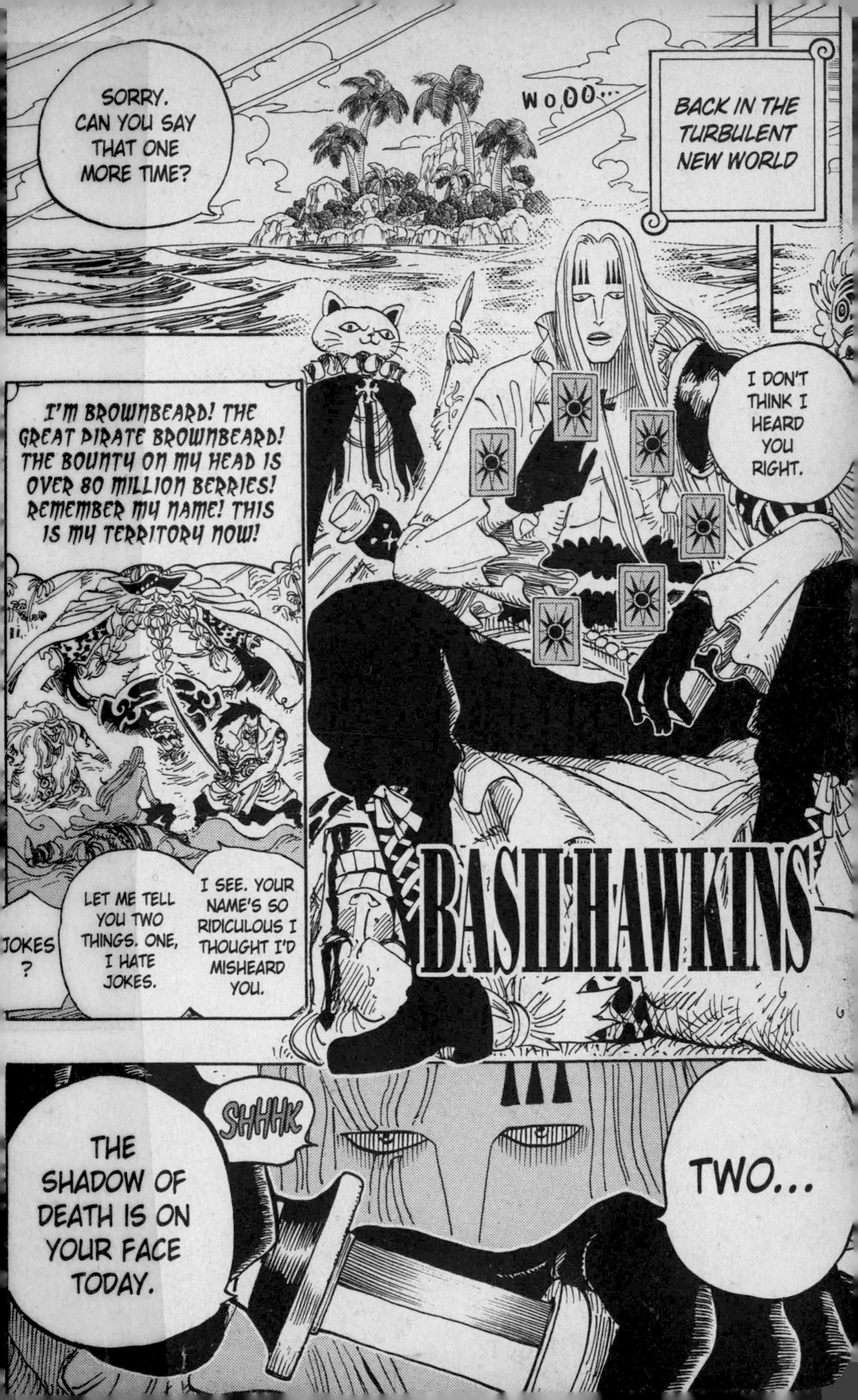
BACK IN THE TURBULENT NEW WORLD
WoOO...
SORRY. CAN YOU SAY THAT ONE MORE TIME?
I DON'T THINK I HEARD YOU RIGHT.
BASIL HAWKINS
I'M BROWNBEARD! THE GREAT PIRATE BROWNBEARD! THE BOUNTY ON MY HEAD IS OVER 80 MILLION BERRIES! REMEMBER MY NAME! THIS IS MY TERRITORY NOW!
I SEE. YOUR NAME'S SO RIDICULOUS I THOUGHT I'D MISHEARD YOU.
LET ME TELL YOU TWO THINGS. ONE, I HATE JOKES.
JOKES?
TWO...
SHHHK
THE SHADOW OF DEATH IS ON YOUR FACE TODAY.

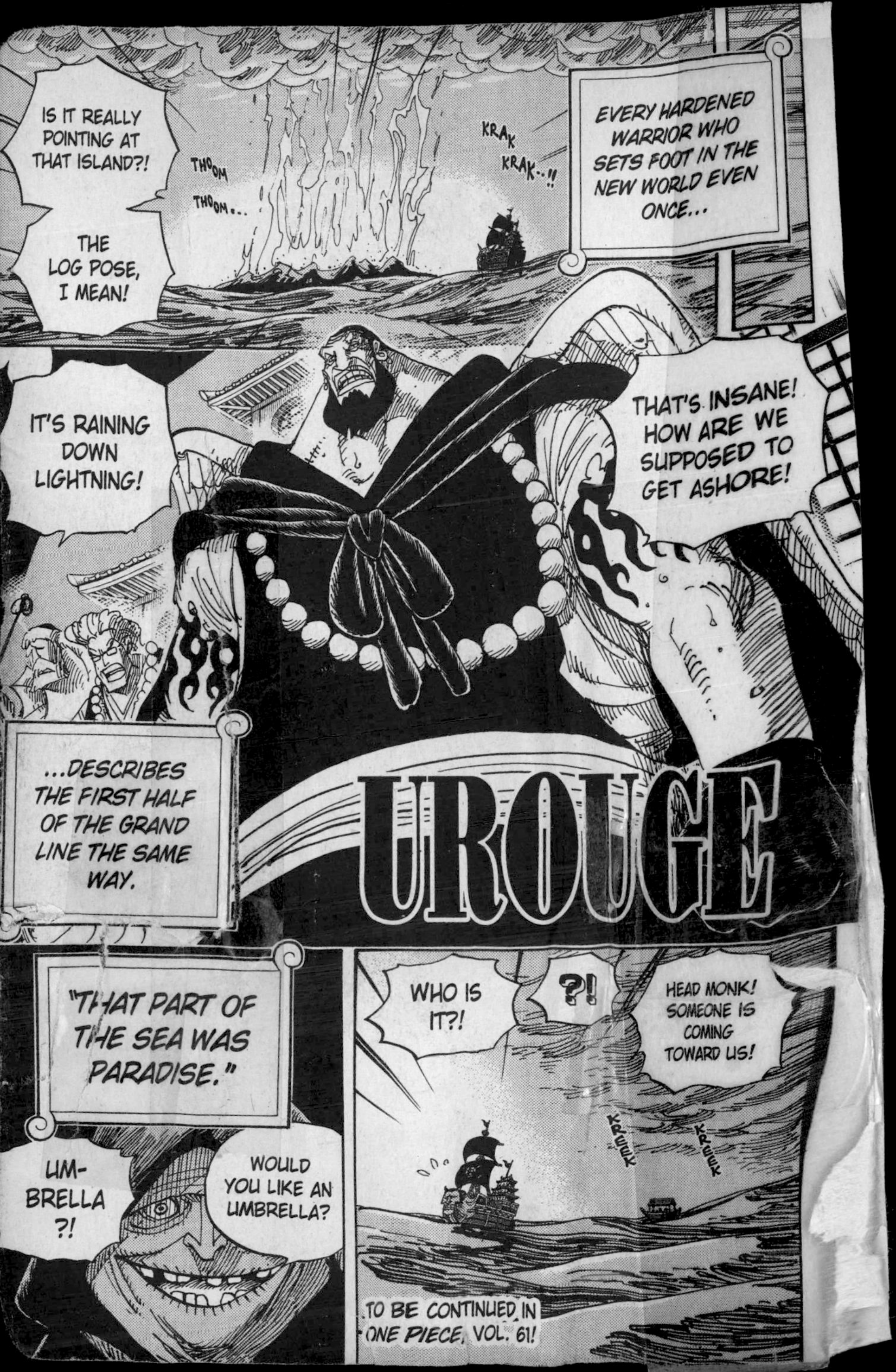
EVERY HARDENED WARRIOR WHO SETS FOOT IN THE NEW WORLD EVEN ONCE...
KRAK KRAK..!!
THOOM THOOM...
IS IT REALLY POINTING AT THAT ISLAND?!
THE LOG POSE, I MEAN!
THAT'S INSANE! HOW ARE WE SUPPOSED TO GET ASHORE!
IT'S RAINING DOWN LIGHTNING!
...DESCRIBES THE FIRST HALF OF THE GRAND LINE THE SAME WAY.
UROUGE
HEAD MONK! SOMEONE IS COMING TOWARD US!
?!
WHO IS IT?!
KREEK
KREEK
TO BE CONTINUED IN ONE PIECE, VOL. 61!
"THAT PART OF THE SEA WAS PARADISE."
WOULD YOU LIKE AN UMBRELLA?
UM-BRELLA?!

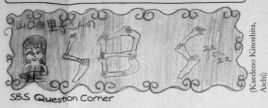

OUR VERY OWN ARCHEOLOGIST, YURIKO YAMAGUCHI!!

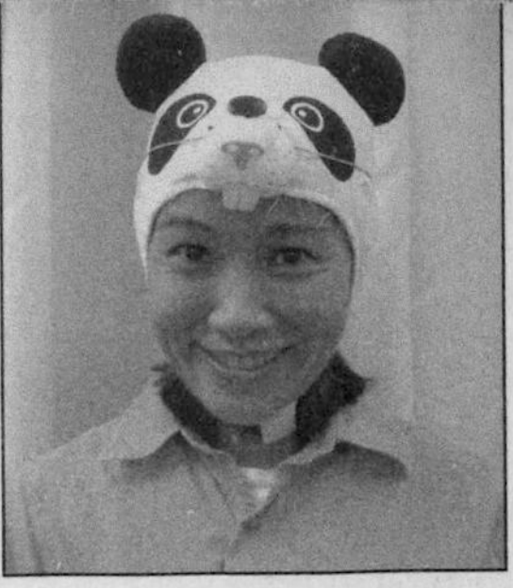

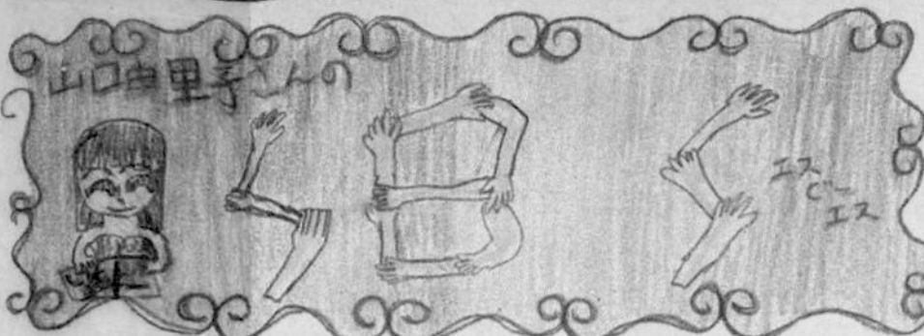
山口由里子さんの
エス
ビー
エス

(Kaedeno Kinoshita, Aichi)

SBS Question Corner

Reader(Q): Yuriko Yamaguchi♡, hello.☀ I'm a 12-year-old that fell in love with Robin's voice! This is a serious question: what was your first impression of Robin? Please tell me!

--Funga

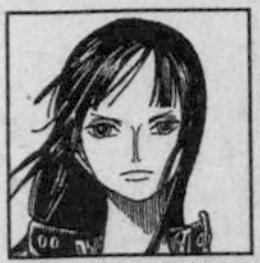

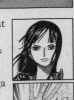

Yamaguchi(Y): She's a really awesome woman!

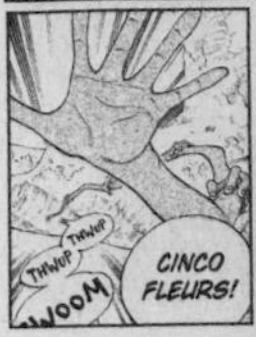
CINCO FLEURS!

Q: Yamaguchi, I have a question! Can you try saying "Cinco Fleur," but replace the "C" with an "St"?

--North 2137

A: St- St- St--Choke!

Q: Dear Yamaguchi: Do you think you have anything in common with Robin? And if there really were Devil Fruits, what kind would you eat? As for me, I'd eat the Flower-Flower Fruit. It could be so convenient!

--Encounter with the Shore

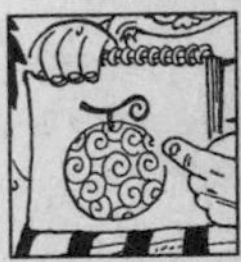

A: What I have in common with Robin is that if I keep my mouth shut, people think I'm as cool as she is. As for which fruit I'd eat, I'd choose the Smile-Smile Fruit. I want to give smiles to people with scary faces and nervous people! (^▽^)

Q: I have a problem, Yuriko! Mr. Oda has disappeared! What do you think happened to him?!

--Fish

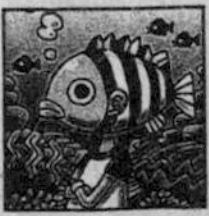

A: Assassination.♡

Q: We always see Robin reading books, but what do you like to read? I hope it's not smut. Right?

--Death Peko

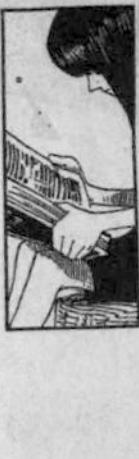

A: I pretend to read books all the time.♡

Q: You have the Flower-Flower Fruit, so Robin must love flowers!♡ Here's a question for you! What kind of flowers would best match the Straw Hat Crew? Just choose whichever flower you think is best!♡

--I Love Cosmos♡

A:

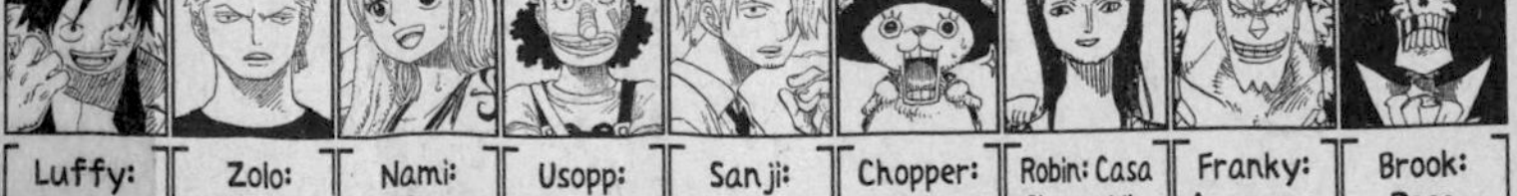

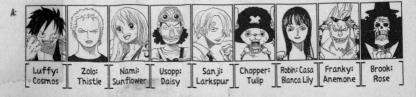

[Luffy: Cosmos] [Zolo: Thistle] [Nami: Sunflower] [Usopp: Daisy] [Sanji: Larkspur] [Chopper: Tulip] [Robin: Casa Blanca Lily] [Franky: Anemone] [Brook: Rose]

Q: Hello! I have a question for you, Yuriko! Robin always keeps her cool! She's always so awesome! In Thriller Bark, she said she was too embarrassed to dock with them. Would you turn them down just like Robin did?!

--I love Zolo and Robin♡

PIRATES DOCKING SIX!!

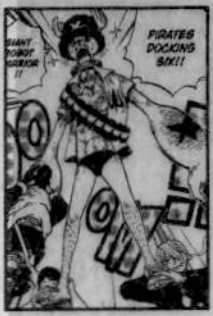

A: I'd be embarrassed, but I'd want to try. How about "Half Docking"?!

Q: To Yuriko Yamaguchi: Are you…my mother?

--My Curtains Stink

IS THAT YOU, MOTHER?

FROM NOW ON... LIVE FOR ME...
...!!

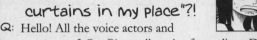

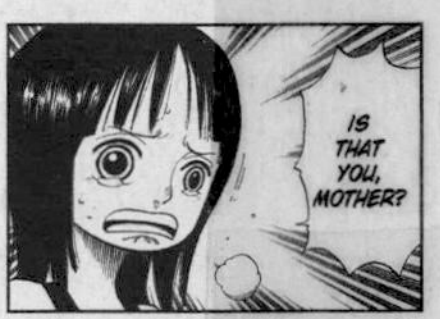

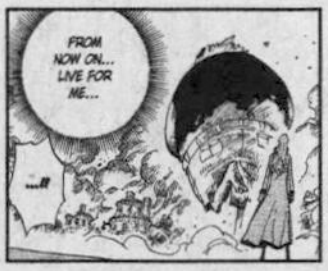

A: From now on, "Wash the curtains in my place"?!

Q: Hello! All the voice actors and actresses of *One Piece* really strive for realism. Do you, Yamaguchi? That means when Franky joined the crew, you grabbed Franky?!

--Nacchi

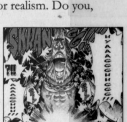

A: I am among the voice actors who go for total realism. Yao (Franky's voice actor) was reluctant, but I really did forcefully GRAB him! Yao, I would like to take this opportunity to apologize for that.

Q: Please tell me your recipe for octopus balls!

--Muujon

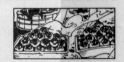

A: One part flour to three parts water, eggs, octopus, green onion, preserved ginger, tempura crumbs, mountain yam (a little), salt (very little), kelp stock (a little), soy sauce (just a dash).
(Making the mix) Mix the flour and water first. Then add the mountain yam, salt, stock, and soy sauce. Oil up the pan, stir fry the octopus, then put in the mix and the rest of the ingredients. Keep an eye on them and flip them when the time is right. You can add Worcestershire sauce or soup stock if you want.

Q: Knowing how well Robin (Yamaguchi) takes care of her friends, I would like to ask a favor of you. Can you draw the Straw Hat Crew?

--Lemonski

A:

Oda: Well, it's about time to go. Thank you very much, Yuriko! Huh? What's this picture?!

ITS A BOMB!

Everyone, run!

Farther! Farther away!

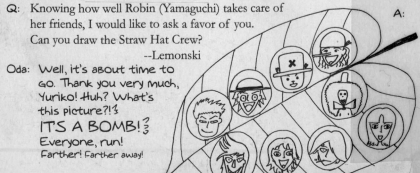

COMING NEXT VOLUME:

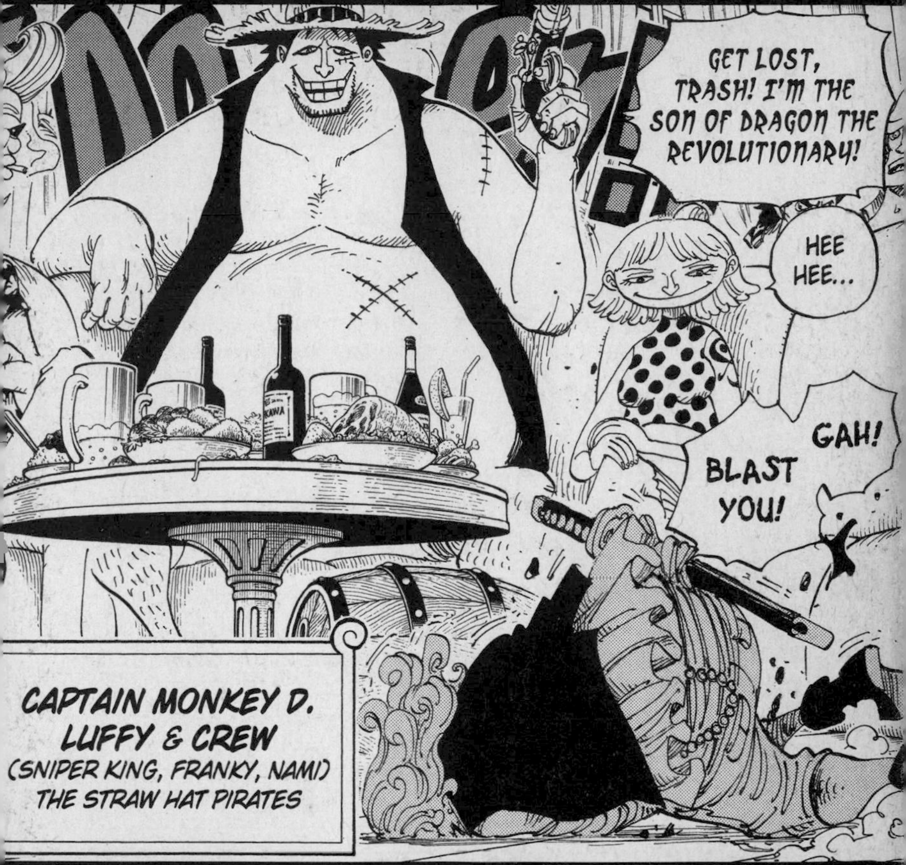
GET LOST, TRASH! I'M THE SON OF DRAGON THE REVOLUTIONARY!
HEE HEE...
GAH!
BLAST YOU!
CAPTAIN MONKEY D. LUFFY & CREW (SNIPER KING, FRANKY, NAMI) THE STRAW HAT PIRATES

After training for a long two years, the Straw Hats are reunited at Sabaody. Waiting for them there are some fierce Navy fighters. Much has changed over the years, but one thing definitely hasn't—a grand new adventure is about to begin!

ON SALE MARCH 2012!